PIERRE BERTON

Niagara

A History of the Falls

M&S

An M&S Paperback from
McClelland & Stewart Inc.
The Canadian Publishers

An M&S Paperback from McClelland & Stewart Inc.
First printing July 1994
Trade paperback edition printed 1993
Original cloth edition printed 1992

Canadian Cataloguing in Publication Data

Berton, Pierre, 1920–
Niagara : a history of the falls

Includes bibliographical references and index.
ISBN 0-7710-1212-8 (bound) ISBN 0-7710-1217-9 (pbk.)

1. Niagara Falls (N.Y. and Ont.) - History.
I. Title.

FC3095.N5B47 1992   971.3'39   C92-094338-1
F127.N8B37 1992

The publishers acknowledge the support of the Ontario Arts
Council for their publishing program.

Cover painting by Gerald Sevier

Typesetting by M&S Toronto

Printed and bound in Canada by Webcom Limited

McClelland & Stewart Inc.
The Canadian Publishers
481 University Avenue
Toronto, Ontario
M5G 2E9

1 2 3 4 5   98 97 96 95 94

"It has all of Berton's narrative verve ... an entertaining and enlightening history." – *The Toronto Star*

"By turns ironic, amused, shocked, horrified and awe-struck, Berton traces [Niagara's] history through the deeds of those who came in contact with it ... all the while walking the fine line between detachment and emotion with agility and grace." – *The Whig-Standard* (Kingston)

"Berton is at his storytelling best; there is something for everyone ... a vintage, full-bodied read." – *The London Free Press*

"A big book crammed with historical data and anecdotes ... a book worth diving into." – *The Calgary Herald*

"A page-turner from start to finish ... every bit as colorful as some of Niagara's better-known stuntmen and heroes." – *Toronto Sun*

"Berton is, without doubt, Canada's historian laureate and **Niagara** is one of his best instalments in this country's ongoing story." – *The Leader-Post* (Regina)

"Classic Berton, everything you wanted to know about the Falls (and more), replete with trademark colorful characters, ripping good yarns ... " – *The Edmonton Journal*

"Delightful and informative ... It should be on everyone's reading list." – *Kitchener-Waterloo Record*

"A welcome book which ensures that its readers will hereafter see Niagara Falls in a different, better way." – *The StarPhoenix* (Saskatoon)

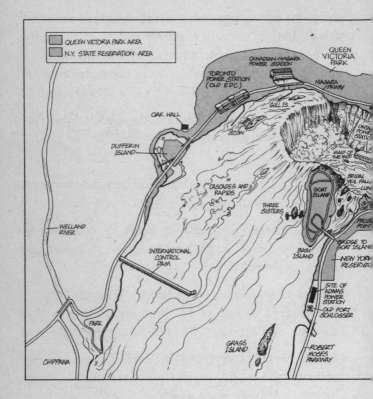

QUEEN VICTORIA PARK AREA
N.Y. STATE RESERVATION AREA

QUEEN VICTORIA PARK

CANADIAN-NIAGARA POWER STATION

TORONTO POWER STATION (OLD E.D.C.)

NIAGARA PKWY

GULL IS.

OAK HALL

SCOW

ONTARIO POWER STATION

DUFFERIN ISLAND

MAID OF THE MIST

BRIDAL VEIL FALLS

LUNA

CASCADES AND RAPIDS

GOAT ISLAND

SITE OF GENERAL

THREE SISTERS

PROSPECT POINT

WELLAND RIVER

INTERNATIONAL CONTROL DAM

BATH ISLAND

BRIDGE TO GOAT ISLAND

NEW YORK RESERVATION

SITE OF ADAMS POWER STATION

OLD FORT SCHLOSSER

PARK

GRASS ISLAND

ROBERT MOSES PARKWAY

CHIPPAWA

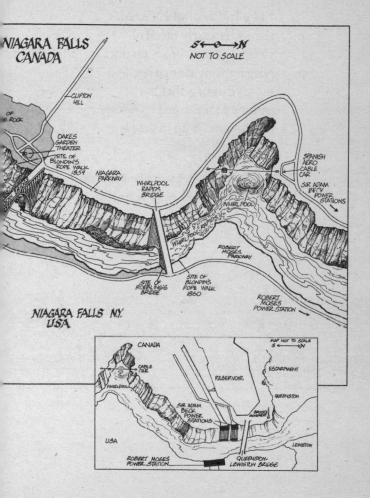

"The Indians hold Niagara claims its yearly meed of victims. It may be so. Or does Niagara thus avenge itself on the civilization that has trimmed and tamed its forests and dressed it up in tinsel-coloured lights?"

– Lady Mary McDowel Duffus Hardy,
Sketches of an American Tour, 1881

BOOKS BY PIERRE BERTON

The Royal Family
The Mysterious North
Klondike
Just Add Water and Stir
Adventures of a Columnist
Fast, Fast, Fast Relief
The Big Sell
The Comfortable Pew
The Cool, Crazy, Committed World of the Sixties
The Smug Minority
The National Dream
The Last Spike
Drifting Home
Hollywood's Canada
My Country
The Dionne Years
The Wild Frontier
The Invasion of Canada
Flames Across the Border
Why We Act Like Canadians
The Promised Land
Vimy
Starting Out
The Arctic Grail
The Great Depression
Niagara

PICTURE BOOKS
The New City (with Henry Rossier)
Remember Yesterday
The Great Railway
The Klondike Quest
Pierre Berton's Picture Book of Niagara Falls

ANTHOLOGIES
Great Canadians
Pierre and Janet Berton's Canadian Food Guide
Historic Headlines

FOR YOUNGER READERS
The Golden Trail
The Secret World of Og
Adventures in Canadian History (series)

FICTION
Masquerade (pseudonym Lisa Kroniuk)

Contents

Maps

Drawn by Geoffrey Matthews

Rendering on pp. ii-iii by Paul McCusker

All illustrations follow pages 128; 224; and 320.

For illustrations used in this book, grateful acknowledgement is made to their sources as follows: The Metropolitan Toronto Public Library: pages 28-29; Section 1, pages 2, 3, 4 (top and bottom); Section 2, pages 4 (top), 5 (bottom). New York Historical Society: page 112; Section 2, page 3 (bottom). National Archives of Canada: Section 1, page 1 (top and bottom). Niagara Parks Commission: Section 1, page 5 (top); Section 2, pages 1, 7 (bottom). Museum of Fine Arts, Boston (M. and M. Karolik Collection): Section 1, page 5 (bottom). Corcoran Gallery: Section 1, pages 6-7. Buffalo and Erie County Historical Society: Section 1, page 8 (top); page 130; page 141; Section 2, page 7 (top); Section 3, pages 4-5. National Gallery of Canada: Section 1, page 8 (bottom). Hulton Picture Library: Section 2, page 3 (top). Local History Department, Niagara Falls (New York) Public Library: Section 2, page 2 (top), pages 6 (top and bottom), 8 (bottom); Section 3, pages 1, 3 (top). Ontario Archives: Section 2, page 4 (bottom). George Seibel: Section 2, page 5 (top). Niagara Falls (Ontario) Public Library: Section 2, page 8 (top); Section 3, page 6 (bottom). Ontario Hydro: Section 3, pages 2 (top), 3 (bottom). Wes Hill: Section 3, page 6 (top). New York Power Authority: Section 3, page 7. State University College, Buffalo: Section 3, page 8 (top). York University Archives, Toronto *Telegram* Collection: Section 3, page 8 (bottom). Library of Congress: page 167. Smithsonian Institution: Section 3, page 3 (top and bottom).

Chapter One

1

In the beginning was the ice.

It crept down the continent as far as the present state of Kansas, advancing, retreating, and advancing again over a period that lasted for two million years. The remnants of that ice are still with us in the glaciers that overhang the Gulf of Alaska, in the Columbia ice fields in the Rocky Mountains, and in the Barnes Icecap that sprawls over the mountain spine of Baffin Island. Its claw marks are everywhere.

The ice destroyed the drainage pattern of eons. It blanketed the weathered Precambrian surface of the North so that wherever it reached vast layers of soil as much as forty yards deep were washed or carried away. It dammed and diverted great rivers, gouged out new inland seas, smothered jungles, buried forests, and crawled up mountainsides, grinding everything in its path – a chill and glittering wall as much as two miles thick.

Twenty times this monstrous frozen barrier slowly built up, inch by inch, and oozed south. Twenty times it shrank and retreated, leaving behind vast ponds of meltwater, the ancestors of the Great Lakes. We know little about the earlier advances because the evidence was obliterated by the ice itself. But we do know something about the last one. Niagara Falls was the child of that most recent incursion, a mere fifteen thousand years ago.

The Niagara is a young river, barely twelve thousand years old, a mere blink in geological history. But the Niagara Escarpment, through which it gnaws its way, is far more ancient, the product of millions and millions of years of geological transformation, first by the laying down of countless layers of sedimentary rocks and then by the slow erosion of ice and water. It is the presence of this ragged cliff of dolostone and shale over which the river plunges that has made possible the second-largest cataract in the world. Victoria Falls, hidden in the heart of

Africa, is vaster but remote, while Niagara Falls is the great Mecca of North America, at the very crossroads of the continent.

Straddling the international border in the industrial heartland of North America – a heartland created largely by its own presence – the Falls in the summer months attracts upwards of twelve million people, more than are to be found in all of Greece. This mass of humanity – kings and princes, presidents and poets, movie stars, painters, honeymooners, would-be suicides, and just plain people – is crammed together in an area that covers no more than twenty-five square miles.

One-fifth of all the fresh water on the planet lies in the reservoir of the four upper Great Lakes – Superior, Huron, Michigan, and Erie. All the outflow is destined to enter the Niagara River and plunge over the Falls. The geography here can be confusing. The Niagara flows north from Lake Erie, not the typical direction of flow in this part of Canada, while the Falls erodes its way south. And the Niagara is more like a strait than a river; it has no valley below the Falls, only a series of spectacular gorges through which the water races on its northward dash from Erie to Lake Ontario. It does not swell in size from source to mouth as other streams do, for there are scarcely any tributaries to feed it. The same amount of water that enters it from Erie pours from its mouth, thirty-four miles downstream.

It is a deceptive watercourse. Its average flow at Queenston is greater than that of much vaster streams such as those western rivers, the Columbia and Fraser, that daunted the early explorers. But there is another, more dramatic aspect to Niagara. The land between the lakes does not slope at an even grade but suffers, instead, an abrupt and spectacular drop, the height of a twenty-storey building, at the Niagara Escarpment. Thus, through a geological accident, Niagara Falls was created.

Its genesis goes back more than 450 million years to a time when much of the Precambrian Shield was submerged beneath ancient seas. Slowly, eon after eon, the debris of the ages was deposited on the ocean floor – a monstrous geological rubbish heap formed from the mounting silt and the myriad shells of small ocean creatures. Layer upon layer of these sediments were compressed and cemented together by chemical action and the pressure of their own weight – forming a sandwich of shales, dolostones, limestones, and sandstones. The various strata of this sedimentary sandwich may be seen today on the exposed face of the Niagara Gorge, the softer shales capped by a hard, uncompromising layer of dolostone, a form of limestone in which some of the calcium has been replaced by magnesium.

When the seas retreated and the water level dropped, the surface of the new land was exposed as a flat, unbroken plain. Little by little, the land began to tilt, spurred on by forces deep within the earth's crust. Down those featureless slopes the rainwater drained, forming streams and rivers that began to erode the rock. As the tilting continued, the plain, now riven by valleys and gorges, became a *cuesta*: a landform that slopes gently back from a steep cliff. In Ontario that cliff is the Niagara Escarpment. Two million years ago it was buried under a creeping blanket of ice.

An ice age begins slowly, almost imperceptibly, when the average temperature drops by a few degrees. Snow falls and lingers. Spring comes later; summers are shorter; winters stretch out. At last the time arrives when the snows of one year do not melt but are carried over to the next winter. As the snow accumulates from that little boreal patch, growing inexorably year after year, gargantuan ice sheets begin to form.

Just as the pressure of the sand and mud piled up over the centuries cemented the geological debris of the Escarpment into stone, so the mounting snowfields, compacted by their own weight, were metamorphosed into ice. Like pitch poured from a spout, the ice was forced by the pressure to radiate out from a central core, overriding and wrecking the old drainage pattern.

As the sun's heat waned and then grew warmer again, the ice sheets advanced and retreated, rearranging the shapes of ancient rivers and lakes. The last of these great sheets clawed its way south about one hundred thousand years ago, ripping up the land, choking the basins of earlier lakes, and burying the entire Niagara Escarpment under tons of ice. One tentacle probed almost as far south as the site of Chicago. Then, about eighteen thousand years ago, the weather mysteriously turned warmer, and once again the ice began its long retreat. Perhaps in some future era it will return.

In the wake of this vanishing rampart, great lakes — greater than those we know today — formed and reformed from the glacial meltwater. Early Lake Erie and its sister, Iroquois, the ancestor of modern Lake Ontario, became separate bodies of water. At the same time, another lake — Tonawanda — a vast, shallow pond, no deeper than thirty feet, lay between the two, just south of and parallel to the Niagara Escarpment.

Tonawanda's outflow spilled over the Escarpment and tumbled into Lake Iroquois from five different passages. Lake Iroquois then reached the foot of the cliff at the present site of Queenston. As the ice withdrew and the land, released from its pressure, slowly rose, Tonawanda's waters pooled at the western end of its bed, and all the spillways except the one at the Queenston site disappeared. That one, 12,500 years ago, became Niagara Falls, seven miles below its present position. Lake Tonawanda continued to shrink to become the Niagara River as it is now seen in the flatland above the site of the Falls.

The cataract dug out a pool at its base, now known as Cataract Basin. Then it began the slow process of undercutting the top layer of the Escarpment that produced the present Niagara gorges. Shale when wet is harder and more impervious to erosion than when dry. So it was that the shales immediately under the protective cap of dolostones began to flake off during the annual cycle of freezing and thawing, encouraged by seepage from the river above working through the cracks and fissures. As the substructure fell away over the years, the ledge of dolostone became so top-heavy that great chunks broke off and plunged into the waters.

That process has continued to this day. The most spectacular modern example is that of Table Rock, a huge platform of dolostone several acres in size that once hung over the gorge near the lip of the Horseshoe Falls. In the last century it was a favourite vantage point for tourists and photographers. Over the years, as the rock beneath it weathered and crumbled, vast slabs of it tumbled away until, bit by bit, Table Rock disappeared.

The same fate befell Prospect Point, directly across from Table Rock beside the American Falls, another popular vantage point, most of which tumbled into the river in 1954. Another much-frequented tourist area, the Cave of the Winds at the foot of the Bridal Veil, or Luna, Falls has been totally altered. Here, another overhanging ledge of dolostone protected visitors, allowing them to walk directly behind the falling water. In 1955 it became so dangerous it had to be dynamited.

Through the process of erosion, the great cataract has created five distinct gorges through which the Niagara River has flowed between Queenston and the present site. That wearing away cannot be halted. All that human beings can do is to try to slow it down.

The shape of each gorge derives from the different volumes of water that once flowed out of old Lake Erie at varying speeds during the retreat of the last ice sheet. These were not constant. Sometimes the ice acted as a dam, changing the direction of flow from the Great Lakes Basin to the sea. There were times when most of the water spilled northeast toward the St. Lawrence. There were other times when it flowed southeast to

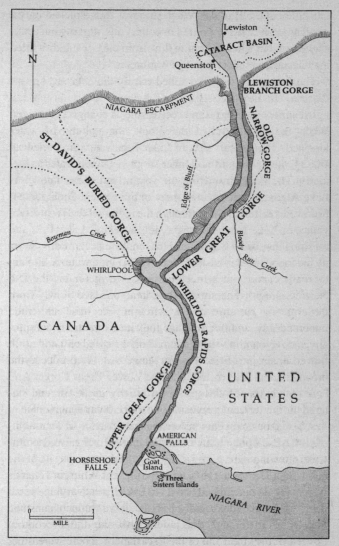

The five gorges of the Niagara River

the valley of the Hudson. When Erie was thus isolated, only a small amount of water poured over the Falls, digging out a narrow gorge, but when the entire flow from the Great Lakes filled the Niagara, a broader passage was created.

The first gorge to be chiselled out by the cataract, known today as the Lewiston Branch Gorge, was a canyon that ran upstream for two thousand feet before it changed character. When the Falls reached that point, the volume of water lessened. The eastern side of Lake Tonawanda had dried up when Lake Erie could no longer supply as much water as formerly. The main flow from the vast inland ocean known as Lake Algonquin (it covered three of the present Great Lakes) followed a different route through the region of the Trent River valley to Lake Iroquois, bypassing ancestral Lake Erie and reaching the sea by way of the Hudson. Erie became temporarily independent of its sister lakes. With so little water available, the Falls carved out a much narrower gorge (called the Old Narrow Gorge). The surrounding land, released slowly from the crushing pressure of the retreating ice, rose and tilted imperceptibly, and the drainage took new directions. Eventually, the Algonquin waters that had once flowed east and north flowed again into Erie. This increased volume produced the broad channel known today as the Lower Great Gorge. And here the cataract, fighting its way slowly upstream, encountered the subterranean remains of a much older watercourse.

A few thousand years before the last advance of ice smothered the Escarpment, an earlier Niagara River flowed northwest, gnawing out a gorge all the way back from the site of the town of St. Davids to the head of the present Whirlpool Rapids Gorge. Re-advancing ice had filled this channel with the usual debris of broken rocks and soil so that it was hidden beneath a mantle of earth and vegetation until the Falls, working upstream from the edge of the Escarpment above Queenston, collided with it.

The softer debris in the buried gorge offered less resistance

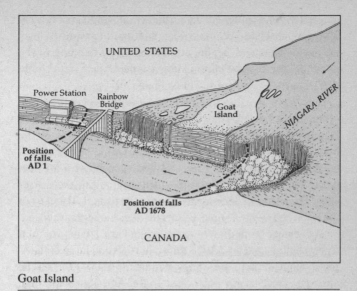

Goat Island

---

than did the hard dolostones of the Lower Great Gorge. The Niagara River could then quickly tumble over the wall of the glacial rubble and scour out the soft clays and sands, creating the Whirlpool Basin and re-excavating the Whirlpool Rapids Gorge. The fascinating Whirlpool Basin marks the intersection of the older and the younger channels of the Niagara River. The evidence is in the northeast wall for all to see.

The retreat of the ice led to the draining of Lake Iroquois and the lowering of the water level of the subsequent Lake Ontario. A new route east through the valleys of the Mattawa and Ottawa rivers acted as drainage for Lake Algonquin, lowering its level and drying up its outlet through Lake Erie.

The land around the Great Lakes, continuing its recovery from the crushing pressure of the ice, slowly tilted south, changing the drainage pattern so that once again the waters of Algonquin flowed out into Lake Erie and surged into the Niagara. As the volume increased, the erosion of the canyon accelerated and widened. The cataract, moving at a rate that may have reached six feet a year, continued to work its way upstream. Thus was begun, at the time of the building of the pyramids, the broader chasm known as the Upper Great Gorge that leads to the present site of Niagara Falls.

Here, some five hundred years ago, the river encountered an obstacle that caused it to split into two channels. This was Goat Island, created of silts and clays that had originally lain on the bottom of the vanished Lake Tonawanda. On the eastern side of the island, the American Falls took shape, on the western side, where the river makes an abrupt, ninety-degree turn, the Horseshoe. The island's sheer northwestern face, rising 170 feet from the basin below the furious waters, divides the two cascades.

The waters immediately surrounding Goat Island are relatively shallow and studded with small islets and large isolated rocks, many of them the scenes of dramatic rescues and rescue attempts. Goat Island is so close to the American shore that only a small amount of Niagara's flow plunges over the edge on that side. As a result, the American Falls are not as effective at erosion as the Horseshoe. The channel here is broken by well-known landmarks such as Bath Island, long used as an anchor for the bridge to Goat. Luna Island divides the American cataract, forming a third waterfall, slender and shimmering, variously known as Luna Falls, Iris Falls, or Bridal Veil Falls.

On the Canadian side of Goat Island, several historic pinpoints of rock stand out from the shore, washed by the spray of the racing river. The Three Sisters islands at the southwest end of the island are the best known, but at one time the Terrapin Rocks, so called because they resembled gigantic tortoises, were equally famous. The water here was so shallow that a slender bridge was constructed out to the rocks and a stone tower built on the very lip of the Horseshoe Falls. The tower did not last out the nineteenth century; the danger from erosion caused the owners to destroy it. But Terrapin Point remains. In 1955 the area was permanently drained of water and back-filled to create an artificial viewing space, perhaps the best of all the vantage points. Here, on the western rim of Goat Island, thousands of visitors look down over the cataract at the very point where the waters hurl themselves over the precipice, 170 feet to the vortex below.

Farther out from Goat Island toward the Canadian shore, the river deepens. Here the current is so strong that the shape of the cataract is constantly changing. Since the first white man, Father Hennepin, reported on the Falls more than three centuries ago, the waterfall has moved about a third of a mile upriver and changed from a gentle curve to a horseshoe bend to today's gigantic inverted V with it point upstream, where the tumbling waters, tearing away at the dolostone, have created a deep notch. It will change again, for it appears to have oscillated between horseshoe-shape and notch-shape over the centuries depending on the rate of recession.

The shape of the American Falls is also changing. Once this fall was likened to a gigantic weir, its crest a straight line between Goat Island and the opposite shore. But once again the implacable river, tearing out the softer shale, has caused the hard dolostone cap to crumble, leaving a familiar V-shaped notch at the western side to destroy the symmetry.

So powerful is the thrust of the water plunging off the Horse-shoe that it has gouged out a hollow beneath the level of the riverbed some two hundred feet deep. On the American side, the pressure of the water is not strong enough to move the piles of talus – broken rock – that are heaped up to more than half the cataract's height.

The Falls can never be totally controlled, even though modern engineers have come close. The cataract can now be turned off at the pull of a lever. And even at the peak tourist periods in the daylight hours of summer, Niagara Falls is not quite what it once was. Today less than half the river's flow (and even less than that in the dark of winter) pours over the precipice. The remainder is carefully channelled into tunnels and canals to feed the great power stations that face each other across the gorge just south of Queenston.

Nobody can see the cataract today in all its splendour as the Victorian visitors in their top hats and bonnets saw it. But then, the Victorians in their turn could not see Niagara Falls as the native peoples and the early explorers saw it – a terrifying display of thundering water, hidden at the end of a dizzy gorge, framed in a luxuriant jungle of foliage, half-concealed by the pillaring mists, unprofaned by the hand of humankind.

Each era has had its own vision of Niagara Falls. Some have seen it as a manifestation of the Deity's omnipotence, others as a Gothic horror lurking among nameless dangers. For every person entranced by its beauty, there has been another seduced by its power. Some have seen it as a backdrop for a non-stop carnival; others have wanted to preserve it exactly as the first explorers found it; and more than a few have wished to destroy it in the interests of science and commerce.

The noble cataract reflects the concerns, the fancies, and the failings of the times. If we gaze deeply enough into its shimmering image, we can perhaps discern our own.

2

Within half a century of the discovery of the New World, the European explorers began to hear whispers of an immense waterfall hidden away in the wild heart of the unknown continent. Jacques Cartier may have had a hint of it from the Indians as early as 1535. Samuel de Champlain was told of it in 1603 and marked it on the map simply as "waterfall." That exotic forest creature Etienne Brûlé, the first white man to reach the Great Lakes, almost certainly saw the Falls sometime before the Hurons killed him in 1633. But he left no personal record of his journeys and adventures.

In the seventeenth century, the Falls was a place of mystery and even magic. A sort of medical missionary, François Gendron, gave a hearsay account, in 1660, of how spray from the Falls was petrified into a form of rock or salt, "of admirable virtue for the curing of sores, fistules, and malign ulcers." Two centuries later, confidence men would still be hawking "congealed spray" from the cataract.

The first eyewitness description of Niagara Falls did not appear until 1683, when Father Louis Hennepin, a Recollet priest who had accompanied René-Robert Cavelier, Sieur de La Salle, on his journey in search of the Mississippi, published his *Description de la Louisiane*, an instant best-seller that went into several editions. Fifteen years later he expanded and revised, not always accurately, his first brief report on the cataract.

A butcher's son from the Belgian town of Ath, Hennepin by his own account "felt a strong inclination to fly from the world" and so joined the austere missionary order of Recollets, mendicant friars who owned nothing but the grey cloak and cowl that was their habit. Hennepin was a mass of contradictions. He wanted to retire from the world, and yet he longed to travel to strange lands and yearned for high adventure in exotic places. Sent on a mission to the port of Calais, he fell "passionately in love with hearing the relations that Masters of Ships gave of their Voyages." Often he would hide behind the doors of taverns, eavesdropping as sailors talked of "their Encounters by Sea, the Perils they had gone through, and all the Accidents which befell them in their long Voyages."

His dreams were realized in 1675 when, at the age of about thirty-five, and no doubt at his own urging, he was selected as one of five of his order to take passage for New France. The ship's company included two great figures of the French regime, François de Laval, the first Bishop of Quebec, and La Salle, the future explorer.

Hennepin and La Salle, whose subsequent westward expedition he was to join, struck sparks off one another from the outset. A single incident suggests a great deal about Hennepin – his prudery, his belligerence, his sensitivity. On board ship was a group of young women, a small contingent belonging to that grand company of more than one thousand *filles du roi*, the "King's Daughters," sent out to New France as prospective wives for settlers and soldiers. The zealous young cleric found their behaviour immodest and took it upon himself to lecture them for "making a lot of noise with their dancing" on the transparent pretext that they were keeping the sailors from their rest. He had no sooner rebuked the women than La Salle rebuked *him*. A cantankerous argument followed, which the touchy Hennepin would never forget. La Salle, he was to claim, turned pale with rage and from that point on persecuted him.

Always a bit of a braggart, jealous of the exploits of his contemporaries, ever eager to take all the credit to himself, Hennepin patronized and belittled the explorer in his accounts, displaying little of the charity associated with his cloth – not the most amiable of companions, one must conclude, in the exploration of darkest America. Later on, when he and two comrades were captured by the Sioux, he managed to make enemies of both his fellow prisoners before their release.

Yet he was certainly courageous, hard working, energetic, adventurous, and, above all, curious, and for that we must be grateful. After Hennepin arrived in Canada in 1675, he was sent as a missionary to Fort Frontenac, on the present site of Kingston, Ontario, then a wild and remote outpost in the land of the Iroquois. La Salle, meanwhile, had obtained the King's authority to explore the western regions of New France. In those days no exploration was undertaken without the presence of a priest. In 1678, Hennepin's superiors ordered him to accompany La Salle on his travels. Nothing could have pleased him more.

Hennepin was to be part of an advance company of sixteen under Dominique La Motte de Lucière charged with the task of setting up a fort and building a barque on Lake Erie. Travel was hazardous in those times. The company set off from Fort Frontenac in savage November weather aboard a ten-ton brigantine, tossed about fiercely in the mountainous waves. Hugging the shoreline for safety, the crew eventually managed to run the ship into the protection of a river mouth (probably the Humber) near the present site of Toronto. That night the river froze and the following morning the entire company was obliged to hack out a passage to the lake with axes.

On December 6 they reached the mouth of the Niagara, which no ship had yet penetrated. It was too dark to enter, and so they stood out five miles from shore, trying to manage a little sleep in their cramped quarters. The following morning, December 7, they landed on the western (now the Canadian) bank at a small Seneca village. Here, the friendly Indians with a single fling of the net pulled in some three hundred small fish, all of which they gave to the newcomers, "ascribing their luck in fishing to the arrival of the great wooden canoe."

To the Indians, and indeed to the early explorers, the lower Niagara and the Falls above were little more than an impediment, forcing a long and weary portage over steep ridges. When Hennepin and several of the party paddled up the river, they found their way blocked by the current of the first of the great gorges through which the Niagara rushes. They were forced to abandon their craft and set off on snowshoes, toiling up the miniature mountain now known as Queenston Heights.

Following the indistinct portage trail of the Indians, they could see, through a screen of trees, the columns of mist rising from the great cataract and hear the rumble of its waters. But they did not pause, for they were anxious to move beyond the Falls to locate a spot where La Salle could build his barque (to be called *Griffon*). They camped that night at the mouth of Chippawa Creek (now the Welland River), scraping away a foot of snow in order to build a fire. The next day, surprising herds of deer and flushing out flocks of wild turkeys, they retraced their steps and spent half a day gazing on Niagara's natural wonders.

Standing on the high bank above the cataract, they peered through a tangle of snow-covered evergreens and deciduous trees, naked and skeletal. They clambered down to the rim of the gorge for a better view, probably in the vicinity of Clifton Hill, a wintry forest then, a neon carnival today. And so Hennepin reached the very lip of the precipice.

See him now on that chill December morning, shivering in his grey habit, staring down into "this most dreadful Gulph" and then averting his eyes because of the mesmerizing effect. "When one stands near the Fall and looks down," he was to write, "... one is seized with Horror, and the Head turns round, so that one cannot look long or steadfastly upon it."

The great cataract was farther downstream then. To Hennepin's gaze, it formed an almost even line from bank to bank, curving gently from the cliffside of Goat Island to what is now the Canadian shore, its crestline only half its present length. On the far side he could see that the cataract between the river bank and Goat Island was broken into two parts, as it is today (the smaller being the Luna or Bridal Veil Falls), while close to the vast overhang of Table Rock on the near shore a fourth jet cascaded into the gorge (and, though he did not record it, there was probably a fifth). That one has long since vanished, as a result of the Falls' implacable backward erosion.

It is said that the priest, who carried a portable altar strapped to his back, went down on his knees to make an obeisance to his Deity, his ears assailed as if by Divine thunder. True or not, it is a plausible fancy, for Hennepin, by his own account, was shaken by the "dreadful roaring and bellowing of the Waters" and by the spectacle of the fearsome chasm, which he and his comrades "could not behold without a shudder." Small wonder! At that point, as each second ticked by, 200,000 cubic feet of water – the equivalent of a million bathtubs emptying – was being hurled into the gorge from the precipice.

These falls were unlike any that Hennepin had seen or heard of. He had probably viewed alpine cataracts in Switzerland, for he had travelled through southern Europe, but this fall defied the conventional image of how a cataract should look. It is its width, not its height, that makes Niagara spectacular. Taken together, the three falls are more than twenty times as wide as they are high. Their massiveness makes them unique. Fifty other waterfalls in the world have more height than Niagara, but of these only Victoria Falls is broader.

Any falls with which the Father was familiar would have been slender – long, lacy columns of tumbling water bouncing from crag to crag like some sure-footed alpine creature. But here there were no mountains, and that astonished and puzzled Hennepin. The river coursed across a flat, forested plain and then, without warning, split in two and hurled itself over a dizzy cliff. "I could not conceive," he wrote, "how it came to pass that four great Lakes ... should empty themselves at this Great Fall, and yet not drown a good part of America."

He could not free himself of the stereotype of the mountain cataract. Europe got its first visual rendering of the Falls in an engraving based on the priest's description. It shows the Horseshoe Falls twice as high as they are broad, the American Falls three times as high. And there are mountains in the distance! That became the basis for all pictorial representations for the next sixty years. Even as late as 1817, the Hennepin version of the Falls, complete with mountains, was appearing on maps of the region.

Later, Hennepin made his way down the steep bank of the gorge, struggling over great boulders and slabs of slippery shale, threading his way between fallen trees and through a frozen web of vines and branches, to stand at the edge of the boiling river and to look up, through the veil of mist, at the

First drawing of Niagara Falls based on Hennepin's description

half-obscured cataract. Here the thunder of the waters was so oppressive that he hazarded the guess it had driven away the Indians who had once lived in the vicinity, existing on the flesh of deer and waterfowl swept over the brink. To remain, Hennepin intimated, was to court deafness.

Among those literary wanderers of the day who sought a wide and appreciative audience, exaggeration was the fashion. Tales abounded of strange and exotic sights in the world's secret crannies – of dragons and devils, half-human creatures, sea beasts, two-headed beings, one-eyed cannibals, and all manner of wild and mysterious fauna. Hennepin was not free of hyperbole. Gazing across at the lesser cataract and watching the sheet of water pouring over the protruding edge of dolostone, he realized it would be possible to walk behind the falling waters. Later, he insisted that the ground under that fall "was big enough for four coaches to drive abreast without being wet." That was a gross exaggeration.

It was in Hennepin's interest, as an ambitious author, to make "this prodigious cadence of water" even more stupendous. In his *Description de la Louisiane*, he created a waterfall three times the true height, boosting it from 170 feet to 500 – a prodigious cadence indeed. In his later revised description of 1697, he added another hundred feet. The book made his reputation in Europe. In Canada it established him as "un grand Menteur," a great liar, as Pehr Kalm, a Swedish naturalist, discovered half a century later. Hennepin did not confine this embroidery to his description of Niagara Falls. In his writings he did his best to undercut La Salle's contributions and establish himself as the real explorer of the Mississippi.

Hennepin's description of "this prodigious frightful Fall" was enough to send shivers up his readers' spines. No doubt that was his purpose. It was to him "the most Beautiful and at the same time most Frightful Cascade in the World." He peppered his descriptions with adjectives designed to awe his readers: "a great and horrible cataract" ... "frightful abyss" ...

"horrible mass of water" ... "a sound more terrible than that of thunder."

It was these overheated descriptions that stimulated in Europeans the macabre vision of the New World – a wild, weird land of dark, impenetrable forests where painted savages lurked behind every tree and a gargantuan cataract foamed and roared in the unknown interior of the continent. Hennepin also wrote of rattlesnakes squirming beneath the sheet of water, and later travellers followed with tales of eels wriggling among the rocks below, of great eagles soaring above the spray, and, at the end of a gloomy gorge, a vast whirlpool, like the Charybdis of antiquity, waiting to entrap the unwary visitor.

Thus was established the image of the Falls as a dread and mystic place. It would take the best part of a century to soften that perception.

3

For most of the eighteenth century the Falls remained almost as remote as the moon. A couple of eyewitness accounts in French followed Hennepin's, but nothing appeared in English until 1751 when a translation of Kalm's travel diary added to the Falls' reputation as a fearsome cataract. "You cannot see it without being quite terrified," he wrote. He described how birds flying over the boiling rapids became so soaked with spray that they plunged to their deaths, of how flocks of water-fowl swimming above the Falls were swept over the precipice, and of how the bodies of bear, deer, and other animals that tried to cross the upper river were found broken to pieces at the bottom of the cascade.

Kalm retold the tale of two Iroquois trapped on Goat Island – an incident that had occurred a dozen years earlier but was still the talk of the region. The pair had gone deer hunting well above the Falls but, tipsy from brandy, had awakened in their canoe to find it heading for the abyss. Paddling frantically, they managed to reach the island before being swept over, but then realized they were trapped between the two cascades.

Faced with slow starvation, they built a rope ladder from basswood bark, tied one end to a tree, and dropped the other down the 170 feet of the Goat Island cliff and into the torrent below. They climbed down the rock face and into the water, intending to swim ashore, but could make no headway against the great eddy caused by the collision of waters from the two cataracts. Each time they tried to escape, the fury of the stream below the Falls hurled them back. At last, badly bruised and scratched, they were forced to haul themselves back up to their island prison.

After several days they managed to attract the attention of some of their comrades on shore, who hastened to the fort at the river's mouth to seek help. The commandant ordered long pikestaffs tipped with iron to be made. Armed with these, two Indians volunteered to attempt a crossing to the northeastern (American) side of the island to try to rescue the starving pair. "They took leave of their friends as if they were going to their death," and then, steadying themselves precariously with a pole in each hand, they managed to make the agonizing journey through the rocks and shallows to the island – something never before or since attempted. The victims, who had been without food for nine days (except, perhaps, for berries and wild grasses) were thus successfully guided to safety.

It took considerable daring and a stout heart to hazard the descent from the lip of the gorge to the slippery tangle of rocks and roots at the river's edge. Hennepin, who had worked his way down the cliff beside the Horseshoe Falls, claimed that the opposite cliff was so steep no one could negotiate it. But one man did.

He was a romantic and adventurous French diplomat, Michel-Guillaume Jean de Crèvecoeur, who visited the Falls with a companion named Hunter in July of 1785. By this time, as a result of the Conquest of 1759, the region was no longer in French hands. The western side was English; the eastern side had just been ceded to the United States following the American War of Independence. Crèvecoeur himself had been arrested by the Americans as a spy in 1783 but had easily established his neutrality (he was a friend of George Washington) and served as consul of France in New York. Now this well-travelled and literate visitor had decided to attempt the perilous descent of the sheer cliff on the American side of the gorge. He and Hunter tied a stout rope to a tree about fifty feet below the crest of the American Falls. Clinging to it and finding footholds in the crevices in the rock, they descended some 150 feet to the bottom, "not without having experienced the greatest bodily fatigue, but also some fearful apprehensions."

Now, nothing would do but that they tackle the Canadian shore. They rode south to the American Fort Schlosser, and there the captain in charge had them ferried across the broad river on a military bateau, accompanied by six soldiers. It was not an easy passage. The current was so swift they were forced to row furiously upriver, close to the shore, for two miles. The experience, in Crèvecoeur's words, was "extremely awful." Just ahead of the bateau he could see the leaping crests of the rapids and, beyond them, the spray of the Falls. A broken oar, he realized, could easily have caused their deaths because once they hit the white water, they would inevitably have perished. Then, "with incredible labour," they managed to reach the mouth of Chippawa Creek.

Many of the large farms on the Canadian side were owned by Loyalists, men who had maintained allegiance to the King in the recent revolution and had been driven from their homes to take up residence on lands supplied them by the British government. One of these, John Burch, entertained the pair at his plantation. Crèvecoeur found the conversation "pleasing and instructive," adjectives that would scarcely have been applied had he been an American patriot.

Following Burch's directions, the two proceeded to another cultivated farm owned by a fellow-Loyalist, Francis Ellsworth, who agreed to act as their guide. Ellsworth took them along the edge of the gorge for more than a mile downstream from Table Rock, where a break in the cliffside allowed them to descend. Gazing down this precipice, Hunter hesitated. Crèvecoeur thought it better that he give up, but finally his companion announced that he did not want to be left behind, and so the three men started down, clinging to trees and shrubs.

They rested briefly in the shade of a large tree on the bark of which were carved the names of others who had gone before. They added their own and then continued their downward scramble until they found their way blocked by an enormous boulder, thirty feet high. An Indian ladder – nothing more than two tree trunks notched by tomahawks – led over it.

From this point the zigzagging route grew more difficult, causing them at times to crawl on all fours, "passing through holes in rocks, which would scarce admit our bodies" or creeping beneath the roots of great trees through hollows made by Indian fishermen.

After an hour of struggle they reached a shelf of rocks that had, apparently, tumbled from the heights the previous spring, loosened by the expansion and thawing of the winter's ice. Some of these boulders weighed several tons, and Crèvecoeur recalled, not without a shudder, stories of earlier travellers who had been lamed or even killed when they fell.

The trio was now about a mile and a half from the foot of the Horseshoe. The entire route was strewn with broken rocks, forming an uncertain pathway that often gave way beneath their feet, increasing the danger of tumbling into the roaring river only a few feet away. "The only way to save ourselves was by laying [sic] down, by which we frequently were hurt. The pending rocks above us added much to the horrors of our situation, for knowing those under our feet had fallen at different

periods, we could not divest ourselves of apprehension...."
They came upon two small cataracts, long since vanished, that
undoubtedly were the basis for the single slender fall that the
Hennepin engraving had shown a century before. Exhausted
and sweating from their exertions, they sat down to catch their
breath and remove their outer clothing. Then, in boots and
trousers, they set off on the next leg of their journey, which
Crèvecoeur called "the most hazardous expedition I was ever
engaged in."

Working their way up and over several high and craggy
boulders, they reached the base of the first of the small falls.
Passing beneath it, Crèvecoeur was reminded of a violent
storm of hail beating upon his head. When they reached the
second fall, he felt he could go no farther. Ellsworth, who had
gone ahead, retraced his steps to shepherd the two through.
Crawling on hands and knees, "expecting each moment to sink
under the weight of water," they finally made it out into the
open air. Hunter by this time was exhausted, and Crèvecoeur
again regretted having brought him. Nevertheless, they gathered their energies and plodded on to the base of the Horseshoe.

"Here I may say with propriety that the most awful scene
was now before me that we had yet seen." It is possible that the
three men were the first humans to hazard a trip behind the
waterfall; the Indian fishermen who frequented the area would
hardly have bothered to indulge in what to them would have
seemed a useless adventure. Into the dark opening between the
sheet of falling water and the dripping face of the Escarpment
the trio made their way "by slow and cautious steps." They
managed to stumble forward for fifteen or twenty yards, gasping in an atmosphere so sultry "that we might be said to be in a
fumigating bath." At that point they retreated hastily, relieved
to feel once more the welcome rays of the sun, "whose beams
seem to shine with peculiar lustre, from the pleasure and gaiety
it diffused over our trembling senses." For Crèvecoeur it was

a religious experience as well as a frightening one. Here, he thought, "was one of the great efforts of Providence, shewing the omnipotence of a supreme being."

The three men, now dripping wet and exhausted, were obliged to work their way back until, six hours after they had begun their descent, they again reached the summit of the gorge – "and who can speak the pleasure we received from our safe return." That evening, after having eaten "voraciously" at Ellsworth's home, the travellers rode on horseback through the woods that lined the banks and then across ploughed fields to the Niagara's mouth, where they boarded a ferry to take them to Fort Niagara on the American side, from which they had set out some days before on what was clearly the adventure of a life-time. Crèvecoeur did not, however, share his adventure with the public (it did not see print for another hundred years). So it was that the European world was deprived of a graphic picture of the terrors lurking at the foot of the cataract until the turn of the century, when the Falls became more accessible.

By that time, western New York was undergoing a revolution in transportation. The "turnpike mania," as it has been called, had reached its zenith. At last it was possible to travel much of the way by stage along gravelled toll roads through the new settlements that were springing up along the old Indian trails. The first tourists were about to reach Niagara.

One of these was the lean, dark, and distinguished Speaker of the Massachusetts legislature, Timothy Bigelow, an inquisitive and witty politician. Bigelow had never been out of New England. Now, in the summer of 1805, with four friends, he determined to see something of the new land to the west and travel overland to the Falls of Niagara. The party left Boston on July 8 and arrived at its destination seventeen days later.

They travelled by wagon or, on sidetrips, to points of interest by more comfortable carriage. They put up at taverns, boarding houses, and, in the larger towns, hotels. They crossed their own settled state and picked up the western turnpike at Albany, New

York, travelling 206 miles through Utica to the road's terminus at Canandaigua. Events were moving swiftly in western New York. Already surveyors' stakes were being driven to extend the toll road all the way to Niagara.

As they moved on west, settlement grew sparser. Some of the new towns, such as Batavia – "a considerable village" – were no more than three years old. Indeed, there was no community with a population of more than six thousand in all of northern New York State. The orchards were newly planted, the stumps of the original forest still disfiguring the cleared land. Bigelow noted "the astonishing rapidity with which this country is settled." At Tonawanda Creek en route to Buffalo, the woods were alive with settlers whose "axes were resounding, and the trees literally falling about us as we passed."

Many of the rivers were unbridged; in other cases, the bridge floors were mere poles, threatening to collapse. On occasion the travellers had to leave their ferry and wade through mud to reach the shore. But, as they rattled across the state, Bigelow felt the buzz of raw new industry – sawmills and gristmills, salt works, silkworm farms, carding machines, cider presses.

From Buffalo, the party drove three miles to Black Rock on the Niagara where they waited an hour for a ferryman. They were appalled by the "wretched machine" that took them across the river – "the most formidable ferry, perhaps, in the world." Horses, driver, wagon, goods, and travellers were all crammed aboard this "crazy flat-bottomed boat" with rotting sides, presided over by "a drunken Irishman, who commanded an Indian and a negro wench, who seemed to be much the ablest hand of the three."

Having reached the far shore without mishap, they spent the night in a boarding house at Chippawa, a circumstance that "required an effort of patience," for the sight of the distant spray had made them eager to see the Falls. Early the following morning, they set off with a guide who took them to the vast overhang of Table Rock, so close to the crest of the Falls that it seemed as if they could almost dangle a foot into the racing waters. Then, ignoring the insubstantial Indian ladders, they rode for half a mile downstream to the Simcoe ladder, built in 1795 for Elizabeth Posthuma Gwillim Simcoe, the wife of the Governor of Upper Canada, who had ventured down it that year in full skirts.

Clinging to it and looking at the projecting ledge above him, Bigelow felt as if he were suspended in mid-air. Another visitor who arrived just before the Bigelow party took one look at the flimsy contrivance and declined to descend. But Bigelow and the others braved the staircase. It proved almost as treacherous as the notched logs that Crèvecoeur had negotiated. The ladder was constructed of log rungs, tied in place with grapevines. Placed sideways to the bank, it was fastened by pieces of iron hoops to twin stumps on the overhang at the top and to a large rock at the bottom.

Once down the ladder, crouching and crawling over the corduroy of boulders, stumps, and slippery shale, the party reached the base of the Horseshoe and ventured behind the sheet. There they experienced, as others had, the tempest that roared out of the cave within – a blast of wind so violent that it sucked the very breath from their bodies. This raging whirlwind was created by the tumbling waters striking the rocks below with such force that the collision seemed to compress the very air around it. Blinded by the power of the spray, the visitors found themselves treading over a crumbling mass of shale, which, agitated by the water, moved alarmingly beneath their feet and was not improved by the eels squirming between the rocks.

Here Bigelow feared for his life. "A false step or sudden precipice, which we might not be able to discern, would have plunged us where nothing could have saved us from instant destruction." He concluded that even if the ground had been firm, the blast roaring out of the cavern was so strong that, had they gone farther, they would have suffocated.

Nothing that followed equalled that experience. The party lingered briefly at the little village of Clifton, then followed the portage road to the mouth of the river, took passage across the lake, moved on to Montreal, and returned home by way of Vermont, having covered 1,355 miles in forty-two days.

The feeling of impotence in the face of indomitable forces that Bigelow had felt – the blind fear of the thundering waters – was commonly reported by Niagaraphiles well into the eighteenth century. To Pehr Kalm in 1750, the sight had been "enough to make the hair stand on end." In 1805, the poet and ornithologist Alexander Wilson, viewing the Falls from Table Rock, wrote of their "awful grandeur" that "seized, at once, all power of speech away, and filled our souls with terror and dismay."

Terror, yes, but not unmixed with other emotions. The spectacle of tons of water thundering into a boiling abyss sent delicious thrills down the spines of the spectators not unlike the titillation produced by the telling of a ghost story or, in modern times, by a well-crafted horror film. Writers and dramatists have always known that one way to capture an audience is to frighten it out of its wits. The revelation of Niagara Falls as a place of horror dovetailed neatly with the appearance of the Gothic romance in literature. Horace Walpole's seminal novel, *The Castle of Otranto*, was published in 1764, and Mrs. Radcliffe's chilling *The Mysteries of Udolpho* appeared in 1794 – one year before the French writer the Duc de La Rochefoucauld-Liancourt, having descended one of the swaying Indian ladders, concluded that "everything seems calculated to strike with terror."

That was the lure of the Gothic – rapture emerging out of terror – and it undoubtedly influenced those early travellers who described the setting in Gothic terms. Niagara had everything – dark caverns, gloomy gorges, furious waters, overhanging scarps, and a monstrous whirlpool.

Like Mary Shelley's Gothic monster (*Frankenstein* was

published in 1818), Niagara was so overpowering that the most literate of visitors often confessed their inability to describe it. That had been a distinguishing feature of travellers' accounts since Hennepin's day. The friar "wish'd an hundred times that somebody had been with us, who could have describ'd the Wonders of this prodigious frightful Fall." Pehr Kalm acknowledged a similar impotence. "I cannot with words describe how amazing it is!" he wrote. Thomas Moore, the Irish poet and composer, came to the same conclusion at the turn of the century. Moore, a friend of Byron and Shelley and composer of "The Last Rose of Summer," announced that it was impossible by pen or pencil to convey even a faint idea of the cataract's power. A new language, he said, would be needed. The great nature painter John James Audubon agreed. He visited the Falls in 1820 at a time when he was embarking on his life's work of painting birds but gave up an attempt to paint the cataract. He would, he said, look upon those waters "and imprint them, where alone they can be represented – on my mind."

Unable to do justice to the Falls by straight description, most visitors fell back on a different literary device to convey some idea of their powers. They described the effect of the Falls on *them*. Moore was one of several who confessed that the spectacle moved them to tears. Timothy Dwight wrote in 1804 that the cataract caused in the visitor a "disturbance of his mind." Dwight was a literate scholar, president of Yale College, and no slouch when it came to descriptive if overheated passages. But he could not or would not describe the Falls. Instead, he described how the traveller *felt* about the Falls: "His bosom swells with emotions never felt; his thoughts labor in a manner never known before.... The struggle within is discovered by the fixedness of his position, the deep solemnity of his aspect, and the intense gaze of his eye. When he moves, his motions appear uncontrived. When he is spoken to, he is silent; or, if he speaks, his answers are short, wandering from the subject, and indicating that absence of mind which is the result of laboring contemplation."

In the second half of the eighteenth century, travellers to Niagara began to use a new word or, more properly, a re-newed word as a kind of shorthand to describe the indescribable. That word was *sublime*. Crèvecoeur had used it in a letter to his nephew in 1785. By the nineteenth century it had become a cliché.

In 1787, Lieutenant John Enys of the 29th Regiment of Foot wrote that it was impossible to give "any adequate Idea of the astonishing Variety which here crowds upon your mind." He added that "it may well be said to be the real sublime and beautifull conveyed in the Language of Nature infinitely more strong than the united Eloquence of Pitt, Fox and Burke...." Any educated Englishman would immediately gain an impression of the spectacle from Enys's reference to the philosopher-statesmen, especially Burke, whose long inquiry into the sublime and the beautiful was published in 1756. When the civil servant and painter George Heriot reported in 1807 that the view from Table Rock was "magnificent and sublime" he was using the word in the Burkean sense, for he linked "a train of sublime sensations" with the terror brought on by fear that the treacherous overhang might crumble beneath his feet.

The Sublime – it had become a noun as well as an adjective – and the Gothic were opposite sides of the same coin, and both fitted the vision of Niagara imprinted on the minds of those who viewed it only through literature. Where the Gothic titillated, the Sublime uplifted. If the Gothic was gloom, the Sublime was grandeur. If the Gothic brought on a sense of foreboding, the Sublime engendered a feeling of awe. Yet both had one thing in common. The Gothic novel and the sublime experience relied on the same basic emotion – terror.

"Terror," Burke declared, "... is the ruling principle of the sublime." His redefining of the word coincided with the European vision of a terrifying phenomenon in the heart of the North American wilderness.

Beauty, in Burke's view, was separate and distinct from the sublime. To be beautiful, in Burkean terms, was to be small and smooth, to have "a delicate frame without any remarkable appearance of strength." That certainly did not apply to the fearsome image of the great cataract that the world had been receiving from travellers since Hennepin's day. A great deal more water would have to plunge over the Escarpment before Niagara became familiar enough, and accessible enough, to be known for its beauty.

Chapter Two

1

Augustus Porter's sylvan bower

2

William Forsyth's folly

3

The jumper and the hermit

1

The exploitation of Niagara Falls began early in the nineteenth century. Sublime the cataract might be to the casual visitor, but shrewder eyes were taking its measure. The potential value of the real estate and the presence of so much raw power had more appeal than the Gothic mysteries of the abyss.

Evidence of this hardheaded approach lay in the name shortly chosen for the new community that grew up on the American side. It would be "Manchester," a title more suggestive of Blake's dark Satanic mills than Tennyson's "flood of matchless might." Manchester would be a mill town, not a spa.

Manchester, which would shortly become Niagara Falls, New York, was built on the blackened ruins of an earlier log community whose leading citizen was Augustus Porter, a stocky surveyor with a moon face and luminous eyes. Porter had first seen the Falls in 1795 as a member of a surveying party on its way to chart the new American wilderness in Ohio Territory, wrested from the British as a result of the War of Independence. Romantics such as Isaac Weld, a travel writer, might tremble "with reverential fear" at the spectacle, but Porter, the shrewd Yankee, looked deep into the cataract and glimpsed the future.

The Falls straddled the new international border. To the chagrin of many Americans, the larger of the two cataracts lay on the British side, with its smaller counterpart on the eastern side of the line. Here, at the heart of the continent, the great east-west thoroughfare of two nations, lay the finest tourist attraction in the world and, as Porter sensed, the source of unlimited power. Porter could hardly wait until the state of New York put the land along the river up for sale, which it did in 1805 – an unthinking move that later generations would have cause to regret.

Niagara Falls power had been used in a small way ever since

1758, during the French regime, when Daniel-Marie Chabert de Joncaire de Clausonne built a sawmill on the eastern bank just above the Falls. An early pioneer and miller, John Stedman, followed to build a gristmill on the same spot. Stedman kept a herd of goats on the island opposite. The animals all perished in the terrible winter of 1780 but bequeathed to the island the name by which it would always be known – Goat Island. Now, with more land available, Porter lost no time in leaving his home at Canandaigua and moving to Niagara. He bought the Stedman property and built a new gristmill on the site of the old.

This was still wild country. Only a little of the forest had been cleared. Wolves howled outside Porter's home, making it impossible to keep sheep. Bears roamed the forest. But civilization was approaching in fits and starts. With his brother Peter, Porter opened a transportation business along the river and established a tannery, a blacksmith shop, and a ropewalk on his property. A carding factory went into operation and a log tavern was built. Some dozen homes became the centre of what appeared to be a growing community.

In 1813 – the second year of the War of 1812 – the British and their Indian allies destroyed it all, burning almost every home in Buffalo, Black Rock, and the new community at the Falls. Yet, in spite of the hostilities, Porter didn't lose sight of his own ambitions. In 1814 he bought two lots along the river that the state surveyor-general had tagged perceptively as "very valuable for water power." One year after the war ended he also bought Goat Island, which, in 1815 under the Treaty of Ghent, was ceded to the United States. It was a bargain, not only for Porter but also for future generations, because Augustus Porter had the good sense to leave Goat Island alone.

At a time in North America when nature was still seen as the enemy and the despoiling of natural sites was accepted as a form of progress, Augustus Porter was the first conservationist. There were those who urged him to dress up his island, clear

45

away the woods, root out crooked trees, and generally tame the environment. He would have none of it. Somebody wanted him to build a vast tavern overlooking the Horseshoe Falls. Porter replied with an emphatic no. In the words of one British visitor, Captain Basil Hall, "his own good taste revolted at such a combination of the sublime and the ridiculous."

For most of the century, until Goat Island was taken over by the state as part of a park system, the Porter family stubbornly resisted all attempts to commercialize it. It remained "an enchanted place" in the words of one visitor, "the noblest of nature's gardens" in the phrase of another. This was no hyperbole. In 1879 the eminent English botanist Sir Joseph Hooker identified on its seventy acres "a greater variety of vegetation within a given space than anywhere in Europe, or east of the Sierras, in America." That same year, Frederick Law Olmsted, the greatest conservationist of his day, wrote that he had travelled four thousand miles over the most promising parts of the continent "without finding elsewhere the same quality of forest beauty which was once abundant about the falls, and which is still to be observed in those parts of Goat Island where the original growth of trees and shrubs had not been disturbed…."

Goat Island was unique. Olmsted emphasized that its luxuriant vegetation could not have existed without the spray from the Falls, which constantly moistened the surrounding atmosphere. This created a natural nursery for every kind of indigenous wildflower, shrub, and tree. As such it became almost as famous as the great cataract itself, for which the Porter family assumed a proprietary interest. One of the younger Porter women, travelling in Europe, was accosted by a flirtatious gentleman who, no doubt attempting to break the conversational ice, remarked that he supposed she had seen Niagara Falls. The lady fixed him with a cool stare. "I own them," she replied.

There was, of course, method in Augustus Porter's mad insistence on keeping the island green. He was shrewd enough to realize that future visitors who came to worship at Niagara's shrine would also be in the mood for a stroll through the sylvan pathways of his unspoiled kingdom – and be willing to pay for it. In 1817, he and his brother built a toll bridge to the island, only to have it swept away by ice the following year. Undaunted, they built a second one farther downstream, reckoning correctly that the ice would break up before it reached the bridge. It was no simple task to complete; one workman, thrown into the raging rapids below, almost lost his life. Basil Hall, who thought the rest of the Niagara scenery of little or no interest, called it "one of the most singular pieces of engineering in the world." Almost seven hundred feet long, it was entered just fifty yards above the crest of the American Falls and soon became the best-travelled walkway in the region.

As the years moved on and the Falls worked their way upstream, as great chunks continued to fall off Table Rock (a six-thousand-foot-square slab in 1818), as the tourists started to filter in and the taverns, mills, and souvenir shops proliferated, the bridge stood as a link between two opposing worlds. As soon as you paid your toll, you left the world of commerce behind. Stepping off the shaky bridge, you entered a different realm – a realm where fringed gentians, wild lobelia, and meadow rue carpeted the forest floor beneath a canopy of hickory, balsam, black walnut, and magnolia; a realm of ostrich, spleenwort, and maidenhair ferns, of grass of parnassus, harebells, and lady's slippers, of orioles flashing orange in the sunlight, of waxwings and thrushes carolling in the tulip trees.

Porter bought Goat Island and preserved it at an opportune moment. The conventional approach to nature was about to undergo a change, and that change was already making itself felt. In Europe, the poets of the romantic movement were heralding a new attitude in which nature was to be worshipped, not shunned. Wordsworth spoke for this new mood when he wrote of hearing in nature "the still, sad music of humanity" and feeling "a presence that disturbs me with the joy of elevated thoughts."

Augustus Porter, the hard-nosed New Englander and enlightened capitalist, didn't have to know his Wordsworth to sense the appeal that Goat Island would have for the wave of sightseers that would descend upon Niagara once the Erie Canal was completed. The Falls were about to become commercialized, and there was little doubt that the new tourists, harried by hackmen and importuned by souvenir hawkers, would sigh with gratitude at being given a chance to take time out and smell the flowers.

2

The idea of gouging out a great ditch, four feet deep and 363 miles long, to join the waters of the Great Lakes with those of the Hudson River had been talked about for a century. George Washington, among others, was all for it. But even after the appointment of an Erie Canal commission in 1810, another seven years of war and political wrangling passed before the first ploughs and scrapers went to work.

Long before the canal opened in 1825, the most myopic bystander could glimpse the dimensions of the change it would bring about. A flood of a different kind was about to descend on Niagara's gorge. The Falls would soon vie with Saratoga Springs as the continent's premier watering-hole.

Once so remote, the great cataract was about to become familiar, at least to the carriage trade. (The masses would begin to come a generation later with the railways.) The uncomfortable nine-day trip from Albany in bone-rattling wagons was obsolete once the upper classes could rest at their ease in eighty-foot horse-drawn canal boats, coasting through quiet waters at four miles an hour. After they reached Buffalo, hacks and ferries were waiting on both sides of the river to take them to the new Mecca, and the hotels were already going up.

The place to go and the place to be seen was William Forsyth's three-storey frame Pavilion Hotel on the Canadian side, with its white portico and broad verandahs. Forsyth built it in 1822, advertised it as a luxury establishment "for noblemen and gentlemen of highest rank," stocked it with "viands from every land" as well as "the best flavoured and most costly wines and liquors," then sat back to watch the world arrive on his doorstep.

He was a supreme opportunist – shrewd, enterprising, aggressive, but also slightly disreputable. His family had come up to the Niagara area from the United States after the revolution – traitors in American eyes, but Loyalists to the British. His own background was clouded. Acquitted of one felony in 1799, he was later jailed for another. He fought on the British side in the War of 1812, sometimes with distinction, sometimes more dubiously. His commanding officer, Thomas Clark, called him "a man of uncouth behaviour" and again, "a man not generally liked," but that was after the conflict when the two were involved in a legal wrangle. This, then, was the somewhat murky character of Niagara Falls' first entrepreneur.

The war was no sooner over than Forsyth built a small inn on his family's property, an establishment that attracted such visitors as the Duke of Richmond because it was the closest to the Horseshoe Falls. But the Duke was not happy with Forsyth; apparently there was trouble with his account. On the other hand, another governor-in-chief, Lord Dalhousie, quite liked him. The innkeeper, he declared, "tho' a Yankee & reputed to be uncivil, was quite the reverse to us, obliging & attentive in every way."

Forsyth set out to monopolize the best view of the Falls for his personal gain. In 1818, he built a covered stairway down the cliff to the foot of the cataract, where visitors could don water-resistant clothing and walk behind the curtain of water. When he completed the Pavilion he came close to achieving his object, for its rear windows looked directly onto a portion of the cascade, and guests had the exclusive use of a pathway that led through a woodlot to the finest vantage point of all. Emerging from the shelter of the trees at Table Rock, they were magically treated to the entire panoply of the cataract, which appeared as suddenly as a lantern-slide thrown on a screen.

In spite of the vast chunk that had toppled off Table Rock in 1818, this intimidating ledge of dolostone still projected fifty feet over the Falls – so close to the crest that one traveller felt he could almost dip his toe into the raging water (the distance was a little less than five feet). The bolder visitors crept to the very lip of the overhang and some, such as Frances Trollope, the writer and mother of the novelist Anthony Trollope, were moved to tears as Thomas Moore had been.

A guide to the Fashionable Tour, as it was called, warned those who attempted to climb down Forsyth's spiral staircase from Table Rock to be wary about going farther. "The entrance to the tremendous cavern beneath the falling sheet should never be attempted by persons of weak nerves," it warned. In spite of her tears, Mrs. Trollope's nerves were not weak. Others might shrink back; indeed, she "often saw their noble daring fail" (a hint of condescension here) as "dripping and draggled" they fled back up the stairs, "leaving us in full possession of the awful scene we so dearly gazed upon."

She clearly relished the experience, which she described in an acerbic and controversial book, *The Domestic Manners of the Americans*. "Why," she asked, "is it so exquisite a pleasure to stand for hours drenched in spray, stunned by the ceaseless roar, trembling from the concussion that shakes the very rock you cling to, and breathing painfully the moist atmosphere that

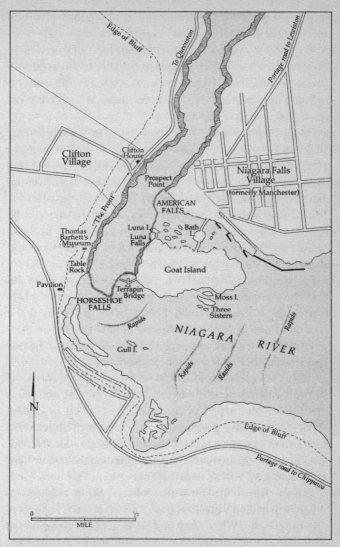

The Falls, *circa* 1825

seems to have less of air than water in it? Yet pleasure it is, and I almost think the greatest I ever enjoyed."

Even she, however, could not hazard the full experience. "We more than once approached the entrance to this appalling cavern, but I never fairly entered it ... I lost my breath entirely; and the pain at my breast was so severe, that not all my curiosity could enable me to endure it."

Flushed with success and encouraged by the canal open for business, Forsyth in 1826 added two wings to the Pavilion and plunged into a series of acrimonious disputes that were to be his downfall. He was a rogue, certainly, but in the struggle for the tourist dollar that was just beginning, all were rogues of a sort. The successful rogues had the political establishment on their side; Forsyth didn't. For all of a decade he battered his head against the unyielding wall of officialdom. One cannot help admiring his stubbornness, if not his greed.

For greed brought him down. He didn't want a piece of the Falls; he wanted it all. This single-mindedness antagonized his rivals. These included John Brown, who had opened the Ontario House a short distance upriver, and two miller-merchants, Thomas Clark and Samuel Street, Jr., who had beaten Forsyth and secured ferry rights on the river in 1825.

All were interconnected. Clark also owned a chunk of Brown's hotel. A powerful figure in the burgeoning community and a former member of the Legislative Council, he had the ear of the lieutenant-governor. He and his partner, Street, were among other things land speculators and money-lenders; the fact that many of the most prominent figures in the region were in his debt gave him an edge that Forsyth could not command.

Forsyth was stubborn to the point of being bullheaded. When Brown built a plank road from his hotel to the Falls, Forsyth ripped it up. When Clark and Street got ferry rights on the river, Forsyth mounted a pirate operation, harassing the partners so aggressively that they couldn't operate.

Charges, countercharges, and lawsuits enlivened the battle.

When Brown's hotel burned down mysteriously, Clark spread the rumour that Forsyth was to blame. When Brown rebuilt it, he found that Forsyth had encircled the Pavilion with a high board fence, shutting off all access to Table Rock and the Falls. But the government had set aside a public strip one chain (sixty-six feet) wide along the river bank as a military reserve. This was Crown property, and Clark persuaded the lieutenant-governor to send a troop of engineers to tear the illegally placed fence down. When Forsyth put it back up, the army tore it down again, an act that many considered an outrageous use of the military over an issue that should properly have been decided in the courts. Forsyth sued; but when the civil suit was finally argued, he lost. He lost again when Brown sued him for tearing up his road. He lost a third time when Clark and Street sued him for ruining their ferry business. That should have been enough, but Forsyth refused to give up. He filed two countersuits and lost those, too.

These civil actions failed to stop the irrepressible hotelier from operating his illegal ferry system. What Clark needed was a criminal action. To effect that, he managed to wangle a licence of occupation – something Forsyth had failed to get – for that part of the old military reserve that lay near his dock. The government reasoned that this would "keep the shore open and free of access to the public who had been shut out by Forsyth." Now the Pavilion's owner realized he could go to jail if he trespassed on what had become the licensed property of his rivals.

In the end Forsyth was beaten down. His attempts to corral the tourist trade at the Falls had failed. In 1833 he sold out – to Clark and Street. The winners immediately focused their attention on an ambitious real-estate speculation, which they named the City of the Falls. In spite of the grandiloquent title, it was an ordinary subdivision of fifty-foot lots to be laid out on Forsyth's old property. Its purpose, they claimed, was to preserve the area from vandalism and commercial enterprise!

Future residents of the City of the Falls were to have the use of a fashionable Bath House complete with Pump Room and Dance Hall. But this attempt to create a miniature Saratoga Springs at Niagara failed. Only a few lots were sold, in spite of an aggressive advertising campaign, while the attempt to pump water up from Table Rock to a reservoir in a tower collapsed when the wooden pipes burst. As a result there was water, water everywhere except in the Bath House, which fell into disuse and subsequently burned. The entire scheme folded, and the investors, including Clark and Street, lost heavily. As for the Pavilion, it was soon superseded by the more luxurious Clifton House, named for the struggling community growing up on the Canadian bank of the gorge.

It was here that the Front was born – that notorious quarter-mile strip, just three hundred yards wide, that ran from Table Rock to the Clifton House and provided a haven for half a century for every kind of huckster, gambler, barker, confidence man, and swindler. Here half a dozen hotels soon sprang up along with a hodge-podge of other shops, booths, and taverns. And here Thomas Barnett built his famous museum with its Egyptian mummies and Iroquois arrowheads.

The City of the Falls had failed, but the Front was its by-product. Those canny promoters, Clark and Street, had used their influence to occupy most of the military reserve, something Forsyth had never been able to achieve. What they could not occupy legally they grabbed anyway. When the new governor sent the army down to stop them from erecting buildings on the reserve, they sued for damages, even though the soldiers had been careful to remove only one stone. The courts, however, awarded the partners five hundred pounds and then gave them a deed to the whole. It would take another protracted court action and many years of protest before the Front finally wound down.

3

The long carnival began on September 8, 1827. The natural spectacle was no longer enough – or so the entrepreneurs believed. If the crowds required further titillation, they would provide it. And the cataract provided a perfect backdrop.

William Forsyth began it before he sold out, with the help of John Brown, of all people. The lure of mutual profit wiped out, at least temporarily, their personal vendetta. Forsyth could not let the Falls go to waste; to him, the thundering cataract, rattling the windows of the Pavilion, ought to be *used*. He was the first of a long line of promoters who felt the same way.

He and Brown roped in an American, Parkhurst Whitney, proprietor of the Eagle Tavern on the other side, and together the trio devised a spectacular feat. If the Falls inspired horror, then Forsyth intended to pour on more horror – albeit slightly counterfeit. He could scarcely send a human being over the Falls (that would not occur to anyone until the start of the next century), but he could send some four-footed surrogates. He and his partners would buy a condemned vessel, deck it out as a pirate ship, and, with a cargo of "wild and ferocious animals," send it hurtling over "the stupendous precipice" of the Horse-shoe Falls. The posters heralding the event anticipated the extravagant style that Phineas Barnum was about to make famous: "The greatest exertions are making [*sic*] to procure Animals of the ferocious kind, such as Panthers, Wild Cats, Bears and Wolves; but in lieu of some of these, which it may be impossible to obtain, a few vicious or worthless Dogs, such as may possess considerable strength and activity, and perhaps a few of the toughest of the Lesser Animals, will be added to, and compose, the cargo....

"Should the Animals be young and hardy, and *possessed of great muscular powers*, and *joining their fate* with that of the Vessel, remain on board till she reaches the waters below, there is great probability that many of them, will have *performed the terrible jaunt, unhurt!*"

The idea of actual living beings plunging headlong into the unforgiving waters was tempting to those who, no doubt, would have welcomed the return of bear-baiting. Certainly the crowds that blackened the treetops, housetops, hotel verandahs, and wagons to witness "the remarkable spectacle unequalled in the annals of *infernal* navigation" were the biggest yet seen at Niagara. Estimates ranging from ten thousand to thirty thousand were bandied about. Stages and canal boats had been crowded with visitors descending on the twin communities. Wagons poured in, crammed with farmers and their families. Five steamboats loaded with thrill seekers arrived from Lake Erie, each with a brass band on deck. Gamblers brought wheels of fortune; hucksters set up stalls to hawk gingerbread and beer. Upper-class ladies arrayed themselves in what the *Colonial Advocate* called "the pink of fashion." Hotels and taverns were overbooked.

At three that afternoon, with the Stars and Stripes at its bow and the Union Jack at its stern, the derelict merchant ship *Michigan* was towed to a point just above the rapids. There was no crew, but effigies of sailors lined the decks. The cargo scarcely lived up to its billing: two bears, a buffalo, two foxes, a raccoon, an eagle, a dog, and fifteen geese.

With an approving shout from the crowd, the *Michigan* entered the first set of rapids. The rest was anticlimax. The ship lost its masts and began to break up before reaching the crest of the Falls. The bears and the buffalo jumped overboard; at least one bear was recaptured and put on display. The ship broke in half, tumbled over the precipice, and went to pieces. One of the geese survived. None of the other animals was found.

The results exceeded the promoters' wildest dreams. So much liquor and beer were consumed in the taverns and hotels that the entire stock was drunk up before half the crowd was accommodated. The message was clear: the Falls was not

The Pirate, MICHIGAN,

WITH A CARGO OF FEROCIOUS ANIMALS, WILL PASS THE GREAT RAPIDS AND THE FALLS OF

NIAGARA,

8TH SEPTEMBER, 1827, AT 3 O'CLOCK.

THE first passage of a vessel of the largest class which sails on Erie and the Upper Lakes, through the Great Rapids, and over the stupendous precipice at Niagara Falls, it is proposed to effect, on the 8th of September next.

The *Michigan* has long braved the billows of Erie, with success, as a merchant vessel; but having been *condemned* by her owners as unfit to sail longer proudly *"above;"* her present proprietors, together with several publick spirited friends, have appointed her to convey a cargo of Living Animals of the Forests, which surround the Upper Lakes, through the white tossing, and the deep rolling rapids of the Niagara, and down its grand precipice, into the basin *"below."*

The greatest exertions are making to procure Animals of the most ferocious kind, such as Panthers, Wild Cats, Bears, and Wolves; but in lieu of some of these, which it may be impossible to obtain, a few vicious or worthless Dogs, such as may possess considerable strength and activity, and perhaps a few of the toughest of the Lesser Animals, will be added to, and compose, the cargo.

Capt. *James Rough*, of Black Rock, the oldest navigator of the Upper Lakes, has generously volunteered his services to manage this enterprise, in which he will be seconded by Mr. *Levi Allen*, mate of the Steamboat *Niagara*—the publick may rest assured that they will select none but capable assistants. The manager will proceed seasonably with experiments, to ascertain the most practicable and eligible point, from which to detach the Michigan for the Rapids.

It is intended to have the *Michigan* fitted up in the style in which she is to make her splendid but perilous descent, at *Black Rock*, where she now lies. She will be dressed as a *Pirate*; besides her *Menagerie* of Wild Animals, and probably some tame ones, it is proposed to place a *Crew* (in effigy) at proper stations on board. The Animals will be caged or otherwise secured and placed on board the *"condemned Vessel,"* on the morning of the 7th, at the Ferry, where the cu-

rious can examine her with her *'cargo,'* during the day, at a trifling expense. On the morning of the 8th, the Michigan will be towed from her position at *Black Rock*, to the foot of Navy Island, by the Steamboat *Chippewa*, from whence she will be conducted by the Manager to her last moorings. Passage can be obtained in the Michigan from *Black Rock* to *Navy Island*, at half a Dollar each.

Should the Vessel take her course through the *deepest of the Rapids*, it is confidently believed, that she will reach the *Horse Shoe*, unbroken: if so, she will perform her voyage, *to the water in the Gulf beneath*, which is of great depth and buoyancy, entire; *but what her fate may be, the trial will decide*. Should the Animals be young and hardy, and possessed of great muscular powers, and joining their fate with that of the Vessel, remain on board until she reaches the waters below, there is great probability that many of them, will have *performed the terrible jaunt, unhurt!*

Such as may survive, and be retaken, will be sent to the Museums at New York and Montreal, and some perhaps to London.

It may be proper to observe, that several Steamboats are expected to be in readiness at *Buffalo*, together with numerous Coaches, for the conveyance of Passengers down, on the morning of the 8th. Coaches will leave *Buffalo*, at 3 o'clock, on the afternoon of the 7th, for the Falls on both sides of the River, for the convenience of those who may be desirous of securing accommodations at the Falls on the 8th. Ample means for the conveyance of Visitors, will be provided at *Tonawanta*, at *Lockport*, at *Lewiston*, at *Queenston*, and at *Fort George*, to either side.

As no probable estimate can now be made, of the numbers which the proposed exhibition may bring together; great disappointment, *regarding the extent of our accommodations* may possibly be anticipated by some; in respect to which, we beg leave to assure our respective friends and the publick in general, that, in addition to our own, which are large, (and will on the occasion be furnished to their utmost limits,) there are *other* Publick Houses, besides many private ones, at which comfortable entertainment can be had, for all who may visit the Falls on the present occasion—an occasion which will for its novelty and the remarkable spectacle it will present, be unequalled in the annals of internal navigation.

August 2, 1827.

P. WHITNEY, *Keeper of Eagle Hotel, United States Falls.*

WM. FORSYTH, JOHN BROWN, *Keepers of the Ontario House and Pavilion, Canada Falls.*

SMITH H. SALISBURY, PRINTER, BLACK ROCK.

simply a static spectacle to be gazed upon and admired; now it could be *used*.

Two years later the first of the Niagara daredevils turned up in the person of Sam Patch, the Jersey Jumper, a twenty-three-year-old millhand who had perfected his curious vocation by leaping into millponds. Patch had been astonishing crowds by his high jumps into raging waters, including a seventy-foot leap into the chasm at Passaic Falls in New Jersey and a ninety-foot plunge from the masthead of a Hoboken sloop. In October 1829, he was invited to the Falls by a group of Buffalo businessmen who had talked of drawing crowds by blowing up a dangerous corner of Table Rock and now saw a chance to mount a stronger attraction.

Patch jauntily obliged and produced a poster attesting to "the reputation I have gained, by Æro-Nautical Feats, never before attempted, either in the Old or New World." He announced he would plummet 120 feet into the abyss from a platform fastened to the cliff of Goat Island between the two falls. The distance was probably less than one hundred feet (the *Colonial Advocate* placed it at eighty-five) because the platform was secured one-third of the way down the cliff.

On a rainy Saturday, as crowds lined both sides of the river as well as the banks of the island, Patch appeared, shed his shoes, and climbed a ladder to the platform. It was only large enough for one man and wobbly to boot, but Patch was unconcerned, acknowledging the cheers of the multitude. Then he stood up, took a handkerchief from around his neck, tied it to his waist, and kissed the Stars and Stripes flying from the stand. He stood erect, feet together, arms at his sides, toes pointing downward, took a lungful of air, and stepped off into the torrent.

"He's dead, he's lost!" the crowd shouted – or so one report claimed. But he was very much alive. His head burst from under the water; the crowd went wild; and Sam, singing merrily to himself, swam into the arms of the nearest spectator and cockily declared that "there's no mistake in Sam Patch!"

October 17th.

SAM PATCH.

To the Ladies and Gentlemen of Western New York, and of Upper Canada.

ALL I have to say is, that I arrived at the Falls too late to give you a specimen of my Jumping Qualities, on the 6th inst.; but on Wednesday, I thought I would venture a small Leap, which I accordingly made, of Eighty Feet, merely to convince those that remained to see me, with what safety and ease I could descend, and that I was the TRUE SAM PATCH, and to show that some things could be done as well as others; which was denied before I made the Jump.

Having been thus disappointed, the owners of Goat Island have generously granted me the use of it for nothing; so that I may have a chance, from an equally generous public, to obtain some remuneration for my long journey hither, as well as affording me an opportunity of supporting the reputation I have gained, by Æro-Nautical Feats, never before attempted, either in the Old or New World.

I shall Ladies and Gentlemen, on Saturday next. Oct. 17th, precisely at 3 o'clock, P. M. LEAP at the FALLS of NIAGARA, from a height of 120 to 130 feet, (being 40 to 50 feet higher than I leapt before,) into the eddy below. On my way down from Buffalo, on the morning of that day, in the Steamboat Niagara, I shall, for the amusement of the Ladies, doff my coat and spring from the mast head into the Niagara River.   SAM PATCH.

Buffalo, Oct. 12, 1829.   Of Passaic Falls, New-Jersey.

The press was predictably ecstatic. "Sam Patch has immortalized himself," burbled the *Colonial Advocate*. "He has done what mortal never did before." The Buffalo *Republican* called Patch's jump "the greatest feat of the kind ever effected by man." Emboldened by the experience, Patch left immediately for the nearby Genesee Falls, leaped from a height of 120 feet before five thousand awestruck spectators, hit the water in a kind of belly-flop, and was instantly killed.

His body was not recovered until the following spring, and as so often happens, there were those who claimed he wasn't dead. So began the Sam Patch legend. "SAM PATCH ALIVE!" ran a headline in the New York *Post* less than a month after his death. People began to see Patch everywhere; some even claimed they had spoken to him. Others wrote poems, plays, stories, songs, novels, even a fake autobiography of the Jersey Jumper. And at Niagara, guides pocketed tips by pointing to the exact spot where Sam Patch had made his last successful leap.

If certain eccentrics were tempted to exploit the aura of the macabre that still hung over the Falls, others were drawn to the cataract by a craving for the sublime and the beautiful. While Sam Patch was drawing the spectators at the lower extremity of Goat Island, a strange young man named Francis Abbott was taking his ease at the upper end where the roar of the rapids drowned out the roar of the crowd. Here, in the core of the island forest, the Hermit of Niagara found the solitude he craved. Abbott had nothing in common with the Jersey Jumper but a watery fate.

In his long, chocolate-coloured cloak, his feet bare, Abbott was a familiar if unusual figure as he wandered, aloof and ascetic, violin in hand, from Goat Island to the shallows where he bathed at least twice a day in the coldest weather, often surrounded by floating chunks of ice.

He had arrived at the Falls on foot on June 18, 1829, a tall, well-formed man carrying a roll of blankets, a flute, a book, and a cane. He put up at Ebenezer Kelly's modest inn on the

American side and asked if there was a library or a reading room in the community. There was. He repaired to it, deposited three dollars, borrowed a book and some sheet music, and then bought a violin. He announced he would stay for a few days.

He stayed longer, for the Falls had captured him – obsessed him. "In all my wanderings," he told the innkeeper, "I have never met with anything in nature that equals it in sublimity, except perhaps Mount Etna during an eruption." He was astonished, he said, that some visitors arrived, gazed briefly on the spectacle, and left – all in a single day. He proposed to remain at least a week. A traveller might as well, he said, "examine in detail all the museums and sights of Paris, as to become acquainted with Niagara, and duly appreciate it in the same space of time."

A week, it developed, was not long enough. He talked of staying a month, perhaps six months. He fixed upon Goat Island as suitably distant from the crowd and asked Augustus Porter for permission to build a hut on its shores. That was the last thing Porter wanted – new buildings disturbing the sylvan setting. But Abbott was allowed to move into the only dwelling on the island, a one-storey log cabin occupied by a family that had, apparently, been on the scene before Porter. They gave him space and let him do his own cooking. When the family moved he had the place to himself – an ideal situation; then, when another family moved in, he left the island and built a small cottage on the main shore directly opposite the American Falls.

But it was Goat Island that seduced him. With the pet dog he had acquired he tramped back and forth along its upper shore until his bare feet had beaten a hard path through the woods. He continued to bathe in a small cascade that lay in the narrows between Goat and its diminutive neighbour, Moss Island.

The Porters had constructed a shaky pier that led from Goat, the main island, above a series of half-submerged rocks to the Terrapin Rocks, three hundred yards out in the torrent. From the far edge of the pier a single piece of timber projected over the cataract. To the consternation of onlookers, the Hermit would saunter out to the rocks in his bare feet and then out onto the timber, walking heel and toe, back and forth, maintaining his balance while his long, unshorn hair streamed out behind him in the wind and the spray. Sometimes he would even stand on one leg, perform an elegant pirouette, then drop to his knees to gaze into the cauldron below. On occasion he would alarm the watchers still more by letting himself down by his hands to hang directly over the Falls for fifteen minutes at a time.

He explained to one of the ferrymen that when crossing the ocean he had seen young sailors perform even more perilous acts aloft on the masts. Since he himself expected to go to sea again, he said, he must inure himself to such dangers. This brief, tantalizing glimpse into his past life served only to deepen the mystery of his background. Who was this man whose uncanny lack of fear and whose flirtation with fate seemed more a matter of cool curiosity than a death wish? Sometimes at midnight he was seen to walk alone in the most hazardous spots; at those times he avoided his fellows "as if he had a dread of man." Who was he?

Probably an English officer on half pay, or perhaps a remittance man. He was well educated and clearly had travelled widely in Europe and Asia. He played several musical instruments, was a fair artist, and on those rare occasions when he was inclined to be sociable could indulge in sophisticated conversation. But at other times he shunned human companionship, refused to speak or listen to anyone, communicated his wishes by writing on a slate, and didn't bother to shave. Then his only covering was a blanket in which he wrapped himself.

He was, in short, a recognizable type, one of the first of a breed of eccentric Victorian Englishmen who would turn up from time to time in remote global outposts – in China ports, on South Sea beaches, in western cow towns, or in Africa's dark heart. For such a stereotype, Niagara offered an ideal setting.

Two years almost to the day from his arrival, Francis Abbott was seen by a ferryman to fold his garments neatly on the shore below the boat landing and enter the water. He seemed to keep his head under for a suspiciously long time, but the ferryman was used to Abbott's odd behaviour and had other duties to attend to. When he next looked, Abbott was gone. Nor was he ever seen alive again, though his body was not found in the river until eleven days later.

His death was as mysterious as his life. Was it accident or suicide? No scrap of paper in his hut remained to provide a clue, even though he was known to scribble away day after day, tearing up the results at night. His faithful dog stubbornly guarded the door and was removed with difficulty. Within, his flute, violin, guitar, and music books lay scattered about. On a crude table were found a portfolio and the leaves of a large book, all blank. Not even his name had been inscribed on them.

His cool flirtation with death and his ambiguous fate were the stuff from which legends are born. Nothing could be more appropriate to Niagara's aura than this uncanny tale, which would be retold in story and verse and even on canvas. Unlike so many others, Francis Abbott sought nothing from the spirit of Niagara – not profit or fame or power – except peace, and that, in the end, is what it provided.

Chapter Three

1

The Fashionable Tour, which was also known as the Northern Tour, began at Savannah, Georgia, in the early spring and wended its way through the various states toward Canada. As a leading guidebook explained in 1830, "the oppressive heat of summer in the southern sections of the United States, and the consequent exposure to illness, have long induced the wealthy part of the population to seek ... the more salubrious climate of the north." The tour wound through Richmond, Washington, Baltimore, Philadelphia, New York, Saratoga Springs, and then by way of the Erie Canal to Buffalo and Niagara Falls before continuing on to Montreal and the New England states.

In the mid-1830s, the popular image of the cataract began to change as more visitors sought it out. The canal era was at its height and the railway era was dawning. The Welland Canal between Lakes Erie and Ontario had opened in 1829. By 1834 a horse-drawn railroad connected Buffalo with the Erie Canal at Black Rock. In 1836, a second line with steam locomotives ran from Black Rock to Manchester. The following May, another horse-drawn line opened between Lockport and the Falls. The twenty-one-mile trip took seven and a half hours, and travellers emerged from the little carriages choking and sputtering, their mouths, ears, and eyes as grimy as their clothes. Matters improved in August when the tandems of trotting horses gave way to steam power.

In spite of such primitive conditions, it was a more comfortable journey than earlier travellers had endured. As a result it attracted a new class of people – well-to-do tourists who, perhaps because they could afford a longer stay, came to see the Falls as both sublime *and* beautiful. "Beautiful and glorious" was the phrase used by Lydia Sigourney, a popular and prolific author of moral verse who produced several cloying poems about the Falls. It was to this class of self-indulgent strangers that the handsome new hotels would cater.

"Beautiful" was also the word that Harriet Beecher (later, Stowe), the future author of *Uncle Tom's Cabin*, used when she came up by stage and steamer through Toledo and Buffalo in 1834. Miss Beecher was enraptured, not terrified. "Oh, it is lovelier than it is great," she exulted. "... so veiled in beauty that we gaze without terror...." As she stood on Table Rock, she felt what so many newcomers were beginning to feel – a sense of peace, of tranquillity and stillness. This represented a considerable literary leap from the Burkean concept of the sublime, but then, Burke was going out of fashion.

From the vantage point of the great overhanging ledge, the young woman not only felt at peace but was also half prepared to deliver herself to the depths below. "I felt as if I could have *gone over* with the waters; it would be so beautiful a death; there would be no fear in it. I felt the rock tremble under me with a sort of joy. I was so maddened that I could have gone too, if it had gone."

The young Nathaniel Hawthorne, then on the verge of a distinguished literary career, also arrived that year by stage from Lewiston, intent on treating the cataract as a shrine. "Never," he wrote, "did a pilgrim approach Niagara with deeper enthusiasm, than mine." In his thinly disguised fictional satire, the future novelist told how he kept putting off his first view of the Falls, saving it up for later as a child saves a sweet, even shutting his eyes tight when he heard a fellow passenger exclaim that the cataract had come into view. Nor did he rush "like a madman" to the scene, preferring instead to revel in delicious anticipation, taking his dinner at the hotel, then lighting a leisurely cigar until, at last, "with reluctant step" and feeling like an intruder, he walked toward Goat Island. "Such has often been my apathy," he explained, "when objects, long sought, and earnestly desired, were placed within my reach."

The tollgate at the bridge gave him another excuse for dally-ing. He signed the visitors' book and pored over several of the entries. He examined a stuffed fish and a display of beaded moccasins. He bought himself a carved walking stick of curly maple, fashioned by the Tuscarora Indians. Only then did he cross the bridge to gaze upon the tumbling waters.

And here he was swept by the same sense of letdown that struck so many other travellers seduced by earlier writers – the ones who had confessed it impossible to describe the indescrib-able. Hawthorne had a vision of the Falls fixed in his head and it didn't jibe with what he saw. He had come to Niagara "haunted with a vision of foam and fury, and dizzy cliffs, and an ocean tumbling down out of the sky – a scene, in short, which Nature had too much good taste and calm simplicity to realize."

"My mind," he wrote, "had struggled to adapt these false conceptions to the reality, and finding the effort vain, a wretched sense of disappointment weighed me down. I climbed the precipice, and threw myself on the earth – feeling that I was unworthy to look on the Great Falls, and careless about beholding them again."

Gradually, Hawthorne came to the conclusion that "Niagara is indeed a wonder of the world" but that time and thought were needed to comprehend it. He cast aside all previous impres-sions and devoted himself to hours of contemplation, "suffer-ing the mighty scene to work its own impression."

As other tourists began to arrive, Hawthorne became amused by the effect the Falls had on them. Most greeted the spectacle laconically. One short and ruddy Englishman peeped over the edge "and evinced his appreciation by a broad grin." His robust wife was so concerned about the safety of their small boy that she didn't even glance at the Falls, while the child was far more interested in his stick of candy.

An American turned up with a copy of Basil Hall's *Travels in North America* and "labored earnestly to adjust Niagara to the captain's description, departing, at last, without one new idea or sensation of his own." He was followed by a sketch artist who complained that Goat Island was in the wrong place. "It should have been thrown farther to the right, so as to widen the American falls, and contract those of the Horse-shoe." Two Michigan travellers appeared to declare that, on the whole, the sight was worth looking at – certainly there was an immense amount of waterpower available – but they would be prepared to go twice as far to contemplate the masonry of the Erie Canal at Lockport.

Finally, a young man in cotton homespun turned up, carrying a staff in his hand and a pack on his shoulders. He stood at the very lip of Table Rock, fixing his eyes on the Horseshoe Falls until "his whole soul seemed to go forth and be transported thither," at which point the staff dropped from his fingers and tumbled over the brink.

Hawthorne lingered until he was alone. Then, as the sun set, he took the winding road down to the ferry landing on the Canadian side to watch as "the golden sunshine tinged the sheet of the American cascade and painted on its heaving spray the broken semicircle of a rainbow." His steps were slow. He lingered at every turn, knowing these glimpses would be his last. "The solitude of the old wilderness now reigned over the whole vicinity of the falls. My enjoyment became the more rapturous, because no poet shared it – nor wretch, devoid of poetry, profaned it: but the spot, so famous throughout the world, was all my own!"

The novelist was not alone in his initial experience of the Falls. Two years later, Anna Jameson, the British art critic, feminist, and travel writer, preparing her book *Winter Studies and Summer Rambles in Canada*, reproached herself because, like Hawthorne's, her first experience had been a letdown. The cataract had thundered in her imagination as long as she could remember. Now she wished she had never seen it, that it had remained "a thing unbeheld – a thing imagined, hoped, and anticipated, – something to live for." The reality of that first sight had displaced from her mind "an illusion far more magnificent than itself – I have no words for my utter disappointment."

She, too, blamed herself for failing to respond to Niagara. Surely those early reports she had read – of astonishment, enthusiasm, and rapture – could not be passed off as mere hyperbole! And yet the cataracts of Switzerland had affected her a thousand times more than the immensity of Niagara.

"O I could beat myself!" she wrote. The first impression of a new experience – that sudden sensation of awe, surprise, and delight – was lost and could never be recaptured. "Though I should live a thousand years, long as Niagara itself shall roll, I can never see it again for the first time. Something is gone that cannot be restored."

On and on she went, in an orgy of verbal flagellation, castigating herself for her obtuseness. "What has come over my soul and senses? – I am no longer Anna – I am metamorphosed – I am translated – I am an ass's head, a clod, a wooden spoon, a fat weed growing on Lethe's bank, a stock, a stone, a petrification – for have I not seen Niagara, the wonder of wonders; and felt – no words can tell *what* disappointment!"

She had come up from Queenston that day – January 29, 1836 – when suddenly her companion checked the horses and exclaimed, "The Falls!" Everything she had read had created an image of the cataract – soul-subduing beauty, appalling terror, power, height, velocity, immensity. But now, as she gazed down upon that distant scene – the Falls half-frozen in a white shroud – she fell quite silent, "my very soul sunk within me." It was not at all what she had expected.

She put up at the Clifton House on the Canadian side, now desolate in winter, its summer verandahs and open balconies hung with icicles and encumbered with snow, its public rooms shabby and chill, its windows broken, its dinner tables dusty. From there she donned crampons, proceeded to Table Rock, and suddenly "could not tear myself away." Like Hawthorne, she sat on the edge until "a kind of dreamy fascination came over me," and watched the sun create an iris across the American Falls. She too had been brought up on the travellers' accounts of terror, awe, and grandeur, and the reality had failed to match that fantasy. Scarcely anything she had read had mentioned beauty, but as an art critic she knew what the emerging school of landscape painters knew. They were teaching the European public to look at nature with fresh eyes.

When she returned that summer, it was not the sublime that she extolled. "The people who have spoken or written of these Falls of Niagara have surely never done justice to their loveliness, their inexpressible, inconceivable beauty," she wrote. "The feeling of their beauty has become with me a deeper feeling than that of their sublimity." The scene before her that evening soothed rather than excited.

Her enthusiasm was tempered by a brief note of disharmony, which later visitors would echo more loudly. "The Americans have disfigured their share of the rapids with mills and manufactories, and horrid red brick houses, and other unacceptable, unseasonable sights and signs of sordid industry." She was pleased that the City of the Falls on the Canadian side had failed to materialize. It would have brought a "range of cotton factories, iron foundries, grist mills, saw mills where now the mighty waters rush along in glee and liberty." The wooden hotels, museums, and curiosity stalls were bad enough, but had the real-estate scheme succeeded, "there would be moral pollution brought into this majestic scene far more degrading."

She reserved her most scathing remarks for the new Terrapin Tower, a forty-five-foot, lighthouse-shaped structure, built in 1833 and perched on the turtle-shaped rocks from which it took its name. Those who ventured to the top of the tower, overlooking the eastern rim of the Horseshoe Falls, were treated to a view of that cascade quite as magnificent as the one from Table Rock, but Mrs. Jameson had no sympathy for the "profane wretch" who designed it.

"It stands there so detestably impudent and *mal-à-propos* – it is such a signal yet puny monument of bad taste – so miserably *mesquin* and so presumptuous, that I do hope the violated majesty of nature will take the matter in hand, and overwhelm or cast it down the precipice...." But the tower stood for forty years, by which time considerably grosser edifices had marred the cataract's beauty.

It was women and poets who felt most strongly about the commercial profanation of the Falls. Caroline Gilman, the Boston-born author and poet who stayed at the Cataract House on the American side that same year, agreed that "this site is ruined." She observed, with distaste, "the beautiful and sublime giving place to the useful and the low." It was the prayer of all persons of discrimination, she wrote, "that Goat or Iris Island may be preserved from this desecration."

She descended the Goat Island cliff by way of the new circular staircase named for Nicholas Biddle, the Philadelphia banker and financier who underwrote its construction so that visitors might enjoy a view of the Horseshoe Falls from the rocks in the river below. As Mrs. Gilman wrote, "here its height and power are fully appreciated." She returned to Goat Island and climbed up the maligned Terrapin Tower to encounter an even more breathtaking view, "the crown and glory of the whole." Her exaltation was transcendent. "I felt the moral influence of the scene acting on my spiritual nature, and while lingering at the summit, alone, offered a simple and humble prayer." At the extreme end of the Terrapin pier she lay down with her head directly over the Falls, like Francis Abbott, and "ceased to pray or even to think.... I gave myself up to the overpowering greatness of the scene, and my soul was still."

Other visitors were beginning to see in Niagara a manifestation of the Creator's great design. Early travellers had described the spectacle as hellish; now it was divine. Mrs. Gilman felt "as if the Great Architect were near," and the poets and artists who followed picked up the theme. To William

Henry Bartlett, sketching prominent Canadian sites in 1836, to see Niagara was "to see God in the excellence of His power."

But the most widely quoted testimonial to the moral and religious inspiration provided by Niagara came from Charles Dickens. The novelist, exhausted by his work on two prodigious novels, *Barnaby Rudge* and *The Old Curiosity Shop*, had embarked on a five-month tour of the United States. He arrived at the Falls by train from Buffalo on a raw, chilly morning in April 1842. The trees were still naked of foliage, and a damp mist was creeping up from the ground. He had reached Buffalo at about five-thirty and was so impatient to see the Falls that he set off immediately after breakfast.

Unlike the contemplative Hawthorne, Dickens could not wait to see the Falls. He kept straining his eyes, "every moment expecting to behold the spray." Each time the train stopped he listened, hoping to hear the roar. At last he saw two white clouds "rising up slowly and majestically from the depths of the earth." Soon his journey ended, and at last he "heard the mighty rush of water and felt the ground tremble underneath my feet."

He did not linger on the American side but stumbled down the steep, slippery bank and climbed over broken rock, "deafened by the noise, half-blinded by the spray, and wet to the skin," to reach the ferry landing. Crossing the Niagara River at a point where the immense torrent of water poured headlong from the heights above, he felt "stunned and unable to comprehend the vastness of the scene."

Where Hawthorne's response to the spectacle had been intellectual, Dickens's was spiritual. "It was not until I came on Table Rock, and looked – Great Heaven, on what a Fall of bright-green water! – that it came upon me in its full might and majesty. Then, when I felt how near to my Creator I was standing, the first effect, and the enduring one – instant and lasting – of the tremendous spectacle, was Peace. Peace of Mind, tranquillity, calm recollections of the Dead, great thoughts

73

of Eternal Rest and Happiness; nothing of gloom or terror. Niagara was at once stamped upon my heart, an Image of Beauty; to remain there, changeless and indelible, until its pulses cease to beat, for ever."

Dickens passed "ten memorable days ... on that Enchanted Ground!" He did not stir, in all that time, from the Canadian side, but wandered to and fro, observing the cataract from every angle and vantage point and at every hour. "To have Niagara before me, lighted by the sun and by the moon, red in the day's decline, and grey as evening slowly fell upon it; to look upon it every day, and wake up in the night and hear its ceaseless voice; this was enough."

2

In gazing upon the tumbling waters, Charles Dickens had never felt closer to God. In the years that followed, more visitors noted evidence of the Deity's work. To many the Falls was a shrine. John Quincy Adams, sixth president of the United States, was one who saw it as "a pledge of God to mankind that the destruction from the waters shall not again visit the earth."

These references to Niagara Falls as a manifestation of the Divine would become even more frequent as the century advanced. It was as if the true believers used the cataract as a crutch to bolster their faith, to reassure themselves that the Almighty was alive and well and manifest in Nature. For with the emergence of the new science of geology, the old faith was beginning to unravel.

The old faith insisted that the age of the Earth could not be determined by the character of its rocks but by the words of the Old Testament, which made it clear that the earth was less than six thousand years old. Against this was the troubling evidence of the Niagara gorge. It was possible to calculate, at least roughly, the speed at which the river had nibbled away at the limestone cliffs, forcing the cataract farther and farther upstream. Anyone who had lived beside the river for any length of time could see the result of that erosion – great platforms of rock crashing into the gorge, piles of talus heaped below the smaller fall, caves hollowed out behind the tumbling curtain.

During the last quarter of the eighteenth century, a number of Niagara observers, on the basis of this evidence, tried to reckon the real age of the river. In 1790, one Niagara observer, William Maclay, pointed out to the surveyor-general of the United States (who had himself been studying the rate of attrition) that people who had lived along the gorge for thirty years insisted that the Falls had moved twenty feet upriver in that time. At that rate, he said, the river was 55,440 years old.

Such calculations did little to shake the religious faith of the masses. As late as 1834, George Fairholme, a "scriptural geologist," argued that the Falls was formed "immediately subsequent to the restoration of order after the Mosaic Deluge" and was now no more than five thousand years old.

Those who held that the earth had developed over an enormous span of eons through a series of gradual changes were considered heretics. Others, attempting to justify the Biblical story, theorized that the earth had developed as a result of a series of sudden, and indeed supernatural, shocks in which mountains had been thrust up almost overnight while gigantic tidal waves had destroyed all life. After each death-dealing upheaval, new life had been reintroduced by God himself, improving by stages until modern man emerged. Now the world was complete and perfect, as the Deity intended.

With these various theories Charles Lyell, the author of the three-volume, trail-breaking *Principles of Geology*, had no patience. "Never was there a dogma more calculated to further indolence and to blunt the keen edge of curiosity," he declared. Always clear-headed, Lyell touched off the revolution in geology that marked the Victorian Age and paved the way for Charles Darwin's seminal work.

Lyell knew and admired Darwin, and yet when he reached Niagara in 1841, he did not share his friend's theory of evolution, a theory that had yet to see print. More than twenty years would pass before Lyell came to accept it. But he knew a great deal about the age of the earth, for he had examined fossils, shells, and strata in his wanderings across Europe. *Principles* had already been published. In these volumes Lyell indicated his debt to earlier observers who had studied the geology of the area. As for Fairholme, he had never visited the cataract and never would. Lyell did, and in just ten days neatly disposed of the theses of the Fairholme school, although many people stubbornly continued to believe them.

He was a handsome man, Lyell, with long, ascetic features and the high dome and broad forehead of a savant. He was the eldest of ten children of a bookish family in Scotland. His father had an abiding interest in nature, and young Lyell was a great one for shinnying up trees, hunting for birds' nests, and collecting butterflies. He was always as much a naturalist as he was a geologist.

Actually, Lyell was trained as a barrister. A sophisticated member of Lincoln's Inn, he was briefly a regular on the circuit court of southern England. In his spare hours, he played the flute and read a great deal of poetry. Milton was his favourite; no doubt Lyell, who had ruined his eyes poring over law books, identified with the sightless poet. He himself would be nearly blind in the evening of his life. His weak vision and his frail physique did not stop him from scaling cliffs and scrambling down river banks in England and Europe, examining strata and collecting old shells and other fossils from prehistoric seas in an effort to discover the origins of river valleys. On these occasions, it was said, he was insensible to both fatigue and heat.

By 1828, when he set off on a nine-month trip through France, Italy, and Sicily, Lyell had abandoned the practice of law. This was the first of several journeys that brought about a revolution in his thinking and would spark a corresponding revolution in geology. His *Principles* argued that there was a natural – not a supernatural – explanation for every geological phenomenon, that the process of geological development worked so slowly that the earth must be much older than was believed, and that modern geological processes (mountain building, for instance) didn't differ from ancient ones. In short, there never was a series of divine cataclysms, and the existence of mankind on earth was relatively short.

Darwin drew heavily on Lyell's methods and style. The *Principles*, Darwin declared, "altered the whole tone of one's mind." Even when observing something never seen by Lyell, "one yet saw it partially through his eyes." It is not too much to say that without Lyell's pioneer work, *The Origin of Species* might not have been written.

Lyell arrived at Niagara on August 27, 1841, and got his first view of the Falls from a point three miles downriver. The sun was shining full on the cataract and there was no building in view to suggest the presence of civilization – "nothing but the green wood, the falling water, and the white foam." To Lyell, the twin cataracts were even more beautiful than he had expected, though not so grand. In geological interest, they were "far beyond my most sanguine hopes." The splendour of Niagara grew on him, as it did on so many others, after several days. "I at last learned by degrees to comprehend the wonders of the scene," he said, "and to feel its full magnificence."

He, too, noted with mild asperity the harsh encroachment of industrialization on the ethereal world of the cataract. The steam railway had arrived, and Lyell wrote that "it has a strange effect when you have succeeded in obtaining some view of the Falls ... to be suddenly awakened out of your reverie by the loud whistle of a locomotive drawing a load of tourists, and of merchants trafficking between the east and west, who discuss the Falls in three hours between two trains." On the other hand, "Goat Island is the most perfect fairyland that I know." He feared that within a decade it would be given over to factories.

Lyell spent his days at Niagara roaming the gorge, climbing the cliffs, and collecting specimens – shells, fossils, and, in one case, fragments of a mastodon skeleton – in order to determine the geological history of the region. His guide, the botanist Joseph Hooker, who had explored Goat Island, told him of the great slabs that had tumbled from Table Rock in 1818 and again in 1828 as the river chewed into the softer strata beneath. Hooker also pointed out an indentation about forty feet long that had been carved in the middle ledge of limestone in the American Falls since 1815.

During the same period, Lyell learned, the river's erosion had also changed the shape of the Horseshoe Falls, while in just four years Goat Island had lost several acres. Various estimates for the age of the river had been advanced by earlier writers. Robert Blakewell had figured it at ten thousand years – a hypothesis Lyell had accepted in his *Principles*. Others, assuming an erosion rate of a foot a year, calculated that the Falls must have started their retreat from Queenston some thirty-five thousand years earlier. Lyell now tentatively settled on this figure. That presupposed that the erosion rate had been uniform everywhere, but as we know – and as Lyell guessed – it would have been faster at some points, slower at others. Was its current average progress more or less rapid than in the past? That he could not determine.

We can see him now in retrospect, a stooped figure because of his poor eyesight, digging into the shale with his trowel and squinting at the fossils he discovered. With the American geologist James Hall he collected specimens both from the beaches of Goat Island and from the overhanging cliffs above the river. They were, he discovered, remarkably similar. From this he deduced that Goat Island had once been under water (Lake Tonawanda, as we now know) and that a prehistoric river had covered the entire area to a greater depth.

Above the lip of the gorge he found traces of that ancient river bank. The following year he came upon a remnant of the riverbed high up on the Canadian side, a mile and a half upriver from the Whirlpool. Thus he was able to show that the Niagara had once been a broader, shallower watercourse (as it still is above the Falls) and that it had been turned into the turbulent stream at the bottom of a deep and narrow gorge by the advance of the cataract. Evidence of that older, wider river, left behind above the gorge walls, gave Lyell the clues he needed.

Lyell's companion, James Hall, had pointed out that the Whirlpool was probably connected with a break in the Escarpment at St. Davids, west of Queenston. This led to a spectacular discovery – the so-called St. Davids Gorge, the buried channel of another prehistoric river running northwest from the Whirlpool to Lake Ontario. Lyell, who charted it, realized that the Falls, excavating its way upstream, had encountered the course of this ancient stream filled with the rubble of the ages – sediments from the older river and lake and soil from ice sheets – and dug it out again. This explained not only the ninety-degree turn of the river but also the presence of the Whirlpool. More geological evidence found later proved the theory correct.

Lyell left the study of Niagara and went on to a knighthood and a host of awards, medals, and honorary degrees. He died at the age of seventy-seven while again revising his *Principles*. "The Falls of Niagara," he wrote, "teach us not merely to appreciate the power of moving water, but furnish us at the same time with data for estimating the enormous lapse of ages during which that force has operated. A deep and long ravine has been excavated, and the river required ages to accomplish the task, yet the same region affords evidence that the sum of these ages is as nothing, and as the work of yesterday, when compared with the antecedent periods, of which there are monuments in the same district."

There was a time when those thoughts would have been considered outrageously heretical. But the work of Hall and Lyell, both of whom published scientific accounts of their findings, put an effective stopper on further controversy among the savants. Today Lyell's ideas are so commonplace that he himself has faded into obscurity. Only the devotees of geological history now remember the half-blind barrister who climbed the great gorge and unravelled some of the mysteries of the ages.

3

The railroads transformed Niagara, exploited it, glamorized it, cheapened it, and created on the banks of the gorge what has been called "the centre of a vortex of travel." By 1845, close to fifty thousand sightseers annually were swarming over the region, a figure that had doubled in just five years. But the onrush had only begun. The promoters of two major lines, Canada's Great Western and New York's Rochester and Niagara (the forerunner of the New York Central), had their eyes on the new Mecca. Anybody who could afford a ticket could soon enjoy a spectacle that had once been the exclusive privilege of the upper classes.

What was needed was a bridge suspended across that terrible chasm to join the two lines. Someone figured that it would immediately attract double the number of tourists, who would no longer be held back by the prospect of a a turbulent ride in a small ferry. The someone was a respected civil engineer, Charles B. Stuart, who had worked surveying both lines. If the toll were as little as twenty-five cents a passenger, so Stuart figured, the bridge would return a profit of 1 percent on the investment in the very first year.

Stuart knew very little about building bridges. He wasn't at all sure that spanning a gorge eight hundred feet wide and two hundred feet deep was practical. He canvassed the leading engineers in Europe and North America and got a negative reception. Only four said it could be done. But within a few years each member of that remarkable and optimistic quartet –

Charles Ellet, Jr., John Roebling, Samuel Keefer, and Edward W. Serrell – would himself build a suspension bridge across the Niagara between the Falls and Lewiston.

The first to respond to Stuart's query was Ellet, impelled by the swift and impetuous enthusiasm that marked his career. Bold, flamboyant, and ambitious, Ellet was fairly dying to be the first man to bridge the river. That had been his hope since 1833 when, after studying suspension bridges in France, he had announced that Niagara offered him his greatest challenge. He did not know, he said, "in the whole circle of professional schemes, a single project which it would gratify me so much to conduct it to completion."

Now, it seemed, he was to achieve that gratification. His qualifications were admirable. He had trained in Paris at the prestigious École Polytechnique. More important, he had already built a suspension bridge, the first in North America, over the Schuylkill River near Philadelphia. Handsome, dark-eyed, slender, and six feet, two inches tall, he looked like an athlete, and though his health was actually precarious, his energies were prodigious. Now he stood on the brink of a brilliant career that would gain him the title of the "Brunel of America" – a reference to one of the best-known builders of railway bridges in Great Britain who was later the designer of the *Great Eastern*, the biggest ship in history.

He was supremely confident that he could span the river. He had told Stuart that "a bridge may be built across the Niagara below the Falls, which will be entirely secure and in all respects fitted for railroad uses. It will be safe for the passage of locomotives and freight trains, and adapted for any purpose for which it is likely to be applied."

He also explained that to be successful it would have to be carefully designed and properly constructed. There were, he said, "no safer bridges than those on the suspension principle if built understandingly, and none more dangerous if constructed with an imperfect knowledge of the principles of their equilibrium." The day would come when Ellet would have rueful cause to remember those words.

That the suspension bridge was both graceful to look at and economical to build was undeniable. Hung on seemingly gossamer cables and curving seductively over a frothing gorge below the Falls, it would be esthetically ideal. Because it required less material than other steel bridges, it would be cheaper. Nor would any other method of construction be practical. Supporting piers would be difficult to construct securely in that treacherous current; worse, they would obstruct both the view and the flow.

The history of suspension bridges, however, was enough to alarm the more conservative engineers – hence the pessimistic response to Stuart's canvass. Vibrations set up by the feet of marching troops or by droves of cattle had caused several such bridges to collapse, often with fatal results, on both sides of the Atlantic. The experts who pooh-poohed the idea of a suspension bridge at Niagara were convinced it would crumple under the vibrations caused by heavily loaded trains. Yet a suspension bridge it was to be.

The bridge was to be built by two companies, one Canadian, one American, acting together. An eminent Canadian, William Hamilton Merritt, promoter of the first Welland Canal, would be president of the Niagara Falls Suspension Bridge Company. His American opposite was Lot Clark, president of the Niagara Falls International Bridge Company, of which Charles Stuart was a prominent board member.

The contest over who should get the contract to build the bridge quickly narrowed down to the two candidates who knew more about suspension bridges than any other engineers on the continent – the colourful Ellet and the sombre German-born bridge builder John Augustus Roebling, the father of the wire rope industry in North America. Ellet had been first on the scene, and that gave him a considerable advantage over his ponderous rival. The newly formed bridge companies encouraged competition to keep down prices. Ellet's cause was helped in July 1847 when he landed a commission as engineer of another suspension bridge to be built at Wheeling, West Virginia – a plum that undoubtedly impressed the directors of the twin firms.

Ellet contracted to build the Niagara bridge for no more than $190,000 and to have it open for traffic by May 1, 1849. It would be about two and a half miles downstream but in full view of the Falls. It would require an eight-hundred-foot span, twenty-five feet wide – large enough for two carriageways, two footways, and a railway track in the centre.

He was ready to start early in 1848, but a serious problem faced him: he must, at the outset, get a line across the torrent. That could not be done in the conventional manner by boat; the Whirlpool Rapids would devour any craft that attempted the feat, and the ferries were too far upstream. At a dinner in a tavern on the American side, he and his colleagues pondered the question. Ellet favoured a rocket. Somebody else suggested a bombshell hurled by a cannon. A few thought a steamer might hazard the crossing.

In the end, the bridge builder accepted a more original idea – one that tickled his sense of the theatrical. A local iron worker and future judge, Theodore G. Hulett, suggested he offer a cash prize to the first boy who would fly a kite to the opposite bank. A covey of kites on long strings immediately appeared above the gorge from the Canadian side to take advantage of the prevailing winds, which blew from west to east. But no one succeeded in spanning the river until a fifteen-year-old American, Homan Walsh, arrived on the scene. Carrying his kite, *The Union*, he crossed to the Canadian shore by ferry just below the Falls and walked along the top of the cliff for two miles to the point where the bridge was to be built.

He waited a day for a favourable wind, then sent his kite aloft, paying out ball after ball of twine as it soared high above the gorge. All day long Homan Walsh kept his kite flying until at midnight, as he expected, the wind died and the kite began to settle. Suddenly he felt an uneven tug, the string went slack, and he realized that his efforts had been in vain. The string, caught in the rocks of the gorge, had snapped.

Now he found himself marooned in Canada: the broken ice in the river was so heavy no ferry could chance a crossing. For eight days he lingered in Clifton, staying with friends, until the river cleared and the service resumed. Back he went to recover and repair his kite, then returned to the Canadian cliffside where, at last, his efforts succeeded. For the rest of his long life – he lived well into his eighties – Homan Walsh liked to tell that story.

A day after the successful flight, a stronger line was attached to the kite string. A rope followed, and, eventually, a cable consisting of thirty-six strands of No. 10 wire. Ellet then built two temporary wooden towers, each fifty feet high, facing each other across the gorge, over which the 1,200-foot cable was passed and anchored.

Now he had to devise a method by which workmen and supplies could shuttle back and forth across the gorge. In the Eagle Tavern, over a pint of ale, he and Hulett worked out a design for an iron basket that could hang suspended from rollers on the cable and be winched from one side to the other by a man turning a windlass. Ellet, with his sharpened sense of publicity, decided upon a personal demonstration – after all, both bridge companies were floating stock in the enterprise, and he himself had subscribed for a substantial amount. Getting into the precarious cable car, the ebullient engineer had himself hauled to the far side and back again. The wind was high, the weather chilly, but Ellet, perched 240 feet above the rapids, was having a wonderful time. The view, he wrote to a friend, was "one of the sublimest prospects which nature has prepared on this globe of ours."

Soon others were clamouring – and paying a fee – for a

chance to experience this most novel of Niagara's thrills. Ellet's contract did not allow him to collect tolls, but he got around that problem by charging a dollar to anyone who would like to "observe at first hand the engineering wonder of bridging the Niagara." As many as 125 people a day took up the offer, three-quarters of them women. One man, so the story went, took one look at Ellet's iron basket and opted for the little rowboat then used as a ferry. Then he walked back to the bridge site to meet his wife, who was coolly descending from the iron basket.

Ellet's spectacular bridge machinery was not the only new tourist attraction at the Falls. The crowds were increasing and entrepreneurs were taking full advantage of the influx. A water-powered inclined railway, completed in 1846, brought sightseers to the base of the American Falls, while the little steamer *Maid of the Mist*, launched the same year, took its passengers directly into the spray of the Horseshoe.

Ellet, meanwhile, was constructing a preliminary bridge to act as a scaffolding from which to build the platform of the subsequent railway span. Actually, he was building two suspension bridges, side by side, and planning to lash them together. He built four massive towers, two on each side of the gorge, to support four cables. Two sets of walkways, each four feet wide and each suspended from two cables, were by now projecting over the gorge on both sides of the river. The sections of the downriver platform had been joined, but the neighbouring walkway was still under construction, projecting one hundred feet from the Canadian bank and two hundred from the American, when a furious gale struck.

The force of the wind instantly wrecked the unfinished portion of the southern section, throwing the floor across the cable that carried Ellet's iron basket. Two men working on the Canadian side managed to reach safety, but three on the American side were stranded. Marooned on the unsteady platform, clinging helplessly to the suspending cables with the floor swaying alarmingly under their feet, they were forced to stay put until the wind dropped. Then, as a twelve-foot ladder was lashed to the iron basket, Theodore Hulett called for a volunteer to try to rescue the trio.

A young workman, Charles Ellis, stepped forward. "I'm your man!" he said. Hulett warned him not to take more than one man at a time into the basket. The basket cable was already under strain because the full weight of the Canadian side of the bridge lay across it. Could it even sustain the additional weight of two men before snapping? Moved by the pleas of the stranded workmen, Ellis gambled that it could. Ignoring Hulett's warning, he allowed all three to climb into the basket. All were brought safely to the American side.

Meanwhile, an extraordinary and totally unexpected event occurred. It had no effect on the bridge construction, but it was so unbelievable it defied common sense. Indeed, it was not credited by those who did not witness it and not understood by those who did. On the night of March 28, 1848, Niagara Falls went dry.

The rapids above the cataract dwindled to a trickle. The twin cascades shrank until they consisted of little more than a few thin streams of water, dripping over the exposed cliff. And the silence! People long used to the roar of Niagara were actually awakened by the unaccustomed quiet. They lined the cliffside and in the torchlight saw long stretches of mud and naked boulders between scattered pools of water.

The following day almost everyone in the neighbourhood was able to explore the recesses and crannies that had never before been exposed to mortal eyes. People walked from shore to shore picking up souvenirs – bayonets, swords, gun barrels, and tomahawks from the War of 1812. A detachment of cavalry trotted up the riverbed. A party of enthusiasts danced a quadrille on a flat rock near the middle of the stream.

On the American side, George W. Holley drove out more than three hundred yards from the Goat Island shore, stood on the lip of the Horseshoe, and with the aid of a team of horses began salvaging huge pieces of timber hanging over the naked precipice.

On the Canadian side, Thomas Street and his daughter rode for three-quarters of a mile down the dry riverbed above the Falls. From Table Rock they walked to the edge of the precipice about one-third of the way to Goat Island, stuck a pole into a crevice, and tied a handkerchief to it. Street looked over at the river below and saw the water so shallow that immense jagged rocks previously hidden by the swirling waters stood out starkly. He shuddered when he thought of how frequently he had passed over these hazards in the *Maid of the Mist*. That same day the rocks were blasted to fragments and removed.

In the evening, the churches were crammed with people who talked fearfully about the end of the world. But before a real panic could set in, a new sound broke the unaccustomed silence – a low growl that caused the earth to vibrate and the air to tremble. A few minutes later, a wall of water crashed over the lip of the Falls and Niagara was in business again.

The explanation for this curious and frightening episode was fascinating. Heavy westerly winds blowing across Erie, the shallowest of the Great Lakes, had driven the bulk of its water over the Falls. Then the winds changed. Much of the water that was left was forced back far to the west. The wind also broke up the ice, which formed a jam in the river near Buffalo, effectively damming it until only a trickle ran between the banks. When the ice jam broke and the wind dropped, the Falls returned to their former glory.

Ellet, having repaired his damaged platforms, completed his service bridge in July 1848. Now it was possible to make a trip from bank to bank as easily as the one the astonished populace had enjoyed so briefly the night the Falls went dry. Ellet was so captivated with the idea that he could not wait for safety railings to be erected on both sides of the span. He called for a horse and buggy and, standing with the reins in his hand "like a

Roman charioteer" in one account, drove himself across the flimsy structure to the cheers of the spectators. Women fainted at the sight, so it was said, while strong men gasped; but then, women were forever fainting and strong men gasping in the records of that century.

Such stunts, so typical of Ellet, not only enhanced his own reputation but also focused public attention on his project. And therein lay the seeds of his downfall. The service bridge was so popular that when Ellet opened it in midsummer, everybody wanted to use it. Within a year it would accumulate a five-thousand-dollar profit in tolls – but for whom? This question added to the nasty wrangle that was developing between Ellet and the bridge companies.

Indeed, Ellet's relationship with the two companies had been testy from the beginning. The international nature of the Niagara gorge did not help. Matters were complicated because the companies were operating under two legal systems. Moreover, there was jealousy between the two presidents, and arguments arose about which company was responsible for paying the contractors. Just as construction was getting under way, a depression struck that delayed shipments of masonry. The companies tried to insist that Ellet act as a salesman to push stock in the venture, something he had not contemplated. They suggested he postpone the project or settle for a lesser structure that would be suitable for wagons and teams only. It did not help matters that Ellet was also at work on the Wheeling bridge and absent from Niagara for days at a time.

Ellet was infuriated by these wrangles. "I have worked hard," he wrote to Lot Clark of the New York company in May, "– expended a great deal to come here – broken up my home – abandoned important interests – deserted my business – have paid away my money, received nothing, and been stripped of all the profits."

Two months later the controversy reached a climax over the service bridge tolls that Ellet was keeping for himself. The bridge companies fired him and, with the help of an obliging Canadian sheriff, seized the bridge. The courts issued an injunction giving temporary control and possession of the structure to the companies. When the injunction was lifted in October, a wild confrontation followed in which Ellet's agents took control of the American side of the bridge with the help of a cannon loaded with buckshot.

Ellet soon gave up the legal struggle that followed. A compromise of sorts was reached: it was said that he was paid off with ten thousand dollars. At the end of December, Ellet, to his considerable relief, relinquished all connection with the Niagara bridge and got on with the job at Wheeling. Niagara Falls now had a bridge suitable for the carriage trade only. Ellet's successor would be his one-time rival, the methodical John Roebling. It was he who would build the world's first railway suspension bridge across the forbidding gorge.

4

Roebling was a far different creature from Ellet. Apart from their engineering expertise, they were as dissimilar as steel and silk.

The deliberate and generally humourless Roebling was as inflexible as the bridges he built. Compared with the impulsive and irrepressible Ellet, he was rocklike. He was the Ironmaster of Trenton – a man of iron with all the virtues of iron, as his eulogist would eventually declaim. "Iron was in his blood and sometimes entered his very soul." Roebling's will was so strong that he used it to ward off seasickness on the immigrant ship that brought him to America in 1831. He *determined* not to yield to the malady, striding about the deck all night, refusing to give in.

Unlike Ellet, who was all sizzle and froth and quick to take umbrage, Roebling was slow to arouse and tenacious in his ambitions. When he built a bridge he supervised every detail, left nothing to chance, prepared himself for every contingency. These Teutonic qualities were apparent when he decided to settle in the United States at the age of twenty-five. Long before he sailed he had carefully surveyed the prospect, state by state, so that he knew exactly where to put down his roots.

He came from the walled town of Mühlhausen in Thuringia, the son of an easy-going tobacconist and a ferociously ambitious mother who channelled all her energies into John, her fifth and youngest child. She entered him in the Royal Polytechnic Institute in Berlin where, according to family legend, he was the favourite disciple of the philosopher Hegel. But it was as an engineer and architect that he graduated, and it was as a farmer that he came to America. With several other countrymen he purchased seven thousand acres of land in Pennsylvania and formed a German-American village that would be called Saxonburg.

Seventeen years later, in 1848, when Ellet parted with the bridge companies, John Augustus Roebling was forty-two, a tall, lean engineer, his long, sombre face lined with deep furrows, his steel-blue eyes unblinking beneath a heavy brow, his beard giving him the appearance of a Biblical prophet.

He had long since given up farming to become the founder of the American wire rope industry. He had come to America while the canal still reigned, when the major communities were linked by a network of manmade waterways. Moonlighting in the winter months as a surveyor and dam builder, he had noticed deficiencies in the Kentucky hemp ropes used to haul canal boats across the Allegheny Mountains on the portage railroad that linked the eastern and western sections of the Pennsylvania Canal. The boats were hoisted into wheeled cradles and dragged by rope hawsers up the inclines, then dropped down on the far side to rejoin the waterway. Under the strain of this system, the thick hemp quickly wore out and had to be replaced.

Why not make the rope out of twisted wire? Roebling asked himself. It would be stronger, lighter, more durable. He fiddled with the idea, built a wire ropewalk on his farm, and eventually taught his fellow Germans his own technique of winding and weaving the strands. But when he approached the canal company, he met a wall of resistance.

Nobody had ever made wire rope in America. The Pennsylvania politicians who controlled the canal wanted no part of the idea; nor, understandably, did the hemp manufacturers. Roebling finally managed to wangle permission to try his scheme on one of the canal's ten inclined railways. But he no sooner had his wire rope in place than his enemies chopped it in two.

The stubborn engineer went to the top – to the president of the state's canal commission – and in a few bold sentences talked himself into a superintendent's job. Soon all ten inclines were equipped with Roebling's wire rope. "God is good!" said Roebling.

But the canal era was nearing its end, snuffed out by the new railroads. Undaunted, Roebling turned his inventive mind to another use for wire rope. He remembered that in his university days he had been impressed by a bridge suspended by chains over a small stream. Indeed, he had written a thesis on the subject. Now it occurred to him that the same principle could be used for a cross-river aqueduct but using wire rope, which was stronger than any chain.

He worked out his plans and calculations in the greatest detail and laid them before the canal company that was about to build an aqueduct across the Allegheny River at Pittsburgh. The idea was unprecedented. In Germany it would probably have been rejected. But Roebling, counting on New World daring, convinced the engineers that his scheme should be tried. If he failed, he faced ruin. But he did not fail, nor did he expect to. In fact, the success made his reputation.

If aqueduct pipes could be carried suspended over a broad river, Roebling pondered, why not a bridge? By 1846 he had built his first suspension bridge over the Monongahela River at Pittsburgh. It lasted thirty-five years.

By 1850, when after a two-year hiatus he was finally awarded the Niagara contract, Roebling had four more suspension aqueducts to his credit. He had also moved his wire rope business to Trenton, New Jersey. There he designed everything himself – not only the new plant but every piece of machinery he installed. His confidence in his abilities was absolute; he trusted no one else. Years went by before he could be persuaded to hire an assistant engineer or draughtsman.

Few others had his certitude. To the engineering profession he was a daring experimenter, possibly a madman. Five chain suspension bridges had already collapsed in Europe. Then in 1850, a wire suspension bridge twisted and crumpled under the tread of marching troops. Why was Roebling tempting disaster?

Robert Stephenson, son of the inventor of the locomotive and one of the best-known bridge builders in England, put no trust in the Roebling concept. He was convinced no suspension bridge could support a heavy train lumbering across its unsubstantial arch. Stephenson's cumbersome and expensive bridges were constructed of tubular steel. "If your bridge succeeds," he told Roebling, "then mine have been magnificent blunders."

Roebling moved implacably forward. Using Ellet's original span as a service bridge, he started construction in 1851. Again he oversaw every detail, planned every step, arranged for any contingency, left nothing to others. Since each Roebling bridge was different from every other, designed for the particular site and circumstance, he was like an artist who puts his own stamp or signature on canvas or sculpture.

Unlike the flamboyant Ellet, he worked without fanfare, often in the bitter cold, without a break. He rarely left the site. A town known, aptly, as Suspension Bridge was springing up on the American side, and from there, by mail, he ran his factory in Trenton, again following every detail himself – from the installation of new machinery to the collection of debts.

He worked as a man obsessed, oblivious to family and friends, shunning holidays, forgetting anniversaries. When the intricate work of cable spinning began in December 1853, he abandoned any thought of Christmas because he trusted no one but himself to oversee the job. "Mrs. Roebling wishes me to come home," he had written to one of his staff. He concluded bluntly, "I cannot."

When, on New Year's Day, 1854, she bore him his fourth son, Roebling heard about it from Charles Swan, his factory superintendent, in a business letter, of all things. He seemed baffled and bewildered. "You say in your last, that *Mrs. Roebling & the child are pretty well*. This takes me by *surprise*, not having been informed at all ... what do you mean? Please answer by return of mail. I myself was a little doubtful about the sufficiency of a 3-inch shaft – must try it now..." And thus, in spite of his puzzlement, he went on with the pressing business of the day.

He had no patience with the conventional thinking that a suspension bridge should be flexible. In these "loose fabrics swung up in the air for the very purposes of swinging" he foresaw future trouble. In Roebling's view, the bridge itself should be as stiff as the wooden aqueducts he had previously designed.

Roebling's two-tiered bridge resembled nothing so much as a gigantic iron girder, stretched across the gorge suspended by cables. It was 820 feet long, 24 feet wide, and 20 feet deep, an oblong metal box, slightly convex at the centre. The railway tracks and pedestrian walk ran along the upper level – the top of the box. Common traffic used the plank roadway at the bottom. In between was a massive nest of trusses, girders, and cables designed to keep the entire structure rigid. Roebling had, in effect, fashioned a single hollow beam as protection against cumulative undulations.

Roebling had made it impossible for his bridge to sway or twist in the wind. A heavy team of horses, Roebling declared, would cause a much greater jar or trembling than a train crossing at five miles an hour. The concept was Roebling's own; it had never been tried before. This was the first time stiffening trusses had been used in bridge building, a radical innovation that would in the future become standard for all suspension bridges.

The span, when completed, weighed a thousand tons. It was hung from four ten-inch cables of wrought iron, each constructed of 3,640 wires, oiled, spliced, reeled, strung, adjusted, and finally wrapped by his own patented methods. As he wrote, with his usual confidence, the finished webs were not only pleasing but "their massive proportions are also well calculated to inspire confidence in their strength." The tension composing each wire, he declared, "is so nearly uniform I feel justified in using the term perfect."

In developing his theory of stiffening, Roebling was intuitive; the principles of aerodynamics were not known in 1854 and would not be for the best part of a century. No other engineer caught on to the fact that a high wind could cause undulations in the floor of a bridge that would build up until the bridge was destroyed.

Even Ellet failed to grasp this principle. The Niagara Suspension Bridge would survive for forty-two years. His own, over the Ohio River at Wheeling, lasted a mere five. Completed in 1849, it was the longest span in the world – more than a thousand feet – but remarkably light and narrow for its length. It lacked the strong mesh of stays and trusses that Roebling insisted upon, and that was its undoing.

In May 1854, a high wind struck Ellet's bridge and collapsed it into a tangle of twisted girders. A reporter for the Wheeling *Intelligencer* had just walked off the structure when the catastrophe occurred. He turned to see it "heaving and dashing with tremendous force." It "lunged like a ship in a storm," the walkway rising almost to the height of the towers, then falling back, twisting and writhing until, in one last determined fling, half the flooring was nearly upside down.

"The great body of the flooring and the suspenders forming something like a basket between the towers, was swayed to and fro like the motion of a pendulum. Each vibration giving it increased momentum, the cables, which sustained the whole structure, were unable to resist a force operating on them in so many different directions, and were literally twisted and wrenched from their fastenings." Shortly afterward, "down went the immense structure from its dizzy height to the stream below, with an appalling crash and roar."

The engineering profession as a whole was baffled by this unexpected development. But not Roebling, who read the account and knew at once what had happened. His immediate reaction was to order additional stiffening for his bridge. From this point on engineers ignored Roebling's principles at their peril. Almost ninety years later one group did. On November 7, 1940, the Wheeling disaster was duplicated, almost blow for blow, when a high wind struck the new Tacoma Narrows Bridge over Puget Sound in Washington State, causing it to shake to pieces.

In July 1854, a different kind of disaster struck Roebling's bridge crew. A plague of cholera broke out, causing sixty deaths in the first week. Roebling didn't stop his own work for a minute. Constantly exposed to the disease, he decided to use his willpower to fight it off, as he had once fought off seasickness. He paced his room all night, refusing to give in. "Keep off *fear*," he declared, "– this is the great secret. Whoever is afraid of cholera will be attacked, and no treatment can save him...." Whether through willpower or plain happenstance, he survived. The epidemic ended in August.

The following January, Roebling's bridge weathered a tremendous twelve-hour gale. "My bridge didn't move a muscle," he said proudly. Less than three months later, on March 8,

1855, with the structure almost complete, he put it to a series of tests using heavy locomotives. That day, a twenty-three-ton engine of the Great Western Railway crossed the span "without the least vibration."

On March 18, when the bridge was opened to the public, a twenty-eight-ton engine carrying twenty double-loaded freight cars with a gross weight of 368 tons crossed the bridge, covering its entire length – the first train in history to cross a bridge suspended by wire cables. "No vibrations whatever," Roebling noted jubilantly. "Less noise and movement than in a common truss bridge."

The first passenger trains, jammed to the roof with people, crossed at the rate of twenty a day. "No one is afraid to cross," Roebling exulted. "The passage of trains is a great sight, worth seeing it." The Niagara Falls, New York, *Gazette* headlined a "Great Triumph of Art." It was an even greater triumph of engineering. For this was the first railway suspension bridge in the world, constructed at a cost of only $400,000. As Roebling reported to the bridge companies, a European bridge would have cost four million "without serving a better purpose or insuring greater safety." Stephenson's heavy tubular bridges in Great Britain were now seen as obsolete. The suspension bridge belonged to the future.

Roebling's Niagara bridge remained intact until, in 1897, it was finally retired to make way for a wider and stronger structure geared to the increase in rail traffic and the heavier rolling stock. But its wire cables were as sound as they had been when Roebling installed them more than forty-two years before. The same could not be said for the two bridges constructed by the other two men – Edward Serrell and Samuel Keefer – who had once been in the running with Ellet and Roebling to span the Niagara.

Serrell was given a contract to build a highway suspension bridge over the Niagara between Lewiston and Queenston. The 1,053-foot span was completed in 1851, damaged by a gale in

1855, and rescued by Roebling, who installed a system of guy ropes to protect it from the high winds. In the spring of 1864, after an ice jam had caused the workmen to loosen the guys, another gale destroyed Serrell's bridge.

Three years later Keefer, an Ottawa engineer, was given the task of building the Clifton suspension bridge two miles closer to the Falls than the Roebling structure. This wooden suspension bridge – 1,268 feet long – was opened in 1869, widened and reconstructed with steel in 1887, and reopened in 1888. Seven months later, on January 9, 1889, a hurricane tore it from the cliffs and dumped it into the river, where it remains hidden beneath the waters to this day.

Roebling's stint at Niagara was scarcely completed before he was contemplating a new and more ambitious suspension bridge. In 1867 he achieved his ambition when he was appointed chief engineer of the Brooklyn Bridge in New York City. Two years later, tragedy struck. Just as work on the bridge was about to begin, on June 29, 1869, he suffered an injury. He was standing on a piling at the ferry slip in Brooklyn when the ferry hit it a glancing blow. Roebling's foot was crushed and some of his toes had to be amputated.

No one considered the accident serious. Roebling, with his usual stoicism, fought off the pain, but his willpower could not fend off tetanus as it had once fought off seasickness. He died six weeks later. A statue was raised to him by the citizens of Trenton, but his real memorials are the bridges – not just *his* bridges, but all the suspension bridges whose graceful ancestor linked two nations at the mid-point of the nineteenth century.

Chapter Four

1

To Isabella Lucy Bird, a spunky if snobbish Englishwoman, Roebling's unfinished suspension bridge appeared infinitely more interesting at first glance than her initial view of the Horseshoe Falls. "The floor of the bridge is 230 feet above the river, and the depth of the river immediately under it is 250 feet!" she wrote. "The view from it is magnificent; to the left the furious river, confined in a narrow space, rushes in rapids to the Whirlpool; and to the right the Horse-shoe Fall pours its torrents of waters into the dark and ever invisible abyss."

This was her second trip to Niagara, but until this moment she had not been too impressed by its surroundings. She was just twenty-three years old, on the verge of a career that would establish her under her married name – Isabella Bishop – as one of the most popular and widely read travel writers of her time. Deeply religious – her father was an evangelical low-church Anglican clergyman – well educated, and more than a little jingoistic and supercilious, she was one of a growing band of peripatetic Englishwomen who were exploring North America as they might have scrutinized the unknown jungles of Africa.

Since the opening of the Erie Canal, a dozen or more women had published lively accounts of their adventures at Niagara Falls, including one appearing in 1848 entitled *An English-woman in America*. At Niagara, Miss Bird was scribbling notes for her own work, which with perfect assurance she would call The *Englishwoman in America*. The two books reflected the political and social bents of their authors. Everything about North America espoused by the earlier writer, Sarah Mytton Maury, a formidable mother of eleven, the youthful Miss Bird decried. That included slavery, Roman Catholics, Irish immigrants, and the Democratic party.

Her first view of the cataract in the summer of 1854 had been disappointing. The Horseshoe Falls were partially obscured by

100

foliage and mist while the American Falls seemed to her not much more than a gigantic millrace. But she reserved her disdain for the growing commercialism that was defacing and degrading the natural surroundings – a collection of mills on the American side and "a great fungus growth" of museums, curiosity shops, taverns, and pagodas on the British.

She had scarcely attained what she called "the proper degree of mental abstraction with which it is necessary to contemplate Niagara" when she was beset by the usual gaggle of hack drivers, urging her to do the rounds of the area for four dollars. She fled to the Clifton House only to be importuned by a new group with another volley of appeals. Most of them appeared to be half tipsy.

In that summer season, the white Clifton House, with its three green verandahs, its huge ballroom, and its crystal chandeliers, was the centre of social activity at the Falls. Balls, picnics, and parties were held, many in the handsome garden at the front of the hotel. Here, to the strains of an invisible orchestra, the anointed danced under flickering torches in a scene that reminded Miss Bird of *A Midsummer Night's Dream*.

The hotel could accommodate four hundred guests, "tourists, merchants, lawyers, officers, senators, wealthy southerners and sallow down-easters, all flying alike from business and heat." But when Miss Bird returned in the autumn, the gaiety was over, and she sat down to a rushed lunch with only twenty-five persons. Her sensibilities were offended not only by the speed with which the meal was eaten – she clocked it at five minutes – but also at the frantic pace that the visitor was otherwise expected to maintain to take in every spectacle.

All Miss Bird wanted to do was to contemplate the Falls in solitude, but that was difficult. She found herself unable to resist the cozening of guides and hack drivers who insisted that she view the spectacle from every angle – from above, below, and even behind – descend the spiral staircase to its base, cross by ferry through its spray, and visit Bloody Run, Burning

Springs, and other points of interest, not to mention the Indian curiosity shops, which seemed to her to have little to do with the Falls.

She was determined to view the Falls from Goat Island, and now, on this second visit in 1855, she found she could travel by hack across Roebling's newly opened bridge to the American side without hazarding the rocky ferry crossing. That, however, meant another infernal squabble with a crowd of some twenty ragged hack drivers, all clamouring for a fare. She and two others guests, a Mr. and Mrs. Lawrence (whom she clumsily disguised in her book with the pseudonym "Walrence"), were scarcely out the door when the drivers all began shouting various prices.

The first offered to do the rounds for five dollars. A second dropped to four dollars and a half and was immediately attacked as a thief and a blackguard, whereupon "a man in rags" offered to take them to Goat Island for three. When she accepted, the first hackman offered to meet the three-dollar price, insisting that his rival was drunk and his carriage wasn't fit for a lady.

A fist fight followed, with much shouting and squabbling, until the ragged man succeeded in driving up to the door. Only then did Miss Bird realize, with sinking heart, that the hack really *wasn't* fit for ladies – the stuffing was quite bare of upholstery, the splashboards were held together by pieces of rope, and the driver was at least half drunk.

Off they went, bumping along the Niagara gorge, 250 feet above the green flood, with no protective parapet to offer security. At the bridge they paid a toll of sixty cents to a man who insisted on coins, saying (as many did at that time) that banknotes were only waste paper. But the view was magnificent.

Having crossed the bridge, assuring the American customs officers that they were not smugglers, they were jolted over the portage road, all stumps and potholes, which the half-tipsy driver made no attempt to avoid. "There now, faith, wasn't I nearly done for myself?" he exclaimed, as he was flung from his seat and almost over the dashboard.

More and more visitors to the Falls were becoming irritated by the commercialization of the Niagara area, and Miss Bird was no exception. Niagara Falls, New York (it had long since discarded the name of Manchester), with its "agglomeration of tea gardens, curiosity-shops, and monster hotels, with domes of shining tin," did not appeal to her. It was not until she crossed Augustus Porter's bridge and paid her twenty-five-cent toll that she began to appreciate her surroundings. Here on Goat Island (she preferred the little-used name Iris Island, conjuring up as it did the goddess of the rainbow) Isabella Bird let her emotions run away with her.

It was a glorious afternoon. A slight shower had fallen, so that sparkling raindrops hung from every leaf and twig. A rainbow spanned the river, and the fresh, clear light shone on the scarlet and crimson leaves of the sugar maple. The droshky drivers and the satanic mills were all forgotten. Here at last she had achieved the full, joyous realization of her ideas of Niagara. She could look out beyond the tangle of the shore at islets garlanded with trees and vines and carpeted with moss. Untrodden by the foot of man, these pinpoints of green foliage were protected by waters that raged and foamed in wild turmoil – beauty and terror in perfect combination. The trio made their way across the island and walked through the shaded groves of ancient trees, then on to little Luna Island to drink in "a view of matchless magnificence."

She could not ignore the darker side. Since 1848, no one could venture onto Luna Island without being reminded of the bizarre tragedy that had occurred on a hot July evening that year. A group of tourists, including a Mr. and Mrs. De Forest, their young daughter, Nettie, and a family friend, Charles Addington, described as "a young man of great talent and promise," disported themselves on the islet. The De Forests and some others returned to Goat Island to rest on one of the benches, De Forest calling out to his daughter to follow and to stay away from the water.

"Never mind – let her alone – I'll watch her," said Addington. The child pulled gleefully on his coat, whereupon he seized her playfully, crying, "Ah! you rogue, you're caught! Shall I throw you in?"

She wriggled out of his arms, took one step too far, and toppled into the roaring river. Addington sprang after her, tried to pull her back, and failed. Both went over the Falls to their deaths, the child locked in the young man's arms, Addington crying out, "For Jesus' sake, O save our souls!" – or so the guide told it. The mangled bodies were found some days later, the little girl still clutching her parasol.

Duly chastened by this dreadful tale, Miss Bird and her companions climbed to the top of Terrapin Tower, where the scene itself transcended everything that had gone before. "No existing words can describe it, no painter can give the remotest idea of it; it is the voice of the Great Creator," Isabella Bird wrote. She shuddered at the sight of the cauldron below, lost in foam and mist, and of the frail bridge that had brought her to this spot, and felt as she came down the trembling staircase that one wish of her life had been gratified.

The mixed bag of impressions continued, rather like a modern television program in which a splendid travelogue is interrupted by squalid commercials. Bath Island, one of the several rocky pinpoints in the rapids above the American Falls, was "lovely in itself, but desecrated by the presence of a remarkably hirsute American, who keeps a toll-house, with the words 'Ice-creams' and 'Indian Curiosities' painted in large letters on it."

Back on the mainland she was again struck by the beauty of the scene. But her enthusiasm was swiftly dampened by a visit to a curio shop, where she bought several overpriced souvenirs. The hack driver, meanwhile, having managed to refortify himself with drink, almost overturned the cab on the way to the Whirlpool. There Miss Bird, who had a distinct flair for the macabre, was transfixed by the impetuous rush of the waters. "Their fury is resistless, and the bodies of those who are carried over the falls are whirled round here in a horrible dance, frequently till decomposition takes place," she reported.

Now she insisted that their guide tell the story of the origin of Bloody Run, a narrow stream that poured over a massive cliff on the American side and into the Stygian chasm. Lawrence protested, fearing the effect of the story on the weak nerves of his wife. But the implacable Miss Bird got her way, confessing, as she gazed into the yawning depths, that "imagination lent an added horror to the tale."

On a sultry morning in September 1763, a body of one hundred British soldiers, forwarding goods from Fort Niagara to Lake Erie, had sat down on the edge of this precipice, at a spot known as Devil's Hole, to take their rest. There they were the victims of two ambushes by Seneca Indians in the pay of the French. The natives tomahawked them on the spot and then hurled the lot – wagons, horses, soldiers, and drivers – over the cliff until the little stream, in Isabella Bird's later description, became "a torrent purple with human gore."

Back at the Clifton House, still yearning to enjoy an uninterrupted view of the Horseshoe Falls, she felt herself put upon again when she was urged to go behind the curtain of falling water. The Lawrences were too nervous – said they couldn't stand the trip – but as an Englishwoman, Miss Bird *must* chance the adventure. The capabilities of Englishwomen, she thought drily, were vastly overrated by Americans. Nevertheless, she felt she had no choice but to uphold the honour of her country and her sex.

It makes an intriguing picture: the very proper Englishwoman, gritting her teeth and doing her duty, dismayed to find she must disrobe to the skin in the Table Rock Hotel and don an oiled calico hood, a loose overgarment (it reminded her of a carter's frock), blue worsted stockings, and a pair of oversized rubber boots. Embarrassed by this odd but serviceable costume, she ran the gauntlet of a group of loiterers and then waded through a sea of mud to the spiral staircase that led down the cliff and under Table Rock. She would have much preferred to sit *on* the rock and drink in the scenery.

In the abyss below, behind the falling water, she experienced the deafening gusts of wind and blinding showers others had described before her. She wanted to retreat, she tried to scream, but her voice was lost in the thunder of the cataract. Her guide, again to her dismay, was a black man, and now as he extended his hand to steady her, she took it – not quite free of the childhood fancy that "the black comes off." She was not used to black people and could not escape the feeling that she was being led to destruction by the darkest of imps.

On the narrow and slippery ledge, no more than a foot wide, behind the curtain of water with the gulf boiling seventy feet below and the gusts of wind acting as a bar to progress, she grasped his hand. The ledge narrowed. She could hardly stand with her feet abreast. She pleaded with her guide to stop, but he could only guess what she wanted to say. "It's worse going back," he shrieked in her ear. She made a desperate attempt to move. Four steps took her to the end of the ledge. With the breath sucked out of her lungs, she could barely stand upright in the face of the gusts. This was Termination Rock, as far as any human being had been able to go; and so, with the guide's help, she turned about and they retraced their steps.

And yet, in spite of all the dangers and all the embarrassments, the shrill importunings of the guides and the nervousness of the Lawrences, she felt emotionally fulfilled. The spectacle before her, half obscured by the lashing spray, left an indelible impression. It was as if she were standing in a magnificent shrine formed by the natural curve of the Falls and the overhanging shelf of the precipice. With her, as with others, the experience was transcendental. "The temple," she wrote, "seems a fit and awful shrine for Him who 'rides on the wings of mighty winds.'" Completely shut out from man's puny works, "the mind naturally rises in adoring contemplation of Him whose voice is heard in the 'thunder of waters.'"

Staunchly refusing the traditional hot brandy that was offered to those who had undergone the expèrience, she took such a severe chill that she came down with what was then called "the ague." She didn't regret her adventure, nor did she boast of it. But she still hadn't seen what she had come to see.

Now she was stubbornly determined to have a good, long look at the Horseshoe. Fending off the hack drivers and "refusing to be victimised by burning springs, museums, prisoned eagles, and mangy buffaloes," she made her way down to the ferry landing, scrambled onto a rock farther out in the water, and there in undistracted solitude she sat, oblivious to everything but the cataract itself.

When at last she arose, the sun had long since set. A young moon shining on the cascading waters made them appear to be composed of drifting snow. She realized with a start that she had been gazing on the vista for almost four hours. The scene that had once disappointed now exalted her.

In one way it was very much as she had expected, yet it was also totally different. She was not the first nor would she be the last of those newcomers who, having read too many accounts of the Falls, found them less than advertised but, as the days went by and the cataract worked its slow magic, changed their attitudes and became worshippers at the shrine.

Her clothes saturated with the mist, Isabella Bird finally tore herself from the hypnotic spectacle, made her way up the cliff, and then at midnight took an omnibus to the railway station near the suspension bridge. There, with the manmade scream of the locomotive drowning out the natural thunder of Niagara, she boarded the train and slept all the way to Hamilton.

2

In the bridge-building years of Ellet and Roebling, the arriving tourists pouring off the new trains at Niagara could not fail to notice a bearded, hawk-faced young artist standing at his easel, painting, painting, painting. Wherever they went – to Goat Island or to the gorge, to the half-finished railway bridge or to the Clifton House – there he was in his cap and high boots, pursuing an astonishing goal.

His name was Godfrey Frankenstein and his plan was to produce the most stupendous moving panorama of Niagara ever attempted. The concept fitted the times, for this was a yeasty period. Europe was coming out of its revolutionary ferment. The potato famine was driving hundreds of thousands of Irish peasants to North America. The eyes of the British world were focused on the remarkable Crystal Palace Exhibition in London. Commodore Perry reached Japan and opened a new window on the East. It was the age of the new – the Morse telegraph and the Singer sewing machine, not to mention the Colt revolver – and Godfrey Frankenstein intended to be part of it.

By 1844, when he first visited Niagara, more than seventy painters had produced hundreds of oils, watercolours, drawings, and engravings of the Falls. To many – and Frankenstein was one – the spectacle was too vast, too theatrical to be squeezed into the narrow confines of the normal canvas. A succession of ingenious artists had already tried their hands at long strip paintings, ambitious panoramas, cycloramas (on a curved backdrop), and three-dimensional dioramas. Mere paint and canvas were not enough, as some of the entrepreneurial artists who preceded Frankenstein had realized. Back in 1728, an ingenious Frenchman had created a new kind of entertainment for his London audience. Known as the Eido Fuksian, it was a scenic tableau entitled *The Cataract of Niagara Falls in North America*. An animated peepshow, it was the wonder of the age.

Through the use of sound, artificial light, and moving stage scenery it achieved effects that at the time seemed almost magical.

Such imaginative fancies were to the nineteenth century what the wide-screen and 3-D motion pictures were to the twentieth. One panorama of Niagara Falls covered five thousand square feet of canvas. Another "unequalled Diorama" in Philadelphia took four years to build and represented "the Rapids and falling sheets of water in actual motion." In London in 1823, stage designers used ten thousand gallons of water to represent the Falls as backdrop for a play. In New York, five years later, William Dunlap's farce, *A Trip to Niagara*, was played down stage before a gigantic moving panorama. In 1851, two ingenious Philadelphia photographers constructed a mechanical marvel that they called *A Physiorama of the Falls of Niagara*. It contained twenty separate scenes.

But it remained for Frankenstein, a German immigrant, to produce, in 1853, the most spectacular and successful moving panorama of all. Frankenstein came from a family of painters that included his father and his four siblings. They moved from Darmstadt, Germany, in 1831 when young Godfrey was eleven years old and already something of a prodigy. At twelve he was apprenticed to a sign painter. At thirteen he left that job and started his own sign-painting business. At nineteen he opened a portrait studio in Cincinnati and two years later became the first president of that city's Academy of Fine Arts. He was just twenty-four when on his first visit to Niagara he decided to devote himself to landscape painting.

To suggest that Niagara was an obsession with him is an understatement. Year after year he was lured back to the Falls. He painted the twin waterfalls by day and he painted them by night. He painted them in the furnace of summer and in the blasts of winter—his easel in a snow bank, icicles dripping from his beard, the freezing spray often congealing on his canvas.

His work was meticulous; every rock, every broken stump, every pebble appeared in the finished paintings, for Frankenstein was intent on producing the most definitive multiple portrait of Niagara ever recorded. He painted the Falls from every conceivable angle: from Prospect Point and Table Rock, from the level of the river and from the heights above, in the moonlight, at dawn, high noon, and sunset. He painted the gorge; he painted the rapids; he painted the Whirlpool from every vantage point. In all, over a period of nine years, he made two hundred studies.

For the last five years of this sojourn, with the help of his two brothers he had been planning an ambitious moving panorama. He selected between eighty and one hundred paintings for the final work – an arduous and exhausting task. Because the end product would stand at least eight feet high and the canvas rolls on which the scenes were painted would each be at least a thousand feet long, he would have to copy and paint an enlarged version of every small sketch on the finished panorama.

He worked like a modern screen director and film editor, creating what was, in effect, a story board for his masterpiece. The paintings were arranged to convey the most dramatic impact: a long view of the subject would be followed by a close-up, a moonlit site with a sunny vista. By juxtaposing scenes painted in 1844 with similar views in 1853, he showed the changes, geological and manmade, that had occurred over nine years.

By these devices Frankenstein's audiences were treated to a short but graphic lesson in the geology of Niagara. Even in a brief nine-year period old landmarks vanished or were transformed. A rock slide in 1847 had caused a huge boulder, four hundred feet square, to topple from Goat Island near the Biddle Stairs, taking with it the seats set out for tourists and the trees that shaded them. That same year most of Gull Island, a gravel bar in the rapids above Horseshoe Falls, named for the roosting birds, was swept away in high water. Three years later almost all of the Table Rock overhang, twelve thousand square feet in size and one hundred feet thick, tumbled into the water with a crash heard for miles. A coachman who had been washing his buggy on Table Rock escaped with his horses, but his vehicle hurtled into the vortex below. In 1852, a great triangular mass of rock, earth, and gravel dropped off Goat Island and over the edge near the Terrapin Tower. A few days later some of the Terrapin Rocks themselves – fifteen thousand cubic feet of dolostone – met the same fate.

No wonder that people flocked by the thousands to the Broadway Amusement Center in New York in 1853 to sit in the dark and goggle at the unfolding spectacle. There on the stage was a huge picture frame within which Frankenstein's carefully arranged scenes moved slowly past on mechanical rollers, controlled by unseen hands. Each of the three rolls, when full, was three feet thick. Like a modern film documentary, the panorama was accompanied by music and by a live commentary by Frankenstein himself. He charged fifty cents admission – no more than his due, for his investment in time and money was in the neighbourhood of fifty thousand dollars.

What the audiences got was a guided tour of the Falls, beginning with an establishing portrait of the two cataracts viewed from a window in the Clifton House. Scenes of repose were followed by wilder spectacles of raging waters and spray – a contrast that never failed to bring applause. As one reviewer exclaimed, "We see Niagara above the falls and far below.... We have it sideways and lengthways: we look down upon it, we look up at it: we are before it, behind it, in it ... into its spray on the deck of the *Maid of the Mist*; tempting its rapids among the eddies above; skimming its whirlpool far below...."

As a climax, Frankenstein had used a sequence of winter landscapes, showing the effects of ice and frozen spray on the trees, with the Falls themselves trapped in a mantle of white. At these novel and unexpected scenes the audience invariably clapped in tribute.

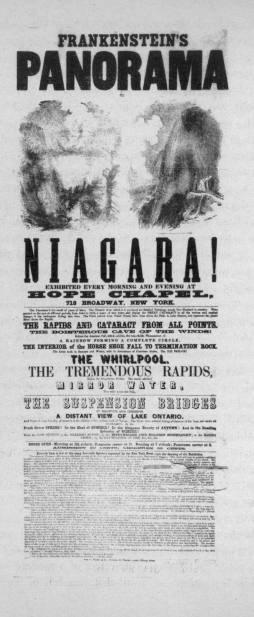

The artist was nothing if not inventive – as much a journalist as he was a painter, quick to capitalize on at least one Niagara tragedy. Shortly after the opening of his panorama in July 1853, a man named Joseph Avery had been discovered clinging to a log wedged tightly between some rocks in the shallow rapids just above the brink of the American Falls. His boat had overturned. Two companions had been swept over the cataract and dashed to pieces on the rocks below. There followed a nineteen-hour suspense story, reported in consecutive editions of the newspapers. Watched by crowds lining both sides of the river, Avery's would-be rescuers hammered together a raft of crossed timbers with a hogshead in the centre, secured by thick ropes. They floated it out on a line through the turbulence, where it too was jammed into the rocks. Avery managed to reach it and free it. As his rescuers tugged and pulled he climbed on board, but the effort was in vain. Once more the raft was caught, and this time Avery could not budge it.

Several more attempts were made to reach him. One man went part way out in a boat and asked Avery to tie a rope around his body so that he could be drawn in to shore, but by now Avery was too exhausted to make the effort.

At last a proper lifeboat arrived from Buffalo. Avery, still on the raft, prepared to leap into it. As the lifeboat reached his perch, it struck the raft, and a cry of exultation rose from the spectators. But moments after the collision Avery was seen struggling for his life in the water. He struck out boldly for Goat Island, but his strength failed; as the onlookers watched in horror, he was borne back slowly and then more rapidly into the fiercest part of the current. On the lip of the Falls, he rose to the surface, flung his hands high, uttered a piercing shriek, and was borne over the crest to his death.

After this sensational story unfolded in several editions of the *New York Times*, Frankenstein added paintings of the scene to his panorama, giving it the effect of a modern newsreel. Then in September, when all that was left of Table Rock toppled into the stream, Frankenstein capitalized on that, too. The rubble had temporarily blocked the entrance to the cavern below the Horseshoe Falls. The artist lost no time in announcing that the only views left of that dark passage behind the curtain were to be found in his panorama. "Table Rock Fallen!" one of his advertisements read. "Passage behind the Great Sheet of Water blocked up! In the Panorama the Passage is still open and the visitors are taken behind the fall as heretofore."

The exhibition played to large crowds in New York until November and then moved on to other cities on the eastern seaboard, heralded as "the most beautiful and truthful Panoramic painting in the world." For the next four years it drew critical plaudits and large audiences everywhere it was shown. Only in 1857 did attendance begin to fall off as another phenomenon of art burst upon the world. That was the year that Frederic Church, one of the best-known landscape artists of his day, first exhibited his remarkable single canvas of the Falls. One canvas against many! It seems, in retrospect, an unequal contest, especially as Church's picture didn't even move.

Or did it? Those who stand beneath it today in the Corcoran Gallery in Washington and stare long enough into the green depths of the water Church created – real water, boiling, coursing, sparkling, churning, skipping in runnels over the ragged ledges in the foreground, bubbling in eddies at the viewer's feet, foaming in one triumphant splurge over the stark lip of the Escarpment, tumbling whitely on the far edge of the horseshoe, may be pardoned if they sense and even *see* the movement. That, after all, was Frederic Church's genius.

3

When Church made his first sketching trip to the Falls in late March 1856, he was in his thirtieth year, tall, handsome, and boyish looking. A talented landscapist, he was facing what many of his contemporaries believed to be an impossible task. Even his mentor, Thomas Cole, then the outstanding landscape painter in North America, had tried and failed to capture either the reality or the essence of the prodigious cataract.

Frankenstein had attempted it in a series of nearly one hundred paintings. Church's bold purpose was to set down on a single canvas everything about the Falls – their raging spirit, their geological significance, their very soul – and to do it with such meticulous accuracy that every curl of foam, every droplet of spray, every slippery rock, and every racing rivulet would seem even more realistic than the stereoscopic views that the new art of photography was making available in the homes of the continent.

Church was a sixth-generation Connecticut Yankee, the son of a well-to-do Hartford businessman who somewhat grudgingly allowed him to follow his natural bent for drawing. He was Cole's only pupil, a member of the Hudson River school of landscape painting, which Cole had helped found. To these high-minded artists, roaming the New York and New England countryside and wandering farther and farther afield in search of subject matter, landscape painting had a loftier purpose than the mere depiction of outdoor views. It must seek to unveil the hidden spirituality in nature, "to speak a language strong, moral and imaginative."

The American landscapists did not see nature as pictorially passive, like the Alps, but kinetic, wild, vital, imbued with energy and power, like the Falls – like America itself. No crumbling ruins for them, no decaying trees; their purpose was to paint life, not death. Alexander von Humboldt, the great geographer-meteorologist, himself a major influence on Church, had charged the landscape artists to paint the heroic, and it was heroic art that expansionist America craved. "Niagara Falls, the mighty portal of the Golden West," in Cole's colourful description, stood as the new symbol of Manifest Destiny. In that phrase, scarcely a decade old, was bound up all America's yearnings, her faith in the future, her unbounded optimism, her unswerving belief in herself. This was the credo that Church himself espoused as a landscape artist.

He was very much a product of his time, a time when science, nature, and religion were, for many, inextricably bound together. Nature was a mirror to reflect God's image, science a method to reveal God's truth. Church, "a Nineteenth Century type of the Puritan," to quote Charles Dudley Warner's unfinished biography, believed in the moral purpose of landscape painting. He would certainly have agreed with his contemporary Samuel Osgood that landscape painting was "a Godlike calling," and with the cleric E.L. Magoon that Niagara Falls was "the most magnificent leaf in the 'mystic volume' in the Book of Nature."

Church himself was an amateur scientist with a wide-ranging knowledge of botany, zoology, meteorology, geology, and geography. He collected rocks and butterflies and devoured accounts of recent scientific expeditions. Humboldt's influential *Kosmos*, a description of the physical universe, inspired Church to follow in the geographer's footsteps through South America to paint mountains, volcanoes, gorges, and waterfalls – heroic landscapes that suggested nature in its rawest and most original manifestations.

But it was John Ruskin who set him on the great adventure of his life – Ruskin who wrote that to paint water was "like trying to paint a soul." For the great English critic, whose influence on American painting was profound, the highest form of art was landscape painting, and the greatest landscape painter of all was J.M.W. Turner, whose ability to paint water realistically was, Ruskin felt, unexcelled. In Ruskin's view, realism in landscape painting was the only "truth" – the link between art, nature, and God. "It will be the duty – the imperative duty – of the landscape painter to descend to the lowest details with undiminished attention," he wrote. "Every class of rock, every kind of earth, every form of cloud, must be studied with equal industry, and rendered with equal precision."

In praising Turner as "the only painter who had ever represented the surface of calm or the *force* of agitated water" Ruskin plunged into an animated discussion of water in motion that clearly had a profound effect on Church. The critic wrote especially of the gravitational forces that changed the form and character of moving water, changed the very look of it, depending on the speed with which it was moving, the obstacles along its route, and the comparative shallowness or depth of the stream bed. Thus did Ruskin link art with science, a marriage that certainly appealed to Church. He had scarcely finished reading the early volumes of Ruskin's *Modern Painters* before he set off for Niagara. He didn't even wait for the snow to melt.

In his three expeditions to the Falls in 1856, Church examined everything paintable. He had followed and experimented with the new science of photography; his own camera-like vision astonished his contemporaries. One pupil wrote that "his vision and retention of even the most transitory facts of nature passing before him must have been at the maximum of which the human mind is capable.... His mind seemed a camera obscura in which everything that passed before it was recorded permanently.... The primrose on the river's brim he saw with a vision as clear as that of a photographic lens...."

Unlike many others, Church was not content to depict the Falls from one or two vantage points. He painted it from above and below, from upstream and down, from near and far – as Frankenstein had. But he went farther than Frankenstein, for his interests were also scientific. He studied the anatomy of the river, painted forms of falling water, made drawings of rock formations, investigated the play of light on tumbling rapids, examined the shallows, peered over the brink, drew the curly waves created by the turbulence of the racing stream, the blasts of spray at the foot of Goat Island, and the abstract lines of foam on the lip of the Horseshoe. He studied the hydraulics of the cataract and the sculptural look of the cliffs. His drawings ran the gamut from the parabolic suspension bridge to the forms and colour of various trees and individual flowers. Much of his work was rough – a few pencil scrawls and some scribbled notations – a form of artist's shorthand, his personal method of committing the Falls to memory. In October he was ready at last to return to his home on the Hudson River to begin work on his masterpiece.

His most important decision was to settle on a point of view for his work. His solution was revolutionary and breathtaking. Most previous artists had painted the Falls head on and from a considerable distance, so that the entire sweep of the two cataracts with Goat Island dividing them filled the canvas. But Church decided to place the viewer on the very brink of the western edge of the Horseshoe and to concentrate solely on the sweep of its great bend. No barrier, psychological or real, would stand between the viewer and the canvas. Against all tradition he included no foreground, no graceful framework of foliage, no clutch of awed sightseers to give the painting scale. It was as if the viewer were actually standing ankle-deep in the shallows overlooking the brink. Modern photography has rendered Church's vision almost commonplace, but in its day, this point of view was a revelation.

The picture is almost entirely taken up with water and sky, the western lip of the Horseshoe sweeping diagonally across the canvas from left to right, then reversing itself to form a horizontal line of white foam slightly above the centreline of the painting. The only evidence of human incursion is the tiny Terrapin Tower in the distance and, on the far American shore, one or two dots that might be people. The sky above glowers and frowns, split by a single ray of white light knifing through the clouds to link up with the broken rainbow that arches over the crescent. In Church's view, the foaming water was a symbol of God's implacable wrath, the rainbow of his everlasting love.

118

The painting was not an accurate representation of the Falls but a kind of Platonic ideal. There was no point on that crumbling bank from which Church's view could be exactly duplicated. Yet he had managed not only to catch the power and energy of the cataract but he had also, in Ruskin's phrase, painted its soul. Everything about the picture was a revelation: he had made the water seem so real, so luminous, so alive that one critic would refer to it as "Niagara with the roar left out." He had for the first time captured the elusive green of the tumbling water, which Dickens and others had admired. And he had abandoned the conventional squarish frame in favour of a wider canvas, 7½ feet by 3 feet, thus emphasizing the boundless, untrammelled geography of the continent.

The picture went on display in New York on May 1, 1857, at the Free Fine Art Gallery on Broadway. It had been bought directly from the painter by a respected New York firm of art dealers, Williams, Stevens, Williams, for forty-five hundred dollars – an unheard-of sum for an American canvas at that time. Of this sum, two thousand dollars was for reproduction rights. The firm also agreed to pay Church half of all future profits above the original twenty-five hundred dollars when the painting was sold. Artist's proofs went on sale for thirty dollars apiece, regular prints for fifteen dollars. To reserve these in advance, some eleven hundred people signed the subscription book.

From the outset the response was ecstatic. The *Home Journal* dispatched "one of the most charming and cultivated women" it knew to a preview. She admitted that she had dreaded the visit, but within five minutes she had completely surrendered herself to Church's composition. "It was there before me, the eighth wonder of the world!" she enthused. "The brown jagged verge above the western section of the Horseshoe *was at my feet*...."

The plaudits poured in. To the *Albion*, the painting was "uncontestably the finest oil picture ever painted on this side of the Atlantic." The *New York Times* called it "the marvel of the western world." Others were equally enraptured: Church's painting was a triumph of colour and form; it was epoch making; it heralded a new era in American landscape painting; it rivalled, nay, it surpassed Turner; it wasn't just a picture of the Falls, it *was* the Falls. Several onlookers tried to describe it in words and failed, just as in a previous century travellers to Niagara had declared the impossibility of putting the subject into words.

Throughout May, Church's *The Great Fall, Niagara* was the rage. Almost every prominent New Yorker, from Horace Greeley to Charles A. Dana to George Bancroft, had been to see it. In one two-week period, 100,000 people lined up to view the picture. The average time given over to its contemplation was estimated at one hour.

After only a month, the painting was spirited off across the Atlantic, partly because its owners wanted to have it chromolithed for sale to the public and also because they hoped for the European stamp of approval. That came from the one critic who could make or break an artist – Turner's champion, John Ruskin.

The manner of that approval went into legend. Ruskin, on carefully examining the painting, could not believe that Church's rendering of the elusive rainbow was not enhanced by a trick of light from a nearby window; it *couldn't* be mere paint. He raised his hand in front of the picture, expecting to see his fingers in the colour spectrum produced by refracted light coming through the glass. Only when the rainbow remained as Church had painted it did Ruskin realize what the artist had achieved. He told a reporter that he had found effects in the painting that he had waited for years to discover.

The London press agreed. The grey and forbidding *Times* applied its own seal of approval to the work by announcing that "the characteristic merit of this picture is its sober truth." The *London Art Journal* echoed those words by declaring "it is truth, obviously and certainly … a production of rare merit … an achievement of the highest order." Church's realistic rendering of water, the "foam, flash, rush, dark depth, turbidity, clearness, curling, lashing, shattering," amazed the critics. All agreed that with Church, American painting had come of age.

That, of course, was what Americans wanted to hear. A writer for *Frank Leslie's Illustrated Newspaper* had predicted that the work would "startle those 'croakers' across the water into a recognition of American genius." In the march toward Manifest Destiny, Frederic Church was now one of the standard-bearers.

The painting toured the English provinces, drawing applause wherever it was shown. It returned to New York in the fall of 1858 to even greater approval. In the words of the *Cosmopolitan Art Journal*, it was now seen as "the finest painting ever painted by an American artist." Meanwhile, Church, travelling through South America in Humboldt's wake, produced another blockbuster, *The Heart of the Andes*, which was also universally acclaimed. He returned to Niagara to do more paintings and was undoubtedly gratified when, in 1876, a prominent banker, William W. Corcoran, bought *Niagara* at auction and hung it permanently in the Washington gallery that bears his name. The price was $12,500 – the largest ever paid for an American canvas to that time.

It hangs there today, among other nineteenth-century landscapes, in its massive gilt frame, and although it is clear that Church was no Turner, it remains a remarkable and respected piece of work. To the modern viewer it evokes, at first, some of the mixed emotions that troubled the mid-Victorians who first viewed the cataract itself and found it wanting. Like the Falls, it requires contemplation to realize the miracle that Church worked with brush and canvas in the days before colour photography.

Of the hundreds of paintings made of Niagara, before Church and after him, this is by common consent the greatest.

Other painters travelled to Niagara, but their numbers diminished. Church had effectively stemmed the flood of artists. To improve upon perfection was, after all, an exercise in futility. Moreover, the emerging science of photography was already changing fashions in art. Six years after *Niagara* was first exhibited in New York, Edouard Manet's controversial *Le Déjeuner sur l'herbe*, shown at the Salon de Refusés in Paris, heralded a new and less representational way of looking at nature.

Frederic Church had become the best-known American landscape painter of his time, but by the next century he would be all but forgotten. He had helped to banish one word from the lexicon of Niagara. The Falls was no longer "an icon of the American sublime," in Elizabeth McKinsey's notable phrase. The terror and mystery were gone and the Falls vanquished. Roebling had bridged the frightening gorge; Church had managed for the first time to capture the awesome power of the cataract. With the funambulists trotting high above the churning rapids on tightropes, could the Falls any longer be called sublime?

Chapter Five

1

On a summer's day in 1858, a year after Church's painting went on display, Jean François Gravelet, a small, well-muscled Frenchman with flaxen hair and a goatee to match, stood on the lip of the Niagara gorge and remarked to a companion, "What a splendid place to bridge with a tightrope."

His companion chuckled at the jest, but Gravelet, whose stage name was Blondin, was deadly serious. He later said that had a rope been at hand he would have started at once, and from that moment on, "wherever I went after that, I took Niagara with me. To cross the roaring waters became the ambition of my life."

The great cataract obsessed him, haunted his dreams that winter, and drove him back to Niagara the following year, where he startled the world by dancing, tripping, mincing, strutting, leaping, and even somersaulting in a variety of costumes – ranging from gorilla to "Siberian slave" – all on a three-inch manila rope, two thousand feet long, stretched 160 feet above the boiling chasm.

The Prince of Manila, they called him, the Conqueror of Niagara. The former epithet is apt, the latter less so. Charles Blondin did not conquer the Falls; he trivialized them. The shimmering cascade became a mere backdrop for a circus act. The thousands who crammed every corner of the gorge that summer did not come to view the Falls; they came to see Blondin defy gravity and joust with fate. The cataract, now only a stage setting, could no longer inspire Gothic terror, but those who glued their vision to the tiny figure trotting with such assurance along that slender filament experienced the same tingle in their spines that earlier visitors had reported when confronted with only the majesty of falling water.

Now the Falls were literally thrust into the background. Although paintings depicted him crossing directly above the thundering Horseshoe, Blondin's feats were performed more than a mile downstream. Yet in later years he himself appeared to believe the legend, for he talked about "crossing this mighty cataract" as if it had been directly below him. When he returned for a second season in 1860, he gave his performances even farther downstream, beyond the railway suspension bridge. Thus the mass of spectators who chose that vantage point to watch the performance had to turn their backs on the Falls – a symbolic rejection of a natural wonder in favour of a human stunt. It was, as one British observer wrote, rather like shutting your prayer book to go to see a pantomime.

To many, Blondin's rope dance eclipsed the Falls. One reporter wrote of that first exhibition: "So intensely engaged was the mind in the event, that we have our doubts whether, among the large crowd present, there was one who even heard the roar of the great Cataract, which was thundering on the ear."

The symbolism was extended to the gorge itself. Blondin had literally caught it in his net. Flung across the chasm was a vast spider web of manila – forty-four guy ropes, measuring twenty-seven thousand feet in all – to keep the tightrope steady, fastened to both banks by means of trees and posts. Over this hempen lattice work the tiny figure in pink tights reigned unchallenged.

Was it the act itself that twenty-five thousand people came to see – or was it their expectation of a darker spectacle? Six days before his first performance, the early birds on the scene had watched in awe as the rope dancer – or "funambulist," to use the popular term – inched his way two hundred feet along the tightrope in a makeshift cable car to test certain guys. Then, to their astonishment and apparent chagrin, he climbed out of the car, turned a somersault on the rope, and sat down as calmly as if he were in a Morris chair. As the Niagara Falls *Gazette* reported, somewhat ghoulishly, "Everybody is disappointed to see him display such agility and courage."

Disappointed. For the first time it dawned on them that

Blondin might actually accomplish what he said he would do and not tumble off the rope to his death below. For many had come expecting to witness Blondin's doom, and now, as he capered above the chasm, they felt cheated. Death, after all, was what the region was infamous for.

It explains why every eye remained glued to the spectacle. Nobody wanted to miss a possible stumble, a terrifying loss of balance. A correspondent for the Toronto *Daily Spectator* told of encountering "a small fellow with a dried-up wizened face who sat in a corner of the enclosure with an opera glass in his hand, which he held fixed to his eyeball from the time Blondin started until he landed." When someone asked him for a loan of his glass, he retorted, "What! I have come from Detroit every week to see that man fall into the river, and do you think I would lose the chance of seeing it now by lending you my glass, even for an instant?"

Nicholas Woods, correspondent for *The Times* who watched Blondin's final performance in the autumn of 1860, believed that "one half of the crowds that go to see Blondin go in the firm expectation that as he must fall off and be lost some day or other, they may have the good fortune to be there when he does so miss his footing, and witness the whole catastrophe from the best point of view." Blondin did not stumble. In 1859 he stood at the head of a long line of daredevils to come, all perfectly prepared to risk their lives for fame and fortune, not to mention the profit of the entrepreneurs who encouraged them.

The greatest natural wonder of all, which had once tantalized the world because of its remoteness in the continental wilderness, was now rendered commonplace by the revolution in transportation. Roebling's bridge and the arrival of the new railways – Canada's Great Western and the New York Central – had thrown Niagara open for business on an unprecedented scale. Now there was an instant audience – and a growing one – for performers like Blondin. It was in the interests not only of the railway companies but also of the hoteliers, the souvenir salesmen, the commercial photographers, and the hack drivers to encourage the kind of spectacle that would soon become a regular occurrence at Niagara.

Blondin did not need to hire a theatre in which to perform. He did not need to sell tickets at the entrance of a marquee. The gorge was his theatre and the railways were delighted to act as his agents. They supplied the customers who, having been inspired by the natural spectacle of the cataract, were happy to linger an extra day or so to view an equally absorbing human drama and, at the same time, help fill Blondin's collection boxes.

The honeymoon was just coming into its own when Blondin walked across Niagara's gorge. "Honeylunacy," as it was sometimes called, was scarcely a generation old, having replaced the "wedding trip" of the upper classes, which was really part of the Fashionable Tour. Now, instead of accompanying the newlyweds to the various watering places, cousins, family, and friends bade them goodbye at the railway station and sent them off to Niagara Falls in the privacy etiquette dictated.

Why Niagara Falls? Half a dozen ingenious theories have been advanced, each more implausible than the last. It has been said that honeymooners went to the Falls to lose themselves in a crowd too busy contemplating the cataract to notice the billing and cooing at their elbows; that the sound of the falling water acted as an aphrodisiac; that the negative ions produced by the cascade served as a stimulant for the marriage bed; that moonlight dappling the water provided a lure to the romantic; that cataracts and waterfalls have always been associated with love, passion, obsession (and, one might add, suicide).

These convoluted explanations fail to identify the real lure of Niagara – that it was accessible and comfortable. Much of the North American population now lived within a day's journey of the Falls where there was pleasant accommodation to suit everybody's purse. Since almost everyone yearned to visit

Niagara anyway, why not combine the trip with a honeymoon and watch Charles Blondin teeter on his rope above the gorge?

For if consummation was the obverse side of the coin at Niagara, death or the prospect of death was the reverse. Brides and corpses were the Falls' stock in trade. As Isabella Bird had discovered, the Falls guides loved to recount dreadful stories of unfortunate tourists sucked into the cataract – stories that no doubt gave more than one new bride an excuse to cling more tightly to her groom.

Back in August 1844, a certain Miss Martha Rigg, reaching for a bunch of cedar berries on a low tree on the bank below Table Rock, lost her footing and fell to her death, 115 feet below. The tale was tailor-made for the entrepreneurs. Miss Rigg's broken body was scarcely in its casket before an enterprising Irishman with a table of souvenirs for sale had set up on the spot a five-foot wooden obelisk with verses recording the tragedy.

> Ladies fair, most beauteous of the race
> Beware and shun a dangerous place
> Miss Martha Rigg here lost her life
> Who might now have been a happy wife.

The monument was so successful that a competitor arrived with his own table of wares, which he installed close by. A spirited tussle ensued, with each man trying to move his goods closest to the fatal spot until the original huckster was forced to remove his obelisk each night by wheelbarrow and install it again the following morning.

Before Blondin's first exhibition, most visitors had been fairly certain he would suffer the fate of the unfortunate Miss Rigg. The *New York Times* thought him a fool who ought to be arrested, while the Niagara *Mail* declared that "Baron Munchausen has evidently come to life again, and has taken up his abode at the Falls." Peter B. Porter refused Blondin permission to anchor his rope on Goat Island for what he called a

ABOVE: The Falls, with Table Rock in the background, right, engraved from a painting by John Vanderlyn in 1803 when the flow of water over the precipice was twice as great as it is today.

BELOW: The Horseshoe Falls from Goat Island, painted in 1830. Note the precarious bridge to the Terrapin Rocks just above the crest.

W.H. Bartlett, the much-reproduced artist of *American Scenery* and *Canadian Scenery*, sketched the massive overhang of Table Rock in 1837.

The fall of Table Rock in 1850. The hackman, washing his carriage, barely escaped
when the dolostone cap crumbled.

ABOVE: One of the locks on the Erie Canal, which
helped turn Niagara Falls into a fashionable spa, rivalling
Saratoga Springs.
BELOW: Like the drawing above, this one was made in
1837 by Bartlett for *American Scenery*. It shows the
Terrapin Rocks, Tower, and bridge.

An advertisement of the Great Western & Michigan
Central shows off Roebling's famous bridge. The painting below was made about the same time by an anonymous artist. The railways made the Falls a tourist centre.

Black and white reproduction does
not do justice to Frederic Edwin
Church's great painting showing the
full sweep of the Horseshoe Falls
from the very edge of the water. The
Terrapin Tower can be seen in the
background, left.

The early days of tourism. How stiff and starched
they look in their toppers and crinolines! Only wealthy
visitors could afford the time and money for such
an adventure.

The daguerreotype, made about 1853, shows tourists
at Prospect Point standing above the lip of the
American Falls.

dangerous and foolish adventure. But the owners of White's Pleasure Grounds on the American side and Clifton House on the Canadian were overjoyed to accommodate him and to charge a fee for everyone entering the enclosures. It mattered little to them whether Blondin fell off the rope as long as he didn't succumb too soon. They need not have worried. He was planning several performances; before the season was out he would engage in eight.

His courage was undoubted. Everyone had heard the story of how on his first trip across the Atlantic, when a fellow passenger tumbled overboard, Blondin had leaped into the ocean and rescued him. But he could scarcely survive in the terrible rapids if, as expected, he fell.

To the astonishment of many, and the chagrin of more than a few, Blondin managed to make his first journey across the swaying tightrope seem as casual and as free of peril as a morning constitutional. He ate a good lunch and turned up at White's Pleasure Grounds in mid-afternoon, with one thousand paying customers watching from special grandstands and thousands more jamming the banks for half a mile above and below the setting. For reasons best known to himself he wore a dark wig, which he doffed along with a vest of purple plush and a pair of white Turkish pantaloons. Then he stepped onto the tightrope in his flesh-coloured tights and started his long descent down the sagging cable, which, at midpoint, was fifty feet lower over the gorge. There he stopped, dropped a bottle on a piece of twine to the *Maid of the Mist* below, hauled up some Niagara River water, drank it, and resumed his journey – uphill this time – to arrive on the far bank triumphant, though bathed in sweat. He rested briefly, accepted a glass of champagne, performed a little dance on the rope, and trotted back across in the space of just eight minutes.

This astonishing performance produced a gush of hyperbole. The Buffalo *Courier* called Blondin "the most wonderful of Frenchmen." The *New York Times* said his walk on the rope

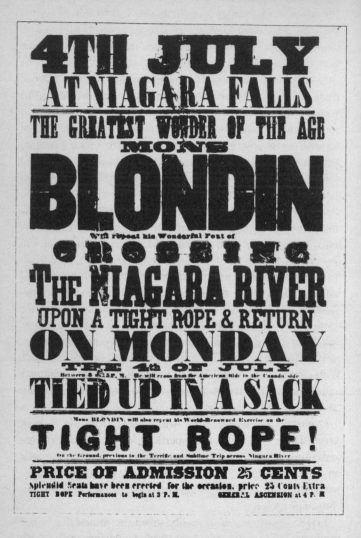

was "the greatest feat of the Nineteenth Century." The Lockport *Chronicle* went the limit. It termed it "the most terribly real and daringly wonderful feat that was ever performed." Three Lockport boys suffered bone fractures that month attempting to duplicate Blondin's triumph in their backyards.

In reality, the chances of Blondin toppling off the rope were about a thousand to one. Previous funambulists had used the horizontal slack wire or had mounted a tightrope fastened diagonally from a height to an attachment tied to the ground. But Blondin had made the horizontal tightrope his own. To him, rope dancing was as natural as breathing.

He had been walking the tightrope since the age of five, when a travelling company of acrobats pitched their tent near the home of his father, a veteran of the Napoleonic wars. Watching a youth in a blue tunic and spangles performing on the slack rope, he determined to attempt a similar feat. He fastened a strong cord between two chairs but, when he tried to walk across, took a tumble that reduced him to tears. Undaunted, he got a stronger cord, stretched it between two gateposts, and using his father's fishing rod as a balancing pole tried again and fell again, spraining a wrist. He did not give up, and when eventually he succeeded, his proud parents were far-sighted enough to enrol him in an acrobatic school at Lyon. Within six months he announced that he was prepared to make a professional debut and did so – hailed by the local press as "the little wonder."

Orphaned at nine and on his own, he soon became famous as a rope dancer. No feat was too perilous for him to attempt. An ambitious perfectionist, he practised each new spectacle until he could perform it with his eyes closed. He was a prodigy without a rival – hard-muscled, impassive, utterly secure in his chosen profession.

In 1851, at the age of twenty-seven, he joined the Ravel troupe of French equestrian and acrobatic performers on their tour of North America. By this time there was no acrobatic performance at which he did not excel. He danced across a tightrope as easily as he strolled down a country lane. As his manager, Harry Colcord, discovered, no human force could detach him from it. Colcord tried, at Blondin's suggestion: shoved, heaved, pushed, without success; his man stayed on the rope.

It was this that persuaded Colcord to climb on Blondin's back during the fifth exhibition on August 17, and to hazard the long trip across the gorge. Colcord later described Blondin as "like a piece of marble, every muscle ... tense and rigid." He said (or perhaps was made to say) that the experience was so nerve shattering that for years afterward he would start up in the dark of the night, "shaking and sweating and screaming to Blondin to save him from Niagara." One suspects here the fine hand of the journalist. If Colcord was so terrified, why did he agree to repeat the original feat – not once, but twice?

Both men were showmen. Like a trapeze artist who pretends to lose his balance, Blondin was forever toying with the crowd. There was the shocking tale of gamblers who, it was said, tried to fray one of the guys to cause his death, on which they had wagered considerable sums. Blondin eventually denied that story, though he waited until the headlines died. No one, apparently, asked how any man but he could have crawled out on that slender cable to the point where he could tamper with the rope.

The press was astonished when Captain John Travis, a crack pistol shot, was persuaded to attempt to put a hole through Blondin's hat from the heaving deck of the *Maid of the Mist*. At Travis's signal, Blondin, teetering on the rope, raised his hat and Travis fired. Blondin lowered the hat to the vessel's deck, and the crowd gasped when they saw a neat hole in the brim. "What makes the feat more wonderful is the fact that the steamer's motion in the rapids was very unsteady," the gullible Niagara Falls *Gazette* remarked. What was really wonderful was that the paper swallowed the hoax whole. Travis, who thought up the stunt with Blondin's cheerful collaboration, fired a blank. The funambulist punctured the hat himself and received a fee for his part in the fraud.

As the summer wore on Blondin continued to top himself at more than one "farewell" performance. He did handstands on the rope; he hung from it by a leg and an arm; he crossed blindfold in a heavy sack made of blankets; he lay down at full length with his balancing pole lashed to the rope; he performed a back somersault; he clung to the rope and hauled himself along it, hand over hand; dressed as a monkey, he pushed a wheelbarrow across; and he balanced on a chair above the roaring waters. When these feats palled, he crossed at night in the glare of locomotive headlights until he was lost to view in the gloom and only the vibrations of the rope told those on shore he was still aloft. He reached the opposite shore and then returned in a blaze of fireworks.

The crowds, wild with enthusiasm, continued to increase. On August 17, it was reported that forty thousand or more were on hand to watch him carry his manager on his back. Whatever the number, the press of the mob was enough to threaten his life. As the 140-pound Blondin toiled up the long incline carrying the 145-pound Colcord plus his 38-pound pole, Colcord saw on the far bank "a great sea of staring faces, fixed and intense with interest, alarm, fear. Some people shaded their eyes, as if yet dreading to see us fall; some held their arms extended as if to grasp us and keep us from falling; some excited men had tears streaming down their cheeks. A band was trying to play, but the wrought-up musicians could evoke only discordant notes."

Colcord realized then that this was the most dangerous moment of the performance.

"Look out, Blondin," Colcord said. "Here comes our danger, those people are likely to rush us on our landing and crowd us over the bank."

"What will I do?" Blondin asked.

"Make a rush and drive right through them."

Tired as he was, the rope dancer realized he had to push right through the surging throng. Calling on one last reserve of energy, Blondin followed his manager's advice and was saved.

He knew that he must continue to outdo his previous performances. A week later, having crossed from the American side in shackles, he hoisted a small stove on his back, walked to the middle of the rope, produced kitchen utensils, condiments, and eggs, lit a fire, and proceeded to cook and fold two omelets, which he lowered on a cord to the *Maid of the Mist*.

The passengers who jammed the vessel were in a frenzy as they tried to seize pieces of the omelets. Some tied fragments in their handkerchiefs to keep as souvenirs. Others crammed the results of Blondin's cooking into their mouths as if hoping that some of his mystique might cling to them. One is reminded of those aborigines who ate the hearts of their more heroic adversaries in the hope of gaining a modicum of their strength.

After his September 8 performance, in which he sat at a table balanced on the tightrope and enjoyed a light repast of champagne and cake, Blondin ended his Niagara season with the announcement that he would return the following year. By that time rope dancing would be the rage, and when spring came, the great funambulist would find himself locked in a contest with a younger but equally adroit rival who would match him feat for feat.

That in no way tarnished his fame or his immortality. More than a dozen daredevils would follow the Prince of Manila to Niagara to equal his performance. But Charles Blondin would always remain supreme. It is his name, and his alone, that springs to mind when somebody evokes the image of a man on a tightrope. Blondin carried the aura of Niagara with him all his life. And when he died, at the age of seventy-three, it was at his English home named, of course, Niagara. There is, after all, no substitute for being first.

134

Standing in the crowd with his sweetheart in the early summer of 1860, watching Blondin on his tightrope, was a twenty-two-year-old Canadian, William Leonard Hunt. As Blondin made his way across the rope, Hunt turned to the girl and hinted that he could duplicate the funambulist's feats. At that, he later recounted, she and her friends "laughed incredulously and began to think they were under the charge of a maniac."

Hunt was no maniac. He meant exactly what he said. That night he went back to Lockport where he was working for a storekeeper and gave his notice. "To the horror of everyone" he announced that he would match Blondin, performance for performance. To everyone's astonishment, he did just that.

Deaf to the protests of his friends, he made preparations "as calmly and as gaily as though I were going to a fair." That led to a breakup with his sweetheart, who could not understand what he candidly admitted was a thirst for glory. But, as he later said, she was not the only one who found his actions incomprehensible. And there would be other sweethearts.

As a youth in Port Hope, Ontario, he had always been in trouble. "I courted peril because I loved it," he was to write. "The thoughts of it fired my very soul with ardour, because it was what others were afraid to face." To the adults of the town, he was incorrigible. Once, when playing hookey from Sunday school, he helped rescue a friend who had fallen through the ice, but that, apparently, wasn't enough. "That boy, that dreadful boy," the townspeople said. "A judgment has fallen upon him at last for breaking the Sabbath…."

This was the era of the travelling circus, with its clown band, its wild animals, its wire walkers, strong men, and trapeze artists. Young Willie was captivated. In spite of his straitlaced father's stricture on witnessing immoral acts, he managed to sneak into the big top and by the age of twelve was emulating the performers themselves. He was wiry and supple and began to train with weights to build up his muscles. He presented his own circus, complete with trapeze acts by himself and his friends; angry parents put a stop to it, and the Port Hope council further discouraged local talent three years later by banning all unlicensed circuses.

His parents got him a job with a local doctor, hoping that would straighten him out and he would go on to medical school. But medicine was not for him. He was totally seduced by the glamour of show business. He built up his strength so that he could lift seven hundred pounds. He strung a rope from the roof of the family barn to the ground and practised aerial feats. A series of tumbles into the manure pile in no way disheartened him. Within two years he had mastered the art. He had an uncanny sense of balance. He learned to stand on his head on the rope, to hang by his heels, to sit on a teetering chair hooked to the rope. He also ran a dancing school and learned to wrestle.

In the summer of 1859, with Hunt's father off on an extended visit to his native England, the editor of the Port Hope *Guide* offered the young man one hundred dollars to perform at a local fair. Hunt demanded five hundred dollars and was promised it – on the condition that he stand on his head above the Ganaraska River. He borrowed a rope from a cousin's schooner, strung it from two buildings on opposite sides of the river, walked slowly across, and returned, to everybody's breathless admiration, without his balancing pole.

Six days later, after delivering a lecture on physical culture (his medical training an unexpected asset), he performed a strong-man routine in the city hall. The climax was a tug-of-war in which he took on a dozen men single-handed, and won. He changed his name to the more exotic Signor Guillermo Antonio Farini, which he kept for the rest of his life.

On the last day of the fair, eight thousand turned out to watch him carry a man across the Ganaraska on his back – a performance cancelled at the last moment by a terrified mayor. In its stead, Hunt/Farini performed somersaults on the rope, stood on his head, and walked blindfold across the river.

His father returned from England and found that the medical student was now better known as a circus performer. "You delight in having disgraced your family by becoming a low, common mountebank," he told him. He'd brought a heap of presents from overseas but refused to give anything to his son. The next day an embittered William left home.

For a while he worked for his uncle's general store in Minnesota but soon wangled a job with Dan Rice's floating circus on the Mississippi, first as a ticket taker and later as a rope walker. His adventures that year, as recounted in his unpublished memoirs, are melodramatic in the extreme. Did he actually shoot and kill a huge black man who thrust a gun through the bars of his ticket cage? Did he really fight a duel with bowie knives in a riverside faro den? Or were these accounts no more than the autobiographical embellishments of a man who thought of himself as another Barnum? Certainly he was reunited with his estranged family, possibly because he bought his father a new farm with his earnings.

Meanwhile he had just issued a series of challenges to Blondin, who ignored him as he ignored every upstart who offered to duplicate his feats. Farini was not as elegant a rope dancer as the Frenchman – he himself admitted that – but he was a better businessman. Blondin's purpose at Niagara was not to make an instant fortune but to create for himself a name and a reputation that would serve as a lifetime annuity. Farini had broader interests that would take him into a variety of adventures, ranging from exotic horticulture to African exploration.

Blondin had been content to take up a collection after each exhibition of rope walking. Farini left nothing to chance. He engaged four excursion schooners to bring spectators from various points on Lake Ontario. He hired four bands to play aboard the steamers and then to entertain the paying customers in the enclosures he had erected for half a mile along the gorge. He had seats for forty thousand, who paid a minimum admission of twenty-five cents but more for reserved space.

No detail escaped his entrepreneurial grasp. He persuaded each of the two railways to pay him a bonus of one thousand dollars. He collected another $2,975 as his share of the steamship fares. Following his first performances he spent all day working with his ticket takers, checking receipts against numbers, and found he had collected $9,393.75. He realized an extra thousand dollars in a wager with a man who bet, foolishly as it turned out, that Blondin would draw a larger crowd. There were also small but unexpected profits from bystanders who on their own passed the hat for him as they had for Blondin. All in all, he collected about fifteen thousand dollars for his performance on August 15, 1860. "Not a bad sum for an hour's work," he remarked airily, but in fact it involved his most difficult feat.

Farini announced that he would descend to the *Maid of the Mist*, drink a glass of wine with one of the passengers, and then return by climbing up two hundred feet of rope. Off he went with a coil of rope over his shoulder – a slight but solid figure wearing buff tights, his long black hair and whiskers streaming in the wind. He fastened his balancing pole to the slack rope, using it as a seat, undid the coil on his back, let it down until it touched the water, and fastened one end to the rope on which he stood.

Below him, the little steamer, crowded with passengers, rocked and swayed in the rapids. Down he went, hand over hand, until, at the halfway point, the dangling rope began to twist. He was forced to coil one leg around it and close his eyes to ward off giddiness. The danger was lost on those below, who thought he was engaging in a new piece of daring.

He clung to the rope until it stopped twisting. Then he continued on down to the deck of the boat, drank the wine, acknowledged the cheers of the crowd, and started up again.

138

He had not climbed sixty feet before he was forced to call down to the men holding the rope to let go because the steamer was rocking so wildly in the current. The wind blowing down the gorge was causing the boat to swing back and forth like a pendulum. Farini figured that if he fell, it would be better to plunge into the water than onto the deck of the vessel.

He twisted a leg around the rope to rest his hands, then continued his climb. After another fifty feet he rested again, relieved that the swinging motion had diminished as the pendulum became shorter. He fought off drowsiness. His arms were stiff and tired, but he had another forty feet to go.

Now he had to stop and rest his arms every ten feet. When he was within twelve feet of his goal he almost gave up. His arms were numb, his hands too weak to bear his weight. Yet he forced himself to struggle on until he was within a yard of his objective.

One arm was now useless, the other almost so. He managed to worm his way up to a point where his nose just touched the horizontal rope. Using every last particle of strength left in one of his hands, he hung on while drawing a leg up as far as possible toward the rope and then, straightening his body, pulled his chest over. There he hung, totally exhausted and at his wits' end to find a way to haul himself upright and continue his walk to the far shore. The only alternative seemed to be to drop into the water.

He continued to push with the leg that was still twisted around the dangling rope. At the same time he threw more of his weight onto his chest, relieving one arm. The arm seemed to be made of lead, but the circulation slowly came back. After a considerable struggle, he was able to get astride the rope. He rubbed his arms and unfastened his balancing pole but was too weak to raise it. He leaned back and threw up his legs, using them to raise the pole until his feet were on the rope. That brought the pole on his knees close to his chin. He bent forward and struggled to an upright position, using his left hand to move the swaying rope from one side to the other as his balance required.

He knew he must make the return crossing, as he had advertised, blindfold and with baskets on his feet. Off he went to the far shore, and with only ten minutes' rest set out again. At one point he pretended to topple from the rope, a piece of showmanship that brought a chorus of screams. No one had screamed earlier when he was in real danger; all assumed that Farini the Great, struggling and dangling above the gorge, had done it many times before. It was, in fact, his first and only attempt of that kind and one that Blondin did not try to equal.

3

In the weeks that followed, Signor Farini matched Blondin feat for feat and sometimes topped him. He stood on his head, hung face downward by his toes, and carried a lanky volunteer, Rowland McMullen, across on his back. When Blondin walked the gorge in a sack, it did not cover his feet; Farini's did. When a manacled Blondin crossed dressed as a Siberian slave, Farini countered by jigging across as an Irish washerwoman. Blondin had taken a stove out onto the tightrope and cooked an omelet. Farini carried a wash tub, lowered a pail into the river, and rinsed out a dozen pocket handkerchiefs. He had no difficulty obtaining these. They were pressed on him by admiring women who gasped at his daring, strove for introductions, ogled him at the receptions and balls held in his honour, and were delighted when the handsome twenty-two-year-old responded to their approaches, not always wisely but sometimes too well.

For Farini was not only a good businessman, he was also an unregenerate flirt. He had an eye for the ladies and they had an

SIG. FARINI

THE INEXHAUSTIBLE!

FARINI THE COMICAL

SIGNOR FARINI WILL ON

ON WEDNESDAY,

SEPT. 5, 1860, AT 4 O'CLOCK, P. M.

AT

NIAGARA FALLS,

introduces himself in his Wonderful and Laughable Character of

BIDDY O'FLAHERTY

THE IRISH WASHERWAOMN,

BY CARRYING OUT UPON HIS CABLE A NEW

PATENT WASHING MACHINE!

WRINGING OUT THE CLOTHES AT THE STRAIGHT ROPE; TWO BOARDS, WITH HIS ARM

Draw up Water from the River AND DO HIS OWN WASHING

Wringing his clothes out to dry upon his Cable where he can leave them and a might without fear of having them stolen. If any one doubts the being washed clean they can go and examine them.

FARINI'S CABLE IS WITHIN A FEW RODS OF THE FALLS

AND CLOSE TO THE FERRY.

TICKETS OF ADMISSION. · · · · 25 CENTS.

Reserved Seats, Twenty-Five Cents Extra.

FRANK SOPER, Agent.

NIAGARA FALLS, Sept. 5th, 1860.   Lossite Print Niagara Falls, N.Y.

eye for him. In his memoirs he is not modest about his appeal, but he had reason to be cocky. With his tanned and bearded face, his long, jet-black hair, his muscular body, and, above all, his reputation as a daredevil, he had no difficulty in attracting women admirers.

After a grand ball given in his honour at Niagara in mid-August 1860, following his first performance, he was presented to "the wives and daughters of some of the most prominent men in America," who showered him with cards and invitations. He was introduced that night to "a very beautiful Southern lady ... with whom in consequence of her being too beautiful to resist," he said, "I commenced a flirtation." He found, however, that he was "encountering an adept at the art." Apparently she matched him simper for simper. Nonetheless, "I did not do so badly for a beginner." Just as he was in the middle of "a pretty series of compliments" another young woman seized him by the arm and bore him off. For the rest of the evening, he said, "my attentions were so evenly divided that to carry on the particular flirtation ... was impossible, so I turned it into a general one and enjoyed myself considerably."

"It is a wonder," he wrote later, "my vanity did not overcome my reason." When he retired for bed, he examined the various cards that had been given him that evening and found himself "in possession of invitations from ladies residing in every State in the Union." The unfinished and unpublished memoirs of Farini are replete with such hyperbole. Yet there is a certain charm in the young man's naïveté and insouciance, especially in those moments of Victorian melodrama that enliven his versions of various encounters.

He tells, for instance, of "a venturesome young lady whose recklessness was a source of much anxiety to me, feeling as I did morally responsible for her safety." He had been escorting her through a passage behind the Luna Falls known as the Cave of the Winds and was standing with some others on the rough rocks near the water's edge when he heard her scream. She had wandered off and, to his horror, tumbled into the rapids and disappeared beneath the foam.

Farini dove in head first and was instantly spun about by a whirlpool that dashed him against a rock. He thought the young woman had been sucked under, but then a movement near the surface caught his eye. He plunged back in and struck his head against her foot. His guide dragged them both out of danger, whereupon Farini performed a form of artificial respiration and with the help of others brought her around. "I picked up the fragile willful piece of loveliness and bore her through the passage, under the Falls, to the dressing room where I laid her on the sofa and administered some brandy and water." Having observed her recovery, the gallant youth departed.

The following day he was invited to dinner by the lady's parents, who insisted she apologize for having caused him so much trouble. Holding out "the prettiest little hands I ever saw," she apologized for being "such a mad, silly thing" and told him she would be forever in his debt. She sat next to him at dinner that night and engaged him in a lively discussion of rope walking. After the meal, Farini excused himself, but only after "Miss V.," as he discreetly called her, gave him her hand. "I felt a gentle pressure as she softly whispered, 'I must see you again before you go.'"

The next morning as he took his customary walk along the shaded paths of Goat Island, he saw Miss V. wending her way through the birch trees in his direction. She seemed uneasy, greeting him with a faltering voice. He suggested a stroll toward the three half-submerged rocks in the rapids known as the Three Sisters. She slipped "her delicate little gloved hand" in his and the two gazed down into the dancing waters. Suddenly, she grasped his arm, as though in terror, and in true Victorian fashion fell insensible upon his breast.

He laid her down and splashed water on her face. She recovered and told him the purpose of her visit – he was "to refuse nothing papa may offer."

"He was talking last night to mother," she told him, "about presenting you with a testimonial, and I knowing your independent spirit was sure that if it assumed a pecuniary shape you would decline it with asperity and deem yourself insulted. To oblige me, I want you to accept what he offers."

To which the chivalrous rope dancer, who had accepted – nay, encouraged – substantial donations following each of his exhibitions, declared that "the act of being of service to yourself is ample compensation and the look and smile you gave me on opening your eyes made me your debtor." In fact, he insisted, the incident had contributed to his popularity. The press had gone mad over the rescue. Every paper had a different version, including one report that had her father insisting that they marry, and that he, Farini the Great, had agreed. As for him, a smile from her was his reward.

"Please do not think me unladylike," the young lady responded, "if I say I wished … wished … no, I cannot say it, it's too indelicate."

"Say whatever you like, Miss V., I am no lover of the conventional."

"Can't you guess?" she whispered. "Can't you form an idea of my meaning?"

He feigned ignorance, urged her to say what was on her mind, offered to turn away if it would save her embarrassment.

"No, no!" she cried passionately. "Do not turn away and I will tell you what my wish was, it was that the account given in the paper was true."

With that avowal, tears sprang to her eyes, leaving Farini nonplussed. He told her that she had paid him the greatest compliment any woman could pay a man, that he had no language adequate to express his admiration for her, but he pointed out gently that she had a romantic and impulsive nature and there were others "whose opinions you must respect and whose happiness you must consult." She would, he declared, think kindly of him for what he had said.

No Victorian novelist could have improved on Farini's version of his final rejection: "At some future date I may meet you on equal terms, both in wealth and love, and then should your mind be unchanged, I will not hesitate to ask the consent of your parents to my being the caretaker for life of a treasure infinitely more valuable than all their money. Such a course as this, I am sure, is preferable to my accepting you in payment of a debt which never existed and showing myself to be more rapacious than Shylock who demanded a pound of Christian flesh for a real debt, while I should be carrying off many pounds for an imaginary one."

At that she called him cruel and cold and, pressing his hand, whispered goodbye. That night, one of the waiters at the International Hotel on the American side brought him an envelope containing five one-hundred-dollar bills and a note of thanks. The family had already left Niagara, but Farini insisted the hotel mail the money to the father. Shortly afterward, the proprietor's wife, Mrs. John Fulton, handed him a note that Miss V. had left for him. It said: "Something tells me that we may never meet again.... Amidst all the excitement and danger of your calling, do not forget that the life you saved is ever yours.... – V."

There were other assignations. After one of his performances in August, Farini found himself involved in an equally dangerous encounter with "a very handsome lady" who struck up a conversation with him following the performance and, seeing his face beaded with sweat, handed him a silk handkerchief to wipe his brow. As he counted the day's proceeds, his mind went back to the incident. Had she forgotten the handkerchief? Or had she left it on purpose? He must find out. He saw that it was embroidered with the monogram L.M., but there was nobody with those initials to be found on the International's register. He tried the Cataract House, and there the desk clerk told him that a Miss Louisa Montague had just returned to Buffalo with a party of friends.

Two days later, his interest was further piqued by a note from the lady herself, suggesting that if he ever visited Buffalo he could return the handkerchief. Before he could seize that opportunity, Miss Montague appeared again at one of his performances accompanied by a woman she identified as her mother, who repeated the daughter's invitation to call. The handkerchief, having apparently served its purpose, was forgotten.

Farini's visit was temporarily sidetracked by the arrival of another young woman, a popular concert singer named Anna Bishop. Miss Bishop, through her agent, was insisting on riding across the gorge on the rope walker's back. "I should like to be pointed out as a woman who risked her life in crossing the Falls on a man's back," was the way she put it. This blatant attempt at self-promotion put Farini off. When he discovered that she was also subject to fits of giddiness, he turned the offer down although, he said, he was "in want of a new sensation ... to keep alive the interest of the public in my exploits."

Now he was free to visit Miss Montague. The events that followed, as set down by the Great Farini himself, formed the perfect melodrama. He was, he says, received by "a very pretty and engaging young lady" who, in her sister Louisa's absence, offered to entertain him. He looked about, observed that "the furniture indicated wealth and good taste, [and] the decorations though rich were not gaudy or ostentatious." The sister's conversation was refined "and had a tone of good breeding." Her appearance suggested that she came from a good family, "but there was a look in her eyes which I did not like and something in her manner not quite in keeping with a well-bred young lady."

He remarked that she herself bore no resemblance to her sister. "Do you think her better looking than I am?" she asked coquettishly, and plumped herself down on the sofa by his side, an action he thought decidedly overfamiliar. She too had been at the Falls, she told him, but he hadn't seen her. "I was there

146

with a gentleman, my friend." Victorian conventions being what they were, this reply caused Farini to have doubts as to whether he was in a respectable house. The phrase "my friend," he noted, was one "applied by women of a certain class to those who support them." He asked whether the friend was a very liberal man, to which she replied, loudly, that it was none of his business. At that, he concluded, "there could be no mistake now concerning the profession of the woman at my side and the character of the house into which I had allowed myself to be invited."

He rose to leave, asking that she tell her sister that he had come but could not stay. At that she gave a loud shriek. "Do your dirty work!" she cried. "I will not be insulted by any of that stuck-up Lillie's fancy circus lovers."

This astonishing turn of events sent Farini into the hall. There he was confronted by a strange man. "He has grossly insulted me, Jack," cried the young woman, whereupon a brutal tussle ensued. While the men exchanged blows the girl struck Farini from behind with a blunt instrument. Nevertheless, he managed to knock Jack unconscious with a piece of iron and tried to get away by heaving a chair through the window.

Now another man named Mose and "a fiendish woman, Sarah," joined the battle, apparently with the intention of robbing him. Kicking and clawing, the foursome kept up the struggle until Louisa Montague herself, accompanied by "the elderly female who passed for her mother," arrived. At this point Farini felt his legs weaken, black spots danced before his eyes, and he passed out.

He woke up in bed in the home of a local jurist, Justice Spetszell, with whom he had spent his first night in Buffalo. A doctor and the comely Miss Montague were standing over him. They told him he had been unconscious for three days, but he was undoubtedly cheered to learn that his two male assailants were in hospital with broken limbs. His nurse was none other

147

than Mrs. John Fulton, of the International Hotel at the Falls, who had rushed to his side on learning of his injuries. Her interest in the handsome daredevil was held by some to be more than motherly, but she brushed this gossip aside. "I am aware," she declared, "that some evil disposed people have wilfully misconstrued the meaning of my intentions toward you, but while I know I have done right and my husband is satisfied, I do not fear the scandal of jealous, narrow-minded sycophants.... I am indifferent to the opinion of everybody, let them think what they like...."

The meek but adoring presence of Miss Montague posed something of a problem until Farini introduced her to Mrs. Fulton as his "night nurse." Mrs. Fulton was baffled at this, since Miss Montague seemed to have no other patients and was, apparently, working gratis. "Sometimes I take more interest in one patient than another," she explained demurely.

"So your interest in this gentleman is not an ordinary one," said the perceptive Mrs. Fulton.

"Yes," came the reply. "It was all my fault." Then, as Farini put a finger to his lips, she became silent.

But Mrs. Fulton would not be put off and soon winkled out the story. "She has plenty of good in her," she told Farini after the two women held a private tête-à-tête. "The poor thing was too confiding and was betrayed by a wolf in sheep's clothing.... When I have gone, she will explain all."

The explanation has all the heart-rending atmosphere of *East Lynne*, the Victorian novel that Mrs. Henry Wood was about to publish. "The terrible girl, who must have been the means of bringing the two scoundrels into the house, had not been there a month.... I lived there as a respectable married woman with a man who had promised to make me his wife but who never kept his word. For his sake I ran away from a happy home and kind parents and I believed his vows and protestations of love and attachment until a few days ago when I discovered that my lover, he for whom I sacrificed home, parents, reputation, and all that a woman should value most, was a married man with two children. It was on the same night that the perfidy of my destroyer was revealed to me that I returned home, only to find you nearly killed. Oh, it was horrible. My punishment seemed to come all at once and I went almost mad. But I must bear everything, the shame, the disgrace, the scorn, and the contempt while he the author of my misery holds his head high and is considered an honourable man." At that she sobbed uncontrollably.

The entire story, reminiscent of the old music-hall favourite "She Was Poor but She Was Honest," was as full of holes as a worn stocking, but Farini accepted it with great gallantry. He was able to report that some time later mother and daughter had been reconciled and that after returning home, "she married a man who really loved her and is now a happy wife and mother."

After several more performances at the Falls, Farini moved on later that same year to neighbouring fairs and carnivals. His amorous adventures, however, were by no means over. At Springfield, Illinois, "the landlord's daughter, who was a highly cultured young lady, somewhat of a blue stocking and a contributor to G.D. Printess's Louisville *Journal*, fell in love with me. I was very much flattered and paid her considerable attention, but not being a covetous man, nor wishing to monopolize so much beauty and genius, I unselfishly left her to shed the bright rays of her talents on more deserving mortals."

Or, at least, that was the way he told it.

4

Although he sometimes drew larger crowds and performed greater feats of daring – letting his taut rope go slack, for instance, so that it swayed alarmingly in the gusts – Farini never achieved the immortality that was Blondin's.

Before Farini completed his series of bi-weekly performances at Niagara, the Prince of Wales arrived on September 15.

The two rival funambulists laid plans to outdo each other with new and greater feats. But it was Blondin who got the attention. Of course Farini offered to take the prince across the gorge, riding in a wheelbarrow on the slack rope, and of course he was refused. In his autobiography he told how he performed before the royal party, dropping from a dangling rope and swimming to safety, then trotting across without the security of a balancing pole. But the press paid only cursory attention. Blondin, on the other hand, drew columns of print – the best part of a page in *The Times* of London.

When Blondin once again carried Harry Colcord across the gorge, and later made his way out onto the tightrope wearing stilts (a feat Farini did not duplicate), thousands came to watch the exhibition – and to gawk at the heavy-lidded heir to the throne. Blondin offered to carry the prince across on his back, and the prince again refused. "I will not endanger your life," he said, "and I will not expose mine." The reporter for *The Times* declared that "one thing is certain … if you do go to see Blondin, when he once begins his feats, you can never take your eyes off him, unless you shut them from a very sickness of terror, till he is safe back again on land."

"Thank God it's over," said the prince when Blondin descended.

It was the Frenchman's feats against which all future performances were measured and it was Blondin's name and memory that provided the magic. Harry Leslie, who crossed the gorge in 1865, advertised himself as "the American Blondin." Professor J.F. Jenkins, in 1871, was "the Canadian Blondin." Signor Henry Bellini, in 1873, was "the Australian Blondin." Marie Spelterina, in 1876, the only woman ever to attempt a rope crossing of the Niagara, was said to "out Blondin Blondin." She crossed backwards, blindfolded, wearing peach baskets on her feet.

In spite of the apparent danger, none of the fifteen or more performers who crossed the gorge on the tightrope was killed –

unless one counts the unfortunate Stephen Peer, a Canadian assistant to Bellini, who in 1887, probably intoxicated after a late party, tried to walk out onto his employer's three-quarter-inch cable wearing ordinary street shoes and immediately plunged to his death.

As time wore on and funambulism became almost commonplace, performers tried to outdo one another by narrowing the rope and increasing their speed. By 1893, after Clifford Calverly established a new record by running across on his cable in a fraction over two minutes and forty-five seconds, tightrope walking at the Falls had begun to pall. One man, Oscar Williams, tried to drum up business in 1910 by repeating Blondin's performance. To his chagrin, only a small crowd turned out to watch him.

For Blondin, the triumph never ended. He performed all his Niagara stunts at the Crystal Palace in London before a huge backdrop of the Falls. He was showered with medals, gifts, money, and jewels. A Blondin March was composed in his honour. The press called him the King of the Tight Rope, the Lord of the Hempen Realm, the Emperor of Manila (a promotion from prince). He toured the globe, performing all his old feats, including that of cooking an omelet high above the heads of the applauding throng. He returned to America and performed them all over again, as women continued to gasp and strong men to turn pale. One young man challenged him to a contest on the high wire, but Blondin gently declined, remarking that he had justly won his prestige and could rightfully claim that he was the greatest performer in the world. He gave his final performance at the age of seventy-two and died the following year on February 28, 1897, of diabetes.

For Farini the Great, the tightrope was only an adventurous way station on a roller-coaster journey through life. During his long career he was many things – strong man, inventor, explorer, writer, painter, sculptor, horticulturist. Nor were his years free from tragedy. In 1862 he performed on the high rope

151

at the Havana bull ring carrying on his back a female partner, identified in one report as his wife. In his unpublished autobiography he makes no mention of her or of the tragedy that followed; undoubtedly Farini did not care to evoke what must have been a dreadful experience. At the high point of the performance in Havana, the unfortunate woman made the grievous error of reaching back to wave at the crowd and toppled off the rope. Hanging by one foot, Farini seized her by the hem of her dress; but it tore away, and she fell headlong into the crowd. She died a few days later leaving a child, who, so the news services reported, was cared for by the women of Havana.

When the Civil War was in its second year, Farini's uncle, who had enlisted in the Union army, asked his nephew to join his staff. Years later Farini told Charles Currelly, the curator of the Royal Ontario Museum, that he had volunteered for the secret service, gone south, and enlisted in the Confederate army. It was his function to ferret out military plans, desert, turn in his information, then head south again and join a different unit. He claimed later to have invented a method of transporting armed men across rivers using pontoons for shoes. The president himself, it is said, watched a demonstration. Farini liked to quote Lincoln's remark at that time: "Young man, don't be afraid, for if you should topple over and get in head down, I'm tall enough to wade you out."

Farini returned to Niagara in 1864, and there he attempted another death-defying feat. He proposed to wade to the very lip of the American Falls wearing iron stilts especially made for the purpose. He succeeded in getting to a point in the shallows halfway between the Goat Island bridge and the brink of the cascade when one of the stilts broke and he found himself struggling in the rapids. With one leg badly injured as a result of his tumble, he managed to reach Robinson's Island, a tiny, wooded bit of rock not far from the Luna Falls. There he sat, marooned and outwardly calm, massaging his injured limb, while a curious crowd gathered. No one attempted to rescue him because it was widely believed that Farini had concocted the entire accident. Hours passed before he was finally taken ashore.

His career in the decade that followed was peripatetic. He took his tightrope act again to Latin America, then in 1866 turned up in England with an adopted child, a young orphan boy he called El Niño. Was this the child his former partner had left in Havana in 1862? Certainly the two were inseparable for the rest of Farini's life. (El Niño eventually married Farini's younger sister.) Farini trained El Niño as a trapeze artist, and soon the Flying Farinis were dazzling spectators at the Cremorne Gardens and the Alhambra Palace in London, the nimble boy playing a snare drum high above the crowd as his adoptive father held him by the nape of the neck.

Farini vanished from public view for more than a year. This was undoubtedly the period when, as he told Currelly, he organized a small circus and took it to the Black Sea, Cairo, and the capitals of Europe. When he returned in 1871, he had put together a new act involving a young woman of spectacular beauty whom he called "Mademoiselle Lulu." He also that year married an Englishwoman named Alice Carpenter; they had no children.

Lulu quickly became the toast of London and Paris, performing the spectacular "Lulu leap" in which she defied gravity by jumping twenty-five feet from the stage to her trapeze bar, executing a triple somersault en route. The crowds were mystified, not realizing that Farini had invented an elasticized catapult that fitted into the stage and propelled her to the bar. Lulu appeared before royalty and was eulogized in *Punch*. Stagedoor johnnies tried to meet her, men of high position sent gifts and offers of marriage; but Lulu remained a recluse until it was revealed in 1878, to the embarrassment of many, that she was actually a man – none other than Farini's adopted son, El Niño.

Meanwhile, Farini had been hired to resuscitate the failing

fortunes of the Royal Westminster Aquarium. He quickly made it pay again by introducing a series of startling acts, the most spectacular of which featured another female protégé, Rossa Matilda Richter, billed as "Zazel, the Beautiful Human Cannonball." Farini had combined his catapult device with a large mortar, complete with flash powder, to send Zazel hurtling from its mouth and through the air into a net. Farini also exhibited a series of human oddities including Krao, the Missing Link, the Man with the Iron Skull, the Hypnotized Horse, Captain Constentenus, the world's most tattooed man, and a group of natives from the Kalahari Desert whom he called "earthmen."

The Kalahari interpreter told him so many stories of diamonds littering the desert that Farini decided to see for himself. Divorced from his wife, he set off in 1884 to America to pick up Lulu (El Niño), now a photographer in Connecticut. Then the two adventurers headed for Africa and the Kalahari, where Farini claimed to have discovered the ruins of a lost city. His explorations brought him some academic notice. His subsequent book about his adventures in the Kalahari was described by the *Era* as "a standard work on its subject."

Farini also brought back a collection of bulbs and seeds that he presented to the Royal Botanical Gardens at Kew. By now he was achieving a reputation as a horticulturist. He had already written *Ferns That Grow in New Zealand*, and now, after cultivating sixty thousand flowering tubers on his estate at Forest Hill, he published his best-selling work, *How to Grow Begonias*. That led to a fellowship in the Royal Horticultural Society. In his spare time, Farini amused himself by writing poems, short stories, and even the lyrics for a song that Anna Mueller, his new wife, had composed.

For this extraordinary man had selected for himself an extraordinary mate – in the Kaiser's court, of all places. She was a prominent and aristocratic German pianist with impeccable credentials – a former student of Franz Liszt, a niece of

154

Richard Wagner, a daughter of the Kaiser's aide-de-camp. Though he was fifteen years her senior, she easily succumbed to his well-honed charms. A seasoned gallant who spoke seven languages, he had a quick and agile mind that few women could resist.

His many activities included that of inventor – at a time when inventors were the folk heroes of the age. The Ontario Archives has three files stuffed with descriptions of Farini's inventions, including a sliding theatrical chair, a new telegraphic apparatus, and a more efficient watering can (for begonias, no doubt). In the old days he had been front and centre on tightrope and trapeze. Now he was a shadowy impresario, lurking in the background, manipulating the careers of such luminaries as Lily Langtry and Sandow the Strong Man. Who could resist him? George Du Maurier is said to have based his sinister character, Svengali, on Farini. Certainly, with his long, jet-black, forked beard, he looked the part.

Farini and his wife returned to Canada in 1899. Madame Farini taught music in Toronto while her husband took up oil painting, a new hobby, exhibiting with such Canadian masters as C.W. Jefferys and J.E.H. MacDonald. He continued to study art after he and his wife returned to Germany. They were caught there in the Great War, detained but not interned, thanks no doubt to his wife's background and influence at the German court. Farini passed the time by writing a thirty-volume account of all the Great War battles from the German point of view. It was never published.

Back in Canada, Farini returned with his wife to his old home town, Port Hope, and there, well past the age of eighty, he continued to paint and to exercise. He walked his tightrope for fun, took five-mile bicycle trips, and exhibited at the Canadian National Exhibition, where in 1923 one of his paintings won an award. He died in January 1929 in his ninety-first year, doomed by a formidable constitution to outlive his own fame and to expire all but forgotten, surrounded by his paintings, his

African mementos, his circus posters, and, of course, his fading memories of the golden summer nearly seventy years before when he had challenged the great Blondin on the tightrope at Niagara and basked in the wide-eyed approbation of "the wives and daughters of some of the most prominent men in America."

5

For decades the rapids of Niagara were overshadowed by the presence of the thundering cataract. Above the Falls, for almost a mile, the river raged and swirled around Goat Island. A mile and half below, the six-foot whitecaps of the Whirlpool Rapids fascinated and repelled those spectators who viewed them from the safe perch of Roebling's railway suspension bridge.

The rapids, indeed, were almost as spectacular as the Falls themselves, but it took Charles Blondin and his imitators to focus attention on what Nicholas Woods, *The Times* correspondent, called "a perfect hell of waters." Woods confessed to "a horrible yearning in your heart to plunge in and join the mad whirl," but even with this thought uppermost in his mind, he admitted, "you shrink instinctively from the dreadful brink."

Woods stood in the enclosure with the Prince of Wales's party in 1860, watching in "a very sickness of terror" as the rope dancer, who had chosen an even more perilous site for his rope walk, more than two hundred feet high above where the "waters boil and roar and plunge on in massive waves at the rate of some twenty miles an hour." William Dean Howells, then a rising literary figure, was also present and marvelled at "their mighty march ... their gigantic leaps and lunges, when they break ranks and their procession becomes a mere onward tumult without form or order." Viewing the rapids was an unexpected bonus to the Niagara experience. He "had not counted on the Rapids taking me by the throat, as it were, and making my heart stop."

The following year, one man, Joel Robinson, did what all had considered impossible. He took a small and fragile steamboat successfully through the raging waters, a feat so terrible that it made him old before his time and was not repeated until 1980, when it became the centrepiece of a motion picture. Robinson was a riverman – a bland designation that disguised the feats of derring-do for which this small but exclusive breed has become famous. Joel Robinson was the first.

He was already famous for his successful rescue and salvage efforts. In 1838, a man named Chapin fell off the Goat Island bridge and into the rapids and was marooned on a tiny islet in the heart of the torrent. Robinson took off from nearby Bath Island and in his red skiff threaded his way to the site and rescued the victim. Three years later he repeated the deed when a man named Allen broke one oar of his rowboat and was marooned on the farthest out of the tiny Three Sisters islands in the perilous rapids on the southwest side of Goat Island. Robinson, using lengths of strong, light cord, managed to haul Allen free.

Until that time, the little islets in the rapids just above the brink of the Falls had all been considered inaccessible. But some time later, in 1855, Robinson was able to salvage the contents of a canal boat trapped precariously on another rocky pinpoint. These exploits took place a stone's throw from the lip of the cascade and called for daring, skill, and iron nerves. A single unwise manoeuvre would have sent Robinson and his skiff plunging over the precipice.

The riverman was tall, fair, and blue eyed, cool and deliberate, easy going, kindly, "gentle as a girl." There was a calmness about him, a serenity that made him a stranger to fear. A first-rate swimmer and skilful oarsman, he loved the river as another might love a turbulent and demanding woman. The rapids delighted him. It was said that he was almost glad when he heard that someone was trapped in them, for it gave him an excuse to plunge in and help.

He was no boaster, but after one of his exploits he enjoyed

157

playing to the crowd. When he rescued Chapin, he climbed up on one of the taller cedars on the little island and waved a green branch to the spectators. When he returned, he distributed a boatload of green boughs to the crowd, who replaced them with coins thrown into the boat and then carried him on their shoulders into the village. Fishing and sailing parties found his presence reassuring. To some, he was indispensable.

When Blondin and Farini were cavorting high above the gorge, Robinson was piloting the little steamer *Maid of the Mist*, which had in 1854 replaced an earlier vessel of the same name. The *Maid* had been built as a tourist excursion craft, shuttling back and forth across the river so close to the Falls that the passengers, dressed in oilskins, were drenched by the spray. George W. Holley, a longtime Niagara resident and chronicler, reported that the journey aboard the *Maid* beneath the spray of the cataract was so impressive that many were not content with a single trip but returned time after time to enjoy the experience. "The admiration which the visitor felt as he passed quietly along near the American Fall was changed into awe when he began to feel the mighty pulse of the great deep just below the tower, then swung round into the white foam directly in front of the Horseshoe, and saw the sky of waters falling toward him. And he seemed to be lifted on wings as he sailed swiftly down the rushing stream through a baptism of spray."

Now, having lost her U.S. landing rights, the *Maid* had become unprofitable, and her owners proposed to sell her as she lay at the Canadian dock. But the only offer received for the vessel was conditional on her being delivered at Queenston. That would mean the unthinkable – a trip downriver, through the rapids and the Whirlpool and then into the gorge below, a journey no one had ever made. But Robinson agreed to make it as captain and pilot and managed to secure two other volunteers, an engineer, James H. Jones, and a mechanic, James McIntyre, as crew.

The vessel was a single-stack paddlewheel steamer, seventy-two feet long with a draught of eight feet, powered by a one-hundred-horsepower engine. When she set off on the afternoon of June 15, 1861, from the dock just above the Niagara Suspension Bridge, few of the crowd that saw her depart expected to see Robinson and his crew again alive. One hundred yards below the eddy in which the *Maid* was safely tethered, the river plunged sharply into the rapids that led directly to the Whirlpool. From there to Queenston, it was "one wild, turbulent rush and whirl of water, without a square foot of smooth surface in the whole distance."

At three o'clock, Robinson took his place at the wheel and jangled the starting bell. With a shriek from her whistle, the little craft swung out into midstream and shot into the rapids under the bridge. Robinson and McIntyre both gripped the wheel with all the strength at their command, only to find themselves impotent in the raging water. Robinson struggled vainly to wrestle the ship into the inside curve of the rapids, but she was swept directly by a fierce crosscurrent toward the outer curve. A jet of water struck the rudder, and he felt her heel over. Another column dashed up her starboard side and carried off her smokestack. The vessel trembled so violently that Robinson thought she would crumble to pieces. Another shock flung him on his back, while McIntyre was thrown against the starboard side of the open wheelhouse.

As she plunged into the Whirlpool, Robinson scrambled to his feet and placed one boot firmly on McIntyre's prostrate body to prevent his rolling overboard. Below the hatches, Jones was on his knees uttering a prayer that he later believed was his salvation. Now, for a moment, the *Maid* rode at even keel. Robinson, seizing the wheel, managed to turn her through the neck of the vortex while receiving another drenching from the towering waves. The rest of the trip was very much as he had imagined it – like the swift sailing of a large bird in downward flight.

Robinson never really recovered his sangfroid. His wife declared that he "was twenty years older when he came home that day than when he went out." He sank wearily into his chair, determined to abandon the river forever. In his neighbour's words, "his manner and appearance were changed. Calm and deliberate before, he became thoughtful and serious afterward. He had been borne, as it were, in the arms of a power so mighty that its impress was stamped on his features and on his mind. Through a slightly opened door he had seen a vision which awed and subdued him. He became reverent in a moment. He grew venerable in an hour."

Chapter Six

1

By the 1860s, after Blondin and Farini had enticed more thousands to Niagara and the new railway suspension bridge had made access easier, the battle for the tourist dollar was becoming more feverish. It was concentrated on the old military reserve on the Canadian side, that quarter-mile-long strip of souvenir shops, taverns, refreshment booths, and inns known to all as the Front. The Front began at the Falls where the old Table Rock had stood. Its downstream terminus was the elegant Clifton House. Two less savoury establishments – Thomas Barnett's Table Rock House and Saul Davis's Table Rock Hotel – crowded as close to the Horseshoe as possible and used every means available, legal or illegal, to seduce the visitor.

Here were sown the seeds of a bitter rivalry between Davis, an out-and-out swindler, and Barnett, an obsessive museum collector as well as innkeeper. Their twenty-year war, which began in 1853 and dragged on into the mid-1870s, was fought without quarter against the gaudiest of backdrops. Here barkers elbowed their way through the crowd or stood outside their emporiums urging the newcomers to view the wonders, not of the Falls, but of those hucksters who had set up shop in their shadow. Roguish Irish girls flirted with passers-by, inveigling them into "Indian" tepees where spurious native curios were sold for outrageous prices. Mountebanks with Malacca canes and derby hats steered the curious toward their own waiting hacks, whose drivers, working on fat percentages, drove the protesting victims to the wrong hotels. Men with oversize cameras offered to take free photographs, then bullied the luckless customers into paying up. "Congealed spray" from the cataract still enjoyed a brisk sale; so did sulphur water allegedly from the Burning Spring a short distance upriver. And everybody peddled the tale of the "maid of the mist" who, it was claimed, was sent over the Falls as a sacrifice to the god who

162

lived there. The tale was as false as the water that refused to burst into flames. This was not Mexico. The local Indians had never indulged in human sacrifice.

The twin communities, one on either side of the international river, had now taken on separate and quite different characteristics. Niagara Falls, New York, was mainly mills and factories – although William Dean Howells did pay twenty-five cents to view a five-legged calf at the entrance to the private park at Prospect Point. Clifton, on the Canadian side, was high carnival.

This dichotomy had less to do with national character than with propinquity. The Canadian village catered to tourists because that was where the tourists wanted to be. The Canadian Falls were far more spectacular than their U.S. counterpart, an incontrovertible truth that some Americans considered a slight to the national endowment. Howells remarked that "my patriotism has always felt the hurt of the fact that our great national cataract is best viewed from a foreign shore." He watched those tumbling waters "with a jealousy almost as green as themselves" and tried to make believe the American Falls were finer, but finally gave up and grudgingly admitted that the Canadian cataract "if not more majestic, is certainly more massive."

The American tourists were easy prey for the human vultures who worked the Canadian side without hindrance from an obliging police force. When John Crist, a Pennsylvania farmer, visited the Falls on July 5, 1866, with his two boys and their aunts, he asked to be driven to Table Rock – or what was left of it. The cabman, instead, deposited the party at Saul Davis's notorious Table Rock Hotel, which paid a commission to hack drivers. Crist was invited to enter the building, which was headquarters for a variety and fancy goods store, a staircase to the river bank, guided tours under the sheet of water, and a photographer's booth. Edward Davis, a son of the owner, assured the unsuspecting farmer that everything within was free. He *must* see the "Boiling Springs," which, he was told, were directly behind the hotel; indeed, the only access to them, Davis insisted, was through the building.

Once inside, Crist and his sons were hustled into one room, the women into another, and all were ordered to don suits of oilskin clothing. The baffled farmer wanted to know what this was all about and was told that the oilskins were necessary "to see the Boiling Springs." There would be no charge, though he might give ten or fifteen cents to his guide if he wished. After that the party was hurried, not to the non-existent Boiling Springs or even to the Burning Spring some distance away, but down the circular staircase in the cliff face to the base of the Horseshoe. Crist didn't want to go, but one of the boys rushed ahead, and so he followed, tipping the guide fifteen cents for a five-minute view of the cascade.

On his return, Crist ordered a glass of beer but didn't get it. Instead, a man at the door ordered him to settle up for the oilskins. The price was five dollars – an enormous sum at a time when labourers received less than a dollar a day.

When Crist tried to leave, he was seized by the coat and hurled back into the room. Three more men, including another of Saul Davis's sons, Charles, now appeared. Crist offered them his pocketbook: "There is one dollar in this purse, all I have got except a quarter."

"You're a damn pretty fellow to come all the way to the Falls with only one dollar in your pocket," Davis sneered. He added that he would keep the entire party imprisoned until he got his money.

When Crist asked if there wasn't a law in Canada whereby he could seek redress, Davis shook his fist in his face. "That's the law in Canada and we're the officers to carry that law out!" he said. He cursed and swore at Crist, who then demanded to see the American consul. Davis refused. The farmer would not get out alive, he said, unless he paid up. At that Crist borrowed four dollars from one of his sisters and was released.

This was no isolated case; at Davis's Table Rock Hotel it was the norm. Threats, abuse, and violence were visited upon the luckless and gullible arrivals who were suckered into believing that the Davis family were philanthropists interested only in providing free views of the cataract. When another American, George Loveridge, protested at being charged twelve dollars, one of Davis's henchmen pushed him across the room and shook a fist in his face. "God damn you," he shouted, "you can't go out of that room without paying what I ask." Thoroughly cowed, Loveridge paid, and with good reason. The Davises were prepared to use force. They seized a luckless Manhattan surgeon by the whiskers and the throat, pushed him through a glass door, and hurled him to the floor, wrenching his back.

The hack drivers aided and abetted this extortion, hustling unwary tourists to the Davis establishment. Appeals to the law had no effect. When a Professor Cooper from New York demanded to see a justice of the peace, Edward Davis cried, "You Goddamned American sons of bitches, you can't move from here till you pay every cent." Faced with a similar request from a Pennsylvania tourist, Edward Davis shook his fist in the newcomer's face and announced that *he* was a justice of the peace.

"If you do not pay your bill, I will smash you," Charles Davis told a Peterborough farmer, John H. Weir. At that, Mrs. Weir burst into tears, whereupon one of Davis's women employees berated Weir as "a damned pretty clod-hopper to take a girl around and not pay your expenses."

The Davis family got away with these swindles because most of their victims lived hundreds of miles away and could afford neither the time nor the money to launch a civil suit. Even when they stayed on and succeeded in getting a ruling, Davis immediately appealed, and few plaintiffs could commit themselves to further appearances. Nor was it easy to obtain witnesses against the family; the hack drivers were understandably reluctant to imperil their main source of income. As the

United States consul, Martin Jones, wrote to the secretary of state, W.H. Seward, "no respectable citizen of Canada who is familiar with [Davis's] Table Rock House speaks well of it, and everyone seems anxious … to get rid of such a nest of swindlers, yet there appears to be no one here of sufficient courage to take an active part in breaking its power."

Davis's depredations received a public airing at last when he sued the Hamilton *Times* for libel in 1868. The newspaper had called his Table Rock Hotel "the cave of the forty thieves," which "needs suppressing periodically." When the suit came to trial, the *Times* was prepared. It paraded before the court a series of witnesses who had been swindled by the Davis family. The judge threw the case out and came down hard on Davis. "This monstrous evil," he said, "ought to be exposed and an end put to it." But an end was not put to it. Davis carried on as before.

Nonetheless, his courtroom loss must have pleased his long-time rival, Thomas Barnett, who had been operating his famous museum of curiosities near the Falls since 1829. Now housed in its new $150,000 stone building, the eclectic museum – said to be the largest on the continent, and also the very first – held close to ten thousand specimens that ranged from stuffed rattlesnakes to Egyptian mummies.

Barnett was also the proprietor of the original Table Rock House. But in 1853, Davis built his own establishment with a similar name, situating it between Barnett's inn and Table Rock itself. With that move, Davis was in a position to intercept Barnett's customers.

The two men were bound to be incompatible. Barnett did not stoop to the kind of chicanery that had made Davis so unpopular. He charged his customers a flat dollar for a trip down his spiral staircase to the foot of the cataract. For another dollar each could buy a certificate proving completion of the trip. It was said that a German prince had offered two dollars for a certificate claiming that he had gone farther behind the

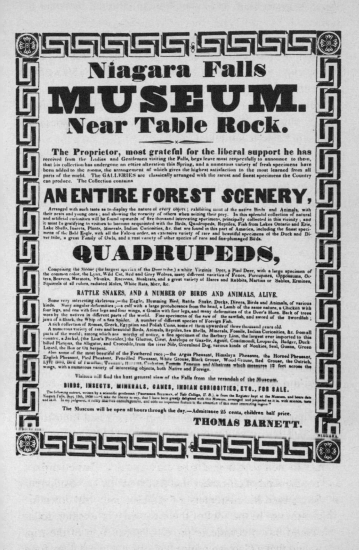

sheet of water than any other human. Barnett declined the bribe.

Barnett was a genuine collector, typical of the breed, so proud of his museum that he often let in visitors for half price and teachers and students for nothing. By the mid-1860s he had on display 150 native Canadian birds, 490 foreign birds, 175 mammals, 38 fish, 42 reptiles, 8,000 entomological specimens, and a confusion of shells, fossils, eggs, coins, statues, paintings, and Eastern antiquities.

He displayed everything that came his way, including the corpse of his own dog. The animal had been born without hind legs, so Barnett had invented a two-wheeled device that, attached to the dog's nethers, aided its locomotion. When the dog died, Barnett had a taxidermist stuff the skin while he removed the skeleton for a second exhibit. Both are still on show in Niagara, complete with the rear wheels.

Barnett's obsession threatened to become his downfall, for he could not stop. The museum expanded, was moved to larger quarters, was rebuilt twice, and, by the late 1860s, was in the process of beggaring its owner. Nonetheless, Barnett found funds to contribute to charity – to the victims of the Quebec fire of 1845, for example, and to the Crimean War fund.

Davis, by contrast, was a jailbird, an American who had served three months of a two-year sentence for fraud in the New York State prison. His relatives lobbied for his release, and Davis himself promised a sum of money to a friend to get him out. The governor was persuaded to give him a pardon, but before that came through Davis was released as a result of "a flaw in the indictment."

He came to Niagara in 1844 and opened the Prospect House on the American side, which he sold to his brother-in-law in 1853 in order to launch his Table Rock Hotel. In the spirited contest with Barnett, few holds were barred. When Barnett got the court's permission to take his customers on a path past

Davis's hotel in order to view the Falls, Davis retaliated by encircling the hotel with a stone wall and exacting a twenty-five-cent fee from every Barnett customer.

That was too much. The government, which still owned the old military reserve on which the Front squatted, cancelled Davis's lease, giving Barnett a monopoly. Davis coolly ignored the order and no one tried to enforce it. Both men had built stairways to the water's edge, and this caused endless recriminations. In 1865, somebody burned down Davis's stairway. Davis tried forcibly to use Barnett's. When Barnett resisted, Davis blasted rocks on his own property so that they hurtled down the cliffside and effectively blocked his rival's staircase. When Barnett successfully obtained an injunction to stop him, Davis responded by charging Barnett and his son with perjury for making false affidavits. Nothing came of that.

Davis regained his lease to the river frontage, but this was quickly seized by the sheriff for non-payment of debt. Barnett bought it, thus gaining the exclusive right to conduct visitors under the Falls. Davis responded with a whispering campaign suggesting that Barnett's stairway was unsafe. He followed that by posting large signs advising tourists not to go under the cataract because of the danger of falling rocks.

The long-simmering feud bubbled into violence and bloodshed on June 24, 1870. Colonel Sidney Barnett, son of the museum owner, was infuriated by Davis's signs posted on his property warning tourists not to proceed down the bank. He tore down the signs, and a wild mêlée with members of the Davis faction followed.

In the confused account of what happened next, certain facts stand out. After the encounter, Sidney Barnett returned to the museum, where he encountered two of Davis's sons, Edward and Robert, apparently in a dispute with his father. The two Davises were seated in a carriage pulling their cart, which contained photographic equipment. Barnett heard, or thought he heard, somebody shout that they were going to kill his father. At that the Barnett contingent, already worked up from their previous encounter, began to hurl stones at the two brothers.

The pair jumped out of their carriage, produced pistols, and started firing, killing one of Barnett's black employees. The two were charged with murder but acquitted on the ground of self-defence. The hapless Sidney Barnett was found guilty of assault and severely reprimanded by the court.

At Saul Davis's Table Rock Hotel, the outrages continued as before with the willing co-operation of hack drivers from both sides of the river, who delivered their protesting fares into the arms of Davis's black enforcer, Ab Thomas, and a white prize-fighter, Jesse Burke, both of whom threatened physical violence if unwanted photographs weren't purchased or the rental of oilskin clothing was refused. Davis was *persona non grata* with the authorities, but his wife was not. She obtained a new lease giving the family access to the foot of the Falls after her lawyer found a loophole in Barnett's document.

It soon became clear that Barnett's preoccupation with his vast collection was driving him into bankruptcy. He made two desperate attempts to recoup by staging the kind of garish spectacle that had once lured customers to the Falls. Neither of these worked, partly because too much commercial greed had already tarnished Niagara's reputation.

First Barnett tried to stage a traditional Indian burial ceremony to attract visitors to his museum. He recruited members of the Six Nations band, suitably painted and dressed in ceremonial garments. Barnett provided an authentic coffin that he announced contained the ashes of twenty warriors from Queenston, dug up from a thousand-year-old burial mound. But even Barnett had to admit that the ceremony was a flop. The chief delivered a funeral oration in his own tongue that lasted two hours, while his followers, lined up in rows, chanted a burial song unintelligible to the visitors. That was followed by a march to the museum garden where the coffin was interred

170

in a pyramidal vault. By that time most spectators had departed.

Now Barnett made a second attempt to attract business. He was convinced that he needed something glamorous (for the Falls, it seemed, had lost their magic). The Wild West beckoned. Why not exploit it?

In 1871, Niagara Falls was virtually on the frontier. On the Canadian side of the border, civilization ended at Lake Huron. The country west and north of the Niagara Peninsula was a no-man's land of lakes, Precambrian rock, and rolling prairie, populated by Indians, fur traders, and buffalo. The Hudson's Bay Company had only recently sold its vast reserve to Canada; it was still mainly empty and wholly mysterious. But the American West was wild and storied, thanks to the dime novels of E.Z.C. Judson, better known by his pseudonym, Ned Buntline. The last spike joining the Central and Union Pacific railroads had been driven only two years earlier. Pony express riders, buffalo hunters, and Indian fighters were the folk heroes of the day. Long before Buffalo Bill Cody created his Wild West show, Thomas Barnett decided to hold one of his own, complete with Texas cowhands, frontier scouts, and Indians on horseback attacking herds of bison.

This ambitious and cumbersome attraction was totally out of keeping with the Niagara ambience, but Barnett persisted. He sent his son Sidney all the way to the western plains to bring back a herd of buffalo. At the North Platte River, Sidney Barnett encountered one Texas Jack Omohundro, who agreed to hire some Pawnee braves to capture the needed animals. That proved abortive. The buffalo sickened and died in captivity, and the United States government, terrified of another Indian war, ordered the unpredictable Pawnees back to their reservation.

Undaunted, Colonel Barnett trekked on to Kansas City, where he sought out the famous scout, Indian fighter, and federal marshal James Butler "Wild Bill" Hickok. With his shoulder-length hair, drooping moustache, and reputation as a gunfighter, Hickok was just the man to manage the exhibition the Barnetts planned for Niagara.

By this time, Saul Davis was crying hoax. The buffalo hunt had been postponed so many times, he declared, that he was planning to sue Barnett for the expenses he had incurred in buying two bears and a quantity of gingerbread to entertain the crowd. Barnett replied drily that Dàvis's best option was to feed the gingerbread to his bears.

The Great Buffalo Hunt was scheduled at last for August 28 and 29, 1872. "No expense has been spared," the advertisements announced, "to make it the most interesting, the most exciting, and the most thrilling spectacle ever witnessed east of the Mississippi" – hyperbolic phrases reminiscent of those that had once been applied to the great cataract itself. Members of the Sac and Fox Indian tribes had been engaged to appear in full war costumes, mounted on fleet ponies from the plains. A Mexican *vaquero* troupe would also participate. Special excursion trains would run to the Falls, and there would be seats for fifty thousand spectators.

Alas, when the great hunt was launched, only three adult buffalo and a calf were still alive to be hunted, and only three thousand spectators turned up to watch. Wild Bill, mounted on a small mustang, loped about after a cow, which had to be goaded to desperation before it would run at all. The show was a fiasco. Barnett's losses came to twenty thousand dollars.

He struggled on in the face of mounting debts, but his days as a Niagara entrepreneur were over. In November 1876, he sold his four buffalo to an agent of P.T. Barnum for seven hundred dollars. The following year his museum and all his other buildings went on the auction block to satisfy his debtors. The purchaser, by the unkindest of all cuts, was Saul Davis.

In 1873, the year after Barnett's abortive buffalo hunt, the new premier of Ontario, Oliver Mowat, besieged by complaints from individual citizens and especially from the U.S. consul at Clifton, decided to act. He established a royal commission under Edmund Burke Wood, a Member of Parliament known as Big Thunder, to investigate crime at Niagara. It sat for five months and in November produced a scathing indictment centring on the person of Saul Davis. Wood noted that the local police consistently turned a blind eye to Davis's misdemeanours because they were beholden to an electoral body "under the influence of those by whose vote they occupy their respective positions."

As a result, the Mowat government appointed a special magistrate and special police constables to clean up the town and especially the Front. Wood also recommended that the government establish a public park on the old military chain reserve "to correct the abuses and protect the public," but Mowat would have none of that. Law-and-order was one thing; the novel idea of the public sector providing parkland for the people was quite another. The Front survived.

The new provisions helped to quell the extreme criminal element at the Falls. (When he achieved his monopoly at Table Rock, Davis no longer needed to swindle sightseers.) But the carnival ran on. Droves of hackmen continued to harass visitors. Barkers still lured the unwary into souvenir stalls, and peddlers peddled everything from German lapis lazuli and Vesuvian lava to caged animals. One persistent showman tried to sell a live bear to Victor-Henri Rochefort, the radical journalist and political gadfly, who had just escaped from a French penal colony. Rochefort felt a certain kinship with the animal, which "turned sadly about in his cage as I had done in mine a few months earlier." He regretted being unable to free his fellow prisoner but reflected that its first act "would probably have been to devour its liberator."

Like so many others, Rochefort was appalled by the tawdry atmosphere that took so much of the grandeur from the spectacle of the cataract. No longer sublime, Niagara was quickly falling into disrepute, suffering from what one journalist called "the disastrous results of a bad name." The American side was disfigured by ugly stone dams, gristmills, outdoor clotheslines, heaps of sawdust, stables, advertising placards, shanties, lumberyards, a pulp mill, and a gas works. On both sides of the river, as William Morris, the English designer, remarked during a visit, "the very pick of the touts and rascals of the world" were assembled.

The hotel clientele was now largely transient, a radical change from the days when well-to-do Southerners would come by the hundreds to stay for several months. The Civil War had brought an end to that; few could now afford to leave their ravaged homes. Cheap fares and fast trains made it possible to enjoy a one-day trip to Niagara without the expense of putting up at one of the big hotels that lined both sides of the gorge. As one old Falls hand described it to the *New York Times*, "if a man should come here and stay two weeks, they would put him in a glass case and have him in one of the Indian museums for sale for a curiosity." As for the hotels themselves, he reported, they "are old – far older in appearance and fittings than those in any other Summer resort in America ... there is no hotel on either side of the river ... where a guest need expect to be treated with anything like civility.... The solid truth is, there is no comfort here. The big hotels are barns, with nobody in them, and there are 4,000 or 5,000 people in 'the Falls' all vying with each other to see who can skin visitors out of the most money in the shortest time."

The saving grace – more than one visitor mentioned it – was the cheerful presence of the pretty girls in the curio shops, where Indian moccasins, beadwork, stuffed birds and animals,

174

natural crystals, canes, rock ornaments, bows and arrows, and souvenir photographs were sold. There were hundreds of these little shops, most staffed by comely Irish women, all flirtatious and affable – "remarkably affectionate in their manners," as one customer put it. "No man likes a stiff and backward girl," he wrote, "and when you go into a store and a pretty 'saleslady' calls you my dear and changes it to my darling before you leave, the effect is as pleasant as it is startling."

The hack drivers, who were present in droves, were a different breed. They pursued customers relentlessly and then insisted, against all protests, in taking them to places they didn't want to go and charging whatever the traffic would bear. One literary traveller, W.G. Marshall, told of "running the gauntlet of fourteen hotel runners, each especially anxious to take us under the shelter of his protection" before escaping and boarding the bus to the Clifton House.

The drivers received a 25-percent commission on every nickel their reluctant passengers paid out. They, in turn, paid a fancy sum for the privilege of using the hack stand at one of the big hotels. At the Cataract on the American side, for example, it cost an annual thousand dollars to secure hack privileges. At some of the larger hotels the amount was said to approach six thousand. No hotel on the New York side was more than a three-minute walk from the railroad station (one, indeed, was directly across the way). Yet every hotel had its omnibus meet the trains and charged each guest twenty-five cents for a one-way trip. When room and board could be had for about three dollars a day, or a single meal for fifty cents, this was a considerable sum.

On the American side of the river, every viewpoint was fenced in by greedy entrepreneurs so that there was no place from which the great cataract could be seen without payment. One farmer who was swirled around the region in 1877 with his wife and two daughters kept a list of all the entrance fees and expenses paid for four persons in a carriage in one day:

175

To Goat Island	$2.25
To Prospect Park	1.00
To Railway Suspension Bridge	1.00
To new Suspension Bridge	2.50
To Whirlpool Rapids, American side	2.00
To Whirlpool Rapids, Canadian side	2.00
To the Whirlpool	2.00
To the Burning Springs	1.60
To the Battle Ground	2.00
To under the Horseshoe Falls	4.00
To "Into the Shadow of the Rock"	4.00
To through Cave of the Winds	6.00
To hack hire	7.00
To fee to driver	0.50
Total	$37.85

He was persuaded to spend this sum – the equivalent of about $530 in 1992 dollars – by a "plausible fair-spoken knave" who got 25 percent of every fee. At the end of the day, one of his daughters was so ill from nervous excitement she could hardly alight from the carriage, and his wife was too exhausted to leave the hotel. Small wonder, then, that the *New York Times* was able to report of the Falls that "its name has become a reproach and a warning throughout the land" and that "Niagara as a summer resort has well-nigh ceased to exist; it remains but a show."

Yet the seeds of Niagara's renaissance were already being sown unwittingly by the get-rich-quick artists themselves. Years later, after the long struggle to preserve the Niagara gorge was won, the first president of the state park paid a back-handed compliment to those who had "outraged public decency by their importunate demands, exorbitant actions and swindling deceits." In hindsight, he said, "we can thank some of those now innocuous offenders for the zeal which their con-duct imparted to the champions of Niagara." Had private greed

176

"not so far overreached itself and had it left even decently tolerable conditions at Niagara, the task of securing the public reservation would probably have been even greater than it was."

3

In the mid-nineteenth century, few North Americans cared about or even thought about the continent's natural beauty. The emphasis was on "progress," which meant carving out roadways, draining swamps, clearing forests, and exploiting natural wonders, such as the Falls, for profit. In the inexorable march westward, those who subdued the wilderness were seen as nation-builders. As one observer has noted, more was written between 1830 and 1850 about the coming of the railroads than about the destruction of the scenery.

Few worried about the Falls. After all, no greedy hucksters could steal or plunder them. It occurred to only a few – poets, painters, European travellers, and American intellectuals – that the environs of the cataract were just as important as the cataract itself.

The idea of actually setting aside a tract of untrammelled wilderness in perpetuity for future generations to admire and enjoy was a novel one. There were no wilderness parks in North America in the mid-century. Canada would not have its first, at Banff, until 1887. The United States acted earlier. Yosemite State Park, built on federal land but managed by California, was opened in 1864. Its first commissioner was the remarkable landscape architect Frederick Law Olmsted, who had created Central Park in New York City and would soon launch a crusade to save what was left of the Niagara Falls environment.

That fight, which lasted for fifteen years, was waged by two groups of people, working on both sides of the international border. The long, tiring struggle that started slowly, almost

177

ineffectually, would involve some of the leading figures of the day, including a number of intransigent politicians who had no stomach for the principle of public ownership of natural attractions. It might be said to have had its beginnings on a warm August afternoon in 1869. Anyone rambling under the green canopy of Goat Island could not have failed to notice three men of substance – bulky and bewhiskered – roaming through the groves, engaged in animated conversation. These were the days before the diet craze, when bulk was considered a symbol of power and eminence, and certainly this was a trio of commanding presence.

The first was William Edward Dorsheimer, a Buffalo lawyer and politician, a powerful backroom influence in the liberal wing of the Republican party, and federal district attorney for the northern district of New York State. Facial hair was also the fashion with men of influence, and Dorsheimer, a big man, made up for his receding hairline with a vast moustache that curled across his jaw to marry up with his full sideburns. The second – broad-shouldered, full-chested, and bearded – was an up-and-coming young Brooklyn architect, Henry Hobson Richardson, who had just received a commission to design Dorsheimer's Buffalo mansion. The third was Frederick Law Olmsted, tall and rugged, with a high dome and a large western-style handlebar moustache that suggested his recent sojourn on the nation's frontier.

These were all men in the prime of life with much of their careers still ahead of them. Richardson, the youngest, was just thirty. He had secured only a few architectural commissions – Dorsheimer's was one – but he was already attracting attention. Four years later he would be acknowledged as the leading architect in North America, putting his personal stamp on a neo-classical form to be known forever after as Richardsonian Romanesque. Dorsheimer was thirty-eight, the son of German immigrants. Within five years he would be elected lieutenant-governor of his state. A successor praised his "courage and tact, fascination and audacity, rare skill on the platform, creditable associations and marked literary attainments." At forty-seven, Olmsted was the oldest of the trio. Most of his adult years had been spent on a personal quest to find himself and to find for himself an occupation that suited his restless nature. At last he had succeeded. Before his death he would be known as the father of American landscape architecture and also the Saviour of Niagara Falls.

An activist who seemed to radiate inexhaustible energy, Olmsted was plagued by inner doubts and subject to various illnesses – digestive problems, sudden headaches, and periods of nervous exhaustion that were at least partly psychosomatic. His career had been an odd mixture of failure and success. He had quit Yale because of a series of fainting spells. He had tried farming and publishing and failed miserably at both. Central Park was his triumph. The design he and his partner submitted was chosen from a field of thirty-three. He was appointed superintendent of the new park and acting secretary of the New York sanitary commission – important posts that he was forced to abandon because, it was said, he couldn't work under anybody.

Off he went to California to manage a mining estate. That failed too, but by this time Olmsted knew where his future lay. The phrase "landscape architect" had scarcely entered the language, but that was what Olmsted intended to be. Central Park and Yosemite had given him direction. His crusade would be to save the American wilderness. Olmsted saw Niagara as a pilot project for a larger and more ambitious campaign. If he succeeded there, he intended to turn his energies to the protection of the entire Allegheny watershed.

The Goat Island "ramble," as Olmsted called it, took some time. Indeed, it was several hours before the three men actually came within sight of the Falls, for the island seduced and held them, and they lingered among its rustic attractions. To them, this tangled, natural garden was living testimony to What

Might Have Been and also to What Might Be Again. It was the only spot within sound of the Falls that had been preserved almost exactly as the first explorers had known it.

Meeting the following day in Dorsheimer's room at the Cataract House and joined by Olmsted's partner – a brilliant young English landscape architect, Calvert Vaux – the three men agreed that the Niagara gorge must be freed of all the unsightly trappings of civilization and restored to its original wild beauty. No manicured lawns for them, no formal gardens or clipped hedges; this was not Europe. Niagara must be restored so that the visitor, standing on the rim of the gorge, would see the Falls as Father Hennepin had seen them, framed by an unruly jungle of native trees, shrubs, and clinging vines.

There was an unseen presence in the room that day, for Frederic Church was there in spirit. He had returned to Niagara in 1867 to paint and found himself surrounded by crowds of rubbernecks, one of whom went so far as to disparage his work. "Pshaw!" he sneered. "You ought to see *Church's* Niagara."

"I painted it," the artist replied, a remark, it is said, that "almost hurled the critic into the abyss."

Church and Olmsted were distantly related, and both, with Richardson, were members of the Century Club in New York. Within those polished walls Church pushed forward his concept of a public park at Niagara. Olmsted, with his experience in California, agreed. Now, in Dorsheimer's room, he and the others planned a campaign to convince press, public, and politicians that the Falls' environment must be preserved.

The campaign moved slowly and quietly for the next decade. It took time for the public to arrive at the conclusion that a small minority had reached – that Niagara was in deep trouble. In 1871 Henry James fired a warning shot in the *Nation*, a magazine that Olmsted had helped found. The fate of Goat Island especially concerned him. He had been told that the Porter family had been offered "a big price" for the privilege of building a hotel on the property. How long would they hold out? he wondered. Why shouldn't the government buy up the precious acres, as had happened with Yosemite? "It is the opinion of a sentimental tourist that no price would be too great to pay," the novelist declared. The following year, a two-volume work, *Picturesque America*, added to the growing outcry when it described the Falls as "a superb diamond set in lead."

Olmsted, meanwhile, had gone temporarily blind – a hysterical reaction brought about by the breakup of his partnership with Vaux. He still sat on the board of Central Park, but a series of acrimonious disputes with Andrew Green, the comptroller, led to another mental and physical breakdown and his eventual retirement from the park commission. The campaign to preserve Niagara remained dormant until, in 1878, Frederic Church jumped into the breach.

Through a well-connected journalist, the painter made an approach to the Governor General of Canada, Lord Dufferin, who had visited the Falls that summer and had been appalled at what he saw. In spite of the political restrictions placed on him by his vice-regal role, the handsome and elegant nobleman thought of himself as an activist – a little *too* active, sometimes, for the Canadian government, which in the matter of building a railway to the Pacific tended to see him as an interfering busybody.

But Dufferin liked to interfere. His ego demanded it. In the transcripts of his speeches, which he sent to the press in advance, he was in the habit of adding bracketed comments – "*(Applause) … (Laughter)*" – so that no one would miss the point. A former member of Gladstone's ministry, he chafed in a position where as the Queen's representative he could reign but could not rule. Now he saw an opportunity to advance a cause that genuinely concerned him, one to which, without ruffling any political feathers, he could make a contribution.

In Toronto that September, in a speech to the Society of Artists, he made the first public announcement that a joint park with the United States was being contemplated at Niagara. He

181

had already met with Governor Lucius Robinson of New York and suggested that the state should combine with the province of Ontario to buy up lands and buildings around the Falls and form a small international public park, "not indeed decorative or in any way sophisticated by the penny arts of the landscape gardener, but carefully preserved in the picturesque condition, in which it was originally laid out by the hand of nature." Dufferin's proposal corresponded with Olmsted's view. The landscape architect may have been irked by the slur on his profession, but he had no wish to see the "penny arts" – formal gardens, carefully pruned shrubs – intrude on the natural beauty of the wild forest.

Governor Robinson agreed with his vice-regal guest, especially about the need for an international approach. As he put it, "the sublime exhibition of natural powers there witnessed is the property of the whole world." Dufferin had already been to see the Ontario government, and Robinson recommended to the state legislature that if Ontario appointed a commission, New York should follow suit. He added a practical note: the proposals, he pointed out, would undoubtedly increase tourist traffic at the Falls.

The legislature at once instructed the Commissioners of State Survey to report on the feasibility of the governor's request. James T. Gardner, the head of the commission, together with Olmsted, would examine the region and draw up a plan of improvement. With commendable dispatch, it was completed and presented to the legislature in March 1880.

The separate statements by the two men presented a devastating indictment of the disfigurement of the Falls' environment. "The Falls themselves," Gardner wrote, "man cannot touch; but he is fast destroying their beautiful frame of foliage, and throwing around them an artificial setting of manufactories and bazaars that arouses in the intelligent visitor deep feelings of regret and even of resentment."

The cancer was spreading. Two more mills and a brewery

had just been built near the bank half a mile below the cataract to "warn us of what is coming." And Goat Island, the jewel of Niagara, was already endangered. A partition suit was in progress, and would-be purchasers were planning, among other attractions, a race course, a summer hotel, and a rifle range. It was even suggested that a canal be cut through the island's midriff with factories lining both banks. The prospect was unthinkable. Many of the trees on the island had been there when Father Hennepin arrived. They remained "the only living witnesses of those important scenes in the dramas of European conquest of America." Would not posterity heap scorn on the present generation for destroying "these living monuments of history" to make way for a race course?

In his accompanying report Olmsted blamed the profit motive for destroying Niagara's scenery. The idea of profit made the worst desecration acceptable. It was "the public's verdict of acquittal"; the idea that Niagara was nothing more than a sensational exhibition for rope walkers and brass bands "is so presented to the visitor that he is forced to yield to it...."

The report made it clear that the state had made a major error early in the century when it decided to sell or lease the land adjacent to the Falls. Now that same land would have to be bought back at considerable cost to the taxpayers. The commission urged that a strip a mile long and between one hundred and eight hundred yards wide be expropriated, the buildings destroyed, and the entire area replanted as close to the original wilderness as possible.

But nobody wanted to pay the cost. Alonzo B. Cornell, who had succeeded Robinson in 1879, was a longtime opponent of the park scheme. Why, he asked, should the taxpayer shoulder the burden of expropriation? Did he really believe that the Falls should be fenced in? "Of course I do," he declared. "They are a luxury and why should not the public pay to see them?"

In Canada, the Ontario premier, Oliver Mowat, who had in 1873 rejected his own commission's recommendation for a public park at Niagara, apparently had a change of heart and unequivocally endorsed the idea, declaring piously that "not in the whole world was there anything more worthy of saving." Yet the saving of money, in the long run, was more important to Mowat than the saving of scenery. On September 27, 1879, when he and three of his Cabinet met with the New York commissioners, it seemed that the international park scheme was a *fait accompli*. But, as in the United States, it foundered on the matter of money.

Mowat wanted the federal government to pay the bill, even suggesting that that had been Lord Dufferin's intention. In 1880, the Ontario premier pushed a bill through the legislature that gave Ottawa the freedom to buy up private or Crown land for a park. In this way he shrugged off all responsibility for the project. But Ottawa wasn't buying. If Niagara was to be saved, it soon became clear, there would be two parks, separate and distinct, one on each side of the gorge.

4

All through the winter of 1879-80, Frederick Law Olmsted had been working on a memorial to accompany the commission's report on the need to preserve Niagara. He had the help of Dorsheimer, Church, and, perhaps more important, a new convert to the cause, Charles Eliot Norton, the distinguished Harvard professor. Among them they managed to secure the signatures of some seven hundred leading politicians, jurists, and writers from Canada and the United States. This remarkable memorial, which urged that the Falls be placed "under the joint guardianship of the two governments" (New York State and Canada), was delivered simultaneously to the governor of New York, the obdurate Cornell, and Lord Dufferin's successor, Lord Lorne.

184

It has been rightly said that no similar petition was ever graced by the signatures of so many illustrious and distinguished persons: the vice-president of the United States, members of the Canadian Parliament, Supreme Court justices, university presidents, high-ranking military men, eminent churchmen, Cabinet ministers, and a bevy of literary luminaries that included Francis Parkman, Charles A. Dana, Henry Wadsworth Longfellow, Ralph Waldo Emerson, Oliver Wendell Holmes, James Russell Lowell, John Greenleaf Whittier, Thomas Carlyle, and John Ruskin.

The governor of New York could – and did – ignore this extraordinary appeal; scarcely anybody on the list was a voter. But with the Governor General pressing him, Sir John A. Macdonald, always sensitive to public opinion, could not. After all, the memorial contained the signatures of some of the most powerful businessmen in Canada. These included a Massey, a Molson, and a Redpath. There was also the principal of McGill University. In June 1880, the prime minister set up a special commission to look into the park proposal. It would be chaired by one of his closest Cabinet colleagues, Sir Alexander Campbell.

Once again, the question of cost frustrated the park proposal. Campbell reported that it would require $375,000 to expropriate the land needed. Even translated into today's dollars, the sum seems picayune, considering the rewards. But regional jealousy – that continuing Canadian bugbear – thwarted the scheme. The Maritime members of Macdonald's Cabinet, with the support of several from Quebec, were firmly opposed. Why, they asked, should Ontario hog all the money? They argued that few tourists from the three impoverished provinces on the chill Atlantic shore would ever see the Falls. If New York State was being asked to pay the full cost, why not Ontario? Why ask the taxpayers of Halifax or Saint John to subsidize a tourist attraction a thousand miles away?

Macdonald compromised and offered to negotiate with Ontario on the basis of joint financing. Oliver Mowat turned him down, and that was that.

In New York, the indefatigable Olmsted refused to give up the battle. In Norton he had a valiant colleague, a man who seemed to know everybody. It was he who had secured many of the signatures on the famous memorial.

Norton was an esthete. Physically fragile – he suffered from long bouts of insomnia – with a high, domed forehead and long, delicate features, he resembled a medieval monk. His was an attractive personality. On first meeting him, Ruskin had remarked on "the bright eyes, the melodious voice, the perfect manner." To Norton, as to Olmsted, the campaign to preserve the Falls was only a step towards a larger vision: a full-scale attempt to awaken America to its natural heritage. He was alarmed – despondent, indeed – over the rapid spread of nineteenth-century industrialism and depressed by what his country was doing to its landscape.

"The growth of wealth, and the selfish individualism which accompanies it (and corrupts many who are not rich), seems to weaken all properly social motives and efforts," he wrote. "Men in cities and towns feel much less relation with their neighbours than of old; there is less civic patriotism, less sense of a spiritual and moral community. This is due in part to other causes, but mainly to the selfishness of the individualism in a well-to-do democracy." Like so many others, then and now, Norton was looking back to a golden age – the "pure and innocent" America, when, at the beginning of the century, his native New England was not begrimed by industrial smoke and the banks of the Niagara gorge were still unsullied.

The phrase "public relations," with all its connotations, had yet to come into use. Indeed, it is difficult to think of Olmsted, and particularly of Norton, as P.R. men. But that is what they were in their fight to preserve the Falls. Unable to move the politicians, they set out like twentieth-century activists to persuade the public by capturing the press.

The Niagara Falls *Gazette*, which represented the commercial interests on the American side, was already mounting a campaign against them. So were the proprietors of the largest pulp mill, who owned seven hundred feet of waterfront. But Olmsted and Norton had better connections. Norton had also helped to found the *Nation*, the most important weekly in the country. Dorsheimer had left Buffalo to become editor of the New York *Star*. Both men had close friends on the Boston and New York papers, and Norton knew intimately every major literary figure in America.

In the summer of 1881, they got themselves a hired gun in the person of Henry Norman, a young Englishman who had recently graduated from Harvard and had impressive literary connections. Norman was sent off to the Falls to write a series of letters to the press – not the terse, two-paragraph epistles that appear in modern newspapers, but full-fledged essays, the length of magazine articles. One, in the September 1 issue of the *Nation,* was unsigned, making it appear that the editors themselves had composed it.

Norman heaped satire on his adversaries. Some people, he wrote, balked at paying twenty-five cents in taxes to destroy a lot of good buildings and replace them with trees "for the sake of a few persons whose nerves are so delicate that the sight of a tremendous body of water rushing over a precipice is spoilt for them by a pulp-mill standing on the bank." But then, what else was to be expected when the governor himself, after listening to a report on the destruction of the Falls' environment, had replied, laconically, "Well, the water goes over just the same, doesn't it?"

The following year, Norton brought in an old friend and skilled propagandist, Jonathan Baxter Harrison, a Unitarian minister turned journalist. His articles, printed in the New York and Boston press, were widely distributed in pamphlet form. When a group of prominent citizens, including both Norton and Olmsted, formed the Niagara Falls Association, Harrison was named its secretary.

A thread of élitism ran through Harrison's propaganda. The "better class of visitors," he wrote, were being kept away from the Falls by the presence of excursionists. Like Norton, he was appalled by the avaricious element in the American temperament. There was little regard for beauty in the national character, he wrote. "The masses in our well-to-do democracy feel no discomfort from hideous ugliness and vulgarity in the objects and scenery around them at home."

But Harrison also put his finger on the real problem. It was not "vandalism and soulless greed" that was imperilling the region but science, "or the changed methods and conditions of life which the modern development of science has produced." Improvements in manufacturing appliances, the rapidly increasing hunger for waterpower to run the burgeoning mills, the changes in mechanical transportation – these highly laudable examples of Yankee ingenuity would soon disfigure Niagara's beauty. The very "progress" that was driving America forward to her manifest destiny was also destroying her heritage. It was a warning that would be heard again and again in the years to come.

None of this high-minded prose seemed to have any effect on the New York legislature. Norton had decided as early as the summer of 1882 that the battle was lost. Nonetheless, he gamely carried on, "not so much to save the Falls, as to save our own souls. Were we to see the Falls destroyed without making an effort to save them – the sin would be ours."

By 1883, however, the tide was turning. Harrison had embarked on a lecture tour and the Niagara Falls Association was mailing thousands of letters to known supporters, urging them to bombard their state legislator with appeals to pass new laws to protect the Falls. Equally important, Alonzo Cornell was out of office and the former mayor of Buffalo, Grover Cleveland, was governor. Cleveland was a close ally of Dorsheimer and an admirer of Olmsted. On March 14, 1883, the legislature passed a bill, which Cleveland signed, providing for the expropriation of property at the Falls and a board of five commissioners (headed by Dorsheimer) to manage the new park or "reservation," as it was officially called.

Three months later, as if to emphasize the schizophrenic nature of Niagara's appeal – a haven for lovers of the idyllic, a focus for thrill seekers and daredevils – the world-renowned British swimmer Captain Matthew Webb arrived at the Clifton House. A former merchant marine officer, Webb declared that he intended to conquer the rapids of the gorge below the suspension bridge. These rapids, in the words of the Suspension Bridge *Journal*, "are not like surf or storm waves. They strike a blow like a sledgehammer and their power is akin to a cyclone."

But Webb was perfectly confident that he could plunge into this fury and emerge unscathed. He was, after all, the conqueror of the English Channel – the first human being to cross from Dover to Cap Griz Nez, a feat he accomplished in twenty-nine hours and forty-five minutes. As a result, he had become a national hero, showered with honours and hard cash, a prisoner of his own success who felt it necessary to top himself over and over again – remaining for sixty hours in a tank at the Royal Aquarium, executing "a Dive for Life" from a high platform into the ocean, imitating porpoises and seals – to the cheers of the crowd. Now he was prepared to attack what he called "the angriest bit of water in the world."

Webb had already examined the Whirlpool and rapids. He was told that he would be tempting suicide but remained confident. "I think I am strong enough and skilled enough to go through alive," he declared. The speed of the river at the rapids was just under forty miles an hour, the depth of the water, ninety-five feet. He planned to leap into the river, wearing only a brief pair of silk trunks, from a small boat just above the suspension bridge and float into the rapids, expecting the "fearful speed of the water" to carry him through. When the going got rough he would dive below the surface and stay there until he was forced to come up for breath.

"When I strike the Whirlpool, I will strike out with all my strength and try to keep away from the suck hole in the centre.... My life will depend upon my muscles and my breath, with a little touch of science behind them."

Webb expected that it would take up to three hours to free himself from the quarter-mile-long Whirlpool. He would then try to land on the Canadian side but if that proved impossible would let the river carry him down to Lewiston.

Nobody believed he could or would do it. Certainly he seemed to understand the seriousness of what he was proposing. Two journalists who interviewed him on July 24, 1883, a few hours before his swim, remarked that "he appeared like a man entering upon an enterprise of the gravest possible concern to himself. The lines of the face were sternly drawn, an occasional drop of perspiration would gather on his brow, and his words, though appropriate and slowly spoken, had an earnestness that was almost solemn."

At four that afternoon, Webb started down the Clifton House hill to the ferry landing, where the ferryman, John McCloy, was waiting for him in a small fishing scow. At 4:15, the watchers on the suspension bridge heard an announcement that the boat was in sight. At 4:20, Captain Webb was seen to stand up in the boat and dive into the river, swimming easily downstream with long, steady strokes. At 4:33, he passed under the bridge and entered the rapids. As he struck the furious wall of water he seemed to stand upright for an instant on top of the highest crest, then dove into the engulfing waves. Now he was lost to sight, but moments later he reappeared farther down the stream. Two or three times he was seen to ride the tops of the waves. Those on the bridge felt confident that he had got through. At 4:35, he reached the last of the rapids before entering the Whirlpool. He sank from sight and was never seen alive again.

Webb's body was found four days later, between Lewiston and Youngstown. There was a three-inch gash in his head, which suggested at first that he had been knocked out and drowned. This was not the case. An autopsy revealed that a wave had struck him with such force that it had paralysed his nerve centres, weakened his muscles, and destroyed his respiration. Niagara, in short, rendered him helpless.

The *Saturday Review* of London called the whole affair "a common scandal ... perhaps the most shocking example which has yet been given of the criminal folly developed by a vulgar love of shows and emotions" – a backhanded attack, perhaps, on the circus atmosphere that Olmsted, Norton, and the others were trying to eliminate.

And yet it required two more years of constant pressure and lobbying to get a final bill of appropriation through the New York State legislature. Again the politicians balked at the cost of buying the land, and the local press echoed their opinion. As the editor of the Poughkeepsie *Eagle* wrote, "we regard this Niagara Falls scheme as one of the most unnecessary and unjustifiable raids upon the State Treasury ever attempted." When the bill was finally passed, Norton wrote enthusiastically to Olmsted: "I congratulate you, prime mover! I hail you as the Saviour of Niagara!"

Concerned at the apparent cost of expropriation – a cost that was highly exaggerated – the new commission kept the proposed reservation to 412 acres, of which 300 were under water. Nonetheless, all the sites from which the Falls were visible would eventually be on public property. The commission now had to deal with twenty-five property owners, some of whom had cared so little for the view of the cataract that they had screened it off with barns, outbuildings, and plantings of shrubbery. They began to ask extraordinary sums for their portion of the river front. The commission took a tough view of that: they "have no title to the rushing waters; they do not own the pillars of spray that rise from the foot of the cataract; … they do not even own the bed of the river … [these] are not subject to human proprietorship; they are the gift of God to the human race."

The owners demanded a total of four million dollars; they got a little less than a million and a half. Of that sum, the Porters would receive $525,000 in compensation for Goat Island. Meanwhile, fences would have to be torn down, gatehouses closed, signs removed, and some hundred and fifty structures demolished. Ponds would have to be drained, banks graded, trees replanted, old roads repaired and new ones built, and viewpoints opened up. Much of the work was delayed by disputes and appeals. Some of it was still being carried out at the century's end. But the reservation became a reality when it was dedicated sixteen years after Olmsted and his friends had taken that first ramble on Goat Island. In the words of Charles Dow, who became commissioner of the reservation in 1898, "it is doubtful whether any measure ever aroused an equal number of public men in all fields of endeavor."

An entirely new principle was evoked in the establishment of the Niagara reservation. This was the first time in history that a state of the Union had used public money to expropriate property for purely esthetic purposes. It was without precedent in the United States, which explains the difficulties encountered by the preservationists. It seems obvious in hindsight; it seemed radical – even insane – at the time.

The preservationists had been careful about nomenclature. This was a "reservation," not a "park" – for *park* connoted geometrical flower beds, cast-iron benches, statuary, and trimmed grass. What Olmsted and the others had always wanted was an approximation as close as possible to the original environment.

At midnight on July 15, 1885, the gates were thrown open to the public. The last quarters had just been collected at Prospect

Point. Goat Island remained open all night. Unprecedented crowds swarmed over the islands, crowded the walls that fringed the cliffside, clambered down to the foot of the cataract, and picnicked on the greensward.

Everything was free. The *New York Times* reported that many who had lived all their lives within twenty miles of the Falls were now seeing them for the first time. Thirty thousand strangers poured into the villages of Niagara Falls and Suspension Bridge, where the hurdy-gurdy shows that had sprung up beyond the limits of the new reservation did a brisk business.

That afternoon, President Dorsheimer formally presented the reservation to the state of New York. "From this hour," he said, "Niagara is free." And so, in a very real sense, it was.

5

Canada was two years behind the United States. In 1880, Oliver Mowat, having refused a federal offer to split the cost of establishing a national park, began to toy with the idea of encouraging a private corporation to take on the task. At that, a number of prominent businessmen, politicians, and speculators jumped joyfully into the fray, solemnly avowing their intention of preserving and beautifying the Falls, while foreseeing a harvest in fees.

The moving spirit was William Oliver Buchanan, a one-time bridge engineer and failed real-estate speculator who saw the private park scheme as a method of warding off personal bankruptcy. Although Buchanan wrote enthusiastically about restoring the Falls' "pristine beauty" and placing "proper restrictions against abuses" while "avoiding as much as possible the artistic and artificial," what he really wanted was the right to build a toll road at the water's edge from the Falls to the Whirlpool, staircases to the top of the gorge, picnic and games grounds, together with hotels and refreshment booths. His

Niagara Falls Reclamation Company foundered when Mowat refused, on principle, to guarantee its bonds.

Nonetheless, Buchanan got a letter of conditional encouragement from the premier and tried again, this time with the help of one of the country's most powerful politicians, the prime minister's friend Sir Alexander Campbell, who had headed the original federal commission. Their Niagara Falls Restoration and Improvement Company again failed to get legislative support and for the same reason: they hadn't been able to raise the money. But that did not stop them from trying again. Undeterred, Buchanan secured the active support of both Campbell and Nicol Kingsmill, a canny Toronto lawyer who was a counsel for the Michigan Central Railroad.

Meanwhile, in the summer of 1883, an English syndicate entered the lists with the dubious assistance of Saul Davis, who hoped to sell his property at a profit. The Niagara Falls Hotel, Park, and Museum Company would, so Davis claimed, "beautify, improve, and establish a system of business that will be a credit to the place" – strange words coming from the man who had almost single-handedly brought the greatest *dis*credit to the Falls. Mowat didn't even bother to respond and the proposal died.

Buchanan, Campbell, and Kingsmill were back in 1883 with a new prospectus for their restoration company. They wanted to expropriate a three-mile strip along the river, 159 acres in size. Again the object was clothed in high-minded phrases, "demanding the removal of the prevailing disfigurements and extortions which have brought the beautiful neighbourhood into world wide disrepute."

These entrepreneurs were really after a franchise to build a miniature electric railway along the Niagara River itself from the Horseshoe Falls to the Whirlpool and a street railway on the bank above. They would also operate an elevator, a steamboat service, restaurants, kiosks, and playgrounds. But it was the railways that would bring in the profit. For the railway era was

194

in full swing in Canada, and both Buchanan and Kingsmill were railway men. The new Pacific railway was already snaking across the western plains, following an orgy of railway building that had changed the face of eastern Canada over the previous quarter-century.

The phrase "conflict of interest" was all but unknown in Canada during the railway era. Railway men, politicians, and promoters were linked together in a loose partnership that crossed party lines. Campbell was a leading Tory, but several of his political opponents were members of Buchanan's syndicate. That was unremarkable. Thomas Keefer, himself a railway engineer (his half-brother, Samuel, had built one of Niagara's suspension bridges), had once said that when the Speaker's bell rang for a division in the Ontario legislature, the majority of members were to be found in the apartments of an influential railway contractor, where the champagne flowed like sarsaparilla.

By the late fall of 1884, when Campbell and Kingsmill presented their plan to an enthusiastic Cabinet, it looked as if it were an accomplished fact. But then, in February 1885, a rival railway syndicate elbowed its way in. The Niagara Falls Railway Company wanted a franchise to build a double-track line from the Falls to Queenston to link up with the Canada Southern Railway. There would be the usual hotels and restaurants, but the railway was the key. Moreover, two of Mowat's most powerful backbench supporters were behind the scheme, perfectly confident that the premier would abandon the rival plan to which he had just lent his approval.

Mowat was in a dilemma. Another proponent of the new railway scheme was the notorious James T. Brundage, an American who operated a nine-acre park at the Whirlpool and controlled an army of hack drivers at the Falls. Having finally quelled the bitter Davis-Barnett feud, the province scarcely needed a new one, but Mowat could not alienate his own political backers.

The ratepayers of Niagara Falls, Ontario (the name "Clifton" had been officially discarded in 1881), along with those of neighbouring municipalities came to his rescue. Up in arms over the railway proposal, they mounted a mass meeting that denounced, in the words of the local council, a plan that would "hand visitors from every clime over to the tender mercies of a well-protected and poorly guarded monopoly." Besieged by politicians and business cronies on both sides, Mowat wriggled out of a final decision by pushing through a new Act for the Preservation of the Natural Scenery about Niagara Falls. The concept of a publicly owned park was far from his mind; the premier was still thinking in terms of private enterprise. A commission of three would select the land for the park, assess the cost, and then choose a private firm to expropriate and operate it under government direction.

The chairman of the commission, another railway man who had the ear of the government, was to be the remarkable Polish émigré Colonel Casimir Stanislaus Gzowski. A commanding figure at seventy-two with a leonine shock of white hair and a vast moustache to match, Gzowski had made a fortune as a railway engineer, contractor, and promoter. He moved in the highest circles, was an honorary aide-de-camp to Queen Victoria, and resided in a handsome Italianate villa known as the Hill, surrounded by a six-acre deer park, on Toronto's Bathurst Street.

He had earned a right to the luxury and social position he enjoyed and the esteem that he certainly craved. At the age of twenty, unable to speak English, he had been dumped penniless on the shores of the United States after two years in an Austrian internment camp. From that unlikely beginning he had managed to fulfil the North American dream – the struggling immigrant with the romantic past who tugs stubbornly on his bootstraps and climbs ever higher.

Gzowski's father was born into the minor Polish nobility and, after Poland was partitioned, became a career officer in the

196

Russian imperial guard. He found an engineering post for his seventeen-year-old son with the Imperial Corps of Engineers. But young Casimir was also a Polish patriot who chose to oppose Russia when his people rebelled in 1830. Wounded, and imprisoned for a time in Austria, he was finally shipped off to America.

He taught music, fencing, and languages to support himself but with his engineering experience in Russia soon found himself working on canals and bridges. Sent to Canada to secure a contract on the Welland Canal, he got a better job through his father's European connection with the new Governor General, Sir Charles Bagot. His rise was extraordinary. When he formed his own contracting firm, his partners were some of the best-known politicians and railway men in the country.

A patron of the arts, a subscriber to worthy causes, a senator of the University of Toronto, he was now above the political hurly-burly. To Oliver Mowat, the partisan Liberal, Gzowski, a prominent Tory, was the perfect choice to head the new commission and extricate him from the dilemma caused by the two rival railway syndicates.

When the Gzowski Commission presented its first report on September 1, 1885, its recommendations were unexpected and, without doubt, unpalatable to the premier. Gzowski totally rejected the idea of a privately run park and opted for a government reserve of 118 acres, to be open to the public free of charge. No hotels, refreshment booths, or other places of business would be allowed to operate within its boundaries. All but three of the current buildings would be torn down. The road along the cliff was to be moved back and the ground within the park limits to "be laid out and planted, not as a showy garden or fancy grounds, but as nearly as possible as they would be in their natural condition." In short, Gzowski's recommendations were very similar to those made by the Americans.

Premier Mowat had not expected this. For six months he shilly-shallied until Gzowski's commission produced a second and final report warning that any further delay would cause "general regret and disappointment." The park would cost half a million dollars, but the report made it clear that the taxpayers wouldn't have to put up a cent. Admission would be free, but the park would be able to pay for itself by small fees – no more than thirty cents a person – from those who wished to hire guides.

Because of the influx of visitors, the commission was certain that the park would quickly free itself of bonded debt. The annual count of arrivals had already jumped from 118,000 in 1882 to 303,400 in the first nine months of 1885, thanks to the opening of the free reservation across the river. Government ownership, then, was "the only policy worthy of being adopted."

Mowat was forced at last into a reluctant decision. In March 1887, the Queen Victoria Niagara Falls Parks Act was passed, and the province of Ontario had its first publicly owned park, to be operated by Casimir Gzowski and his fellow commissioners as trustees for the government. On Queen Victoria's birthday on May 24, 1888, the park was opened to the public, who streamed through the handsome gate, named, not without irony, for Oliver Mowat. A reporter for the Toronto *Evening Telegram* described what he saw during a press preview: "To the visitor who has not seen the Falls for four or five years, the change in the scene would be most striking. Here along the river bank but two short summers ago, stretching in a solid row of attached buildings, were established numerous fancy goods and relic bazaars, regular gulling establishments, where exorbitant prices were charged for insignificant articles to unsuspecting foreigners and other visitors who were bent on carrying away some memento of their trip to America's greatest natural wonder. But the voice of the fakir is heard no more, the photographer has folded his tent and departed, the very storehouses, which held their wares, have vanished, and in their place, green in the garb of springtime, stretch the broad acres of the new park, tastefully laid off into walks and drives and planted at intervals with young trees, which will ere long shoot out their spreading foliage and afford a grateful shelter to the sweltering picnicker or tired tourist who can hardly satisfy himself that he has not yet seen enough of the rugged grandeur of this charming spot on which nature has lavished her chosen gifts."

Although there was some controversy over the ten-cent fee to use some of the artificial walks and covered bridges and the fifty-cent ride in the elevator to don waterproof clothing at the foot of the cascade, Gzowski's solution to Mowat's dilemma met with general approval. It was not only the public and the journalists who applauded. Saul Davis was also elated. For his various properties along the Front, that incorrigible rogue received the sum of $175,000 – or exactly one-third of the total amount spent on saving Niagara from the motley crew of mountebanks of whom he was the crowning symbol.

Chapter Seven

1

Early in 1890, Edward Dean Adams, president of the newly formed Cataract Construction Company of Niagara Falls, New York, set off for Europe on a journey of inquiry. The preservation movement had barely achieved its goal, and now a new and antithetical campaign – of which Adams was the spearhead – was under way to put the Niagara River to commercial use. His company was proposing to bore a vast tunnel as much as two hundred feet below the streets of the town of Niagara Falls, with a view to harnessing the waters of the cataract.

This was a daring – some would say foolhardy – project. Even though plans had been drawn up and the first sod was about to be turned, nobody had an idea of how any power that was generated was to be transmitted. Would it be by compressed air? By shafts, belts, and cables? By water pressure? Or could that most newly discovered of all scientific miracles, electricity, be brought into play? That was Adams's task overseas – to study power transmissions in England and on the continent and to plan a sensible course for an enterprise that was operating blindly, albeit decisively, at Niagara.

With his heavy-lidded eyes and his weak chin, partially disguised by a soup-strainer moustache, Adams was not a prepossessing figure. Yet his background in railway reorganization had given him, at forty-four, an enviable reputation in banking and financial circles. He was seen as a financial wizard and fixer who, among his several accomplishments, had just rescued the New Jersey Central from bankruptcy. His company was only three years old, the latest in a long line of enterprises that had been trying to tap the power of the great cataract for a variety of projects, some visionary, some eccentric. One man wanted to employ the Falls' "inexhaustible" energy to create a City of Fountains at Lewiston. Another wanted to use the tumbling waters to power a single colossal water wheel attached to a drive shaft 280 miles long, to which local industries could be connected. Inherent in all these schemes was the almost unanimous conviction that the Falls, undeveloped by man, represented a terrible waste.

Waste – that was the key word. As early as 1857, the prospectus of an early, short-lived enterprise, the Niagara Falls Hydraulic Company, had spoken glowingly but with some frustration of "a power almost illimitable, constantly wasted, yet never diminished – constantly exerted, yet never exhausted – gazed upon, wondered at, but never hitherto controlled." Thirty years later, the inventor Sir William Siemens echoed those sentiments when he declared that "all the coal raised throughout the world would barely suffice to produce the amount of power that continually runs to waste at this one great fall." To the scientists and engineers it seemed almost appalling that this stupendous 170-foot drop should be nothing more than a pretty cataract for the rubbernecks to gaze upon.

A waste, yes, but how to make use of it? The French had operated small mills using Niagara water above the crest as early as 1758, but it was not until 1847 that Judge Augustus Porter, the owner of Goat Island, came up with a feasible plan to use the drop to turn mill wheels. Porter contemplated an ambitious "hydraulic canal" three-quarters of a mile long. It would start from a point above the American Falls and cut across the neck of land circumvented by the river, running directly through the village before emptying its water over the high bank of the gorge – a miniature Niagara of its own. Such a millrace, Porter predicted, could operate "thirty run of mill stone."

After Porter's death in 1853, another entrepreneur, Horace Day, took over and for the next seventeen years worked sporadically on the canal, deepening it, widening it, and lengthening it. He had only one customer: Charles Gaskill's flour mill. By 1877 he had completed a mile of canal and was bankrupt.

The canal, together with the land and water rights, was put

up for auction by the sheriff of Niagara County on May 1, 1878, at the Spencer House in Niagara Falls, New York. Only a few turned up to bid on what was considered a white elephant; the first offer was a mere $5,000. Then, as the bidding dragged on, a Buffalo tanner and miller, Jacob Schoellkopf, raised his hand, and, to everyone's astonishment, offered $67,000 for the package.

A self-made man, with a heavy Teutonic face and a short beard, the fifty-eight-year-old Schoellkopf had a history of buying up bankrupt tanneries and making them pay. Now a leading citizen of Buffalo, he determined to use the same techniques to resurrect the bankrupt canal. When the auction continued after lunch, another bidder, emboldened by Schoellkopf's offer, raised the price. Schoellkopf responded with a successful bid of $71,000.

Off he went to Buffalo to tell his wife, Christina. "Momma, I bought the ditch," was the way he put it.

She was not entranced, nor was his partner in the milling business, George Matthews. "What'll you do with all that water, Jacob?" he asked. "You can't use it and you can't sell it." But Schoellkopf knew how to use it. He completed the canal, and by 1882, seven industries, two of which he controlled, were using its power, supplied by water turbines that operated machinery through shafts, belts, and pulleys.

Schoellkopf saw another use for waterpower. Three years before, Charles Francis Brush, inventor of the arc lamp, had installed the first street lighting system in Cleveland. Schoellkopf built a small powerhouse on his canal, installed one of the first Brush generators, and began to supply power for sixteen street lamps in Niagara Falls, New York. That caused a sensation. Railroads ran excursions to the site and torchlight processions celebrated the miracle.

Brighter street lights, however, could not direct attention from the growing number of commercial eyesores taking power from the canal. That alarmed the conservationists while failing to satisfy the engineers. As Professor George Forbes, an internationally known consulting engineer, pointed out, "not only is this hideous in itself, but it is repulsive to the engineer, because of the great waste. They use only a few feet of the fall, and waste over 100 feet."

Waterpower could be used to drive machinery, but few contemplated converting it into electricity. By the mid-1880s, Thomas Edison's new invention, the incandescent bulb, was being used to light certain buildings, while Brush's arc lights were illuminating streets in several major cities. But for the most part (Schoellkopf's tiny generator was an exception), this power came from coal, not running water, and could be transmitted for short distances only. Hydro power was put almost entirely to mechanical uses. The rushing waters were carried by flumes or pipes to individual shafts known as wheel pits. At the base of a pit, a wooden water wheel (later replaced by a metal turbine) revolved to drive the machinery by a series of belts and pulleys. The system was inefficient because the wheel broke if the water pressure was too great. Gaskill's flour mill could risk only a twenty-five-foot drop – using only about one-sixth of the potential energy of the available falling water.

With the strip of land along the gorge expropriated for the state reservation and no longer available for industry, some new method of employing the Falls' power had to be devised. In 1886, Thomas Evershed, the white-bearded divisional engineer of the New York State canal system, came up with the breathtaking solution of boring a tunnel underneath the village to carry water from a point well above the Falls to a discharge point far below. Evershed's tunnel would be two miles long and at least 160 feet deep. It would make possible an industrial district above the Falls, well beyond the limits of the reservation. Wheel pits would be sunk into the rock at twenty-five-foot intervals and the power "cabled off to any point desired, running any number of mills and factories of any size, from the making of toothpicks, to a Krupp's foundry."

The proposal thus continued the traditional "mill over wheel pit" system, in use throughout North America. Evershed planned twelve lateral canals to supply water to 238 individual wheel pits, each driving its own machinery. He proposed dockage, streets, and railroads to accommodate the industrial city of mills (each of five hundred horsepower) that he contemplated upriver from the cataract. It was, as one writer put it, "one of the most daring and colossal, yet practical of modern enterprises." In one minute, the Evershed tunnel could carry enough water to supply a city of ten thousand with power for fifteen minutes.

But the costs of the project could not at that time be covered by selling the power locally. More and bigger customers were needed. Until power could somehow be transmitted to Buffalo or to some other large centre, Evershed's plan would not be financially feasible. There was then no certainty that this could be accomplished. Yet such was the optimism engendered by the scheme that a new company was formed to put it into operation, with Evershed as its engineer. In spite of the general ignorance about electrical power, the company in its prospectus was sunnily optimistic: "It is conceded by leading practical electricians that it would be entirely practicable now to light the city of Buffalo (distance 20 miles) with power furnished by Niagara Falls, and the opinion is rife among scientific men that ways will be found in the near future for transmitting this power to much greater distances, and for using it in many new ways...."

The ways had not yet been found, however, and the company's cheery futurism was not calculated to attract hard-headed businessmen. The original plan to raise $1.4 million foundered. The very size of the project – one that dealt with hydraulic forces far greater than anyone had ever attempted to harness – frightened off investors. By 1889, the company had become the Niagara Falls Power Company. A sister corporation, Cataract Construction (the two firms had interlocking

206

directorates), was created to build the project. Its president would be Edward Dean Adams, the New York banker and general all-round fixer.

Adams inherited Evershed's unsolved problem. The village of Niagara Falls had a population of about five hundred. Who, then, would use all the power, and how could it be transmitted? Could Buffalo, with a population of 255,000, be reached by any of the known methods? Would electricity come into its own at last?

The one man who might provide the answer was the Wizard of Menlo Park, Thomas Alva Edison, the greatest inventor of his day. It was Edison who designed and introduced the electrical distribution system for incandescent lighting by direct current. Edison, who was, of course, aware of the Niagara scheme, was about to return to the United States from a European sojourn. The promoters couldn't wait. In September 1889, the inventor received a terse cable from Niagara: "HAS POWER TRANSMISSION REACHED SUCH A DEVELOPMENT THAT IN YOUR JUDGEMENT SCHEME PRACTICABLE?"

Edison cabled back from Le Havre: "NO DIFFICULTY TRANSFERRING UNLIMITED POWER. WILL ASSIST. SAILING TODAY."

But neither Edison nor any other engineer who examined the Evershed plan could agree that the scheme made sense commercially. Power could certainly be transmitted to Buffalo, but at prohibitive cost. No way could be found to transmit heavy loads cheaply over long distances. Nor had anybody yet devised a method of reducing the voltage – of transforming it – to a safe and useful pressure once it reached its destination.

Cataract Construction was operating on pie-in-the-sky. As Dr. Henry Morton, president of the Stevens Institute of Technology, said that same September, "something new ... must be developed in order to meet the requirements of such a problem as you propose." Indeed, the problem was daunting. Adams and his colleagues were proposing to develop hydraulic power on an unprecedented scale when the use of such power was still relatively unexplored. They had no experience to go on, no examples to follow. They didn't yet know whether electricity could or would be used – or whether they would have to fall back on cable drive, compressed air, or water pressure.

In spite of that problem, they were determined to forge ahead, blindly but optimistically, and build Evershed's discharge tunnel under Niagara Falls. Micawber-like, they were convinced something would turn up.

Adams left in February to study the science of power development and the art of transmission in Europe. He visited Switzerland, Germany, and France, all of which had made some progress in transmitting electrical power by direct current. The possible value of alternating current was also being argued and championed as a more effective method of transmitting energy over longer distances.

Adams soon realized that a simplification of the Evershed plan was not only necessary but also feasible. Instead of building a costly series of lateral canals, each transmitting power to one mill or factory, it would be more practical to concentrate the source of the power at a single spot. It could then be transmitted from a central station to individual industries and "enable the mill owners to be as perfectly independent as if they each had their own wheel beneath their mill as originally planned."

The Cataract president was also proposing something that had never before been attempted – a prestigious competition among the world's biggest engineering firms for the biggest power development in the world. To mount it, he selected Sir William Thomson – the future Lord Kelvin – the world's most famous physicist. Thomson and four leading scientists from Great Britain, France, Switzerland, and Germany would form the International Niagara Commission that would, in turn, select up to twenty-eight such companies to be invited to compete for a series of prizes to be awarded for projects dealing with the development, transmission, and distribution of the Falls' power.

That set off a whirlwind of activity. Fifteen European and five American companies took up the challenge and jumped into the competition, which was due to close January 1, 1891. Long before that, however, Adams's company took a bold step forward. It started to build a discharge tunnel – a tailrace to take away the waste water – before knowing how the power would be distributed. It was a considerable gamble, for no existing system seemed adequate to the size of the project. The company's directors were simply assuming that one would be found.

Thomson and his four fellow commissioners spent an exhausting six days examining the submissions. They awarded four prizes for pneumatic projects, four more for electrical, but no first prize for a combined project that would involve the hydraulic development and electrical distribution of power. In short, the main purpose of the competition had not succeeded. As hordes of workmen blasted away at the rock far below the village, no feasible method of getting power beyond Niagara Falls had yet been discovered.

What was needed was a visionary: neither Edison nor Thomson, both of whom were committed with near missionary zeal to the concept of direct current, but somebody who could free himself from that scientific strait jacket and work out a way by which electric current could be transported over hundreds of miles. Only then could the Falls be made to release its power.

In fact, just such a man existed. Indeed, he had already worked out the principle of an alternating-current motor, a system that would, in the end, be universally adopted. The son of a Greek Orthodox priest from the little village of Smiljan, Croatia, on the Austro-Hungarian border, he was, without doubt, the most extraordinary scientist in the world.

His name was Nikola Tesla.

2

He was almost too good to be true. No Baron Munchausen would have dared to imprison his saga within the limits of a tall tale. By the nineties, he was for a brief time the most celebrated scientist in the world. The Tesla coil, which he invented in 1891, is still widely used in radio and television sets. The tesla, a unit of magnetic induction, honours his memory. He stands at the very threshold of the age of electrical power – the Slavic genius who made it possible. Yet his name is hardly known outside the scientific community.

There is something uncanny about Tesla, something almost mystical. His senses, according to his own account, were all amazingly acute. While he was under strain, his hearing was so sensitive that he could note a thunderclap 550 miles away. During one nervous breakdown, he was able to hear a watch ticking three rooms away. When a fly lit on a table beside him, the thud it produced caused him agony. A carriage rumbling down a street seven miles distant seemed to shake his entire body. He could feel the vibrations caused by a train whistle twenty miles off so powerfully that they caused him to tremble. He needed little sleep – no more than two hours a night – but during one illness he could not rest unless his bed was anchored in rubber cushions.

There were times when the sun's rays seemed to strike with such force on his brain that they would stun him. He had to summon all his willpower to pass under a bridge because he would experience a crushing pressure on the skull. In the dark, he was like a bat, detecting the presence of an object or a person at a distance of twelve feet by a sensation in his forehead.

He was incredibly restless, unable to sit still for more than a few moments, his brain never at ease. In his younger days, when he went for a stroll he counted every step; when he sat down to a meal, he could not enjoy it until he had calculated the cubic contents of every plate, cup, and piece of food set before him. He preferred to do things in threes because he favoured numbers divisible by three.

Born in 1856, destined by his father for the church, he became a scientist who was also a poet and a philosopher. He loved music, food, and wine and spoke eight languages, including English, without an accent. He dressed like a dandy in a Prince Albert coat, derby hat, and stiff collar. His handkerchiefs were always of silk, never linen. He was so fastidious that he invariably wiped his cutlery with eighteen linen napkins before every meal. He threw away each pair of gloves after a few wearings. But he wore no jewellery – couldn't stand it. In childhood, he had had a violent aversion to earrings on women, and the sight of a pearl would almost give him a fit. "I would not touch the hair of other people," he recalled, "except, perhaps, at the point of a revolver. I would get a fever from looking at a peach, and if a piece of camphor was anywhere in the house, it caused me the keenest discomfort." When he was twenty-eight he wrote, "Even now, I am not insensible to some of these upsetting impulses."

At six foot six, Tesla was a commanding figure, clean-cut and wiry, his jet-black hair parted in the middle. With his intense blue eyes and Slavic profile, he was a magnet for women, whose interest was perhaps piqued by his supreme indifference to the opposite sex. The great Sarah Bernhardt once deliberately dropped her handkerchief in his presence. Tesla picked it up absently and returned it without bothering to look at her. Not even the Divine Sarah, apparently, could be allowed to interrupt his train of thought. Marriage, Tesla once said, would take him away from his work.

He was a voracious reader with a compulsion to finish everything he started. Once he set out to read the works of Voltaire, without knowing that they had been published in close to one hundred volumes, available only in small print. As one biographer reports, it almost killed him, but he found no peace until he had finished every last one.

He was blessed with a photographic memory. As a youth, he had learned the entire body of logarithmic tables by heart. He could memorize a page of type or a visual pattern almost in an instant. In dangerous situations or in moments of elation he was subject to inexplicable flashes of light over which he had no control. There were times when he felt hot and the air about him seemed filled with tongues of living flame.

Tesla was obsessed by water wheels and turbines. As a child of four, with the help of his older brother, Dane, he devised a unique wheel, smooth and without paddles, that spun evenly in a stream's current, with a twig serving as an axle. That was the genesis of an idea that returned to him years later when he invented a smooth disc turbine without buckets.

Neither his incurable curiosity nor his exotic imagination knew any bounds. He experimented ceaselessly. He took his grandfather's clocks apart to see what made them tick. He tried to build a motor using sixteen June bugs to power it through the rapid fluttering of their wings. He once tried to fly by hyperventilating himself until he was convinced he was lighter than air. He used the family umbrella as a parachute, fell on his head, and knocked himself out. But he did fly, in his imagination, on make-believe journeys to far-off realms.

He had difficulty distinguishing the real from the imagined. He saw objects and scenes before his eyes that others could not see. Often these were accompanied by strong flashes of light. As he later recalled, "when a word was spoken to me, the image of the object it designated would present itself vividly to my vision and sometimes I was quite unable to distinguish whether what I saw was tangible or not."

If he witnessed a funeral or some other nerve-racking spectacle, "inevitably, in the stillness of the night, a vivid picture of the scene would thrust itself *before* my eyes and persist despite all my efforts to banish it. Sometimes it would even remain fixt in space, tho I pushed my hand through it." To rid himself of these hallucinations he would try to concentrate on something else: visiting cities, fancied or real, and making friends with the people of his imagination who were "just as dear to me as those in actual life, and not a bit less intense in their manifestations."

As an inventor he had no need of models, blueprints, or drawings of experiments. He pictured everything, in detail, in his mind. He claimed to be able to perfect a conception without touching anything. "It is absolutely immaterial to me whether I run my turbine in thought or test it in my shop," he said. "I even note if it is out of balance."

By his own account he was accident prone. "I got into all sorts of difficulties, dangerous scrapes from which I was extricated as by enchantment," he wrote. "I was almost drowned a dozen times; was nearly boiled alive and just missed being cremated. I was entombed, lost and frozen. I had hair breadth escapes from mad dogs, hogs, and other wild animals. I passed thru dreadful diseases and met all kinds of odd mishaps and that I am hale and hearty today seems like a miracle." On three occasions doctors despaired of his life. He caught malaria at fifteen. A year or so later he was bedridden for nine months with cholera. At twenty, in Budapest, he suffered a complete nervous breakdown, which he conquered through a gruelling program of calisthenics.

His concentration and self-discipline were awesome. He tried to see how long he could stop his heartbeat by willpower (a test halted by the family doctor). He learned to force himself, when he was eight, to put aside anything that gave him pleasure – mouth-watering cake, say, or a piece of fruit. He would give it to a friend, and, as a result, "go through the tortures of Tantalus, pained but satisfied." If he was faced with a difficult and exhausting task, he would attack it again and again until it was done.

Ideas chased each other at breakneck speed through Tesla's fevered brain. Niagara Falls, which perhaps owes more to him than to any other scientist, took hold of his imagination at an early age. At fifteen he began to experiment with various water turbines. During his bout of malaria, when he read voraciously, he opened an old book and found a steel engraving of the Falls. It fascinated him. In his mind he saw how a great wheel might be made to turn under the cataract's tremendous power. He told his uncle of his daydream – that some day he would go to America and harness the runaway waters of the Falls. Years later he remarked, "I saw my ideas carried out at Niagara and I marvelled at the mystery of the mind."

In his teens he had begun to fiddle with the concept of a substitute for direct current. Examining a new direct-current dynamo that could be turned into a motor by reversing the current, he experienced a thrill of excitement. The design could be improved, he declared, by switching to alternating current. Nobody took him seriously, and the practical method eluded him at the time; but he filed the problem in the back of his mind.

Several years later, in 1882, during a walk with a friend through a park in Budapest and while in the midst of reciting Goethe's *Faust*, the full solution came to him in a flash. He seized a stick and drew a diagram in the dust. "See my motor," he said. "Watch me reverse it." To him, the image of the motor was "wonderfully sharp and clear and had the solidity of metal and stone." It was an emotional moment: "Pygmalion seeing a statue come to life could not have been more deeply moved." In one breathtaking flash of intuition, Nikola Tesla had not only devised a motor but had also arrived at the principle of the rotating magnetic field produced by two asynchronous alternating currents, out of step with each other. In that instant he had changed the course of science and paved the way for the exploitation of Niagara Falls power.

The time would come when almost all the electricity in the world would be generated, transmitted, distributed, and turned into mechanical power by the Tesla Polyphase System. For the first time it would be possible to send high voltages on slender wires for hundreds of miles. Thanks to this obscure Croatian, a new age of electric light and power was about to dawn.

But the new age had not yet arrived. In 1882, Tesla went to work for Continental Edison in Paris, determined to push his new discoveries. In this he was bitterly disappointed. Thomas Edison believed in direct current the way Billy Sunday believed in God. Tesla was told firmly that he must never so much as mention the subject of alternating current. In spite of this, when he left Paris for North America he carried with him a glowing recommendation from the manager of the French plant. All the material possessions he brought to the United States were four cents, a book of his own poems, a scientific treatise, and a package of calculations outlining his plans for a flying machine. As one of his biographers, Margaret Cheney, has noted, "at twenty-eight he was already one of the world's great inventors. But not another soul knew it."

The rumpled Edison hired him but refused to discuss Tesla's views on alternating current. "Spare me that nonsense," he said. "It's dangerous. We're set up for direct current in America. People like it, and it's all I'll ever fool with." As Edison was to admit, many years later, that was a monumental error.

Edison knew nothing of Tesla's background and cared less. Apparently he believed the young immigrant came from some savage corner of the globe, for he once shocked Tesla by asking if he had ever eaten human flesh. The robust and practical American had little in common with his poetic and intuitive new employee. Edison worked him hard, often until five in the morning. When Tesla offered to improve one of Edison's direct-current motors to lower the cost and save on maintenance, the older inventor said casually, "There's fifty thousand dollars in it for you – if you can do it." Tesla succeeded, but Edison didn't pay up. "You don't understand our American humour," he explained.

Disappointed, Tesla quit and set up his own company in New Jersey to manufacture the new arc lights. Within a year he was bankrupt. The man who had made a quantum leap in electrical progress was reduced to eking out a living by digging New York sewers at two dollars a day.

Then, a year later, his fortunes changed. Tesla, it developed, was exactly the kind of inventive genius that George Westinghouse was seeking. Next to Edison, Westinghouse was the best-known inventor in America, a powerful six-footer of commanding presence, unfailing courtesy, and lively imagination. His crowning achievement was his invention of the railroad air brake.

Unlike Edison, Westinghouse was a convert to alternating current. He bought up forty patents from Tesla for $60,000 plus a royalty of $2.50 for every horsepower generated under the Tesla system. He also made him a consultant at two thousand dollars a month, a princely sum that enraged Edison and set the stage for a titanic struggle between the two inventors. Thus was launched "the battle of the currents."

Edison, who had invested a good deal of time and money in the development of direct current, attacked savagely, mounting a scare campaign designed to give the impression that alternating current was incalculably dangerous. He issued pamphlets with the headline "WARNING!" in red letters, alleging that dangers lurked for anyone who tried to use the Westinghouse system. He paid schoolboys twenty-five cents apiece for stray cats and dogs, which he proceeded to electrocute with alternating current before groups of reporters. The anti-nuclear campaign of a later century seems almost placid when compared with Edison's hard-driving attack. He lobbied the legislature at Albany to pass a law limiting electric currents to eight hundred volts. He even managed to persuade the warden of Sing Sing prison to "westinghouse" a condemned murderer using alternating current. The electric charge that had killed the dogs and cats was too weak; the condemned man survived and had to be electrocuted a second time – a grisly spectacle that one reporter said was worse than a hanging.

Westinghouse fought back with public lectures and pamphlets. He had his eye on Niagara Falls and also on the upcoming World's Columbian Exposition at Chicago. In 1892, when the Edison company was swallowed up in an amalgamation that became General Electric, the new firm went head to head with Westinghouse's company in an effort to secure contracts for lighting the exposition and building turbines for Niagara. Westinghouse won. His firm would install all power and lighting equipment for the first electrified fair in history – using Tesla's alternating current.

Meanwhile, Adams's Cataract Construction Company was proceeding with its discharge tunnel under Niagara Falls, still not knowing how it could deliver power to Buffalo. The first sod had been turned on October 4, 1890, after Adams got back from Europe. The old bell from the Cataract House, which had once summoned guests to dinner, sounded again after a long silence as six carriage-loads of dignitaries debouched at Shaft No. 1. Captain Charles E. Gaskill, a shaggy Civil War veteran, one-time flour miller, and chief customer of the old hydraulic canal, now president of the Niagara Falls Power Company, gave the opening address. "A great future is in store for us," he proclaimed. "… As each year passes we will see great industries located along the Niagara River … adding wealth to this already favored region, making of it the seat of the greatest manufacturing city in the world."

The magnitude of the undertaking was unprecedented. It was, in the words of one journalist, "a triumph of human enterprise which out rivals some of the bold creations of Jules Verne." Thirteen hundred workmen were blasting their way, day and night, through the solid rock, 160 feet below the town. The horseshoe-shaped tunnel, eighteen feet wide, twenty-one feet high, and seven thousand feet long, would displace 300,000 tons of rock; it would require twenty million bricks to line it and two and a half million feet of oak and yellow pine to shore it up. This gigantic tailrace would carry off the excess water that the hydraulic canal above the Falls would deliver to turbines in wheel pits 140 feet below the powerhouse to produce 100,000 horsepower of electricity. But the question of how that electricity was to be distributed remained unanswered.

Sir William Thomson's commission had leaned toward electricity over compressed air as the most attractive method of transmitting power to Buffalo. But Thomson himself stubbornly opposed alternating current. Finally, in 1893, the new Lord Kelvin came round. In October of that year, the Niagara Falls Power Company awarded Westinghouse the contract to build the first two generators at Niagara. As a form of compromise, General Electric was given the contract to build the transmission and distribution lines to Buffalo, using the Tesla patents. George Westinghouse had clearly won the battle of the currents.

The change of attitude towards alternating current was certainly helped by the Westinghouse exhibit at the Columbian Exposition that year. The big fair, which introduced the zipper, Edison's motion-picture projector, and Little Egypt's hoochie-koochie dance, was lit entirely by electricity and known as the White City. In the Electrical Building, Tesla himself, clad in white tie and tails, indulged in scientific wizardry, reversing metal eggs at great speed on a velvet-covered table and receiving through his body currents of a potential 200,000 volts – his clothing emitting halos of splintered light that brought gasps from the spectators.

Tesla was now the man of the hour, a brilliant lecturer and a flamboyant personality, hailed by his contemporaries as "the greatest living electrician." A bulletin announcing a lecture at St. Louis that gave a brief account of his life was so popular it sold four thousand copies on the city streets in a single day, "something unprecedented in the history of electrical journalism." It was reported that his lecture in the Great Music

Entertainment Hall that evening was heard by a larger audience than had ever before been gathered together on an occasion of that kind. Complimentary tickets to the event were sold by scalpers at five dollars each.

Tesla thrilled his listeners by promising a brilliant electrical future. Niagara Falls, he told interviewers, had enough horsepower to "light every lamp, drive every railroad, propel every ship, heat every store and produce every article manufactured by machinery in the United States." He foresaw a time when "we will be very likely to be able to heat our stoves, warm the water, and do our cooking by electricity, and in fact, perform any service of this kind required for our domestic needs." Again, these words have a certain resonance for the nuclear age.

In mid-1892, even before the method of transmission had been approved, Cataract Construction plunged ahead with the design of the generating station a mile and a half above the brink of the Falls. Edward Dean Adams was determined to go first class. The most prominent architect in America, Stanford White, would be given the job – a difficult one, since structures like these had never before been attempted. Adams's instructions were that it had to be attractive, "artistic in grandeur, dignified, impressive, enduring and monumental.... It should express in its design, the purpose of its construction." By the use of roughly trimmed native stone – "as the old inhabitant had recommended by building his home of that material" – its character would "be defensive against the storms without, and protective of the valuable machinery enclosed therein."

The company, which had already assembled a considerable acreage of land, now set up a subsidiary to develop a village to house the workers, also to be designed by White. Adams called it Echota, from the name of a Cherokee capital, loosely translated as "place of refuge." Adams's plan was practical as well as esthetic. He needed to attract and retain skilled labour.

His workers, unlike others in similar communities, would enjoy an unusual luxury. In their neat, shingled houses they would all have electric light.

The pace of development accelerated. The tunnel was finished in 1893. The following summer huge electricity-powered cranes lowered the massive twenty-nine-ton double turbines – the largest of their kind so far produced – into the wheel pits. Tesla's polyphase motors, also the world's largest, followed. Stanford White's handsome powerhouse, capable of delivering fifteen thousand horsepower, was completed in 1895. The following spring the town of Niagara Falls was lit for the first time by electricity.

That summer of 1896, Tesla himself arrived at the Falls accompanied by Adams and Westinghouse. He pronounced the powerhouse "wonderful beyond comparison," but his sensitive nature was badly shaken by the enormous size of the dynamos. "It always affects me to see such a thing," he declared. "The shock is severe on me." As for transmitting power to Buffalo, Tesla was as certain of that as he was of the coming dawn. "The problem has been solved," he said emphatically. "Power can be transmitted to Buffalo as soon as the Power Company is ready to do it…. It is one of the simplest propositions. It is simply according to all pronounced and accepted rules, and is as firmly established as the air itself."

Buffalo's civic authorities were not blessed with this Slavic certitude. When the power arrived at last on November 16, the mayor waited until shortly after midnight before pulling the switch. The quiet ceremony, scheduled for the dark of the night when carping opponents could be deemed to be safely in bed, had gone unadvertised and unnoticed until the city fathers were sure that Tesla's system would work. But that morning, Buffalo's streetcars were running on Niagara Falls power, and when Cataract Construction's "power banquet" was mounted the following January, Tesla was chosen to respond to the mayor's toast to electricity.

Well he might be, for he had saved the Westinghouse Company from collapse or merger by an act of singular generosity. The House of Morgan, which controlled the General Electric Company, was waging a price war to eliminate "costly competition." The Westinghouse Company was badly overextended because of the expensive campaign to put the country on a system of alternating current. To fend off GE the firm would have to consolidate with some of its smaller competitors. The stumbling block was the royalty contract with Tesla. His patents covered powerhouse equipment, motors, and every other use of the alternating-current system. Already, it was said, the accrued royalties amounted to twelve million dollars. In a few years, at $2.50 per horsepower, Tesla would become a billionaire, while Westinghouse would sink under the financial burden of the contract.

George Westinghouse himself met with Tesla and asked him to give up his royalties, explaining that he held the fate of the company in his hands.

Tesla asked if Westinghouse proposed to continue his missionary work for the alternating-current system he had invented.

Westinghouse replied that Tesla's polyphase system was the greatest discovery in the field of electricity and no matter what happened, he intended to continue to put the country on an alternating-current basis.

"You have been my friend," Tesla told him. "You believed in me when others had no faith; you were brave enough to go ahead when your own engineers lacked vision.... Here is your contract and here is my contract – I will tear them both to pieces ..."

And so saying, he ripped up the documents and tossed them into the wastebasket.

3

The final quarter of the nineteenth century has been called the Great Age of Heroic Invention. It was probably the last time in which a single genius, working by himself in basement or woodshed, could come up with a device or process that would change society. The electric light, the telephone, the motion-picture projector, the gramophone, and the automobile were all products of this yeasty period. Inventors like Edison, Westinghouse, and Bell were popular heroes, to be emulated by younger men. Now, with enormous quantities of raw electrical power available, North America stood on a threshold.

In a single decade, Niagara Falls, New York, *né* Manchester, became the centre of the electro-chemical and electro-metallurgical world. It began in 1893, when Charles Martin Hall announced that he was moving his Pittsburgh Reduction Company to the Falls. The manufacture of aluminum as a commercial product requires enormous quantities of electric power. Hall's first contracts with the Niagara Falls Power Company called for an immediate fifteen hundred horsepower with the option of buying one thousand more.

A few short years before, aluminum had been one of the rarest of all manufactured metals. Now, at Niagara, Hall was proposing to produce one thousand pounds a day. His company would shortly change its name to Aluminum Company of America – ALCOA. Its product would have an extraordinary influence on both industry and everyday life.

Hall was a prototype for the nineteenth-century inventor – an enthusiastic and curious young man who worshipped George Westinghouse. In 1886, when he hit on the discovery that made him famous, he was just twenty-two. His twin dreams, to make a great scientific breakthrough and to grow rich as a result, exactly fitted the ethos of the times.

As a boy he had had an abiding curiosity about how things worked. Using chemicals taken from the kitchen shelves, he carried out experiments in the woodshed, or in a cupola above the family home in Oberlin, Ohio. He read everything that had been published about Westinghouse, but then, he read everything that dealt with science, from an old chemistry book of his father's to the *Scientific American*, at that time the Bible for young men of a scientific bent.

Aluminum had been isolated as an element in 1825. A strong, light metal that didn't tarnish, it could have a hundred uses if only a way could be found to produce it cheaply. It was the third most abundant element in nature; as a French scientist had said, "every clay bank is a mine of aluminum." Yet it was being extracted only in tiny quantities. In the early 1880s when young Hall was attending Oberlin College, it was worth fifteen dollars a pound. When his professor, F.F. Jewett, asked the class if any of them had actually seen a piece of aluminum, Charles Hall was the only one to raise his hand.

Jewett then turned to the class and said, "If anyone should invent a process by which aluminum could be made on a commercial scale not only would he be a benefactor to the world but he would also be able to lay up for himself a great fortune." In the America of that day, as the hugely successful Alger books made clear, anything was possible. Hall turned to a classmate and whispered, "I'm going for that metal."

Starting in 1881, Hall began an intermittent series of experiments hoping to find a cheap method of separating aluminum from clay. First, he tried heating the clay – aluminum silicate – with carbon. It didn't work. Then he tried to fuse the mixture by exposing it to burning charcoal and potassium chlorate. That didn't work. He tried heating calcium chloride and magnesium chloride with clay, hoping that aluminum chloride would distil off. That didn't work either.

He kept on trying. In 1884 he achieved a higher temperature using another homemade furnace and bellows. He tried experimenting with various catalysts at these higher temperatures, again without results. All this time he had been completing his studies at Oberlin College. After graduating in 1884, he set up a laboratory in his woodshed. He abandoned the idea of reducing aluminum silicate chemically and hit on an alternative plan. "It looks as though electrolysis would be my only hope," he told his sister, Julia.

He secured a single-burner gasoline stove and wrapped a cylindrical iron shell lined with fire-clay around it. In the centre of this shell, above the burner, he placed a fire-clay crucible.

Now he had to find a solvent for the alumina clay. He had decided that water wouldn't work because the aluminum, if produced by electrolysis, would immediately react with it. The chlorides hadn't worked, so he experimented with a variety of fluorides. These didn't work either. Some wouldn't melt; others wouldn't dissolve the alumina. Finally he tried a double fluoride, sodium aluminum fluoride, known as cryolite. To his elation, it not only melted to a red-hot fluid but when pinches of alumina were thrown in, the clay dissolved "just like sugar in water," in Hall's ecstatic phrase. With a borrowed battery, he passed an electric current through the solution. What he achieved was pure aluminum.

The results were startling. Even before moving to Niagara Falls, Hall's Pittsburgh Reduction Company was able to offer aluminum for less than a dollar a pound. In little more than a decade the price would drop to eighteen cents. In a single flash of inspiration, a youth only a year past voting age had given Niagara Falls its first major industry and made the United States the largest aluminum-producing country in the world.

Hard on the heels of Hall came another inventor, the immaculate and methodical Edward Goodrich Acheson, a self-taught chemical wizard who had just discovered how to make silicon carbide, or Carborundum. Next to diamond dust, it was the hardest abrasive known to man. Acheson had been forced to drop out of school at the age of seventeen, but what he lacked in formal training he made up in reading and in enthusiasm. He read everything, from the Alger-inspired *Try Again, or the*

FRANK LESLIE'S ILLUSTRATED NEWSPAPER

NEW YORK, OCTOBER 25, 1879.

To go "behind the sheet" in 1879, oilskins were provided — at a price — though many an unwary tourist thought they were free.

ABOVE: The great Blondin casually straddles the rope stretched across the gorge. To him, it was nothing more than a country stroll.

BELOW: Blondin's great rival, Bill Hunt, a.k.a. Signor Farini, hangs by his heels from the slack wire.

ABOVE: Crowds were commonplace when Blondin performed.
BELOW: With Harry Colcord, his manager, on his back, Blondin performs the most spectacular of his feats.

ABOVE: Saul Davis's notorious Table Rock Hotel, "the cave of the forty thieves," overlooks the Horseshoe. His stairway down the gorge wall is just visible in the foreground of the photograph.

BELOW: The famous "Front," *circa* 1862. Davis's stairway is the in the foreground; Barnett's Museum is beyond Robertson's pagoda. In the distance, right, is the Clifton House, where the élite always stayed.

ABOVE: Barnett's Museum in 1862. It was moved several times. The collection, much enlarged, can still be seen at the Falls.
BELOW: In its day, the Clifton House was the finest hotel at Niagara. Cupolas and pagodas were the architectural whimsics of the time.

A bedraggled Annie Taylor photographed just after she emerged, slightly stunned, from her barrel, which she later put on display. Her manager, F.M. "Tussie" Russell, poses with her, but this barrel is actually a replica of the lost original.

The famous Falls ice bridge, *circa* 1900. It's doubtful if anyone stayed at the "hotel," which wasn't much more than a closed-in shack. Note the inclined railway on the American side, in the background.

James Harris, photographed as he was brought to safety by breeches-buoy in 1918. The scow, from which he was saved, can still be seen in the rapids.
BELOW: Red Hill, his saviour, poses with the barrel that later took him through the Whirlpool on a trip that almost killed him.

Trials and Triumphs of Harry West to early works on metallurgy. Like Hall, he devoured the *Scientific American*. Edison was his hero; chemistry and electricity were his passions. He was scarcely out of school before he had patented a rock-boring machine for coal mines. That was the first of sixty-nine patents that he would take out in his lifetime. George Westinghouse bought several and thus helped him on his way.

Acheson went to work for Edison at Menlo Park and later in Europe. He saw the need for a new abrasive – diamond dust was horribly expensive – and when at last he set out on his own, he began a series of experiments, hoping to find one. He soon noticed that clay got harder after being impregnated with carbon, and he wondered whether or not a mixture of the two might be fused if subjected to several thousand degrees of heat.

In March 1891, using a small iron crucible, Acheson carried out his experiment, thrusting a carbon rod, connected to a generator, into a mixture of clay (aluminum silicate) and carbon. The results were disappointing; apparently nothing had happened. But Acheson took a second careful look and saw a few bright specks attached to the rod. He stuck one of these on the tip of a pencil and drew it across a pane of glass. To his astonishment and delight, it cut the glass like a diamond.

By 1892, Acheson's Carborundum Company was making about twenty pounds of the product a day, and the price was dropping. But Acheson realized that if he were to succeed he must make much larger quantities for sale at a much lower price. The abrasive had been selling for $576 a pound   half the price of diamond dust, but still prohibitive. Acheson was determined to bring the price down to *eight cents* a pound. For that he would need substantial amounts of electrical power, and that was available only at Niagara Falls.

Without telling his board, he signed a contract with the Niagara Falls Power Company for one thousand horsepower a day, with an option for a later amount up to ten thousand horsepower. It was a daring move. Acheson was contemplating increasing production by a factor of twenty at a time when his original plant at Monongahela, Pennsylvania, could sell no more than half the Carborundum it produced. No wonder, then, that when he finally told his board, the directors resigned on the spot.

The mass walkout did not faze him. He pressed on, thinking big, planning the largest electric furnace in the world. It was scarcely in operation before he made a second spectacular discovery. Engaged in some high temperature experiments on Carborundum, he accidentally produced graphite and gave Niagara Falls another industry.

The example of both Hall and Acheson, who signed up for Niagara power even before the Cataract company had developed it, brought a flood of electro-chemical and electro-metallurgical firms to Niagara Falls, New York, seeking cheap and plentiful power. Thus was established a symbiotic relationship between the power companies and the chemical industry. Without power, the industry had no future, but without industry, the companies had no customers. It had once been assumed that Buffalo would be the major customer. Now it was clear that the industry would concentrate on the spot, as close to the power source as possible, just as Evershed had contemplated.

Jacob Schoellkopf's foresight in snapping up an apparently useless hydraulic canal was paying off. By 1896 he had completed a second generating plant, this one at the water's edge in the Upper Great Gorge. Rivalling the newly opened plant of Niagara Power (to be named for Edward Dean Adams), it had the largest penstocks in the world and took advantage of the full drop of 210 feet to produce 34,000 horsepower. Hall's Pittsburgh Reduction Company contracted for half its output.

By the end of the nineties, the availability of cheap power had brought eleven major companies to Niagara. By 1909 the number had risen to twenty-five. Jacob Schoellkopf did not live to see the dawn of the new century, but so great was the demand for power that his successors started work almost at

226

once on an addition to the river plant with four times the original capacity. In 1918 Schoellkopf's Hydraulic Power Company merged with Niagara Falls Power. Though the name Niagara Falls Power Company was retained, Jacob's sons and grandsons controlled the new consolidated enterprise.

Most of the companies lured to Niagara by cheap power were new firms that would soon merge with others to become industrial giants with names like Union Carbide, Anaconda, American Cyanamide, Auto-Lite Battery, and Occidental Petroleum. They gave the world acetylene, alkalis, sodium, bleaches, caustic soda, chlorine – a devil's brew of chemicals produced by electrolysis or electrothermal processes. Ironically, the very waters that produced the new power – so clean, so serene – were themselves poisoned by the residue of the chemical boom, while their surroundings were infected by contaminants that would lie dormant and undiscovered for more than half a century.

No such paradox was apparent at the time. The flamboyant Tesla had declared publicly that Buffalo, Tonawanda, and Niagara Falls would merge into the greatest city in the world – a statement that fuelled the boosterism that had seized the region. "NIAGARA LEADS THE WORLD," the Niagara Falls *Gazette* trumpeted. In the machine age there was little place for the sublime. The hum of Tesla's great motors took precedence over the roar of the cataract. In the minds of many, the Falls were obsolete.

One who held to this view was Lord Kelvin himself. Kelvin echoed the hopes of the electrical industry when he stated baldly in 1897, "I do not hope that our children's children will ever see Niagara's cataract." As far as he was concerned, the Falls could be shut down. He believed that "the great power of the waterfall of Niagara is destined to do more good for the world than even the great benefit which the people of today possess in the scenic wonders of this renowned cataract. The originators of the work thus far carried out, and now in progress, hold a concession for the development of 450,000 horsepower from Niagara Falls. I do not believe that any such limit will bind the use of this great natural gift, and I wish that it were possible that I might live to see the future's grand development."

4

"Humanity's modern servant," as Edward Dean Adams called electricity – "the giant genie" – had changed the course of history, heralding a newer and brighter era. Nature at her most awesome had been subdued. The harnessing of her power touched off a wave of optimism about the future. Niagara's mighty forces would benefit humanity not only materially but also morally. Electricity was clean and pure, a symbol of peace and harmony, in contrast to coal – grimy and corrupt, hidden in the murky bowels of the earth. The Columbian Exposition – the famous White City – pointed to Utopia.

The first of the Utopians was a flamboyant entrepreneur named William T. Love, who in 1893 proposed to build a "Model City" at Niagara. This carefully planned community would be big enough to hold a million people, with thousands of acres set aside for parkland that was advertised as "the most extensive and beautiful in the world."

Hyperbole abounded. Love's metropolis, according to his brochures, would be "the most perfect city in existence." It was destined, indeed, "to become one of the greatest manufacturing cities in the United States," backed as it was by unlimited power from the Falls. And like the Falls, which dwarfed everything around them, the Model City would dwarf all previous developments. "Nothing approaching it in magnitude, perfection or power, has ever before been attempted."

Love literally beat the drum for his project, hiring brass bands and choruses to sing its praises, producing pamphlets trumpeting the advantages of cheap and sometimes free sites, and free power for new factories. He even managed to address a joint session of the New York State legislature (an uncommon privilege), which gave him, in effect, *carte blanche* to expropriate and condemn property and divert all the water he needed from the Niagara River for his power project. The centrepiece of his plan would be a seven-mile, navigable power canal, bringing water to a point above the Model City, where the drop to the river would provide 100,000 horsepower.

Love actually laid out streets and built a few houses and a factory before he ran out of money. The depression of the nineties was blamed, but one cannot escape the conclusion that Love's reach was far beyond his grasp, and that depression or no depression his grandiose real-estate scheme would have foundered. He had managed to dig no more than a mile of his proposed canal, which lingered on, long after his death, a soggy monument to his failed ambitions. Over the years rains filled the ditch; children used it as a swimming hole in the summer and a skating rink in the winter. More than eight decades after his vision, Love's canal was once more in the headlines, a symbol not of the purity of Niagara's power but of its corruption. Utopia had become purgatory.

One year after William Love proposed his Model City, another idealist, a one-time bottle-cap salesman and small-time inventor, proposed his own version of Utopia at the Falls. His name was King Camp Gillette, and what he envisaged was a mammoth city that would make Love's look like a village. It would not be just another city; it would be the *only* city on the continent, housing almost the entire population of the United States and feeding on the Falls' apparently limitless power. Gillette called it Metropolis, and, as he described it, it bears an uncanny resemblance to Fritz Lang's film of the same name, produced thirty-two years later.

Gillette's detailed plan for Metropolis, published in a 150-page paperback book entitled *The Human Drift*, might

One of the huge apartment buildings in Gillette's Metropolis

have been dismissed as the ravings of a lunatic save for one thing. The following year, 1895, he had a second intuitive flash and invented the Gillette Safety Razor. With his picture on every package of blue blades – curly black hair, drooping moustache – he soon became one of the most widely recognized human beings in the world.

He was also one of the most puzzling – a product of invention's golden age, an example of the Alger hero, and an embryonic millionaire who railed against the system that nurtured him, who taught that the doctrine of individualism was a disease, who lambasted both wealth and competition. He was out to destroy capitalism, which he thought of as a dirty, rotten and inefficient system. Would he have postulated his revolutionary theories had his invention and subsequent wealth come first? Perhaps; perhaps not. For the fact remains that Gillette held to that philosophy for the rest of his life – until his death in 1932. Indeed, he used his wealth to promote his ideals. By 1910 he was rich enough to offer Theodore Roosevelt a million dollars to act as president of his Utopia, a position that the hero of San Juan Hill quickly declined.

Gillette was in his fortieth year when he published *The Human Drift*. The son of a small businessman and part-time inventor who had lost everything in the Chicago fire of 1871, he set off on his own as a travelling salesman, eventually peddling bottle stoppers for the Crown Cork & Seal Company. It was William Painter, the inventor of the Crown cork, who gave him the piece of advice that eventually led to the invention of the safety razor: "Try to think of something like Crown Cork; when once used, it is thrown away and the customer keeps coming back for more."

With Painter's words percolating quietly in his subconscious, Gillette had his first flash of inspiration. Looking out of his hotel window in Scranton one wet day, he noticed a grocery truck that had broken down on its way from the wholesalers to the railroad depot. The resultant traffic snarl convinced

231

him that there must be a more economical and efficient system of distribution. What was needed, Gillette reasoned, was a world corporation to replace the present system.

As its frontispiece, *The Human Drift* carried a photograph of Niagara Falls. But, though Gillette was obsessed by the idea of building a garden city on a scale never before conceived, the beauty of the waterfall and its value as a natural attraction escaped him. In Gillette's concept, nature must be bent to man's will and replaced by a vast and rational pattern of geometric parks, lawns, flower beds, and hedges. It was Niagara's raw power that interested him – that and its size.

This was an era when bigness was worshipped for its own sake. The turbines at Niagara were the biggest in the world. So were the powerhouses and the industries, not to mention the Falls themselves. Bigness spilled over into architecture. The modern skyscraper had been made possible by the addition of the electric motor to Elisha Otis's earlier elevator. The biggest buildings in the world were under construction, but none so gargantuan as those Gillette projected.

A big man physically, he thought big. His plan for Niagara Falls would have dwarfed the cataract. He foresaw a city of sixty million – almost the entire population of the United States at that time – housed in twenty-four thousand gigantic apartment houses, each twenty-five stories high, each accommodating twenty-five hundred tenants, all feeding on Niagara's "unlimited power" and "free from all the annoyances of housekeeping." Like so many others of his time, Gillette was obsessed and elated by the prospect of so much power locked up within those waters. "Here is a power," he wrote, "which, if brought under control, is capable of keeping in continuous operation every manufacturing industry for centuries to come, and, in addition, supply all the lighting facilities, run all the elevators, and furnish the power necessary for the transportation system of the great central city."

Gillette's great central city was designed as a vast rectangle,

135 miles long and 45 miles wide. There was nothing vague in his grandiloquence. He had worked it all out to the foot and drawn up detailed plans showing cross-sections of apartment buildings, floor plans of typical apartments, and a bird's-eye diagram of the city itself. Seen from the air, Metropolis would resemble nothing so much as a giant beehive – hexagonal high-rises, surrounded by star-shaped lawns and flower borders, each building exactly six hundred feet in diameter, each with its 250-foot dining-room. He went so far as to detail the materials – steel, firebrick, and glazed tile of various colours. There would be, he said, fifteen thousand miles of avenues, "every foot of which would be a continuous change of beauty."

Metropolis would be "the heart of a vast machine, to which more than a thousand miles of arteries of steel, the raw material of production, would find its way, there to be transformed in the mammoth mills and workshops, into the life-giving elements that would sustain and electrify the mighty brain of the whole, which would be the combined intelligence of the entire population working in unison, but each and every individual working in his own channel of inclination." Metropolis "would make London, Paris, Berlin, Vienna, and New York look like the work of ignorant savages in comparison."

Money would not be needed in Metropolis. Each citizen would work for a given number of hours a week. Élitism would not exist. The citizens would select what they needed, without money and without the price tag, from a variety of emporiums where goods "all of the highest grade and quality" would be arranged "in attractive display," the products of "the highest developed intelligence."

These pretentious phrases and glowing descriptions also have a resonance for our time. What Gillette envisaged was a benevolent dictatorship, and he outlined it with all the fervour and naïveté of a Marxian idealist extolling the workers' paradise. Free food and clothing for all – just for the taking? "Many will maintain that the people would abuse the privilege, but

233

such would not be the case," he argued. "For under a state of material equality there is no incentive to hoard up, and no one would load themselves down with the care of clothes which they did not need and could not wear. And no one would fill their apartments with a lot of useless trash and furniture which is neither useful nor ornamental, and would be in the way."

As for the Falls, in Gillette's ideal city they would cease to be seen. The entire Metropolis would be built on a vast three-level platform, one hundred feet thick, that would cover the entire countryside, Falls, gorge, and all. Within the lowest of its three chambers would be installed all the water pipes, sewers, and power lines. A middle chamber would be a transportation corridor – a subway. Above that a third chamber, fifty feet high, would be reserved for strolling and recreation. Domes of glass would provide light for a perpetual garden. How the Falls could be fitted into this the author did not say. Nor did it really matter. In spite of his offer to Roosevelt and the publication of two more books, nothing ever came of King Camp Gillette's grandiose concept.

In 1896, two years after the publication of *The Human Drift*, another worshipper at the cult of bigness matched Gillette's conception with one of his own, which he called the Great Dynamic Palace and International Hall. Leonard Henkle, a Rochester inventor, drew up a detailed set of architectural plans for his gigantic project. Half a mile long and forty-six stories high, it would stretch across the Niagara River just above the brink of the cataract. There are echoes of Henkle's conception in the work of Paolo Saleri, the twentieth-century "arcologist" in Arizona, whose high-density megastructures have aroused such controversy. Unlike Gillette, Henkle proposed to "combine the most imposing grandeur of art with the natural beauty of Niagara Falls." But he, too, saw the cataract primarily as a power source, which, he claimed, would supply all the needs of every city in the United States and Canada.

None of these visionary schemes for Niagara ever reached

fruition, but one Utopian dreamer did achieve his objective. Henry D. Perky, a health fanatic, determined to build "the cleanest, finest, most hygienic factory in the world" on a hilltop overlooking the American Falls. He succeeded in doing just that.

A tall, bespectacled figure, his face half concealed by a luxuriant walrus moustache, Perky had enjoyed an extraordinary career. Raised in Ohio, he had started life as a schoolteacher, switched to manufacturing, and then switched again to law. He headed west to Nebraska, became a state senator at the age of twenty-five, and then, with his health failing, decided in 1879 to move to the crisp mountain air of Colorado.

There, drawing on his experience as a railroad lawyer, he built the Denver Central, organized a mammoth industrial exposition, and constructed the first steel passenger cars in the world. Yet he still suffered dreadfully from stomach troubles; indeed, his health deteriorated in spite of the mountain atmosphere. He tried various remedies before hitting on the idea of eating whole unground wheat. That seemed to do the trick, or at least he thought so. But boiling the grain was a laborious process and produced an unpalatable mush. The search for a tastier product led to his greatest invention.

In 1891 Perky devised a machine that would separate the whole wheat kernel into fibres in such a way that its nutritional value wasn't lost. These fibres would then be made into biscuits and baked. Eaten with milk or cream, they made an acceptable breakfast cereal. Thus, in 1893, Shredded Wheat was born in a Denver cracker bakery, and the ailing Perky was transformed, so it was said, from an "almost abject and physical wreck" to perfect health.

Henry Perky was the last of a triumvirate of health addicts who helped change the breakfast habits of the continent. The Battle Creek Sanitarium, operated by the vegetarian Seventh-Day Adventist sect, had already spawned W.K. Kellogg, the future Corn Flakes king, and C.W. Post, whose Grape-Nuts,

Postum, and Post Toasties were fixtures on the grocery shelves. Now Perky, as much an evangelist as a merchandiser, proposed to make Shredded Wheat a household word. At first he had thought only in terms of manufacturing the machine that created the product. But why sell the device to let others profit from the cereal? The real money lay not in the shredder but in the shredded cereal.

A quirky health faddist, Perky was convinced he had found the answers to the world's ills. He blamed the educational institutions for not emphasizing the benefits of natural foods. He set out to proselytize the globe and incidentally to sell his Shredded Wheat, for he was convinced that mankind's propensity to do evil sprang from bad nutrition.

He set up a small factory in Worcester, Massachusetts, in 1895. But manufacturing was not enough; he needed missionaries to peddle the finished product. The Oread Castle caught his eye. A monumental pile of battlements and towers perched on a hill in the finest residential section of town, it had once been a girls' finishing school. In this Gothic environment he established a school of nutrition, underwriting both board and tuition for the young women who studied under his direction and who were then sent out to spread the gospel. He lived among them, took his meals with them in the dining-room, and trained them as after-dinner speakers and lecturers. He was himself a lively, if eccentric, speaker, a master of the broad gesture and staccato delivery. Sometimes he embroidered his enthusiastic arm-waving addresses by indulging in his hobby of Swiss yodelling, at which he was adept.

Perky soon realized that lectures, articles, and even books – he had already published one entitled *The Vital Question* – were not enough to sell Shredded Wheat. If he was to spread the word he must do something spectacular. He would not wait to bring Shredded Wheat to the people; he would, instead, bring the people to Shredded Wheat. The obvious site for such an attraction was the one place where hundreds of thousands

236

congregated. He had had his eye on it since his first visit in 1895. At Niagara Falls he would build a temple to nutrition that would attract thousands of visitors annually.

He knew exactly what he wanted. Standing with his vice-president, William Birch Rankine (who was also secretary-treasurer of the Niagara Falls Power Company), on the site of the old Augustus Porter mansion on Buffalo Avenue, he exclaimed, "If I am to come to Niagara I must have this property ... I want my conservatory to be located on the State Reservation with the rapids of Niagara in front of them [*sic*] where nobody but God Almighty can interfere with them."

He bought a 1,300-foot strip along the avenue facing the rapids – an old residential district that had once housed Niagara Falls' first families. There he planned his conservatory, a handsome 65,000-square-foot complex of buildings, unlike any other factory in the world. He promised to spend ten million dollars on the site and hire one thousand workers to make his dream come true. When that news was published in 1900, the community went manic. "Crowning Triumph For Niagara Falls," read the huge block headlines in the *Gazette*. "It Sounds Like a Dream, Reads Like a Fairy Tale, Seems Too Good to Be True But Is Positively True." The paper reported, correctly, that it was "the biggest piece of news affecting Niagara Falls."

Perky's special railroad car spirited the mayor, the council, and the press to his Worcester plant, where they were served a Shredded Wheat drink, Shredded Wheat Biscuit Toast, roast turkey stuffed with Shredded Wheat, and Shredded Wheat Ice Cream. They diplomatically pronounced the meal delicious and waxed even more enthusiastic about the promised factory and the prospects for their community.

Perky's industrial centre opened in May 1901 and fulfilled his promise that it would be "one of the largest and most far-reaching in its design of any in the country." In an era when factories were virtually windowless – dark, stuffy, and airless – Perky had planned buildings for the future. His vision went beyond Shredded Wheat. He wanted to turn Niagara Falls into an industrial paradise and was not above using a little personal clout to achieve his ends. He threatened D.O. Mills, head of the Industrial Paper Company, "Stop that malignant smoke in your plant else I won't come to Niagara."

In this last crusade he was largely unsuccessful. But his own "Conservatory of Natural Science," as he called his complex, was everything he had dreamed of – "a temple of cleanliness," in one description, containing two hundred tons of marble. Covered in glazed, cream-coloured brick, it was one of the first factories to be air-conditioned, with the heat automatically controlled. Its 844 windows carried thirty thousand panes of glass, making it "the cleanest, finest, most hygienic factory in the world." The women working on the line wore white aprons and caps; the men wore white jackets. A sign posted in the biscuit-packing room read: "This is the only time in our entire process of manufacturing where our products are touched by human hands. Every provision is made to ensure absolute cleanliness."

The company was one of the first to install men's and women's rest rooms – and these were decorated with marble and mosaics. In one spacious dining-room, the women were served a free lunch. (In the men's dining-room, lunch cost a dime.) The complex boasted 13 bathtubs and 13 showers for employees, as well as 104 sinks. The reception room looked like the lobby of a palatial hotel, complete with palms and a gigantic globular chandelier containing thirty-six electric lights. Reading rooms for the public, their floors covered with handsome rugs, lay off the main lobby. There were also an eight-hundred-seat theatre and a roof garden from which visitors could view the Falls.

Perky's bold venture paid off. The factory was soon playing host to 100,000 visitors a year. When they tired of munching on Shredded Wheat they could enjoy the music of the company's choral society or its marching band. Perky was an enthusiastic amateur musician who played several instruments, his favourite being the violin.

Every box of Shredded Wheat, Perky decided, would carry a picture of his plant, making it one of the best-known buildings on the continent. It was this graphic trademark that made Shredded Wheat and Niagara Falls inseparable.

Perky died in 1904. Eventually, Shredded Wheat was gobbled up by the National Biscuit Company – NABISCO. But each package still bears a small picture of the great cataract as a kind of homage to Henry Perky, the Utopian businessman who saw his dream come true.

Chapter Eight

1

In the dying days of September 1889, the year that saw Edward Dean Adams take over as president of the Cataract Construction Company, a young Englishman named Arthur Midleigh arrived at Niagara Falls, Ontario, disconsolate, bored, and not a little frustrated.

This was the twilight of the Victorian Age, when certain adventurous Englishmen sought fleeting fame in the far corners of the world – assaulting the rapids of the Congo, climbing the Matterhorn, pursuing wild boars in the Punjab, exploring the cannibal islands of the Pacific. Arthur Midleigh caught the fever. One cousin had ascended Mont Blanc. Another had gone after tigers in the jungles of India. Midleigh opted for the life of a cowboy in the American West, lured there by Ned Buntline's romantic novels of Indian wars and reckless gunfighters. He had gone out to Wyoming in 1888 to work on a ranch, only to discover that Buntline's Wild West was a fiction. The buffalo had long since vanished; the Indians were depressingly friendly; the bad men had all been shot or – worse – had settled down to a respectable existence.

As for the life of a cowboy, Midleigh found it boring, filthy, and wearisome: to his disgust, he had become nothing more than a common herdsman. After the best part of a year of bunkhouse life, he decided to go back home.

On his way back to England, Midleigh – a dashing figure with his unshorn locks, sombrero, and chaps – decided to stop briefly at Niagara Falls. He had, unwittingly, come to the right place, for he was determined to perform some impossible feat and thus return home in triumph. There were more impossible feats waiting to be performed at Niagara than at any other place on the continent.

The town itself reflected Midleigh's sombre mood, for here, as in the so-called Wild West, all was anticlimax. The tourist

242

season had ended. The itinerant peddlers had packed away their beadwork and knickknacks, folded their tents or shut their booths, and departed. The crowd of tourists was already thinning, and in the newly created Queen Victoria Park, the gravel pathways were yellow with the falling leaves of autumn. As Midleigh discovered, it was no longer difficult to get a room at the Clifton House.

There, in the ornate lobby, he was regaled with tales of derring-do in Niagara's waters that fired his imagination. It must have seemed to him that the community was crowded with would-be heroes, intent on making a name for themselves by plunging into the rapids, or riding the crest of the waves in a barrel, or even tempting the cataract itself. For some of these, a single deed of daredeviltry was not enough; they had to keep topping their previous feats – or at least pretending to do so. That very month, two of the most famous stunters, Carlisle Graham and Steve Brodie, had faked plunges over the Horse shoe Falls.

Everybody was talking about Graham's fall from grace. A weedy cooper from Philadelphia, he had, since 1886, made four successful trips in his own barrel through the same Whirlpool Rapids that had once doomed Captain Webb, the channel swimmer. They called Graham the Hero of Niagara, a title he felt he had to live up to. In late August, after testing the cataract with an empty barrel, he announced that he would go over himself. On September 1, he claimed to have done just that – a feat no human being had ever accomplished. Graham was quickly exposed as a fraud, and when Brodie, the man who claimed to have jumped off the Brooklyn Bridge, made a similar boast a few days later, his flimsy tale was easily disposed of and he left town hurriedly.

Then, a few days before Midleigh checked in at the Clifton House, a twenty-year-old youth from Youngstown, New York, performed a genuine feat of daring that outdid all of Graham's heroics. Walter G. Campbell decided to take a borrowed rowboat through the Whirlpool Rapids and into the vortex itself. The year before, a Syracuse undertaker, Robert William Flack, had been battered to death while attempting the same feat in his specially built boat, the *Phantom*. Although Campbell was hurled from his craft by a monstrous wave, he managed to swim the rest of the way, right through the white water that had killed Captain Webb and into the Whirlpool itself. He made it to safety at the upper end on the Canadian side and emerged, exhausted but game. "Tell the people that I have accomplished the greatest feat on record," he said as he reached shore. "OUR OWN, OUR NOBLE HERO," the Suspension Bridge *Journal*'s headline called him.

None of this was lost on Arthur Midleigh, who had come to America seeking adventure, had failed to find it, and now saw it staring him in the face on the lip of the Niagara gorge.

Midleigh was determined to accomplish some exploit that no one else had attempted. When he learned that nobody had dared to row from shore to shore in the rapids above the Falls, he knew he had found what he was seeking – something to brag about when he returned to England. His trip to North America would not be a dead loss after all.

He had hired a guide to take him around the area – a young man from St. Catharines named Alonzo Gardner, who earned a slim livelihood steering visitors to hotels or showing them the best vantage points from which to view the Falls. Gardner had brought his new wife, Suzanne, a sloe-eyed French-Canadian girl, with him to Niagara. Now, with the tourist season over, the newlyweds faced a long and unprofitable winter.

Midleigh and Gardner stood on the edge of the upper rapids and surveyed the spectacle below – the shallow, frenzied river coursing over the ledges of shale and swirling around the submerged rocks whose coarse snouts, erupting from the foam, hinted at the dangers below.

Midleigh was not fazed by the speed of the current. Why, he boasted to Gardner, he had held his own in a punt in a stream running twice as fast. Like many upper-class Englishmen, he was proud of his athletic abilities. "If I can find a fellow with a decent amount of skill in rowing, I am going to cross," he said, for he knew he would need two men on the oars.

Gardner did his best to dissuade him, but Midleigh paid no attention. Soon word got around that another adventure seeker was planning a daring escapade, and Midleigh began to be approached by well-wishers on the street and in the Clifton House.

He suggested that Gardner join him in the venture, but the new husband had no intention of risking his life. When Midleigh offered fifty pounds to anyone who would help him row across the river, several volunteers appeared, but Midleigh preferred his guide.

"Now, Gardner," he said, "you need the money. I'd vastly rather have you, and I'll make it up to you, mind you, a hundred pounds if you'll say the word."

This was a tempting offer. Gardner talked it over with his black-haired wife, who had no real idea of the dangers involved. In 1889, a hundred pounds – five hundred Canadian dollars – represented a small fortune. With that they could buy a house in St. Catharines. Suzanne told her husband to do what he saw fit. So, reluctantly, he accepted Midleigh's offer.

In spite of the lateness of the season, crowds turned up on both sides of the river when the pair appeared, ready to set off from the American shore. Gardner gave his trembling wife one last kiss; then they pushed off in their frail craft to the cheers of the onlookers, a British Ensign fluttering from the bow, a Stars and Stripes at the stern.

When they set off they were about 700 yards upstream from Goat Island. Midleigh figured that the boat would be swept downriver about a quarter of a mile during the crossing. That would allow them to land safely on the Canadian side about 250 yards upstream from the crest of the Horseshoe.

He had not reckoned accurately the speed of the current,

which increased as they reached the middle of the rapids on the American side. Now Midleigh realized that no tide he had ever experienced had come close to the fury of the deceptive river. He tried to retreat to the American shore, then changed his mind. The crowd was shouting to him to make for Goat Island. Gardner pointed to it. Midleigh tried to turn the boat about, and at first it looked as if he might make it.

On the American shore, Suzanne had fainted. The crowd, seeing the boat turn into the tip of the island, cried out that the pair was safe. When she recovered, she uttered a prayer of thanks.

What the onlookers could not see was that as the boat turned toward the island, it was being driven into the overpowering current on the Canadian side. Its tired occupants could no longer control it. As it surged toward the cataract, it struck a protruding rock. Midleigh and Gardner leaped out onto the rock while their craft, partially filled with water, lurched into the current and was swept over the cataract.

Their plight was not immediately apparent to the crowd on the American shore, for it was masked by Goat Island. But it was not long before Suzanne Gardner learned that her husband and the Englishman were marooned on a rock sixty feet from the island and some 250 feet from the brink of the Falls.

It was impossible to shout to the pair, for the roar of the Falls drowned out all other sounds. Nobody seemed to know what to do, and as darkness fell and lights were brought out, the watchers on Goat Island decided to wait until morning.

At first light somebody suggested that a stick of wood might easily follow the same course as the boat. Some of the onlookers tied a cord to a pine board and sent it into the current from the island's upper tip. To their relief, it followed the same course. Midleigh and Gardner waved back to show they'd retrieved it.

Now the would-be rescuers had a method of communication. They hauled the board back and sent it out again with some food and a message: "Be of good cheer. We will bring a boat over and fasten it to a hawser." By the time a boat could be found, however, darkness had again fallen. All rescue attempts were abandoned until the following morning. All night long Suzanne Gardner waited on the Goat Island shore, never taking her eyes off the stranded pair.

The next morning the banks of the river were black with spectators. More food went out, and the two men devoured it gratefully. Now a rescue boat was also sent out, unoccupied, for no one would risk the trip. It too followed the current directly to the rock. But as the two men prepared to leap into it, the hawser tightened; the craft was dashed against the rock and broke into pieces.

The rescue party of volunteers decided on a different solution. Instead of a boat, they would send out a piece of heavy timber. "Cling to that, one at a time," the note said, "and we will take you off."

It took some time to find a suitably stout beam, and it took more time to fasten the hawser in such a way that it would not slip off. Indeed, the entire rescue operation seems to have proceeded at a glacial pace. Finally, one end of the hawser was fastened to the bank, and the makeshift life raft was dispatched.

Once again the current took the piece of wood out to the rock. Midleigh and Gardner shook hands, and then Midleigh jumped into the water and clutched at the timber so forcefully that it rolled out of his grasp. It quickly righted itself, but Midleigh was gone. For an instant his head was spotted above the angry water farther down the river. Then he vanished as the crowd on the shore groaned. Gardner dropped to his knees in prayer. Suzanne, her mind deranged by her vain and sleepless vigil, was taken off to hospital.

Another night passed with Alonzo Gardner alone on the rock, his predicament now the subject of intense excitement, curiosity, and pity. With the news of Midleigh's death, the railroads added excursion trains. By ten the next morning, some twenty thousand people were on hand to watch the drama unfold.

In order to prevent a second disaster, the rescue party decided to send out a harness made from belts and straps taken from a hotel fire escape. These were floated out to the exhausted guide, together with a hook with which to fasten the makeshift harness to the timber. An accompanying note told him that his parents had arrived, and Gardner, who had been searching the crowd vainly for Suzanne, recognized them and waved. At that, his mother dropped to her knees while his father wept and groaned aloud. Members of the crowd closest to the pair began to sob in sympathy.

Gardner retrieved the harness and put it on carefully. With the hook in his right hand he propped himself up with his left, crouching as the beam swirled toward him, prepared to spring onto it as soon as it reached his perch. He let the timber pass by, intending to slip the hook over the rope at its head. Just as he tried to do so, the hawser tightened and the timber began to leap and twist in the rapids, like a fish on a line.

Before Gardner could hook onto the rope, the timber had gone too far. Fifty men tried to haul it back upstream while it cavorted like a thing bewitched, lashing first the water and then the rock. Then, as a howl of anguish rose from the shore, the timber struck Gardner and knocked him off the rock and into the rapids.

His head could be seen briefly rising above the water, then submerging again. At the brink of the chasm the upper half of his body rose for an instant with the arms uplifted. Then he was gone.

His body and Midleigh's were found two days later farther down the gorge.

There is an eerily Victorian postscript to this unhappy tale, almost too melodramatic to be true. But it was reported that Suzanne Gardner, her mind unhinged by the experience, escaped twice from the institution in which she was held and was found each time standing on Tower Rock overlooking the rapids, gazing into the mists of the waters that had engulfed her bridegroom.

2

The urge to win attention by performing some audacious feat was not confined to upper-class Englishmen with time on their hands, such as the unfortunate Arthur Midleigh. At Niagara Falls it was almost endemic, especially in the summer, when the Whirlpool's challenge seemed too much to resist, but also on those chill winter days when the odd phenomenon known as the ice bridge formed in the waters below the cataract. There were certain years when the ice stretched from shore to shore in a wild, rumpled mass. When the bridge was pronounced solid – when all the small chunks of ice hurled over the Falls had congealed into a craggy expanse of hummocks and clefts – men and women risked their lives in a race to be the first to cross. Watchers overhead on the newly completed Upper Steel Arch Bridge would gather by the thousands to follow these wild scrambles, whose winners achieved sweet celebrity for at least five minutes.

Ice bridges did not form every year: a special set of circumstances was required. The great ice bridge of 1899 was the most massive in human memory, and the longest lasting. It formed and reformed over a two-month period, appearing first on January 9, breaking up on the eleventh, reforming again on the sixteenth, breaking up again on the twenty-second, and then reforming for a record stay.

The winter of 1899 was particularly cold; for days the thermometer stayed below zero. Shifting winds blew clouds of spray over the rocks, trees, and shrubs until they seemed to be sheathed in alabaster. Weeks of freezing weather had caused large sheets of ice to form on the surface of Lake Erie. A thaw followed, and as the ice began to rot, a high wind from the west sprang up, breaking the ice into fragments. These chunks were swept into the entrance of the Niagara River, where the current bore them downstream. At the same time, more ice formed on the reefs and bars, narrowing the river's channel.

Trainloads of spectators lined the banks to watch the awesome spectacle of a river of ice racing relentlessly toward the Falls. As it was forced among the rocks of the upper rapids, it broke into smaller, uneven pieces, and these were hurled over the brink hour after hour in a mighty frozen cascade.

Great jagged blocks of ice squeezed through this narrow gap and with such force that their edges were worn as smooth as if sliced by a monstrous knife. At first the water foaming out of the Niagara Falls Power Company's tunnel farther downstream broke up the mass. Then, as the weather grew colder and more ice piled up, all the blocks were wedged together into a solid ice bridge, "as pretty as any that graced the gorge." Out onto this craggy expanse, where the hummocks rose as high as thirty feet and fissures radiated off in every direction, Harry Applegate ventured on the morning January 10. He was the first of several to make his way from the American shore to the Canadian and to get his name in next day's newspapers.

Over the next ten days the ice bridge twice broke up and reformed. In spite of the obvious dangers, several more people succeeded in making the crossing and gaining a few moments of fame. By January 20, seasoned veterans of earlier ice bridges declared this one safe, and small groups of thrill seekers headed out over the treacherous surface.

The river below the Falls was fifteen hundred feet across and almost two hundred feet deep. Just behind was the full force of the cataract. Yet so strong was this frozen bridge that hundreds were able to cross from shore to shore. Even horses had occasionally made the trip on ice bridges formed in previous years. Those who crossed took its measure before venturing out onto the broken expanse, noting the fissures and crevasses to be avoided and the great hummocks to be climbed or circumvented. Although they realized that the longer they remained on the ice, the greater was the danger, they were often forced to take a roundabout course to achieve their goal. Sooner or later, they knew, the unwieldy mass would move again. The route was uneven. The hummocks denied any sure footing. People stumbled, never knowing where the tumble might take them. At times the route ran up the slippery slopes of a great mound, at others down between the walls of a deep crevasse.

With the winter season at its height, thousands crowded into the two Niagara communities to witness the spectacle. The first shanty appeared on the ice on January 20, and others soon followed. If the ice held there would be curio shops, Indian tepees, photographers' shacks, makeshift saloons, and even buildings identified as "hotels." Since this was an international no-man's-land, liquor could be dispensed freely, if not cheaply.

Old-timers who remembered previous ice bridges looked forward to the informal winter carnival – the crowds on the ice, singing and laughing, paying top prices for coffee and sandwiches, the cliffs echoing with their shouts. Men planted flags on hillocks to record that they'd been the first to clamber to the top. Others explored crevasses to estimate the thickness of the ice. Some of these were thirty to forty feet deep, suggesting that the ice itself, most of which was submerged, was more than one hundred feet thick.

On Sunday, January 22, a young travelling salesman from Buffalo, Charles Misner, headed off for Niagara Falls with his friend Bessie Hall of Johnstown, Pennsylvania, a student at Slocum's School of Shorthand in Buffalo. Misner was eager to cross the ice bridge but Miss Hall hung back. Indeed, the sight was fearsome. High winds in Erie had again broken up the huge floes that covered the lake, driving them down the Niagara and over the Falls, damming the lower gorge and causing the water to rise. Squeezed by the pressure of the water, the ice had formed into towering hummocks in the centre of the river. It took all of Misner's powers of persuasion to convince his pretty companion that the ice bridge was safe.

It wasn't. Even the great Upper Steel Arch Bridge, built the previous summer (known later as the Falls View or Honeymoon Bridge) – the greatest metal arch in the world – was threatened. The ice piled up against the supporting pillars to a height of eighty feet, crashing into the steel work and rending the metal. Already gangs of men were preparing to blast the frozen monster away with dynamite.

Misner and his companion picked their way gingerly over the ice. Two hundred yards out from the *Maid of the Mist* landing, they found a boulder of ice and sat down to enjoy the scenery. Half an hour passed. Misner noticed that many of the others on the ice had returned to shore. But he felt perfectly safe, and when Miss Hall remarked that she could hear a singing noise under her feet, he told her it was only her imagination.

At last, feeling that they had seen all that could be seen, they started back toward the American shore. They had not gone far when, by gestures, a crowd on the bank indicated that they could not reach the boat dock: the ice had broken away from the shore, leaving a stretch of water too wide to cross. To get to land, they would have to work their way down to the Steel Arch Bridge.

Misner now felt the first stirrings of disquiet. He said nothing to his companion, who was herself showing alarm. The farther they went, the more anxious they grew. A crowd had gathered on the banks and on the bridge above. The couple began to hear sounds as of something falling.

They were now hurrying as fast as possible. Ahead lay a large fissure in the ice, three feet across. Misner tried to bridge it by filling it with chunks of ice in order to help Miss Hall over. He could see black water a hundred feet below and knew that one unsure step would mean death for both. He prepared himself to jump across the gap when he heard a loud report like that of a cannon, followed by grinding and crashing. The great ice bridge had torn loose from its foundations and was starting to move downstream toward the Whirlpool. It was 4:10 p.m.

Their only hope of escape lay on the Canadian side. Grasping his companion's hand, Misner started across the frozen river. Almost immediately he felt the ice part beneath his feet. Bessie Hall fell full length between two great ice boulders. Had Misner not been holding her with a sure grip, she would have gone to the bottom or been crushed between two grinding chunks of ice. He managed to pull her free just before the pieces collided.

The ice was carrying them past the Upper Steel Arch Bridge. Near them on the moving mass was another person who hadn't been able to reach the American shore, a boy who had saved himself by climbing onto an ice hillock. As he passed under the bridge he grasped one of the girders and climbed safely into the superstructure. But Misner and Miss Hall, unable to reach the bridge, were swept past and carried downstream for another two hundred yards. Misner could see on the American side the end of the tunnel from the power station. Its tailrace, shooting out at a rate of eighty-five miles an hour, created an undertow so strong that it sucked in anything that passed by. Astonishingly, they passed it in safety. A few yards later they heard a shout from the shore. For the first time in memory the ice bridge had come to a sudden standstill. It was now about 5 p.m.

Looking up, they could see thousands of people lining the banks, urging them to hurry. They set off for the Canadian side, stumbling, often vanishing from sight in one of the gullies, then reappearing to the cheers of the crowd. Often they were forced to leap blindly into ravines five or ten feet deep. At one point, Bessie Hall tried to give up, but Misner persuaded her to keep going. From time to time he was forced to leave her briefly while he ran ahead to scout the best way to cross the ice. Some of the spectators, believing that he was leaving his friend to her fate, grew angry and began to shout "Coward!" One man announced that if Misner reached shore alone he would shoot him on the spot. But Misner was determined to save them both.

At last, after forty-five minutes of struggle, they crossed a fifty-yard expanse of slush and reached the Canadian shore to a mighty cheer from the crowd. There, in Misner's own words, "willing hands stood waiting to receive us and to congratulate us on our almost miraculous escape from certain death."

Within hours the waters of the river were again jammed solid. The new ice bridge was larger and stronger than any that season. It remained in place for a record seventy-eight days until April 11, when the spring thaw finally caused its breakup. To the very end, the ice bridge of 1899 became a target for acts of bravura. The day before it finally disintegrated, five adventurous Canadians managed to cross to the American side and return, dragging a scow with which they propelled themselves across the major gaps.

3

Late in July 1901, Annie Edson Taylor sat in her dreary little room in a boarding house in Bay City, Michigan, and contemplated a bleak future. She was broke, lonely, and despondent. She knew she was too old to continue in her career as a dancing teacher. Who wanted to learn the arts of the ballroom from a bulky and shapeless woman of sixty-three, with coarse features and a rasping voice? Having exhausted her savings, Annie Taylor now faced the poorhouse. There was no social security at the century's turn. You begged, you took charity, or you starved.

All her life she had been a private entrepreneur, making her own way, traipsing from town to town, but always solvent. Now what was left for her? The three traditional women's jobs – stenographer, teacher, telephone operator – were reserved for younger women. If only, she thought, she could do something that no one else had ever done, then perhaps the world would take notice and reward her. In this fantasy she was kin to Arthur Midleigh, though her purpose was fortune as well as fame.

This was the year of the great Pan-American Exposition in Buffalo, and, as Annie's copy of the New York *World* made clear, tens of thousands were heading for Lake Erie to take in the big fair and then go on to see the sights at Niagara Falls. Just a few days before, on July 15, Carlisle Graham, the obsessive cooper, had restored his tarnished reputation by taking a five-foot, cigar-shaped, metal barrel on another perilous ride – his fifth – through the Whirlpool Rapids. Trapped in an eddy, Graham was retrieved from the barrel badly bruised, just before he almost died of suffocation.

Annie put down the paper and sat in thought. Then it came to her, as she wrote later, "in a flash." Suddenly this flabby and overweight woman decided to do what younger and more athletic daredevils had shrunk from doing. She would become the first human being to go over Niagara Falls in a barrel.

On the face of it, she seems the unlikeliest of candidates for the brief but blazing celebrity that such a venture would bring. Yet her career was that of a survivor. She was a nineteenth-century rarity – a determined and independent female entrepreneur who had suffered her share of misfortune yet had always overcome adversity.

As a child she preferred playing games with boys to dressing up dolls. She devoured adventure stories, her brain "teeming with romance." Her marriage to David Taylor, more than a dozen years her senior, was not happy. When he died of wounds suffered in the Civil War, she was left on her own.

She enrolled in a four-year teacher-training course in Albany on borrowed money, completed it with honours in three, and decided to make her way to San Antonio, Texas, then on the very rim of the western frontier and unreachable by either rail or water. She left New York on a White Star steamer in 1870, stopped off for a month in Cuba, sailed on to Galveston, took a train to Austin, and arrived at her destination by stagecoach. There she was able to board with the family of an old school friend. She got a job teaching at a nearby public school and within a year was made vice-principal.

For the next three decades she lived the life of a vagabond, moving restlessly from one city to another. In her autobiography, written after the Niagara adventure, she presented herself as a woman of pluck and audacity who was forever being set upon by miscreants. In San Antonio, she said, she was attacked in her boarding house by burglars who chloroformed her in an attempt to make off with the rent money she was collecting on behalf of the absent landlord, her friend's father. In 1873 she left San Antonio and was scarcely out of town when the stage on which she was travelling was attacked by three masked robbers who ordered her to hand over all her money. "I'll blow out your brains," one threatened. "Blow away," she cried. "I would as soon be without brains as without money!" They departed empty-handed, she recounted. There is, in her writing, a suspicious fuzziness, a lack of detail, and an absence of dates that encourages scepticism.

She moved to New York City where she enrolled in a dancing school and emerged as a qualified instructor in dancing and physical culture. Off she went to practise her new profession in Asheville, North Carolina, Chattanooga, Tennessee, Birmingham, Alabama, and again, San Antonio. She travelled across Mexico, took passage to San Francisco, then headed back to New York by train. Once again masked gunmen appeared, lined up all the passengers, and emptied their pockets of valuables. Since Annie had hidden her money and jewellery she had nothing to show and so lost nothing; "nor was I a bit afraid," she later wrote.

She survived fire and flood. She was in Chattanooga in March 1886 when the Tennessee River rose fifty feet and swept away hundreds of homes. She was in Charleston, South

Carolina, the following August when an eight-minute earthquake caused 110 deaths and hundreds of injuries. Walls crumbled, buildings toppled, pavements heaved, but Annie merely rose from her chair to examine a thermometer and note that the mercury had fallen twenty-six degrees in an hour.

She claimed that she had survived "three ocean storms" and "three serious fires," but "on none of these occasions did I ever for a moment lose my composure." A boast, perhaps, but who can quarrel with it? A woman prepared to plunge over the Falls in a barrel is not the sort who trembles at a pointed pistol or panics when the elements turn ugly. But in 1892, a fire in Chattanooga wiped her out, and she was forced to resume her gypsy like wanderings across the country, giving dancing lessons.

As she aged, grew grey, and lost her figure, there were fewer and fewer students. For one brief, exotic interval she travelled to Europe, the guest of a wealthy friend. When she returned to North America, she settled in the Michigan lumbering town of Bay City on the shores of Saginaw Bay, and there, by launching a furious advertising campaign, managed to open a dancing school. But she could do no better than break even and so closed her doors and set off once more to San Antonio, Mexico City, and El Paso, then back north to St. Louis, Chicago, and Bay City.

The pickings grew slimmer. "With the utmost economy and prudence I could not live decently," she wrote. Younger, prettier, and more athletic instructors were getting the business. She could, of course, have become a scrubwoman, but that her pride would not allow. "I didn't want to lower my social standard, for I have always associated with the best class of people, the cultivated and the refined. To hold my place in that world I needed money, but how to get it?"

She lived on the charity of her relatives, but it was given so grudgingly that she decided to have no more of it. For two years she had been obsessed by the problem of money and how to get

257

enough to keep up appearances – for appearances meant a great deal to Annie Taylor. "I was always well dressed," she wrote, "a member and regular attendant of the Episcopal Church, and my nearest neighbour had not the least idea of where I got my money...."

But what could a woman in her sixties do for a living in 1901? "All kinds of wild ideas ran riot in my brain. My thought was, if I could do something no one else in the world had ever done, I could make some money honestly and quickly." She might even be able to pay back what she had borrowed.

It was at this point that Annie Edson Taylor became an improbable aspirant for immortality of a sort at Niagara Falls.

4

Niagara Falls, when Annie Taylor arrived with her barrel, was known as the Honeymoon Capital of the World, but might as easily have been called the Suicide Capital of the World. By 1900, close to one thousand men and women were known to have hurled themselves into the abyss, either on the spur of the moment or after several days of careful planning. As one police officer noted that year, "there seems to be a hypnotism about it that allures people into its power. They go there in sound health and it seems to fascinate them with its grandeur and rainbow beauty. As soon as troubles come they begin to think about the place. When ... bats begin to flit about in their belfries, they begin to think the Falls is calling to them. And although they are twenty-five miles away they cannot seem to shake off the influence, but head for the place as though they were bewitched, and then the papers report Another Man Missing."

The policeman might easily have been describing John Lazarus, a stocky sixty-year-old from Mount Carmel, Pennsylvania, who arrived at Niagara Falls, New York in February

1900, and engaged a hack to take him about for some leisurely sightseeing. First, however, he stopped at the United States Express Company, where he wrapped up all his belongings, including a gold watch, three pocketbooks, cash, and personal papers, and dispatched them to his brother, a doctor in Bloomsburg. He asked for pen and paper, wrote a letter, and sent that off, too.

He climbed back into the hack and asked the driver to show him all the points of interest – just another tourist doing the rounds. But that was not enough for John Lazarus. Everybody was talking about the new belt line, known as the Great Gorge Route, that had opened the previous July. This fifteen-mile scenic tour by electric sightseeing trolley ran along the base of the gorge to the new suspension bridge at Lewiston. From Queenston at the bridge's western end, the trolleys rattled along the Canadian cliff and returned to the American side by the Upper Steel Arch Bridge. Even in winter the view was magnificent, and John Lazarus had no intention of passing it up. At the railroad office he bought a ticket but refused to take any change. For the next two hours he relaxed and enjoyed the spectacle that unwound before his eyes.

When he returned, Lazarus left his grip and topcoat at the station, announcing he would be back in ten minutes. He did not come back. Instead he set off for the bridge to Goat Island (successor to Augustus Porter's original structure), stopped at the centre span and – a tourist to the end – spent some time gazing into the hypnotic waters below. He walked back to the first span, appearing totally unconcerned. Suddenly he climbed over the railing and hurled himself into the rapids to his death.

Like Lazarus, a remarkable number of suicides indulged themselves in a leisurely tour of Niagara's attractions before steeling themselves to make that final leap. One such was a handsome twenty-year-old man, who arrived in wintertime wearing an expensive chinchilla coat and a silk hat, and registered at the Spencer House on the American side as C.F. Stanley of Cleveland. In lieu of luggage he left a gold watch.

His real name was Karl Stevens. Four of his relatives had died of consumption, the great scourge of that era. Fearing that the disease would claim him, too, he decided to cheat it by ending his life, a wholly irrational decision since he himself suffered no symptoms. He enjoyed a midday meal at his hotel and then, like Lazarus, hired a carriage to take him on a tour of the Falls. He had never touched liquor, but now, to strengthen his resolve, he began to move from saloon to saloon, gulping down glass after glass. By four that afternoon he was wildly drunk and heading for Goat Island.

He spent two hours on the island before returning to the bridge that led to the mainland. It was closed for the night but an official offered to open it so that Stevens could leave the park. Seeing Stevens's condition, he took his arm, but as the two walked over the bridge, Stevens broke away, climbed over the railing, and leaped into the rapids below.

But he still could not bring himself to end his life. Instead, he seized a projecting ledge of ice and climbed up on it. Rescuers arrived with ladders and ropes and were joined by John McCloy, the veteran ferryman who had already saved several lives.

Stevens waited, arms folded, perfectly still on his perch, standing out from the bridge's pier on the upstream side. McCloy coiled a rope around his body and then made his way down the ladder fastened to the bridge railing on the downstream side. He landed knee-deep in the shallow rapids and started upstream toward his quarry.

Half an hour had elapsed since Stevens had made his awkward plunge. In all that time he had neither moved nor shown any interest in the rescue attempt. Fighting his way through chunks of floating ice, McCloy unwound the rope from his body, gained a secure foothold, and prepared to tie it around his

260

victim. Just as he reached the ledge, Stevens plunged into the water, and with strong, steady strokes began to swim upstream. When McCloy tried to seize him, he rolled over on his back and was carried downstream out of sight and over the Falls.

Was Annie Taylor, too, attempting suicide? Certainly there were those who thought she was. But when a Bay City reporter asked the obvious question she snapped at him. "I am too good an Episcopalian," she said. "My people were Christian people and I was brought up in affluence and properly educated and instructed."

Still, there was a certain fatalism in her decision as she went about securing a suitable barrel that August. "I might as well be dead," she declared, "as to remain in my present condition." Death was certainly in her mind. "It would be fame and fortune or instant death," she wrote. In one way or another, the barrel symbolized escape.

She went down on her hands and knees to sketch out a full-scale diagram of the barrel she wanted. She cut a number of staves out of cardboard, laced them together, and called a local cooper, John Rozenski, to come to her house. Always careful of her reputation, she suggested he use the side door so that the neighbours wouldn't see him and suspect a scandal. She swore him to secrecy and asked him to build the barrel. Horrified, he refused. "Mein Gott, woman!" he said, "you will be killed, and me to help; I cannot do such a thing!"

He finally consented and the barrel was built. Annie picked out every stick of lumber herself, making sure that each piece was perfect – sturdy staves of Kentucky oak, each one an inch and a half thick and oiled individually to shed water. When it was finished, the barrel stood four and a half feet high, the staves secured by ten two-inch iron hoops, bolted to the barrel at four-inch intervals. It weighed 160 pounds.

Annie searched about for a suitable manager and found one, she thought, in Frank M. "Tussie" Russell of Bay City, who acted as a small-town promoter of high-diving carnival acts.

Russell was thirty-five, a short man with slicked-down hair parted in the middle. Annie told him she was forty-two. In fact, she was old enough to be his mother.

She told Russell she needed money, not for herself – she did not want him to know of her straitened circumstances – but to help pay off the mortgage of a ranch somewhere in Texas. He was not to mention the matter of money to the press: that would be too venal. He was simply to say that she was shooting the Falls "in a spirit of bravado."

She had only a vague idea of how money was to be attracted. Perhaps she thought that if she passed the hat the crowd would be generous. Russell knew better, but he was no Farini. It did not occur to him to approach the railways or to sell seats for a view of the spectacle. He talked only of later appearances in dime museums, and that was not quite what the refined Mrs. Taylor had in mind.

That September, a less discriminating woman, Martha E. Wagenfuhrer, was packing in audiences on the vaudeville circuit by describing her thrilling ride through the Whirlpool Rapids. The wife of a professional wrestler, she had borrowed Carlisle Graham's barrel and plunged into the turbulent waters to emerge badly battered and dreadfully seasick, but alive. She had chosen the afternoon of September 6 to perform the feat, for she had hoped that President McKinley, then attending the Pan-American Exposition, might be in the audience. McKinley, however, having seen the Falls, returned to Buffalo, where on that same day, in the Temple of Music, he was mortally wounded by a deranged anarchist.

The following day the shooting vied for headlines with the death of still another stuntwoman, a burlesque performer named Maud Willard, who was a friend of Martha Wagenfuhrer. Miss Willard and Carlisle Graham had worked out a double performance in which she would ride the same barrel through the Whirlpool. On her emergence, he would leap into the water and, wearing a life preserver and a ring to support his head, swim alongside and follow the barrel down the gorge to Lewiston.

The plan failed because Maud Willard insisted on bringing along her pet fox terrier for company. When the barrel was sucked into the Whirlpool and held there by the current, the dog not only used up much of the air but also jammed the intake hole with his muzzle. Tossed and buffeted for six hours, and caught in an eddy in the vortex, she died of suffocation. The dog survived, and because a motion-picture company was filming the stunt, Graham was obliged to complete his swim alone for the cameras.

Miss Willard's death did not deter Annie Taylor. She was more concerned by the attitude of the authorities on both sides of the river, who wanted no more stunts. But she was confident she could give the police the slip. She kept her intentions secret until September 22, when Russell announced in the Bay City *Times-Tribune* that an unnamed client was planning to go over the Falls in a barrel. He declined to give her name or her motivations.

On October 11, he arrived at Niagara Falls, New York – by this time a thriving industrial city of twenty thousand – to reveal to the press that Annie Edson Taylor was about to brave the cataract. "She is a widow, forty-two years old, intelligent and venturesome. She has scaled the Alps, made dangerous swimming trips, and explored wild, unknown countries," he announced, slipping into the hyperbole of his calling.

But when Annie stepped off the train at the Falls on October 13, she did not look like an experienced adventurer. She stood five feet four inches in her cotton stockings – a stout and almost shapeless figure in a voluminous black dress, her features fleshy and her greying hair concealed under a broad-brimmed hat. She was determined to make both her fame and her fortune. Fame she achieved; fortune eluded her.

She lied about her age, admitting to forty-two years, believing that the press would prefer a younger woman to make the plunge. Some journalists went along with the charade. One described her as "agile, athletic and strong"; another said she cut a sturdy, graceful figure. But others, more sceptical, put her age at fifty. She was thirteen years older than that.

Annie's lie was a gross miscalculation. It would have been cannier for her to announce (lying again, but with more wit) that she was seventy-three. In the inevitable lecture series that followed, few would be intrigued by a grossly overweight, fortyish prude. But a seventy-three-year-old widow tempting the great cataract! That might have been different. One can imagine the newspaper stories:

> Annie Taylor, a septuagenarian widow, looking
> remarkably young for her 73 years, today became
> the first human being to conquer Niagara Falls in a
> barrel. At a time when most people of her age have
> a foot in the grave, the amazing Mrs. Taylor, active
> and bold, in spite of her advancing years ...

But Annie was no Barnum. She insisted on the proprieties. She would not, she declared, make her way through the town to the point where her barrel was to be launched already dressed for the trip. It would be unbecoming, she said, "for a woman of refinement and of my years to parade before a crowd in a short skirt."

Russell found an expert riverman to help launch the barrel: Fred Truesdale, a sturdy teamster with a bold black beard, who had been hired by previous thrill seekers to send barrels containing cats and dogs over the Horseshoe. No one knew whether or not the animals survived, but none of Truesdale's customers had followed through on the feat itself.

Truesdale tested the barrel, dubbed *Queen of the Mist*, on October 18, supplying a cat for the journey. Russell watched from Terrapin Point on Goat Island, accompanied by the

ubiquitous Carlisle Graham and another daredevil, Bill Johnson, who had celebrated the Glorious Fourth that year by jumping, manacled, from the *Maid of the Mist*.

Truesdale tossed the barrel into the river from the Canadian
shore. Spinning, tumbling, tossed high on the crest of the
waves, it wallowed through the rapids before being hurled over
the brink. The barrel was retrieved, but whether or not the cat
survived remained a matter of conjecture. The Niagara Falls
Gazette and the *Cataract Journal* said it had. The Buffalo
Express and the *People's Press* of Port Welland said it hadn't.
Russell wasn't saying anything.

The crowd gathered on Sunday to watch Annie go over. She
failed to appear, and Russell gave the press a confusing variety
of excuses. The most plausible was that the photographs
Annie had intended to sell on the site had not been developed.
After all, she was almost broke.

She apologized later to the reporters for her absence. "I do
not wish to be classified with the women who are seeking noto-
riety," she said. "I am not of the common daredevil sort. I feel
refined and I know that I am well educated and well connected." The barrel trip was postponed to Wednesday afternoon, October 23. "I have no fear whatever," said Annie.
"When I make up my mind to do a thing, nothing can stop me."

Heavy winds caused a second delay, and the presence of
Carrie Nation, the axe-wielding prohibition advocate, shuttling between the exposition and the Falls, briefly crowded
Annie out of the headlines. By this time, few believed she was
prepared to make the trip. The *People's Press*, in its headline,
suggested it was all "A GIGANTIC HOAX!"

But she was determined. "If I say I will do a thing, I will do
it," she said, her voice trembling. "I hate a weak, vacillating
person who says they'll do a thing and then backs out. I value
my word of honor. If I thought it were necessary, and I had
given my word that I would step in front of a cannon and be
shot to pieces, I would do it!"

She remained true to her promise. At half-past one on the afternoon of Thursday, October 24, she was ready.

There was a small hitch when Truesdale's assistant, Fred Robinson, bowed out. "I ain't going to be a party to the murder of any woman," he announced. The local police chief had scared him off by threatening to arrest him for manslaughter if Annie perished. Truesdale replaced him with a cheerful youth, Billy Holleran.

Wearing a long black skirt with matching jacket and a black, wide-brimmed hat, and looking and acting "as if she were some plain, stout woman on her way to Sunday morning service," Annie emerged from Truesdale's house with her manager and walked to her boat as a crowd of well-wishers chorused goodbyes. "I will not say goodbye," she said, "but *au revoir*." Peter Nissen, better known as "Bowser," who had made headlines tempting the rapids the year before in his boat (aptly named the *Fool Killer*), was present to pump her hand.

In order to elude the police, who were making a half-hearted attempt to stop what the authorities regarded as a potential suicide, Russell had decided that Annie should push off from Grass Island in midstream a mile and a half above the cataract. There she was photographed with her barrel, and there, at her request, the members of her entourage and the press retreated to the far side of the island while she, hidden in the reeds, modestly peeled off hat, jacket, and outer skirt. Then, attired in a short black skirt, blue-and-white shirtwaist, black stockings, and tan slippers, she pronounced herself ready for the ordeal.

There she stood, with the waters swirling only a few feet away – a lumpy figure with a pudding of a face, resolute, unafraid, and totally confident that she, at sixty-three, could accomplish a feat that no other human being had managed, and from which younger and more athletic daredevils had shrunk. What was she doing here – a woman of "refinement," as she constantly reminded the press – indulging in a common stunt mainly suitable for exploitation in the music halls that

266

she despised? Many in the crowd that day must have seen her as a figure to be laughed at or pitied; that she was not. What Annie Edson Taylor was doing, as she prepared to enter her barrel, was to shake her fist at Victorian morality, which decreed that there was no place but the almshouse for a woman without means who had reached a certain age.

Her only concern was the Whirlpool, in whose grip Maud Willard had suffocated. She had a terror of the Whirlpool Rapids, she said, and had given some thought to the problem of air inside the closed barrel. "I will have the barrel filled with air by a bicycle pump," she said. "I believe I can live fully an hour, or perhaps two, with the cover closed."

She squeezed through the opening of the barrel and buckled herself into the special harness, designed to hold her fast to the bottom. Protected from buffeting by two cushions and a pillow, she gripped a strap on either side as a further stabilizing precaution. Three airholes, stopped with removable corks, had been drilled into the barrel. After the two-inch thick cover was fitted into place, Billy Holleran worked away for twenty minutes with a bicycle pump at the airholes to replenish some of Annie's air. "I'll give her enough gas to last her for a week," he cried enthusiastically.

Truesdale heard her call in a weak voice that a chink was letting in light between the staves. He stuffed it with a rag. At 3:50 he rowed his boat directly for the Canadian shore, pulling the barrel with the help of another boat. As he reached the main current and the barrel was pulled alongside, Truesdale heard a faint tapping from within.

"What is it?"

"The barrel is leaking," Annie said.

"How much water is there in it?"

"About a pailful."

"Well, that will not hurt you. You will be over the Falls and rescued in a few minutes and the water will help to keep you awake. We're going to cast off now. Goodbye."

"Goodbye," replied Annie faintly.

The crowd, having been put off twice, was thinner than it had been the previous Sunday, but the shores were still heavily lined with spectators as the barrel bobbed off in the current, heading directly toward the brink of the Horseshoe.

On the inside, Annie Taylor felt the barrel glide away until it reached the suction of the rapids. It paused for a moment, and then, thrown into the angry waters "like a thing of life, fighting for its prey" (Annie's words), it zigzagged through mountains of spray until it reached the first sudden drop – about forty feet – half a mile above the Falls. It caught on a fragment of drift-wood, turned over, gave a lurch, and plunged to the bottom of the river. She could hear the hundred-pound anvil at the base grind in the riverbed, but then the barrel popped to the surface and continued its race downstream. She knew that if it moved too close to the huge rocks on the Canadian shore it would be dashed to bits, but she felt no fear, resigned "to whatever fate had in store for me. I knew that my motives were pure and exalted though my life were to pass."

The barrel paused in midstream. It turned over, from side to side, righted itself, and entered the smooth, swift current that rounds the bend in the river. Now the roar of the cataract, "like continuous thunder," assailed her ears and she realized she was on the brink of the precipice. She placed a small cushion under her knees, clasped her hands tightly, relaxed every muscle, and dropped her head on her bosom as the barrel went over. The sensation, she said later, was one of indescribable horror. "I felt as though all Nature was being annihilated."

She felt no impact when the barrel struck the water; she simply knew it had dropped below the surface. No sound reached her. She felt alone, forsaken. About a minute passed and then she felt the barrel starting upward. It shot out of the water ten or fifteen feet into the air, dropped and plunged again, and was hurled back into the cavern behind the sheet of water. There it

268

was picked up by the force of the waves, dashed around in mid-air and dropped onto the rocks. She could feel herself being whirled about and lifted like "butter in a churn." She felt her strength ebbing but remained calm. The gusts below the Falls shot the barrel into the *Maid of the Mist* eddy, a minor whirl-pool, in which she feared she would be trapped. But then she heard the barrel grate on the rocks and knew she was safe. Her head dropped forward but she did not hear the barrel being opened until a fresh breeze struck her.

She heard a male voice: "The woman is alive!"

"Yes, she is," Annie gasped.

Carlisle Graham and several others had been waiting on a big rock a few feet from the shore. "Kid" Brady, a well-known featherweight boxer and a good swimmer, had stripped to his trunks and, clinging to the rock, was able to grasp the rope attached to the barrel and with help pull it to safety as the crowd of onlookers cheered.

Graham helped work the lid off the barrel and peered in, not knowing whether its occupant was dead or alive. A limp hand, blue and benumbed, gave a feeble wave. The crowd cheered again, but Annie was too far gone to squeeze out of the barrel by herself.

A hoop was removed; it wasn't enough. A saw was called for, and part of the barrel was cut away. Through this opening Annie Taylor was finally dragged, blood streaming down her clothing from a gash in her head.

"Have I gone over the Falls?" she asked wearily. And then, "I'm cold. I've lost my power of speech. I want to go home."

She was so dazed that she had difficulty walking. Graham and another helper each took an arm and guided her across a plank from the rock to the shore. Bedraggled and unkempt, she looked her age as she was bundled into blankets, taken to her boarding house, and wheeled before a blazing fire. The scalp wound, caused by the incessant bumping of the barrel against the rocks, was superficial. There were no broken bones. She was, however, suffering badly from shock.

She managed only a few words for the press. "If it was with my dying breath," she said, "I would caution anyone against attempting the feat. I will never go over the Falls again. I would sooner walk up to the mouth of a cannon, knowing it was going to blow me to pieces than make another trip over the fall."

5

The local press went wild over Annie's exploit. The Niagara Falls *Gazette* claimed that she deserved "foremost rank in the list of those who have dared to toy with Nature...." To the *Cataract Journal* she was a "woman of indomitable resolve, of lion-like courage and a woman who had the strength of her conviction." The Buffalo *Courier* declared that her exploit was "the climax of Niagara wonders."

The New York papers didn't gush. Indeed, they almost missed the story because most editors refused to believe it was true. The *Times*, in its imperious fashion, made a habit of sneering at Falls stunters. When Robert Flack lost his life in the Whirlpool Rapids, the *Times*' callous headline had read: "ANOTHER NIAGARA CRANK DISPOSED OF."

Annie's home-town paper, the Bay City *Times-Tribune*, predicted Fame and Fortune for Mrs. Taylor. She received an immediate offer of two hundred dollars to appear during the closing week of the Pan-American Exposition, but her expenses in equipping the barrel and paying her helpers quickly gobbled that up. Russell managed to secure her a week at Huber's Museum in New York for a fee of five hundred dollars, but, to his fury, she declined. Dime museums were not for her, especially in her emotionally drained condition.

She returned to Bay City to be greeted by her long lost brother, Montgomery Edson, a blacksmith. The two, who hadn't seen each other for twenty-five years, embraced warmly. But when Edson started to reveal his sister's real age, she disclaimed all relationship. She was still intent on presenting herself as a woman in her early forties.

Fame was fleeting, fortune illusory. Russell booked her into a series of store window appearances in Saginaw, Detroit, Sandusky, Cleveland, and Cincinnati. There she sat with her barrel and her black cat, advertised as the same animal that had survived the test plunge over the Falls. For this she grossed no more than two hundred dollars.

Annie's weight had dropped from 162 pounds to 135, and she was still feeling the bruises from her ordeal. She turned up at the Charleston Exposition, but heavy rains kept the customers away. Back in Cleveland, she and Russell found themselves broke, depending on the city's charity. At this point, Russell decamped with Annie's only assets, the barrel and the cat. "If she had been a beautiful girl, why we could have made thousands," he was quoted as saying. But poor, greying Annie failed to electrify the crowds.

She was obsessed with getting her barrel back; it was, she felt, the key to financial success. Then she found that Russell had sold it to a Chicago theatrical company that was planning a stage play entitled *Over the Falls*. She raised some money by publishing a quickie pamphlet about her exploits, and with the proceeds she hired a lawyer to locate the missing barrel. Private detectives traced it to Chicago where on August 14 the stage company was displaying it in a department store window to advertise their play.

Annie made straight for the city and with her lawyer's help served a writ on the stage company, retrieved her barrel, and took it back to Niagara Falls. She estimated its temporary loss cost her fifteen hundred dollars, and she warned that if anybody tried to steal it again, "I have a pistol and I know how to shoot."

Now she discovered that Carlisle Graham had also betrayed her by staging a re-enactment of her Falls plunge to add to the

271

film that had been made of his own adventures. Graham hired both Truesdale and Billy Holleran to set up the scene and sent his own empty barrel over the cataract while the cameras rolled. He did not hire Annie to play herself, probably because she objected to being portrayed in a medium that was considered socially disreputable. If the dime museums were indecent in her eyes, so were the raunchy nickelodeons. Annie saw herself as a lecturer on a platform, not a cheap sensationalist in a flickering peep show.

Annie hired a new manager, William A. Banks, who booked her in a number of state fairs. Then he decamped, not only with the precious barrel but also with her stock of pamphlets and photographs. Worse still, Banks had engaged his attractive young girl friend, Maggie Kaplan, to pass herself off as "the Heroine of Niagara Falls" and to sell Annie's stolen pamphlets to the gullible. It was all too much: many of those who had paid to see the real Annie – wrinkled, dour, and dowdy – began to wonder if she *was* the genuine article.

At this point, Annie's barrel vanishes from history. It was said that Banks sold it for five hundred dollars (the cat had long since disappeared). Annie immediately ordered an exact replica of the famous cask and with it by her side became a familiar figure on the sidewalk outside the New England Restaurant in Niagara Falls, New York, seated in the shade, peddling souvenir postcards, being photographed with tourists, or selling copies of a new autobiography in which she revealed more than a trace of bitterness over her failure to make a fortune from her adventure. "None of the thousands of people who have come to see me," she wrote, "ever thought of the brain to plan such a trip and the courage to make it."

She remained convinced, against all the evidence, that she represented a lucrative investment. In 1903 she went to New York City to try to raise some financial backing. "I am sure if I appeal to the generous members of the Stock Exchange, they will help me in my adversity," she said. There was no response, and so she returned to her souvenir stand in the summer and travelled the lecture circuit in the winter, making just enough money to pay her bills.

In 1906, in spite of her earlier statements that she would rather brave the cannon's mouth, Annie Taylor began to talk of a second Falls plunge. Now, close to her seventieth year, she still didn't want to appear as a money-grubbing stunter. She no longer talked of needing funds to support herself or to pay off the mortgage on a ranch somewhere in Texas. Instead, she portrayed herself as a philanthropist, eager to help old friends down on their luck. Later she talked of raising enough money to build a home for the aged and another for homeless young women.

Nothing came of these plans. On July 25, 1911, a new daredevil appeared to rival Annie's exploit. He was a roistering, British-born tavern keeper named Bobby Leach, and he represented everything the refined Mrs. Taylor loathed. He was a pool shark, a hard drinker, a tough and colourful spinner of yarns who sported a derby hat cocked over one eye, kept a cigar clenched in his teeth, and flaunted a diamond tie pin. He was, in short, a character, who had no trouble getting press coverage and putting Annie Taylor in the shade.

Leach was no stranger to Niagara stunts. Back in 1896 he had twice attempted the rapids successfully in a barrel. Now, in a special steel cask, the forty-seven-year-old high-flyer repeated Annie's feat while the motion-picture camera whirred. He emerged from the barrel bloodied, battered, and blind drunk, shouting, "Ain't nobody got anything on me now!"

For Annie, this was the final indignity. Her shining adventure had been profaned by a common roustabout! She pleaded with the press not to associate her name with Leach's "in any way, shape, or manner." For her, life had reached its climax in October 1901. After that, it lumbered slowly downhill. She tried to write a historical novel; it failed. She managed to make her way to Europe, only to find that the despised Leach was prospering in the vulgar English music halls. For the rest of her life she was a prisoner of her own exploit. She even tried to reconstruct her story on film – the motion picture having become respectable – but the results were never shown.

She continued to eke out a living based on the fading memories of her famous plunge. Hack drivers pointed her out on Falls Street to tourists – a frail, shrivelled, half-blind figure, her face a mass of wrinkles, still proudly posing with her barrel. By 1919, unable to see properly, she went into business as a clairvoyant. Later she offered to give electric and magnetic treatments – the newest therapeutic fad – to Falls residents. There were few takers.

The press had all but forgotten her. When other daredevils tempted the Falls or the rapids, her feat was recalled as ancient history, but no one checked to see if she was still alive. Only when she entered the county infirmary (the poorhouse) was there a brief flurry. Annie resisted this ignominy until the last. "I've done what no other woman in the world had nerve to do," she told Louis Elmer, commissioner of charities, "only to become a pauper."

That was in February 1921. She was eighty-three years old but was now stubbornly insisting that she was only fifty-seven and in the prime of life. The terrible pounding she took during the barrel trip, she said, had caused her to age prematurely. Frank Russell emerged to declare his regret that his former client had been reduced to penury. "She had an aversion against going on the stage," he explained to the Bay City *Times-Tribune*.

A week after her admission to the infirmary, the Niagara Falls *Gazette* rediscovered Annie Taylor and found that she had not lost her sense of the dramatic. "I have crossed the Atlantic Ocean four times," she said, "the Straits of Florida fourteen times, have made several trips across the continent and visited the Hawaiian Islands." On she went, talking of trips to Quebec and France, of journeying through Mexico with the widow of a former Mexican president, and, of course, of the famous tumble over the Falls.

She remained to the end what she had always been – resolute, proud, a little snobbish, and always optimistic. "Through misfortune and other people's dishonesty I lost all of my fortune," she said. "It is quite a change for me to come here when I have been used to being entertained in senators' homes in Washington and travelling extensively; but I feel that it is no disgrace and if all my plans materialize, I shall not remain here long."

Two months later, on April 29, she died. How ironic that she should have been buried in Strangers' Rest, a section of the Oakwood Cemetery where other Niagara heroes had been laid! For there her body lies, side by side with Carlisle Graham, a man she despised. Her shade was saved from further indignity, however, when Bobby Leach died. He, too, would almost certainly have occupied a neighbouring plot had he not ended life in New Zealand – and in the most mundane and hackneyed manner. He slipped on an orange peel, fell, and succumbed to complications.

Chapter Nine

1

In the fall of 1901, when Annie Taylor plunged over the Horseshoe Falls, the exploitation of Niagara's power was entirely in the hands of Americans. With considerable daring – some might call it recklessness – they had thrust their country into the electrical age and seen that gamble pay off. The power that they drew from the great cataract was, of course, reserved for American industries. Canada, with its small population, was not a lucrative market, nor had the cautious Canadians shown any interest in developing power on their own.

Indeed, for all of the previous decade Canada seemed to have been mired in the past. In 1891, when an American syndicate was already boring its tunnel under Niagara Falls, New York, and exploring the possibilities of hydro power in Europe, the *Canadian Electrical News* was pooh-poohing the idea of long-distance transmission as commercially unsound. In 1892, the year the Americans hired Stanford White to design their generating station, the manager of the Toronto Electric Light Company, J. J. Wright, insisted that alternating current was far too dangerous to be practical.

The majority of Canadian businessmen clung to the idea that steam would always be the main source of power for industry. It was not until April 1900 that the Toronto Board of Trade set up a special committee to get the facts about electricity. Its chairman was Walter Massey, of the famous farm implements firm, himself a progressive entrepreneur. But even at that late date the committee concluded that electricity would remain "a secondary force, a handmaid or servant of steam or some other primary power." This, in spite of the fact that eleven major industries, all using hydroelectric power, were already operating on the American bank of the Niagara River.

The Americans themselves helped to hold back power

development in Canada. For most of the nineties, exclusive rights to develop electricity from the Canadian falls were held by the Canadian Niagara Power Company, wholly owned by Americans. The company made no move to harness the Horseshoe; why go to any expense in Canada until its American parent, the Niagara Falls Power Company, had used up all the available power on the other side? It did not put a spade into the ground until 1901, and when its hydroelectric plant finally went into operation in 1904, all the power was transmitted across the river to American industry.

A second American company, known as the Ontario Power Company, had been incorporated in 1887. It took several years to secure a franchise and did not get around to building a powerplant in Canada until 1903. Another two years went by before it was able to generate electricity. Again, most of the power was transmitted to U.S. customers across the river.

Canadians were shaken out of their torpor in 1902 when the great coal famine struck Ontario industry. Suddenly, the country's dependence on the United States was brought home graphically. A series of bitter strikes in the anthracite mines of Pennsylvania sent the price of hard coal in Toronto – used extensively for heating – soaring from three dollars a ton to a peak of more than nine dollars. Indeed, there came a time when Canada ran out of hard coal, and even the soft coal used in manufacturing was in short supply. Wood, peat, and coke all proved ineffective. Factories closed, hundreds were thrown out of work, and, as winter approached, ordinary people began to shiver. Even when the famine ended in the fall, coal was scarce because Americans controlled the transportation systems, and American customers got preferential treatment.

The coal famine turned the eyes of Central Canada toward Niagara. As the Berlin (later Kitchener) *News Record* argued, "Niagara Falls is worth serious consideration." If it were harnessed for Canadians, the Falls would make western Ontario independent of the soft coal fields and provide cheaper power than steam. Berlin, a rising industrial town, became the centre of a growing campaign for public power in Ontario.

The shortage had another result. It stimulated a trio of Canadian businessmen to resolve, at long last, that a Canadian company should also exploit the waters of the great cataract.

The three men who in 1902 formed the syndicate that became the Electrical Development Company were among the most powerful industrialists in Canada. All were in the prime of life; all were experienced financiers and builders. Frederic Nicholls, general manager of Canadian General Electric, would be the technical expert. Henry Pellatt, who ran the Toronto Electric Light Company, and William Mackenzie, who controlled the Toronto Street Railway Company, would be their own best customers.

The eloquent Nicholls had been identified with electrical development in Canada for more than a decade. In 1896 he was elected president of the National Electric Light Association of America – the first and only Canadian to hold that post. A fervent supporter of John A. Macdonald's National Policy of high tariffs, he was a leading spokesman for the manufacturing interests. Nicholls had published and edited the *Canadian Manufacturer* and also served as secretary of the Canadian Manufacturers' Association. He and his group had been able to seize control of Canadian General Electric when its American parent ran into financial difficulties. As vice-president and general manager of CGE, the forty-six-year-old Nicholls had the motivation to exploit the power of the Canadian Falls and the drive to get what he wanted. In the assessment of the Toronto *News*, "he was a man of skill, courage and enterprise."

With his round, pink face, his slightly popped eyes, and his military moustache, Henry Pellatt looked more like a Colonel Blimp than a hard-nosed financier. Actually, he was both. He had started in his father's brokerage business and took over running it. By 1902 he was up to his armpits in utilities, power,

Powerplants on the Niagara River

and mining, "the Cecil Rhodes of Canada", as one financier called him. Perhaps the most enthusiastic amateur soldier in Canada, he was lieutenant-colonel of the 2nd Regiment of the Queen's Own Rifles. And he was such a romantic royalist that he would within the decade erect, on one of Toronto's most prominent ridges, the fairytale castle Casa Loma, for which he is best remembered.

The third member of the triumvirate, and, as it developed, the most important, was William Mackenzie. He had begun his career in Kirkfield, Ontario, as a schoolteacher. He failed in the lumber business, took a job cutting railway ties, and gravitated from that into major contracting. His fortune rested on a five-thousand-dollar loan coaxed from the Mother Superior of a Montreal convent where his wife, a Roman Catholic, had been a student. For the rest of his career, Mackenzie, a Conservative and a Calvinist, would build his growing empire on borrowed funds.

A major contractor during the building of the Canadian Pacific Railway, Mackenzie, with his strapping partner, Donald Mann, had also amalgamated and electrified the Toronto tramway system. Since 1896 Mackenzie had been busy cobbling together Canada's third transcontinental railway, the Canadian Northern, out of a "series of disconnected and apparently unconnectable projections of steel hanging in suspense." (Those were the words of a colleague, D.B. Hanna.) The dapper Mackenzie, with his sharp features, his neat imperial beard, and his agile mind, knew his way around the financial world. Blunt-spoken, tough-minded, and secretive, he had, in the words of the *Canadian Courier*, "a sphinx-like attitude towards the public."

When the Montreal *Standard* produced a list of twenty-three men who formed the basis of Canadian finance, Nicholls, Pellatt, and Mackenzie were among those named. Indeed, their joint activities dovetailed neatly, to the benefit of all three. Nicholls, until 1902, was president of Mackenzie's transcontinental railway. Mackenzie was one of ten major shareholders in Nicholls's Canadian General Electric. Nicholls also sat on the board of Pellatt's Toronto Electric Light Company, while Pellatt was a director of and broker for Mackenzie's Toronto Street Railway Company. Conservatives all, fellow members of the exclusive Toronto Club, they were also among the most prominent of Toronto's social élite.

On January 29, 1903, the syndicate was granted the right to take water from the Niagara River at Tempest Point above the Falls and to generate 125,000 electrical horsepower. The Niagara Falls Queen Victoria Park Commission was strapped for funds and set the price at a mere $30,000. The prospect was – to use a word then new in the language – electrifying.

In 1905, in an address to the Empire Club in Toronto,

Nicholls rhapsodized over the "invisible and mystic power which men call electricity." In a single poetic sentence, he delineated the magical qualities of the new energy, which was only then beginning to captivate the public. It would, he explained, "be transmitted along slender copper wires to great distances, and having silently entered our mills, factories and power houses, over still more slender wires, will, like the genie out of the bottle, expand into a force that is terrifying when uncontrolled."

Nicholls did not dramatize, of course, the enormous profits to be made by those who controlled the genie. That year he and his partners created the Electrical Development Company as a publicly traded stock company. They then sold their $30,000 franchise to the new corporation for a staggering $6,100,000. Each took only $10,000 in cash, the rest in shares.

It was a breath-taking financial coup. They had got all their money out, made a profit, and created a six-million-dollar company with very little risk. Next they raised $5 million for construction through the sale of public bonds. But then, who could blame them for seeing an electrical future that the members of the park commission, in their myopia, had failed to grasp when they sold for $30,000 a franchise the worth of which would increase a thousandfold within twenty years?

Now these late arrivals proposed to outstrip the other two power companies operating on the Canadian side. Theirs would be the biggest and the best. The power station would be installed on a twelve-acre stretch of reclaimed riverbed, raised, in Nicholls's colourful phrase, "from the most turbulent part of the upper rapids at Tempest Point." That was no exaggeration. When workmen sent down sounding rods to gauge the river bottom, the flow was so fierce that it bent the metal at right angles. Nothing could be accomplished until a great wall of rocks and earth was thrown up to hold back the raging waters.

The problems the new company faced were unique, for

nothing of this sort had ever before been attempted. The waters of the river, diverted down into a deep well 150 feet below the powerhouse, would rotate the big turbines at the bottom. Shafts would carry the power up to rows of generators on the ground floor of the building. The waste water would be drained away through a 2,000-foot tunnel, 150 feet below the river level. It would run to a point directly behind the Falls and discharge its effluent into the cataract itself. The tunnel would be thirty-three feet wide, the largest of its kind in the world according to the company's boast.

Construction began at the lower end of the tunnel in 1903. A shaft 150 feet deep was sunk in the bank at the edge of the Horseshoe Falls, and a second construction tunnel driven at right angles out to the very brink, 700 feet of it under the water, to the point where the excavation for the main tunnel would commence. To save both money and time, the contractor, Anthony C. Douglass, an American from Niagara Falls, New York, decided that the debris from both tunnels would not be hauled back to shore and up the connecting shaft. Instead, it would be dumped into the chamber that the river had gnawed out between the falling sheet of water and the limestone face of the cliff over which that water tumbled.

But to accomplish this, he needed to rip a hole in the wall of the escarpment. A small opening was made near the ceiling of the construction tunnel, but thick clouds of spray from the cataract burst in. Obviously a larger opening was needed through which the tailings could be removed and the water allowed to drain out, leaving a clear passageway.

Douglass then had eighteen holes drilled into the rock face and loaded with ten cases of dynamite. The blast that resulted tore a jagged hole in the cliff, but it still wasn't large enough. Meanwhile the tunnel, open to the spray, was filling up with water.

Douglass had a flat-bottomed boat lowered down the shaft in

the river bank. The tunnel was now so full of water that the boat couldn't clear the roof and had to be weighted down. Three miners with several boxes of dynamite and coils of copper wire then boarded the boat and started off down the tunnel, lying on their backs and propelling the craft with their hands and feet.

When they reached the opening, they placed the dynamite around it, attached the copper wire, and headed back to the shaft. Just as they reached it, their boat sank under them. They climbed to safety, and a moment later a tremendous explosion rocked the gorge. But the hole in the cliff face still wasn't big enough.

The only solution was to apply the dynamite to the face of the cliff behind the fall of water, a dangerous enterprise. The company's chief engineer, Hugh L. Cooper, and its resident engineer, Beverly R. Value, donned rubber suits and roped themselves together like mountain climbers. Starting from the Scenic Tunnel, long a tourist attraction, the pair headed for the opening that had previously been blasted. They scrambled precariously along the cliff face, blinded by the intensity of the spray and buffeted by the force of the wind created by the intense pressure of the falling water. Soaking wet in spite of their precautions, chilled to the bone, and thoroughly miserable, they finally reached the opening in the tunnel wall.

Here they were battered by two forces of water   the back lash churning up from the base of the Falls and the powerful jets of spray coming at them from every side. Again and again they made this journey, risking their lives each time, until they had secured four tons of dynamite around the opening, chaining the boxes into position to prevent them from being torn away by the incessant blasts of water.

This effort worked. The obstructions were at last removed, and the water ran out of the tunnel, which, as Nicholls later told an Empire Club dinner in Toronto, "is as dry and pleasant as this room."

Meanwhile, a trickle of protests against a private Canadian company harnessing the Falls was growing to the dimensions of a tidal wave. Neither Mackenzie's city transit company nor Pellatt's electrical utility was popular. Both were known for gouging the public and giving inferior service. Moreover, the proponents of public power were bringing their case before the public, and it was a popular one.

The Electrical Development Company knew that it had to put up a good front, and this was undoubtedly one reason why Pellatt hired his friend E. J. Lennox, one of the country's best-known architects, to design the powerhouse. As a result, what might have been a plain brick box became instead a neo-classical palace that in its every line seemed to suggest both power and grace. Lennox set it on the bank half a mile above the brink of the cataract, the point where the river is at its most turbulent. It was ninety-one feet wide and forty feet high, clad in pale Indiana limestone. A colonnade of massive stone pillars extended along the entire 462 feet of its front. From there visitors could goggle at the line of eleven great generators, each weighing close to two hundred tons, filling a hall so vast it was large enough to accommodate five regulation hockey rinks.

The Canadians had finally outdone all their rivals, including the Americans. But would this impressive architectural gem, perched on the very lip of the thundering river, be symbol enough to withstand the popular appeal of the public power movement?

2

The probability that Toronto – Hogtown, as its rivals called it – would gobble up all the Falls power did not sit well with the smaller communities of southwestern Ontario. Solid industrial towns such as Berlin and Waterloo, 70 percent of whose populations were of Germanic origin, knew that they would have to fight for their share. The only way to provide a large enough market to justify transmission of power from the Falls was to work together. No single community could go it alone.

Such was the concept that a Waterloo manufacturer, Elias Snider, brought to the local board of trade meeting in February 1902. Two days later, his friend Daniel B. Detweiler, vice-president of the neighbouring Berlin Board of Trade, preached the same gospel. The twin communities must set up a joint committee, "the sooner the better," to look into the possibility.

From that day on, the campaign for cheap public power – "the people's power," as it came to be called – gathered momentum, led by Snider and Detweiler. For their communities, public power made sense. All inland towns suffered in competition with those on the lakes, which did not have to pay high freight rates to bring in coal by rail. Hydroelectric power was cheaper, but why let private industry gouge the manufacturers with exorbitant prices and poor service when a publicly owned company could provide cheaper electricity more efficiently? That was the message that the two businessmen carried to other neighbouring communities.

Popular sentiment was on their side. Suspicion of Big Business, imported from the growing antitrust movement south of the border, helped give the campaign a much-needed shove. Besides, the people of Waterloo had first-hand knowledge of the advantages of public ownership. It was one of the few municipalities that had opted for a publicly owned street railway and gas distribution system. Toronto, on the other hand, was in thrall to Mackenzie's inadequate and inefficient privately owned transit service, which was notoriously indifferent to both public and political criticism. As Detweiler wrote to Snider, "If the new Toronto Co'y should get started they no doubt would look mainly to their own interests first and then sweat the Public all they could stand same as other Co's." After all, the same business cronies were involved. "The Ontario legislature must choose," the Toronto *News* declared. "The time for decision has arrived. The people, or the Corporations?"

"The rising clamour of the multitude," as *Saturday Night* called it, was amplified in February 1903, when seventeen municipalities, mostly from southwestern Ontario, met in Berlin to issue "the first, faint blast" in the campaign for public power. It was important enough for the mayors themselves to attend with their aldermen to hear the report of the joint committee set up the year before. It was a tentative document that merely asked for provincial legislation enabling municipalities to buy, sell, and distribute electric power.

Up rose the mayor of Toronto to toughen the resolution. He proposed that the government build and operate the transmission lines itself. The seconder, who helped push the resolution through, was the mayor of London, Adam Beck.

Almost immediately Beck took up the campaign for public power. Within a year he was its leader. His name would be linked forever with the principle of publicly owned hydroelectric power in Ontario. His larger-than-life statue would dominate Toronto's University Avenue, opposite the Ontario Hydro building. The great generating stations flanking the Niagara gorge would all bear his name. Hated, feared, despised, and admired – even venerated – in his lifetime, he would eventually attain the status of provincial idol.

Since Beck's childhood, his life had centred around waterpower. He came from a family of Lutheran millers who had been using water to turn their mill wheels in the old days in Baden, Germany. As a boy in Baden, Ontario – Waterloo County – Adam Beck built miniature dikes in the little brooks that ran into his father's millpond. From his earliest days, he was challenged by the potential of water and the question of how it could be further channelled to serve mankind.

The German immigrants were devotees of the work ethic. At the age of ten, Adam found his summer holidays interrupted when his father took him to the family foundry that ran in conjunction with the mill. "Slap him if he doesn't work, or I'll slap you," he told an employee. The younger Beck, who never went to university, learned to work a ten-hour day. For the remainder of his restless life he found it difficult to take a prolonged holiday.

Beck soon learned the value of community co-operation, for those were the days of barn raisings and quilting bees, when people banded together to help each other out. That concept would fire Beck's later obsession to attain a publicly owned hydroelectric system.

When Beck was twenty-two, his father's business failed, and the family moved to the United States. But Adam stayed in Canada, determined to make it on his own. He took various jobs – one in a brass factory and another, later, in a cigar factory. Then, discerning an unfilled need, he started a cigar-box company in the heart of the Southern Ontario tobacco fields. There the young workaholic did everything from sharpening his own saw to delivering the product in a two-wheeled handcart.

By 1898, Adam Beck was well enough off to enter politics. In 1902 he was elected mayor of London and soon revealed his social philosophy when he refused to extend the lease of a privately owned local railway. Beck was determined that the city itself should run the line. Although in politics he was nominally a Conservative, the term, in those days, did not have the connotations it later acquired. The Ontario Liberal party, rusty in office under George W. Ross, contained the die-hards. The Conservatives, led by James Pliny Whitney, were more progressive. In the provincial election of 1902, narrowly won by the Liberals, Beck ran as a Conservative and was elected to the legislature. That, of course, was the year of the great coal famine and also of the gift of the franchise to develop Niagara power to a private concern, the Electrical Development Company.

With the municipalities demanding that a commission be set

up to look into the whole thorny question of public power and most of the press on their side, Ross could not refuse. In August he bowed to the pressure, put Elias Snider in charge, and made Beck one of the commissioners. From that moment the cigar-box manufacturer began to dominate the movement. As his biographer and colleague, W.R. Plewman, has said, he went at it "as naturally as Queen Victoria of England went to the centre of any stage upon which she had occasion to stand."

He was forty-six years old, an assertive and dynamic person-ality – eloquent, impetuous, aggressive, and often unbending in his pursuit of "power for the people." A handsome man with steel-grey eyes, he had the profile of a romantic stage actor to fit his own theatrical nature – aquiline nose, aggressive jaw, high forehead. In repose, it was said, he seemed "to be carved in granite." A self-made man, he dressed like an aristocrat in clothes of British cut, and he acted like one, too, for he was an avid horseman and breeder who, when he found the time, rode pink-coated to hounds.

In 1905, an aroused electorate, disenchanted with the creaky thirty-four-year-old Liberal regime, threw Ross's government out of office. James Whitney became premier, and Beck was named minister without portfolio. He might more aptly have been called "Minister of Public Power." One of Whitney's first moves was to refuse to ratify the agreement his predecessor had made with the Electrical Development Company to allow it to generate an additional 125,000 horsepower from Niagara Falls. Whitney also pledged that no more franchises would be granted until a thorough examination into Niagara power had been conducted. "The water power of Niagara," he declared, "should be as free as the air."

Beck, meanwhile, had found the villain he needed in his own campaign. He attacked the EDC from the public platform and in the legislature and declared that the agreement with the private company was worthless. It was supposed to protect the public, but, he said, "the promoters get the capital stock for nothing, the total cost of acquiring and developing the property being borne by the proceeds of the bond issue." Thus began a long and bitter wrangle between Beck and the private power interests.

In July, Premier Whitney appointed his own three-man commission of inquiry to examine the subject of electrical power. Beck, who was already a member of the Snider commission appointed by the previous government, would be chairman of this new body. That position did not prevent him from stumping the province, attacking the private companies for charging too much and pointing to the benefits for industry in cheap power generated by a publicly owned company. For, although Beck also emphasized the advantages of power in the home, "Power for the People" really meant power for industry. Niagara Falls was seen, correctly, as the source that would create an industrial heartland in Southern Ontario. The manufacturers who demanded public power did so, not out of any political philosophy, but simply because they knew it would be cheaper.

The two commissions – Snider's and Beck's – submitted their reports within days of each other in the spring of 1906. To Snider's fury, much of the data gathered by his own commission when it appeared in the press was credited to Beck. Snider never forgave Beck for that. Beck, in his turn, had no faith in the Snider commission, which had, in effect, been superseded by his own. Snider's report recommended a municipal co-operative that would own both the generating plants and the transmission lines. Beck was not proposing public ownership of the generating plants, but he did want the province to build the transmission lines. In addition – and more significantly – he urged the creation of a provincial hydroelectric power commission mandated to regulate the private companies.

Beck had no intention of letting his report gather dust on the legislative shelves. The night it was tabled he organized a massive demonstration. Fifteen hundred people wearing cardboard badges bearing the words "Cheap Power Convention" marched on Toronto's Romanesque city hall (a Lennox building) and then paraded to the legislative buildings in Queen's Park, where they received Whitney's promise – appropriately guarded – that the government would either supply power itself or regulate that business in the public interest.

Beck's cause was further advanced by the revelation that the Electrical Development Company intended to charge Canadians a much higher price than its American customers, even though the transmission costs in Canada were lower. He was nervous about Whitney's intentions, worried about the possibility of weak legislation. A seasoned political friend gave him some advice. "Why do you wait? Why take a chance? Why not draft your own bill and tell the cabinet what you want passed?" Beck did just that, with the help of the province's chief justice. Then he campaigned for press support, inviting reporters into his office, eloquently outlining his dream, and giving the newspapermen the kind of black-and-white story they liked – the People versus the Vested Interests.

Beck got exactly what he wanted. In May 1906, the government created the Hydro-Electric Power Commission of Ontario, known to succeeding generations simply as "the Hydro" or, later, "Hydro." Beck would be its chairman. Its power was astonishingly broad, but such was the strength of the public power movement that scarcely a voice was raised against it. The new commission would distribute power to the municipalities and it would also regulate the private companies. Hydro would not generate power itself but was given wide powers of expropriation.

The Electrical Development Company fought back on two fronts, in the Canadian newspapers and in British financial circles. In those days, much of the daily press was literally for sale. The EDC was able, through an advertising agency, to buy space in both the letters-to-the-editor columns and the editorials of some newspapers. At the same time the company tried to frighten the British from investing in the province. The strategy backfired by angering the premier, who told Nicholls that it had only injured the EDC's cause.

Beck now faced a second battle. On January 1, 1907, the ratepayers of the various municipalities would have to give their councils permission to enter into contracts with Hydro. An intense public relations battle took place, with Beck and his engineers campaigning across Ontario like evangelists, spreading the gospel of Hydro and depicting the private interests as greedy scoundrels.

Beck cleared the 1907 hurdle. At the municipal elections, twenty communities voted for the proposition. But they still had to approve a $2,750,000 bond issue to pay for the municipal network that would deliver the power. The fight was on again, reduced once more to a good versus evil struggle by Beck's propaganda. The villain was "the Electric Ring ... the Most Dangerous Ring in Canada." That meant the EDC.

The newspapers plunged into the battle. The Toronto *World,* which supported Beck, attacked both the Electrical Development Company and the rival *Globe.* "Both are public enemies," it cried. In fact, the *Globe* favoured public ownership but believed in fair play for the private interests. Yet the private interests themselves were hardly playing fair. The *Globe,* the *Mail,* the *News,* and the *Star* were all being paid advertising rates for letters, articles, and editorials supporting private enterprise. "A perfect deluge of letters" (Whitney's phrase) – some anonymous, others with fictitious names or such noms-de-plume as *Veritas* or *Citizen* – was appearing in newspapers in major centres in the province. All, apparently, were the work of a Toronto advertising agency with money to burn. The *World* was offered and turned down $350,000 to change its shrill policy. It was, in fact, losing so much advertising that it found itself in financial trouble and asked the government, vainly, for advertising help.

On January 1, 1908, the municipal electors again gave Beck

what he wanted – a solid vote in favour of the bond issue. Now Whitney found himself in a dilemma. Three of the country's most powerful capitalists controlled the EDC. If that company failed – and it too was in financial straits – Canada's credit abroad would be badly compromised. Yet the premier, facing a provincial election that year, could scarcely halt the growing pressure for public power. The best he could hope for was that one of his appointments, John S. Hendrie, minister without portfolio and a former mayor of Hamilton, might serve as a brake on Adam Beck's ambitions. Hendrie, a member of the three-man Hydro-Electric Power Commission, was sympathetic to the private power lobby.

But Beck's ambitions had already damaged the EDC; talk of expropriation had hurt its credit badly. Mackenzie stepped in with a dazzling series of mergers and realignments that placed it under the umbrella of his newly organized Toronto Power Company. Now the EDC, its transmission lines, and its contracts with Mackenzie's Street Railway Company and Pellatt's Electric Light Company were all part of the same package. Mackenzie assumed direct control, with his partners in subordinate positions.

Whitney easily won the summer election in 1908, and Beck was returned with a huge majority. But he remained obdurate in his near fanatical opposition to Mackenzie. When, in August, Canadian General Electric submitted the lowest tender to build the Hydro line, Beck tried to block the contract because Mackenzie's colleague, Nicholls, controlled the company. Whitney stepped in and persuaded the vengeful Hydro chairman to allow CGE to have two-thirds of the project.

The first sod for the transmission line was turned on November 18 at Exhibition Park in Toronto. Whitney was on hand to make a conciliatory speech. "We have undertaken to safeguard the interests of the people," he said, "but only with the assurance that it will not be at the expense of private rights."

In actual fact, the premier was growing more and more disenchanted with the private power lobby. Mackenzie brought suit to try to prevent Toronto and London from taking power from Hydro. The Whitney government immediately introduced an act placing these contracts beyond the jurisdiction of the courts. That touched off a vicious press campaign in Montreal, London, and New York, designed to convince the financial world that the "socialist legislation" would damage Canada's credit in the money markets. The British press was especially vitriolic. The *Financial Times* of London wrote of "an outrageous parody of lawmaking," and the *Monetary Times* referred to "bullying legislation which takes away the first right of the British subject."

All such comments were published in a widely distributed pamphlet whose purpose was to force the federal government to disallow the act. A petition for disallowance was heard in October, but Hydro went forward with construction anyway, convinced, correctly, that Ottawa would throw out the case. Whitney had never had any doubts about that. The London manager of the Bank of Montreal had already told him privately that Canada's credit was in no way harmed. The press campaign had not only nettled the premier but, by its intemperance, had also turned many London investors against the private power interests. The battle between Beck and Mackenzie, two strong and stubborn personalities, was over, at least for the moment.

When the power was switched on in Berlin on the night of October 11, 1910, the premier referred to the long and bitter struggle. "We have been attacked, vilified, and slandered," he said. "Large sums of money have been expended in creating and fomenting prejudice and ill feeling against us. And still larger sums have been expended in conducting a campaign against us outside of Ontario. Our opponents left nothing undone that could be done, and men of influences, from the humblest man in the land up to the Prime Minister of Great

Britain, were approached in the endeavour to destroy our power legislation and render it impossible for the wonderful new force to be used and enjoyed by the people.... We, Adam Beck's colleagues, can never forget his steady confidence in the result and the bravery and pluck with which he stood up against all attacks."

This was Adam Beck's triumphal moment. The movement for public power had been launched in Waterloo and Berlin by Snider and Detweiler. But Snider, who had broken with Beck because of his leak of information to the press, was no longer in the picture. It had been Beck's day, and his alone. The streets, garlanded with foliage, bunting, and strings of coloured lights, were lined with people standing three deep as the representatives of thirty-four participating municipalities were driven through town. Some ten thousand crowded into the community's largest skating rink, festooned with banners proclaiming "Power at Cost" and "We Are Proud of Our Boy, Adam Beck." At the end of the proceedings, after everyone had had his say and before the festive banquet – cooked for the first time with electricity – the premier took centre stage. There stood a young woman, Hilda Rumpel, dressed in red, white, and blue and wearing a crown of bulbs, which in a moment would glow with electric light.

Whitney had already called for three cheers for Beck. Now, with his voice breaking slightly, he said, "I have been asked to press the button which will turn on the people's power. I am proud and happy to do it in the name of the province. But with your approval I propose to use a true and tried influence, one in which we all have learned to have unbounded confidence."

In the semi-darkness he turned and beckoned to the Hydro chairman, standing in the background. "Give me your hand," he said. As the crowd cheered he grasped Beck's hand and used it to press the button. The darkened rink was instantly enveloped in a blaze of light, while Hilda Rumpel's crown sparkled.

"Congratulations," the premier said to Beck, "and thanks from Ontario."

Beck had already spoken. "The work is not finished," he told the crowd. "It has only begun. Let us gird our loins and earnestly, honestly, and indomitably go on, and on, and on until this great public service serves all our people and serves them well. That is our ambition, that is our aim, that is our ideal."

3

Our dreams exceeding by thy bounteous spray;
With power unrivalled thy proud flood shall speed
The New World's progress towards Time's perfect day.

Thus did Benjamin Copeland in his 1904 poem, *Niagara*, capture the euphoria that greeted the growing use of Niagara's power. Two years later, H.G. Wells visited Niagara and wrote enthusiastically about the "noble masses of machinery," so clean, so noiseless, so irresistible, heralding, in Wells's view, a world in which the greatness of life was not to be found "in such accidents as mountains or the sea" but in a world that human beings would create, as they had created electric power. To Wells it did not matter if the Falls ceased to flow, provided its waters "should rise again in light and power ... in cities and in palaces and the emancipated souls and hearts of men."

Wells was captivated by the wave of optimism engendered by the great age of heroic invention at the turn of the century. But with the Canadians also preparing to tap the cataract for hydro power, a few voices began to express their opposition to the kind of future that the novelist was envisaging. The very future of the Falls as one of nature's great showplaces was in doubt. What if unlimited water should be diverted from the two cascades by power-hungry industrialists and power-hungry governments? Lord Kelvin himself had said he hoped the Falls would have vanished by his grandchildren's time.

These ominous forebodings touched off the Second Battle of Niagara, as it was called, to save the Falls. A series of articles in newspapers and leading periodicals began to harp on the uncertain future of the great cataract. Niagara, "saved from the hand of the catch-penny sharper ... has fallen into the hands of the catch-million capitalist," a writer in *Outlook* declared. *World's Work* identified the catch-million capitalists as those early twentieth-century whipping boys, the Vanderbilts, the Morgans, and the Astors, fair game in those trust-busting days for any muckraking journalist. These were the men behind the Niagara Falls Power Company, the New York Central Railroad, and General Electric.

The key figure in the new preservation campaign was J. Horace McFarland, president of the American Civic Association and editor of the "Beautiful America" column in the influential *Ladies' Home Journal*. "Every American – nay, every world citizen – should see Niagara many times, for the welfare of his soul and the perpetual memory of a great work of God," McFarland wrote. And yet, he warned, the Falls was about to be "sacrificed unnecessarily for the gain of a few."

"Shall we make a coal pile of Niagara?" he asked his readers in 1905. He urged them to write letters to the White House and to Rideau Hall, the governor general's residence in Ottawa. Thousands responded. Clubs and newspapers took up the cry. Under McFarland's prodding, Theodore Roosevelt mentioned the subject in his annual message to Congress. When McFarland asked the president for suggestions to prevent the destruction of Niagara, Roosevelt gave him a forthright reply: "Get as many intelligent citizens as you possibly can to write urgently upon this subject to their representatives and Senators in Congress. That will help mightily."

Tens of thousands of letters swamped Congress and had

their effect. In March 1906, the International Waterways Commission, which had been studying the problem, advised that no more than thirty-six thousand cubic feet of water a second be diverted from the Canadian falls and half that amount from the American side. Any greater diversion, the report declared, would be dangerous. "It would be a sacrilege to destroy the scenic effect of the Falls."

Roosevelt sent the report to Congress, whereupon the private power companies besieged Washington with attorneys, engineers, promoters, and lobbyists issuing contradictory statements designed to kill its impact. But the House Committee on Rivers and Harbors, chaired by Theodore Burton of Ohio, resisted the pressure and put the recommendations into a law "for the preservation of Niagara Falls."

In 1909, a new international treaty established the amount of water that could be diverted from the Falls. The United States would be allowed a total diversion of twenty thousand cubic feet a second, slightly more than the Waterways Commission had recommended three years before. The Canadian diversion would be held at thirty-six thousand. For the time being, at least, the Falls was safe.

A commission appointed by the United States war department had recommended that the entire gorge area for three hundred feet back from the cliff be purchased as a national park and that the buildings along the crest be removed, together with the Schoellkopf power station at the foot as soon as it became obsolete. Few of these recommendations were followed. The proposed park was considered too expensive; the factories kept working and were not removed until 1945, and the power station operated until 1961 and was not torn down until 1965.

The preservation movement had concentrated on the beauty of the cataract and its surroundings, successfully preventing the bulk of the water from being looted for private gain. But the humanists behind the Second Battle of Niagara could do nothing to suppress the carnival atmosphere that had been a part of the Niagara environment for the best part of a century; nor is there any evidence that they wished to do so. It was neither feasible nor necessary to deny tourists who were lured to the Falls the attractions they expected. Indeed, both communities had every intention of using the Falls as a backdrop for fun and frolic.

In 1910, the Twin Power Cities of the World, as the press dubbed them, mounted a successful carnival built around the magic of electricity. But electricity was already losing its novelty, and electrical exhibits had less and less drawing power. After all, every town had become a "White City." When the two communities tried to repeat the spectacle the following year it was a near flop. The program promised a gigantic automobile parade, with five hundred illuminated cars – "three miles of electrical enchantment." But the auto, too, was becoming commonplace. Henry Ford had just introduced his Model T. The parade fizzled out. "Prince Nelson the Great" was supposed to walk a tightrope across the gorge, his costume emblazoned with 180 miniature lights. But the prince got cold feet and failed to turn up.

A feeling of *déjà vu* hung over the affair like a pall. The crowds were large – as many as one hundred thousand persons – but they didn't spend much money. The hotels and restaurants failed to prosper. The organizing committee had made the colossal error of hiring a non-union press to print the official program. Labour was beginning to feel its strength, and this gaffe kept many away.

Strapped for funds, the organizers had gambled a good chunk of their budget on one event. It cost at least one thousand dollars in gold (some reported five thousand), but when it was over no one begrudged that. For this was the only spectacle that looked to the future and not to the past. Without the presence of Lincoln Beachey, the carnival would have been more than a disappointment. He helped save it from disaster.

The automobile may have lost its excitement, but the airplane had not, and Beachey was a pilot who knew no fear. The Niagara Falls *Gazette* called him "one of the nerviest aviators in the country." "He will fly anywhere and over any obstacle and is known as the man who will take more chances than any aviator in the world," the *Cataract Journal* told its readers.

Variously depicted as "fearless," "intrepid," "dauntless," and "daring," the twenty-four-year-old Beachey, clean-shaven and debonair, had in less than a year become the best-known stunt flyer in North America, if not the world. Wearing an ordinary business suit with white shirt and tie rather than a pilot's leather jacket and helmet, he barnstormed about the country in his specially reinforced Curtiss pusher biplane. Beachey was already developing his vertical "death dive," which saw him plummet straight down from the clouds, pulling out only at the last possible moment. He came so close to the ground on these dives that he was once able to scoop up a handkerchief with the tip of one wing. On another occasion at Dallas, Texas, he made a vertical dive onto a race track, flew straight under the starting wire, and pulled out without touching either the wire or the ground.

Beachey would collect his gold only if he piloted his flimsy craft immediately above the Horseshoe Falls and then flew downriver directly *under* the Upper Steel Arch Bridge. The closest bridge to the Falls, its arch supported a roadway of 840 feet, only 150 feet above the river. To meet the conditions, Beachey would have to zoom down from the crest of the Horseshoe almost to the water's surface, fly under the bridge between its two massive pillars, and then climb again to a safe height. He agreed at once.

Beachey flew in from Buffalo on the afternoon of June 26, making the fourteen-mile trip in sixteen minutes. Thousands cheered as the plane landed on the American side, and the following day hundreds paid a fee to examine it. A little after five that afternoon, as bells rang and whistles blew, Beachey took his plane into the air in the teeth of a high wind and rose several thousand feet above the Falls while crowds on both shores cheered.

He swept down the gorge, circled round, and made a second pass at the Falls to lose altitude. He soared up the river above the Falls, circled back toward the crest, his speedometer clocking eighty miles an hour, then suddenly dove at a forty-five-degree angle directly into the wall of mist rising high above the river.

Blinded by the spray, he had to shut his eyes for a moment. The drop was so swift that the engine stalled briefly, then coughed into action. As he pulled out of the dive, he spotted an open space between the two bridge supports and swept through, just twenty feet above the furious water, on what he later called "one big, beautiful joyride."

A second bridge, the cantilever structure built by the Michigan Central Railroad in 1883, now barred his way. But Beachey easily lifted his craft over it, circled about, and raced back over the Falls again before landing to the cheers of the crowd. He was, that day at least, "the most talked of aviator in the world." In banner headlines, the *Cataract Journal* announced that he had saved the carnival.

Beachey moved on to greater triumphs. In 1913 he added to his reputation by looping the loop over San Diego Bay. He challenged Barney Oldfield, the great automobile racer, to a contest, and won. In the Palace of Machinery at the Panama-Pacific International Exposition in San Francisco, he made the first indoor flight in history. In that city on March 14, 1915, fifty thousand people watched him take off from the polo grounds in a light monoplane built especially for him. Down he came in a terrifying vertical plunge from 3,500 feet. But he had misjudged the speed of his descent. As he tried to pull out of the dive at 500 feet, both wings broke off the plane and it crashed into San Francisco Bay. "The Silent Reaper of Souls and I shook hands," he had written of an earlier flight. "Today the old fellow and I are pals." But the friendship ended on that sunny afternoon. Before his body could be hauled from the wreckage of his plane, Lincoln Beachey had drowned.

4

By February of 1912, when he won his second life-saving medal, William "Red" Hill had established himself as a local hero and also as something of an eccentric. He was obsessed by the Niagara River – drawn to it as if by an irresistible force. It haunted his dreams, controlled his waking hours, held him captive. To Hill, the Niagara was an old friend; he knew its every current, eddy, and whirlpool; he knew it in every season – knew it and loved it.

It had been that way since his father, Layfield Hill, impatient with anyone who feared the river, had swum out into the current with five-year-old Red on his back to give him a taste of Niagara, the temptress. The following day he pushed his son, fully clothed, into fifteen feet of water. "Sink or swim!" Layfield cried. Young Red swam.

He was born with a caul – a membrane covering the fetus – and so, following a mystic tradition, was believed to have second sight. His wife, Beatrice, claimed that he often awoke suddenly in the dark to announce that he would find a body in the morning. More often than not he was right, as he was right about the weather, which he could predict with uncanny accuracy, simply, he said, by listening to the roar of the Falls.

It was once believed that a child born with a caul bore a charmed life. Certainly Red Hill's life seemed charmed. He took chances and survived. The river had no terrors for him, but then, it is also said that a person born with a caul is in no danger of drowning. Neither flood nor fire fazed him. At the age of nine, when his parents' home burst into flames, he rushed back barefoot into the inferno to rescue his two-year-old sister, Cora, who had been trapped inside. For that he was awarded his first life-saving medal.

He often skipped school to study the river. Once, after he had been absent a fortnight, the principal tackled his parents. What, he asked, has happened to young Red? Young Red, as it turned out, had spent each day from 8:30 in the morning until four in the afternoon tossing sticks and bits of driftwood over the Falls and into the rapids. All his life, Hill continued the practice, throwing in logs, tin cans, lifebelts – anything that would float – until he could guess the exact spot at which an object would end its journey. As with logs, so with a corpse. Over his long life, Hill would pull 177 bodies from the waters of the Niagara. He got a fee for every one.

No day went by that did not see Red Hill patrolling the river. Beatrice soon gave up trying to keep his evening meal warm for him. He was off at 8:30 a.m., gulping down a cup of coffee before heading for the waterfront. Sometimes he would be away for two or three days, spending his nights in a sheltered nook known as the Cave. No more than ten feet square, it had been worn out of the cliff six hundred yards below the Falls. "There's nothing to worry about," he'd tell his wife when he returned. "The river can't do me any harm."

He had no steady work. He ran a taxi service for a time and also a souvenir store. He did odd jobs. He bootlegged whiskey from his back door. His real vocation was the river.

He achieved celebrity in 1910 after Bobby Leach, in a new barrel, again successfully tackled the Whirlpool Rapids. Hill swam out to haul Leach to shore and retrieve the barrel. When he returned, somebody bet him two dollars that he didn't have the courage to take the barrel through the lower rapids. "I'm your man," cried Red Hill, and, to Leach's fury, leaped into the barrel and rode all the way to Queenston unscathed.

Now, two years later, on a freezing February day in 1912, he was about to exchange local celebrity for wider fame. Two weeks earlier another great ice bridge had formed on the

Niagara, stretching for a thousand yards below the Falls. Red Hill, as usual, had erected his shack not far from two other shanties some distance out from the Canadian shore. From there he peddled coffee, sandwiches, and, of course, hard liquor.

It was bitterly cold. The thermometer stood at zero Fahrenheit, and the mist that usually pillared skyward had turned to sleet. No more than twenty-five people had braved the weather to remain on the ice when, at noon, Hill heard an ominous rumble beneath him. He knew at once that the ice bridge was breaking up.

Calling for everyone to follow, he raced for the *Maid of the Mist* landing on the Canadian shore. Most followed his example, leaping the widening gap of water and slush between the slow-moving mass and the bank. But four people failed to recognize the danger.

Hill called for men and ropes to help these stragglers – two teenagers from Cleveland, Burrel Hecock and his friend Ignatius Roth, and a young Toronto couple, Mr. and Mrs. Eldridge Stanton. The two boys, childhood friends, had arrived that morning and were frolicking on the ice when they encountered the Toronto couple. The Stantons lived in Rosedale, then a new subdivision on the northern edge of Toronto. Eldridge Stanton was well known in musical circles. He sang in the Schubert choir and had taken a leading role in a light opera, *Three Little Maids*, on the stage of the city's Royal Alexandra theatre. His attractive dark-haired wife, ten years his junior, was a camera enthusiast. The pair had often come to Niagara for sightseeing and to visit friends, and now, as Mrs. Stanton produced her camera, she offered to photograph the two Cleveland boys. The quartet quickly became friends and decided to stay together exploring the hills and valleys of the great frozen mass as they threaded their way back toward the concession shacks.

Suddenly, with a loud cracking sound, the ice bridge, anchored to both shores, shook itself free and began to move down the river. The four found themselves standing on a vast moving floe from which smaller chunks were breaking off. The two youths immediately rushed toward the Canadian shore while the Stantons headed in the opposite direction, only to find a dark channel twenty feet wide barring their way.

Hill dashed across the moving ice, leaping over fissures and rounding great hummocks, calling to the couple to make for the Canadian shore. Stanton grasped his young wife's hand and followed the riverman. But when they encountered another channel of slush lying off the Canadian shore, the Stantons panicked. Hill urged them on; the slush, he said, was thick enough to take their weight. But they turned back, and the two youths followed them.

The great floe on which all four were marooned was already passing beneath the Upper Steel Arch Bridge. They stood helplessly on the American side of their frozen platform, escape still cut off by the open channel. Firemen from American towns stood ready with rescue lines but could not reach them. Canadian firemen dropped ropes from the bridge, to no avail. Hill and others raced along the Canadian shore, clambering over hillocks and boulders, to keep pace with the moving ice.

As the floe passed the outflow of the Niagara Falls Power Company's tunnel, its back section broke off and ground to a halt on the American shore. Had the marooned quartet been standing at that end they could have been saved. Now their only hope was to try to return to the Canadian side.

The two youths rushed on ahead, with the Stantons stumbling along behind. Mrs. Stanton fell. "Oh, let me alone!" she said, "let me die now." Her husband tried to drag her to her feet, and Hecock, hearing his call for help, turned back. In doing so he sacrificed his life.

Roth kept going. The great floe was now some seven hundred yards downstream from the Upper Steel Arch Bridge. Hill threw the youth a rope. Roth seized it and, calling back to his companions to follow, plunged into the slush. Hill leaped from the bank into the water, grasped the youth, and dragged him, half unconscious, his clothes frozen solid, to safety. But the other boy and the man, with a hysterical woman on their hands, remained on the crumbling, drifting floe.

By this time the banks were lined with spectators. The Whirlpool Rapids were only half a mile downstream. The trio would have to escape before the ice plunged into that maelstrom. The block on which all three were standing broke into two pieces, leaving Hecock on one and the Toronto couple on the other.

On the Michigan Central Railroad bridge, members of a repair crew lowered a rope weighted with iron, while another workman fashioned a makeshift line from three coils of insulated telephone wire. Hecock grasped the dangling rope as he passed below it and plunged waist-deep into the water, battered by the ice as the men above tried to yank him free. When at last the lifeline tightened, they began to haul up the numbed Hecock, who, in turn, tried to climb upward, hand over hand. He was dangling forty feet above the water when his strength left him. His frozen hands slipped, and he tried to grip the rope with his teeth. But he could not hold on, and suddenly he was gone, swallowed by the ice-choked river as the crowd above groaned.

Stanton saw it all. His wife, on her knees, weeping uncontrollably, closed her eyes. Then, as the current moved the floe out into midstream, Stanton was able to seize the knotted telephone line dangling from the bridge. He was trying to tie it around his wife when, to his horror, it broke. A second lifeline was dropped, and Stanton tried again to save his wife; but the twenty-mile-an-hour current was too swift. The floe swept beyond the bridge before he could reach the line.

The spectacle of the two, clasped in each other's arms, then dropping to their knees as if in prayer, would remain with Red Hill all his life. An instant later the rapids overturned their icepan. Their bodies were never found.

Hill received a second life-saving medal from the Royal Canadian Humane Association for his efforts. And for the rest of time, the Niagara ice bridge was declared off limits to everyone, residents and visitors alike.

5

The chairman of the Hydro-Electric Power Commission of Ontario was a man obsessed with power – not only the power that the Falls could provide but also the power that he himself could wield. Adam Beck was an autocrat. He wanted no interference from politicians peering over his shoulder. Hydro was his child, and he wanted to run it in his own way, at arm's length from the Ontario government.

In one sense that was admirable. There would be no political patronage under Beck – no incompetent friends of the government bungling matters, as had happened in the federal government's Intercolonial Railway in the Maritime provinces. But there was another, darker side to Beck's personality. He was quite prepared to dissemble, and even to lie, in order to keep the government unaware of his ambitions for Hydro. He was miffed in 1915 when the new premier, William Howard Hearst, appointed an auditor to examine Hydro's books. The government had received no accurate financial information from Beck since 1909 and wanted some answers. Beck was even more miffed when the auditor came down hard on Hydro for spending four million dollars more than the new legislature had authorized. The auditor declared that there wasn't even a semblance of legislative control over Beck's commission and referred to his "seemingly defiant disobedience of the Act."

In this harsh condemnation shrewder politicians might have seen some hints of what was to come, but Adam Beck, MPP, was riding high with both press and public. His Hydro Circus, a horse-drawn caravan, was travelling to rural communities

308

trumpeting the advantages of electrical appliances and equipment. Beck himself often arrived in his Pierce Arrow automobile to address the crowds. A witty popular song, "Oh! What a Difference Since the Hydro Came," emphasized the enthusiasm with which the public greeted Beck's achievement. His white-knight stance as the saviour of the people from the greedy private interests had made him a folk hero to go with the real knighthood he was awarded in 1914.

With his haughty aristocratic features, he did not look like a man of the people. If he was obsessive about public power, it was the single-minded obsession of a fanatic. Beck was like a collector whose energies are channelled into an insatiable desire for rare porcelain or eighteenth-century watches. He couldn't let go. He wanted more, no matter what the cost, and more was never enough.

His empire was expanding at a furious rate. When Hydro began operation in 1910 it was delivering 2,500 horsepower to ten municipalities. At the outset of the Great War it had already expanded into a network of ninety-five municipalities, requiring 77,000 horsepower. By the end of 1916, with wartime demands increasing, Hydro was delivering 167,000 horsepower to 191 municipalities. The following year, with hundreds of newly constructed munitions factories all demanding power, Hydro was providing 330,000 horsepower.

Hydro had been designed as a middleman that would build and operate the transmission lines while buying its power from private concerns. That original concept had been sold to the municipalities, to the provincial government, and to the public. But Beck wanted more. He did not want to be dependent on others; he wanted to generate his own power.

The idea had been percolating since 1914, when he had approached the ailing premier, Whitney, to gain his support for a mammoth generating plant at Queenston. A year later he asked Whitney's successor, Hearst, to back the idea. It would cost $10 million, he said, to produce 100,000 horsepower, and take three and a half years to build. Beck apparently pulled the figure out of a hat – the estimates occupied a single sheet of paper. Later, they were revised. In January 1917 the cost was estimated at a little more than $24 million to produce 300,000 horsepower. That was the only estimate the government ever received. The enabling legislation placed before the ratepayers on the January 1916 municipal ballot carefully made no mention of costs or horsepower. It simply asked authorization "to develop, or acquire, through Hydro, whatever works may be required for the supply of electrical energy or power."

What Beck was planning was a huge project that would take its water from the mouth of the Welland River at its confluence with the Niagara at Chippawa, above the Falls, and convey it by a long canal to Queenston. The net fall would be 294 feet. With the efficiency of newly designed generators, Hydro at Queenston could develop two to three times as much power as the stations nearer the Falls were producing.

Beck, in the meantime, was casting covetous eyes at the Buffalo-owned Ontario Power Company, which took its power from the foot of the Falls, using no more than the original 170-foot drop. This company had been awarded the major share of the Canadian horsepower allotted under the treaty of 1909. Beck knew that Ontario Power was not using all the water that the international agreement allowed: four thousand cubic feet a second were going to waste. And so Beck "acquired" this potential power source in 1917 for $22 million. At about the same time he accused the Electrical Development Company of "stealing water" – exceeding its legal maximum – a charge that enraged Sir William Mackenzie, who, like Beck, had received a knighthood. Mackenzie wrote to the premier protesting Beck's "despicable calumny."

Beck's ambitions were stimulated by the wartime power crisis. As the demands of the munitions plants increased, he wrapped himself in the flag. He wanted the government to stop the sale of private power to the United States on the grounds that it was needed for the Canadian war effort. His intention was not entirely patriotic. Industry south of the border now paid more for Canadian power than Canadian industries did. By persuading the government to cut off that lucrative source of profit, Beck would weaken his rivals. But Hydro had just become an exporter itself, through its recent purchase of the Ontario Power Company, and Beck had no intention of revoking the contracts with U.S. industries it had inherited. This time, however, Beck didn't get his way. The United States was also at war and threatening to cut off exports of coal to Canada. Ottawa refused to place an embargo on power exports.

By 1917 Ontario was faced with a shortage of 70,000 horse-power, much of it brought on by Beck's own sales efforts, which had prompted householders to buy such things as electric irons and heaters. The Canadian government ordered all power interests to develop electricity to the maximum, regardless of their legal restrictions. With power blackouts now a regular inconvenience, Beck had no trouble getting legislative approval for his pet Queenston-Chippawa project. Nobody knew how long the war in Europe would drag on, but it was obvious that more electric power would be needed.

Now Beck's implacable rival, the dapper Sir William Mackenzie, struck back. He argued that Beck's plan to divert water from the Niagara River for the Queenston plant contravened an earlier agreement the EDC had made with the commissioners of Queen Victoria Park. Mackenzie's firm applied for an injunction to stop the project. It failed. Mackenzie tried to get the federal government to disallow the Ontario legislation. That failed, too. The defeated Mackenzie, strapped for cash, was finally prepared to sell out to Hydro.

A long and acrimonious series of negotiations followed, with Beck intransigent as always, refusing even to stay in the same room with Mackenzie's nominee, R.J. Fleming. W.R. Plewman reported that the premier thought both men were acting childishly "and would have taken pleasure in banging their heads together." The long-drawn-out arguments cost the tax-payers dearly and did not end until December 5, 1921, when Hydro bought out all of Mackenzie's interests for $32,734,000 – more than five million dollars above the price that Mackenzie had been prepared to accept in 1918.

During this time, Beck was determined to press on with his new project at any price, but he did not tell his political masters that costs were escalating. Nor, apparently, did they ask. As far as the premier was concerned, the job would be done for about $25 million, a figure that Beck continued to cling to in the face of all evidence to the contrary.

Eight thousand labourers were toiling night and day, blasting an eight-mile tunnel out of solid rock to carry the water from Chippawa to the cliffside at Queenston. Fourteen gigantic shovels were at work, five of them larger than any others in the world. Seventeen million cubic yards of earth and rock had to be moved – an amount five times greater than the volume of the great pyramid of Cheops. Four hundred and fifty thousand cubic yards of concrete had to be poured. Beck, it turned out, was building on a hitherto unprecedented scale, dwarfing the American plants across the river. This would be by far the largest hydroelectric plant in the world, and Ontario Hydro would be the world's largest power company.

For all of this turbulent period, Beck misled not only the government but also the other members of the commission. Expenditures were running wildly ahead of estimates, but Beck withheld that information. The big shovels were not operating under ideal conditions and could do no more than half the work advertised by their manufacturers. Wartime pressures had escalated wage rates. And the original estimates had been distorted by Beck and his staff, who were eager for official approval and didn't want to see the project aborted.

Time and again Beck had submitted estimates to the municipalities that he knew were unsound. Sometimes he had persuaded the provincial legislature to approve money for one purpose, then used it for another. He had issued cheques without the sanction or knowledge of the Treasury Board or even of his fellow commissioners, knowing that otherwise they would not be authorized. Beck had had no compunction about misleading the government in which he was a Cabinet minister. He had got approval of his huge project on the basis of a single sheet of paper estimating the cost at about $10 million, later raised to $24 million. The government had no inkling of the real bill until three years after the start of construction.

In 1919, a new political movement, the United Farmers of Ontario, swept into power under its leader, E.C. Drury. Beck himself was out of political office, swamped by the tidal wave. He had had considerable clout with Hearst; he had none with Drury, who after an investigation of Hydro accounts found that construction costs were far out of line. An audit revealed that the cost of the Niagara project would be at least $40 million. Within six months that was revised to $50 million and then to $65 million. Even this figure was low. When all the bills were in, the price had soared to $84 million.

Beck had exceeded his estimates in another way. Instead of producing the original 100,000 horsepower that he had forecast to Whitney in 1914, or the 300,000 horsepower agreed to in 1917, the new plant would produce 550,000 horsepower.

Beck tried to stall Drury off as he had successfully obstructed his predecessors. In October 1921, the premier and his cabinet met with the Hydro chairman to get some explanation of the soaring expenses. Beck promised he'd have it in a week. But two months went by with Beck pleading pressure of business. He finally replied with feeble excuses, blaming "conditions which could not have been foreseen" and "results which could not have been anticipated."

It was time for that old Canadian standby – a royal commission that would head off a politically embarrassing confrontation between the tough-minded Drury and the resolute Beck. Thus, when the big project finally opened with much fanfare on

313

December 29, 1921, "a pall seemed to hang overhead," in the words of W.R. Plewman, who was there.

The royal commission, under the chairmanship of W.R. Gregory, produced its report in March 1924, and it was devastating. It came down very hard on the Hydro chairman, who, it said bluntly, "has shown an absolute lack of frankness." He had recognized no obligation to keep the government informed about costs or expenditures. His estimates had been "inadequate or unsound" and it was clear that he knew it. He had often "been arbitrary and inconsiderate in his dealings with his colleagues and with the government."

"It seems inconceivable that the Commission should have regarded cost so lightly and that the financing of this great work could have been carried on by it in such a loose way," the report said. No government, it declared, "should accept with confidence estimates prepared by a promoter of a scheme." Beck had hoodwinked a successions of premiers, but the premiers themselves were also to blame. They had let Hydro become a law unto itself. The Ontario government, dazzled by Beck's charisma, had never kept in touch with the work through an independent representative. Beck got money "almost for the asking" not only from the government "but by diverting millions which it [Hydro] held in trust for other purposes."

The Gregory Commission could not, however, ignore the "inestimable" value to the province of the Queenston-Chippawa plant, no matter what the cost. Some other figures turned out to be wrong – but on the right side. The canal, designed to carry 15,000 cubic feet of water a second, was capable of 18,000, and perhaps more. Beck had planned to develop 500,000 horsepower, but the plant, which had an efficiency of 90 percent, was capable of developing 550,000. That indicated "a fineness of design seldom, if ever, attained in a work of this character. It is, in short, a magnificent piece of engineering."

That would serve as Beck's epitaph. By finagling and dissembling, by vague promises and outright lies, the bullheaded Hydro chairman had got his way. Would his dream have come true if the government had known early in the game what the final cost would be? Sir Adam Beck clearly didn't think so. He died in 1925, his name linked forever with the campaign for public power in Canada. When the Tennessee Valley Authority was brought into being in 1933, Ontario Hydro served as a model. Franklin Roosevelt, when he was governor of New York, had been a close student of Beck's project.

There were other monuments in addition to the one on University Avenue, Toronto. In 1950, Beck's enormous power-plant was renamed Sir Adam Beck Generating Station No. 1. Two more stations would follow, also carrying Beck's name. History may not have forgotten the autocrat's financial leger-demain, but the public has long since forgiven him his flaws. He got the job done, and that, in the long run, is all that seems to matter.

Chapter Ten

1

Red Hill came back from the Great War at the beginning of August, 1918, some said to die. A sniper with the 75th Battalion – the "Jolly 75th" as it was known – he had been wounded twice. Worse, his lungs had been permanently damaged in the abortive gas attack on March 1, 1917, a few weeks before the battle of Vimy Ridge. When the wind blew the Canadians' gas back into their own lines, causing fearful havoc, Hill was one of the victims. The army doctors finally sent him home to recuperate. "I just hope it's not too damp where you live," one told him, ignorant of Niagara's incessant spray. There were those who thought he would be dead before the year was out.

He was scarcely home before something happened to restore his spirits and spur his recovery. It was a call for help, and it won him his third life-saving medal.

On August 6, a huge steel sand scow, used for dredging the hydraulic canal on the American side of the river above the Falls, broke loose from its tugboat and drifted with increasing speed toward the crest of the Horseshoe. Two deckhands were aboard – Gustav Lofberg, a fifty-one-year-old unmarried Swedish seaman, and James A. Harris of Buffalo, a fifty-three-year-old father of five. As the scow hurtled down the rapids, the two men struggled to open the hatches. "We're going over! We're lost!" Harris cried. Fortunately, they managed to get the hatches open, water poured in, and the scow settled until it scraped the ledges of rock just above the brink of the cataract. There, as crowds gathered, it caught and teetered precariously. Bystanders rushed to telephones to call the fire departments of both towns and the life-saving station at Youngstown, New York.

It was crucial to get a line aboard, and the men on the scow knew it; they began tearing away timbers to build a crude windlass. Firemen sped to the shore with a small life-saving gun,

318

which sent a five-hundred-foot length of rope arching toward the marooned craft. It fell short. They tried again, but the second line also splashed into the water.

Within half an hour an army truck arrived from Youngstown with a larger gun, which was placed on the roof of the Toronto Power Company's generating plant below the bank, about 750 feet from the scow. This time the light line reached the scow and was caught by one of the men. A heavier rope was paid out, and then a breeches-buoy was winched across. As it sank into the water under its own weight, the two men struggled with their improvised windlass.

Then the buoy itself – a sling big enough to carry one man – got caught in the current about halfway to the scow and twisted around the rope until the line was hopelessly fouled. By then it was two o'clock in the morning. A call went out for a volunteer to untangle the lines. Red Hill shouldered his way through the crowd and stepped forward.

As the watchers on shore held their breath, Hill hauled himself out to the sling, hand over hand, in the glow of powerful searchlights. Hanging by his legs, he tried to untangle the lines, but it was too dark to see properly. He made his way back to the roof of the powerplant, where a large sign, illuminated by the lights, told the marooned men: "WAIT UNTIL DAYLIGHT."

At dawn, Hill ventured out again. All five power companies on both sides of the river had used their turbines to keep the water level as low as possible. Hill, floundering in the water on the sagging cable, was close enough to the scow to hear Lofberg, who had once survived a hurricane at sea, tell Harris, "It's out of our hands. Don't worry. We only got to die once."

At last, Hill managed to untangle the lines, and the buoy reached the scow. The men were hauled to shore one at a time in the basket. Harris went first. "You go ahead, Jim," said Lofberg. "I'll stay behind and man the ropes because I know how to handle them better than you." After he hauled himself to shore, Lofberg, who had never lost his nerve, asked for a plug of chewing tobacco and announced that he was going to go as far back on land as possible and lash himself to a tree. "Then I'll know I'm safe," he said. The scow resisted all efforts to dislodge it from the rocks and can be seen to this day, a battered hulk lashed by spray, not far from the old Toronto Power station.

Red Hill went back to his old ways, doing odd jobs, bootlegging, plucking corpses from the river for a small fee, and restlessly roaming the lip of the gorge, examining the currents and passing on the Hill tradition and his own knowledge of the river to his eldest son, William "Red," Jr. The boy promised he would devote his life to the river. "The river will keep you poor," the father told all his boys, "but in return it will give you a reward greater than money. I can't put it into words."

Drinking beer with old army buddies in the Canadian Corps Association headquarters, Red Hill would often dream up bizarre schemes for making money. At one point he planned a gigantic sweepstakes in which one hundred barrels of different colours would engage in a race over the cataract. None of these projects ever materialized.

He became known as the guardian of the Niagara. The press called him the Wizard of the River and the Master Hero of Niagara Falls, but he wanted only one title, "riverman," and he asked that they use it. His phone number, 717, became well known to police and firemen who got into the habit of calling it when a body had to be recovered or a stranded tourist rescued.

The Niagara was a cruel river. Its sharp rocks battered corpses and stripped them of their clothing. Hill once dragged a body to shore by its necktie – the only article of apparel left. Often the bodies had to be retrieved from difficult places: the bottom of the gorge at the Whirlpool was one. Hill would haul the remains to shore and lash the corpse to Dead Man's Tree, which had fallen halfway into the water. Then, with the body wrapped in burlap and tied to a pole, he'd carry it four hundred

At the turn of the century, this young woman found it easier to pose, not before the Falls, but before a painting of the great cataract.

Construction of the cofferdam for the generating station of the Electrical Development Company. (later the Toronto Power Company) in 1903.

Across the river, fifteen years earlier, the Americans built this huge discharge tunnel to get rid of the waste water used by the Niagara Falls Power Company.

ABOVE: The main stairway of the office building at the Adams powerplant could grace the rotunda of an Italian palazzo.
BELOW: Hacking out the wheel pit for the Adams powerplant, the first to be build at the Falls. The date: June 25, 1900.

The Upper Steel Arch Bridge, also known as the
Honeymoon Bridge, lies shattered on the ice jam that
caused its destruction in 1938. It was replaced by the
famous Rainbow Bridge.

The river as enemy: a rock slide sends the Schoellkopf power station (above) crashing into the gorge in 1956, two years after similar erosion had doomed most of Prospect Point, railings and all.

Dewatering the Falls: in a vain attempt to remove the rubble that hides so much of the American Falls, U.S. Army engineers dried up the cataract for five months in 1969. In the end, it was decided to let nature take its course.

ABOVE: Lois Gibbs, housewife turned activist, holds a lively press conference on the condemned school site of the old Love Canal.

BELOW: Young Roger Woodward, the only human being ever to go over the Falls protected by no more than a life jacket, is hauled aboard the *Maid of the Mist*, July 9, 1960. The experience changed his life.

feet up the wall of the gorge, an exertion that could take four hours.

In July 1920, Hill was hired by a fifty-eight-year-old barber from Bristol, Charles G. Stephens, to help him attempt to rival Annie Taylor and Bobby Leach by tumbling over the Horseshoe in a barrel. The "demon barber," as the press dubbed him, was no stranger to close calls. After a serious illness at the age of five, he had been given up for dead and was actually placed in a coffin. Before the lid was closed and the death certificate was signed, the doctor decided to make a final examination. He was more than a little taken aback when the small corpse suddenly looked up at him with his eyes very much alive. By the time he reached his teens, Stephens was robust enough to work for a time in Welsh coal mines.

Later he became a barber, but barbering was too dull for him. And so he proceeded to indulge in a series of stunts on the British music-hall circuit. Crack marksmen shot sugar cubes off his head; knife throwers split apples fastened to his neck. He made a performance of entering lions' cages, first to kiss one of the beasts, then to thrust his head into a lion's mouth, and finally to shave one of his customers in the cage while the animals looked on. Now, having successfully leaped off the Firth of Forth bridge, he decided to take on the Falls.

A mild-looking man, tall and slight, with a bushy moustache and greying hair, he ignored the pleas of his wife, Annie, and their eleven children to give up the scheme. He was in it for the money, he admitted. Once he had conquered the cataract he could take his barrel back to the music halls and show a motion picture of his feat. He had already hired a camera crew to produce the film.

Stephens's barrel weighed six hundred pounds and was built of two-inch-thick Russian oak held together by steel hoops. It was padded with cushions of duck feathers made by Hill's wife, Beatrice, and ballasted by an anvil. A harness would keep Stephens reasonably steady, and an oxygen tank and mask would keep him from suffocating.

There is some argument as to whether Hill tried to dissuade Stephens or encouraged him. Certainly he helped him launch the barrel. Bobby Leach was one who expressed serious doubts. He took one look at the contraption and announced that the Englishman would never survive the trip over the Falls. The barrel, he said, wasn't sturdy enough – an assessment backed up by Richard Carter, captain of the *Maid of the Mist*.

In order to circumvent the authorities, who were trying in a half-hearted way to prevent further barrel adventures, Stephens checked into a hotel in Hamilton under an assumed name. He spent the early morning reading his Bible, enjoyed a brief breakfast, and then set out for the Falls. He had written out two cables; the appropriate one would be sent to his wife when the adventure was over and included a message for his manager. The first read: "FEAT ACCOMPLISHED. TELL DAN," the other: "PROFESSOR STEPHENS LOST IN THE ATTEMPT."

At 8:30 on the morning of July 11, 1920, at Snyder's Point, three miles above the Falls, Stephens prepared to enter the barrel, which had been painted with zebra stripes for easy identification. He took off his jacket and his red plush vest with its two rows of medals – some won in the Great War, others given for feats of daring – and handed them to Hill with four hundred pounds sterling for safekeeping.

"Don't worry," he said. "I'll be back to get it in a short time."

"Good luck, Charlie," Hill said. "I'll be waiting down below for you with a doctor and an undertaker."

As the barrel was towed out into the current, apparently a hoop snapped off. In spite of this, Hill cut the barrel loose, then raced back down the river bank to see it tumble over the Falls and vanish into the foam. By this time the word was out, and crowds were streaming down to both banks to witness the barrel's recovery. They waited in vain. At noon all hopes had faded, for Stephens's three-hour supply of oxygen would have been used up by then. Suddenly a black object appeared in the foam and drifted toward shore. "There he is!" somebody shouted. But it was only a broken stave. During the rest of the afternoon more fragments were washed ashore. Obviously, the river had reduced the barrel to kindling.

All night long Hill and others searched for Stephens's body. They found only an arm, torn off at the shoulder, still attached to the safety harness. It was identified by a tattoo showing two hands clasped around a floral garland with the inscription *"Forget me not, Annie."* Stephens must have tied the ballasting anvil to his feet. When the bottom was torn out of the barrel by the force of the water, he had been wrenched from his harness and sucked into the maelstrom.

Instead of scaring off future thrill seekers, Stephens's tragedy seemed to stimulate them. Within a month authorities in both cities logged inquiries from nineteen people asking permission to ride a barrel over the Falls. No sensible civic father was going to give anybody permission to plunge over the Horseshoe in a barrel, or in anything else. On the other hand, the daredevils brought in business. The police made a show of banning any such performance, but the truth was that anybody who really wanted to pull it off could do so with only a modicum of secrecy.

Jean Lussier, a thirty-five-year-old salesman, circus stuntman, and racing-car driver from Springfield, Massachusetts, had no trouble evading the authorities when he decided to hurl himself over the brink in a rubber ball of his own invention. Eight feet in diameter, the ball consisted of a light steel framework covered with canvas and lined with thirty-two inner tubes inflated to a pressure of thirty-five pounds. A 150-pound weight would serve as ballast. After two Akron rubber companies had declined to build the contraption, Lussier eventually put it together himself in his garage.

At two in the afternoon of July 4, 1928 – the biggest tourist day of the year – Lussier, wearing a blue-and-white bathing suit, took up a seated position in the ball. He secured himself in a harness, taped a small aperture shut, and was towed from the American shore into the middle of the stream.

At 3:20 the big orange ball was cut loose. At 4:25 it plunged over the crest of the Horseshoe. As it went over, it bounced into the air like a child's toy, tearing away the ballast so that Lussier found himself dropping head first into the waters below.

As the ball bobbed down the river, Red Hill commandeered a rescue boat and strained at the oars to reach it before it was pummelled to destruction in the Whirlpool Rapids. Hill managed to tie a rope through one of the wire loops on the outer skin. Then he began an exhausting journey, fighting the current, toward the safety of the shore.

It wasn't easy. The ball weighed close to nine hundred pounds because water continued to leak into it. Even if Lussier were saved from the rapids, he might easily drown as the level rose inside his odd craft. Heavy and unwieldy, the ball swung back and forth, forcing Hill to seesaw his way toward the bank. When at last he reached it, the ball had to be ripped open with knives. Lussier, badly bruised and bloody from gashes suffered in his dramatic dive, was slightly stunned from the impact but alive. The plunge, he said, was "like a big ski jump." A vast mob surrounded him, cheering, laughing, and praising his pluck.

Like so many others, Lussier expected to get rich from his adventure. He didn't. He toured with his ball and for small fees displayed it at the Niagara Falls Museum, Thomas Barnett's original enterprise. As a sideline he cut small pieces from the inner tubes and sold them to tourists at fifty cents apiece. His profits did not end when the inner tubes that had gone over the Falls were all chopped up. As he later remarked, "I must have cut up and sold 450 ... when I'd run short I'd go over to the Falls garage and they'd give me any discarded tubes too badly patched for use."

Lussier became a fixture in Niagara Falls, New York, where he worked as a machinist, recounting his story to those who would listen and announcing, from time to time, new stunts. These included a projected plunge over the American Falls, something that had never been attempted because of the mountain of rocks at the base. It didn't come off. Lussier died in 1971, forty-three years after his feat.

In 1930, two years after Lussier's plunge, Red Hill tried his best to persuade another daredevil to abandon his plans to attempt the journey over the Falls in a one-ton barrel. It is hard to believe that George Stathakis was entirely sane. A forty-six-year-old Greek short-order cook and a self-styled mystic and philosopher, Stathakis needed money with which to launch a literary career. He had written several philosophical texts in his native tongue and even paid to have one, *The Mysterious Veil of Humanity through the Ages*, translated into English. In this rambling, incoherent tract, Stathakis claimed to have lived for a thousand years, to have visited the North Pole, and to have seen Niagara Falls long before it had receded to its current site.

Now he was planning a new book to be called *From the Bosom of Niagara*, which, he said, would form part of a trilogy tracing the story of mankind from ancient times into the distant future. Proceeds from the barrel stunt, he believed, would pay for the publication of these works -- "the dream of my life."

The heavy barrel, ten feet long and five feet in diameter, with steel bumpers at each end to help cushion the shock of impact, did not impress Red Hill. He tried to talk Stathakis out of the venture, but the Greek was not to be dissuaded. Supremely confident, he set off at 3:35 on the afternoon of July 5, accompanied by a 105-year-old turtle named Sonny Boy. Stathakis said the turtle would recount the story of this adventure if its master succumbed.

In the turbulence below the Falls, Hill and his son Red, Jr., waited and waited, long after the crowds had vanished from the shoreline. There was no sign of the barrel. Since Stathakis had enough oxygen for only three hours, Hill concluded by night-fall that he must be dead. In fact, the Greek had suffocated. His barrel was trapped for fourteen hours behind the curtain of water and did not come out until dawn of the following day.

Hill, after hauling the battered barrel to the shore, worked for several hours cutting through the scores of bolts that held the lid tight. So securely had the eccentric Stathakis locked himself inside that it was quite possible, if he were not already dead, he would have expired from a lack of air while his rescuers struggled to release him.

His corpse was strapped to a water-soaked mattress. Sonny Boy, however, was alive. Hill set up a tent on the lawn of the Lafayette Hotel on the Canadian side, from which he ran a taxi business. Here, for a fee, he displayed both the barrel and the turtle until a couple from Buffalo made off with Sonny Boy, apparently intending to hold it for ransom. Hill gave chase in one of his own vehicles, but the thieves escaped. The riverman then hired a detective who tracked down the reptile. Hill continued to display Sonny Boy for profit, but contrary to Stathakis's forecast, the turtle wasn't talking.

The following winter a different kind of disaster made international headlines. While daredevils were plunging over the cataract and testing their courage against the rapids, the river was continuing its slow work, nibbling away at the soft shales concealed beneath the harder platform of dolostone. The eroded shape of the Horseshoe Falls bore witness to this implacable attack.

On Saturday, January 10, 1931, the familiar even crest of the American Falls was destroyed as a huge chunk toppled into the gorge, creating a wedge-shaped indentation 150 feet deep and 130 feet wide, about three hundred feet from Luna Island. It was a spectacular event witnessed by only a few stray tourists. Gerald Cook and his wife were standing at Prospect Point at 5:35 that afternoon when they heard a furious rumbling they mistook for an earthquake. The ground around them shook so fiercely that their small son began to cry in terror. A few minutes later they saw the crest of the Falls seemingly move outward as large pieces of rock were hurled into the air. The dry shale layers above the river level, attacked by weather and internal seepage, had finally crumbled.

Arthur Baker, a local man, was at Prospect Point with a friend from Cleveland when they too heard the rumbling. They turned to face the Falls in time to see a section about one hundred feet deep crack off and fall into the gorge, creating a prodigious splash that rose fifty feet above the crest. A few seconds later another section gave way. Chunks of rock continued to fall that night and the following day. The last piece broke off at 2:30 Sunday afternoon.

The entire contour of the American Falls was altered, and the change in appearance was the greatest in living memory. The crash brought thousands of tons of rock down and piled them up below the cataract. Fears were roused that the rest of the cascade was threatened. The pile of broken boulders – some as big as houses – now reached halfway up the waterfall, obscuring a section of it and lessening its beauty. Rivulets of water coursed through this stone jungle, sending up a curtain of opaque white vapour that further shut off the view.

The attention of the world, naturally, was focused on the Falls. Many feared that the American Falls was "committing suicide," to use a newspaper phrase. On Sunday, Goat Island was jammed with spectators, some of whom had travelled a hundred miles to view the great gash that nature had created. The world's press arrived to speculate that the Falls itself, moving inexorably back toward the site of ancient Lake Tonawanda, would be diminished until it became merely a series of rapids. That, however, was centuries in the future.

That spring, Red Hill himself caught the fever that had gripped earlier daredevils. He had warned Stathakis that his barrel was unsafe, but now the riverman was determined to ride it through the Whirlpool Rapids and on to Queenston. He had performed the feat the previous year in a small steel barrel of his own design; in a burst of braggadocio, he announced he would make the trip again, this time in "the death barrel." It almost became his tomb.

Hill made the attempt on May 31, after alerting a motion-picture crew. Wearing a rugby football helmet and a life jacket, he climbed into the barrel at the *Maid of the Mist* landing and let the current take him through the rapids and into the Whirlpool. His cumbersome craft could not slip around the vortex as his small barrel had done the previous year. Instead, it was sucked into the centre and there, for the next two hours, it circled slowly. As water leaked into it, Hill grew panicky, and at last he thrust a distress signal – a small Union Jack – through one of the two air holes that had been drilled at one end. To Beatrice Hill, standing on the shore with her baby, Wesley, in her arms, the flag was the first indication that her husband was still alive. Her eldest son, Red, Jr., was beside her. That morning she had noticed that he was wearing his bathing suit under his street clothes.

"That barrel is jinxed," young Red had told her. "I'm not just going to hang around and let Dad die." Now it drifted within a hundred yards of the shore, and he heard his father's muffled voice cry out, "Get a boat and get me out of here before this thing sinks. It's filling with water."

But there was no boat available. Somebody borrowed a 250-foot rope from the fire hall, but all attempts to lasso the barrel failed. The craft was sinking deeper and deeper, and Hill's death now seemed only a matter of time; at most he had half an hour left before he would drown or suffocate.

Young Red was already tearing off his outer clothing, and as the babble of the crowd fell to a hush, he fastened the rope around his waist and plunged into the maelstrom. He fought the current for twenty minutes before the force of the waves hurled him against the barrel. Treading water, he managed to fasten

328

the rope to one of the hooks on the outside before swimming back to shore. At that a mighty roar went up. Beatrice Hill fainted. But the ordeal of Red, Sr., was not over. Twelve men hauling on the rope, struggling against the suction of the current, would have to get the barrel back to shore and open it with little more than ten minutes to spare.

Inch by inch they pulled the barrel to safety. Hill emerged bruised, but alive. "I'm damned glad to be out of there," he said. Then he turned to his son and shook his hand. "You have more guts than I have," he told him.

He was determined to continue the journey on to Queenston, but his friends talked him out of that – or thought they had. The following day he quietly returned to the river and completed the trip without mishap. It was his final stunt. The motion-picture cameramen who had promised to film the journey failed to show up, and so there was little profit in it for Hill. "I'm all washed up on this racket," he said. "I've run these rapids three times and all I've got to show for it is two barrels and some photographs. There's no money in it and I'm through.... I'm not giving any more free shows.... Never again will I fight the Niagara."

2

By the time Red Hill finished his stunt, the Richest Man in Canada had become a fixture at the Falls. Niagara thrives on superlatives, and so it seemed proper that the Richest Man in Canada should choose the Greatest Natural Wonder in America as his headquarters.

He was a sombre figure with a weathered face, looking older than his fifty-seven years. His had not been an easy life. He had struggled in poverty for the best part of half a century but was now wealthy beyond imagination. He could have indulged himself anywhere in the world and, indeed, owned several houses, including one in London. But in 1924 he had chosen to make Niagara Falls his main domicile. There he lived in baronial style and dispensed the largess that his new-found wealth made possible.

His name was Harry Oakes, and his saga, which ended with his murder in the Bahamas in 1943 by villains unknown, is the stuff from which melodramas are made. Fiction could not compare with the tale of the young medical student who, on graduating from Bowdoin College in Maine, announced, "I am going to find a gold mine and make my fortune." After more than fifteen years of unremitting and unrewarding toil, he did just that. In fact, Harry Oakes improved upon his prophecy. He found *two* gold mines, both fabulously rich.

He was the quintessential prospector: the man who treks from camp to camp and country to country whenever a gold strike beckons, undefeated by setbacks, ever optimistic that the end of the rainbow is to be found just beyond the horizon. As a young man he had scrapped his plans to become a doctor when he learned that medical men rarely made more than three thousand dollars a year. When in the winter of 1897-98 the news of the Klondike strike electrified the continent, Oakes headed north. He picked and panned in the Yukon valleys, found nothing, and in 1899 joined the next stampede, drifting in an old boat for seventeen hundred miles downriver to the golden sands of Nome, Alaska. Once again, he failed to fulfil his dream.

He moved on to other goldfields – to Manila in the Philippines, and Western Australia. Again he found nothing. He made a small fortune growing flax, of all things, in New Zealand, and then headed for California. He sought gold in Death Valley but found only rattlesnakes. Flat broke, he ended up in Swastika, a small mining camp not far from Kirkland Lake in Northern Ontario. And there, at last, he struck it rich.

In January 1912, working with three brothers, Tom, George, and Jack Tough, and swathed in five pairs of pants to keep out

330

the minus 52°F weather, Harry Oakes staked a series of claims that became the Tough Oakes Mine. Here was a treasure trove. The ore that came from the first shaft was almost fifty times richer than the average for Ontario.

That wasn't enough for Oakes. He trudged around the western shore of Kirkland Lake and there, in July of the same year, he staked the claims that became the famous Lake Shore Mine. Far richer than Tough Oakes, it was to become the second-largest gold mine in North American history after the Homestake in the Black Hills of South Dakota, the one that provided a fortune for William Randolph Hearst.

It took Harry Oakes more than five years of continuous struggle to raise enough capital to create a producing mine. Nobody would buy his shares or even take them instead of cash. The local grocer preferred to give him credit. Toronto's Bay Street, the mining centre of Canada, wasn't interested. Sir Henry Pellatt, the lord of Casa Loma, turned him down. To finance Lake Shore, Oakes was forced to sell his share of Tough Oakes for $200,000.

At last a group of Buffalo financiers showed interest. Oakes lost no time in making a deal. He hired a private railway car, brought them to Kirkland Lake, entertained them royally, and scribbled out an agreement on a sheet of brown wrapping paper. It gave them half a million shares of treasury stock at what was soon seen as a rock-bottom price. Original shares in Lake Shore went for 32.5 cents. Before Harry Oakes went to his grave, each was worth more than sixty dollars.

In 1922, the newly wealthy Oakes treated himself to a round-the-world cruise. On shipboard, he encountered a tall, blue-eyed Australian named Eunice McIntyre. She was twenty two; he was forty-eight. The contrast went beyond age. She was easy going, gentle, and innocent. He was three inches shorter, thickset, violent, and opinionated. They were married the next year.

He made enemies of some. Others thought him half mad, for

he had odd habits – whistling under his breath when people spoke to him or shuffling about in a little dance. He was also subject to sudden fits of temper. He fired every mine manager he ever had and on one occasion, so the story has it, got rid of seven employees in one day because his skis weren't put where he wanted them. But he fed his men well, even installing a greenhouse at Kirkland Lake so that they could have fresh vegetables. He built a skating rink for the children and gave away toboggans and books at the local school.

This was the man who, back in 1924, was planning a baronial mansion at Niagara Falls – a man rendered uncouth by years of grubbing in the clay, whose table manners were atrocious, who had forgotten how to use a knife and fork, and who often spat grape seeds across the table at formal dinners. He knew what he wanted. One day when he was walking down Bay Street in Toronto, he saw a Canadian Pacific poster showing the mountaintop dream castle of Ludwig, the "mad king" of Bavaria – the same castle that Disney later copied for his first theme park. "Something like that. That is what I want," said Harry Oakes, and something like that was what he eventually got.

He was anxious to get out of Northern Ontario to escape the con men who were constantly buttonholing him, demanding that he invest in their schemes. He needed a retreat in which to hide. He chose Niagara Falls, Canada, partly because of his successful connection with neighbouring Buffalo and also because he saw Niagara as the gateway to his adopted country. The park along the river appealed to him, and he revelled in a dream in which the entire area would be cleansed of its factories and transformed into one gigantic piece of parkland.

In 1924, after his wife had given birth to their first child, Nancy, he searched the community and settled upon the home of Paul Schoellkopf, president of the Niagara Falls Power Company across the river, whose grandfather, the Buffalo tanner, had founded the family fortune by his purchase of the Porter hydraulic canal. Oakes paid half a million dollars for the property.

The Schoellkopf mansion was not baronial enough for Harry Oakes, in spite of the legend that some of the panelling had come from the rooms that Cardinal Wolsey once occupied at Hampton Court. He had the place remodelled in Tudor style, a job that took four years. In its refurbished form the house contained thirty-five rooms, seventeen bathrooms, and air-conditioning – an almost unheard-of luxury in those days. The grounds held a swimming pool and a five-hole golf course. In the best English tradition, the one-time prospector named it Oak Hall.

By the time the family moved in – the same year that saw Jean Lussier take his rubber ball over the Falls – Harry Oakes had become an influential figure in Niagara. The city benefited from his generosity. He bought a sixteen-acre farm and turned it into the Oakes Park Athletic Field. During the Depression, which hurt him not a bit, he provided jobs for the unemployed by restoring the original portage road from Lake Ontario to its former site; it became Oakes Drive. When the second Clifton House burned down in 1932, he bought the land to keep it out of the hands of developers. Then he bought the Lafayette, on whose lawn Red Hill had pitched his souvenir tent. He gave both properties to the Niagara Parks Commission, which simplified its title in 1927 and now controlled both Queen Victoria Park and others in the region. In return the commission gave him two small lots on Clifton Hill, the road that ran down from the ridge of the same name. Two hotels – the Falls View and the Park – stand on those lots and are still in the family. In 1934, Harry Oakes was named the ninth member of the commission. The Lafayette and Clifton properties, saved from development, became the Oakes Garden Theatre.

He was a man used to getting his own way. Once, playing a

round of golf on his private course, Oakes lost his temper because he couldn't chip out of one of the bunkers. He called in a bulldozer and razed the offending sand pit. On another occasion he became irritated by the smoke pouring out of the Ohio Brass Company's factory not far from Oak Hall. He solved that by buying the building and shutting the plant down. The company moved elsewhere. The building, now part of the Marineland amusement complex, remains entirely smokeless.

He had no time for panhandlers of any variety, but, with the Depression at its height, he gave a handout to anyone who wanted to work for it. When an unemployed man knocked on the door, he was handed a shovel and was paid two dollars for half a day's labour, a fair wage in those hard times. Oakes insisted that all payments be made in two-dollar bills, a curious fancy that created a problem for his foreman, not to mention the stores and banks in the area, which were soon faced with a banknote shortage.

Oakes had tried to escape the importuning visitors clamouring for his attention, but there was no refuge. Strange cars lined his driveway until he installed a gatehouse to keep them out. Fortune seekers scaled the walls of his estate in order to waylay him. The Richest Man in Canada had to sneak out of his own house by a back entrance in order to play golf. Each day a mountain of letters awaited him from all over the world, pleading for financial help.

He was, by most estimates, the greatest single contributor to the Canadian treasury, for he was paying as much as three million dollars a year in income taxes. It was his habit to make handsome donations to both the Liberal and the Conservative parties – 60 percent to the party in power in Ottawa, 40 percent to the Opposition. In 1930, with an election slated for the summer, the Liberals, who then formed the government, asked Oakes for extra money to fight the campaign. He obliged, it is said, on the promise that the new government would make him a senator. But the Liberals lost the election, and the

Conservative government of Richard Bedford Bennett got even by taxing him $25,000 for the lands and the parks he had contributed to Niagara.

Oakes was devastated when he learned of the tax. He clutched his throat, found it impossible to breathe, and took to his bed, wheezing, choking, and gasping. The doctors told him that he was suffering from a severe bronchial attack, but his biographer, Geoffrey Bocca, has called the bout of asphyxiation almost certainly psychosomatic. "The great man lay between his silk sheets, breathing with the greatest difficulty, surrounded by medicaments, guarded by nurses, and contemplated his future with the deepest gloom."

Born an American, Oakes had become a naturalized Canadian. But it was costing $17,500 in taxes every day of his life to live in his adopted country. As he saw it, he was getting nothing in return. The Bahamas beckoned; there, the income tax was unknown. Oakes was convinced that the Bennett government was singling him out for special treatment. He figured out that 25 percent of the gold taken from his mine was going to the public coffers in some form of taxation. He shuddered when his accountant told him that if he were to die suddenly his heirs would owe the government four million dollars.

Oakes didn't want to leave Canada. He told the government he was prepared to pay in kind rather than in cash – specifically, in Lake Shore mining stock. That, he was told, was impossible.

His biographer records a shattering telephone call from Minister of Mines Wes Gordon, in Ottawa. "I have to tell you, Harry," Gordon said, "the government is planning to increase taxes on some of the higher producing mines. You know what that means? Yours."

Once again, Oakes felt a throbbing in his bronchial tubes, but he held his temper. "Does that apply only to mines?"

"I am afraid it does."

"Damn it, man," Oakes burst out, "why don't you tax other

industries that are doing well, to the same degree? Why do you always pick on mines?"

"The government feels –"

"Damn the government! Tax the gold mines if you want. That's your privilege. But don't tax the gold mines alone. Increase the tax on the automobile factories. They are doing well. Wheat has gone up, so tax the farmers. Herrings have gone up. Tax the fishermen."

"That's not the way the government sees it, Harry."

Oakes's chronic bronchitis began acting up, as it always did when he was under stress. "All right," he said, between gasps, "have it your own way. But I am warning you now, Gordon, if you just pick on my mine and a few others that are really paying, I shall quit."

"What do you mean?" the startled minister asked.

"I mean I shall quit Canada."

"You wouldn't do that."

"Wouldn't I. Just wait and see."

He was as good as his word. The government tried to persuade him to change his mind. He wouldn't. He had encountered Harold Christie, a prominent Bahamian real-estate man, who proposed the Bahamas to him as a tax-free haven. Oakes now jumped at the suggestion.

In spite of his philanthropies at the Falls, he was not a popular figure. He had, indeed, been called the Most Hated Man in Canada as well as the richest. Now he became the target of a national fury for deserting the adopted country that had provided his fortune. The loss of his tax revenue would mean that ordinary families would have to share more of the burden.

Harry Oakes didn't care. In 1934 he went off to warmer climes and to an eventual violent death. During the war, Lady Oakes deeded Oak Hall to the government. In 1959 the Niagara Parks Commission bought the estate, which became its headquarters.

3

On the afternoon of January 25, 1938, Mrs. Jack Cowie heard a sharp report, like a thunderclap, followed by a rumbling sound that caused her small house to tremble. It sat on the river bank close to the *Maid of the Mist* landing on the Canadian side downstream from the cataract. Mrs. Cowie's husband was employed as a watchman, guarding the two little tourist boats drawn up for the winter not far away. Now, as she ran for the window, Mrs. Cowie saw that the house was in the path of a moving wall of ice.

As the house shook under the impact of the advancing floes, her year-old baby, Phyllis, started to giggle while five-year-old Herbie began to cry. She scooped up both children and ran from the building, slipping on the ice and gashing an arm in her haste. Herbie's pet spaniel, Laddie, romped about barking, thinking it all part of a game. But as Mrs. Cowie realized, it was deadly serious.

Jack Cowie ran up, dashed into the house, and doused the coal fire in the stove. Sloshing through ankle-deep water, he rescued the family's canary before the coal gas forced him out. Then, with the help of a fishing rod, he pulled their bedraggled cat from under the floor of the house. It was later revived with hot water bottles.

The Cowies' house was a ruin. The ice had pushed it fifty feet up the bank and deposited it in the middle of a roadway. Cowie went back to try to salvage a few items and was almost killed when the building toppled over on its side. He escaped through a window and maintained a vigil all night in a cave, while his wife and children moved in with friends.

The Cowies were minor victims in the worst ice jam in thirty years, and the most costly in history. Shorelines vanished under the irresistible advance of the ice. Both *Maid of the Mist* tourist craft were damaged. Fishermen's shacks, summer cottages, and boat houses were ripped apart. Docks were torn to pieces. As the ice climbed higher and higher, the piles of broken rock, known as talus, below the American Falls were smothered by a mountain of ice.

This gargantuan ice jam, which stretched downriver to within a few hundred yards of the Whirlpool Rapids Bridge, threatened to wreck the old Ontario Power Company generating station near the foot of the Falls. The ice climbed seventy-five feet up the bank, almost smothering the building, squeezing in through windows and doorways, clogging the elevator shaft, and covering the huge generators. Soon, all that could be seen of the building was its roof line.

But the worst threat of all was to the Upper Steel Arch Bridge, also known as the Falls View Bridge, which the press was now calling the Honeymoon Bridge. As the Cowie family struggled with their own problems, maintenance crews were working until midnight vainly trying to remove some of the mounting ice from the bridge's abutments. At four o'clock on the morning of the twenty-sixth, they were called back to work, but by seven-thirty they were forced to abandon their task and flee for their lives across the giant ice hummocks to the Prospect Point elevator on the American side.

Kurt Blommstern, the maintenance supervisor, barely made it. One of his colleagues sank through the ice to his waist but was pulled to safety. Soon the elevator itself was jammed with ice, and workmen were forced to reach the bridge abutments by a series of rope ladders dropped over the cliffside.

That morning, Red Hill called the Niagara Falls *Gazette* in New York to announce that there was no hope for the bridge; it was sure to collapse. Shortly after noon, two of the reinforcing girders were torn from the upriver side. Watchers on the shore could hear the rivets snapping as the steel gave way. The east end of the bridge began to settle. A bulge appeared in the floor. Cross-members at the base of the eastern tower were twisted out of shape. The Niagara Falls Power Company opened the intake to the old Edward Dean Adams powerplant on the American side of the river above the Falls. The water forced into the power tunnel gushed out, dislodging some of the ice near the bridge and easing the pressure on both abutments.

In spite of optimistic pronouncements from the International Railway Company, which owned the bridge, most people now believed the structure was doomed. That night a crew of men stationed on the bridge dangled a series of huge twelve-by-twelve timbers, each twenty feet long, over the side of the bridge to workmen below in an attempt to strengthen the downriver side. One employee stood at the bridge entrance, his eyes focused on a disturbing crack, an inch and a half wide, in the floor of the bridge. His orders were to turn a floodlight on the work force if the crack should widen, giving the men time to escape.

At four the following morning all bridge traffic was halted. At 11:30 a.m., the bridge company called its men off the job. By this time it was obvious that nothing could be done to save the bridge. The upright support was off the upstream abutment by seven inches; a second rupture had also occurred in the upper structure. Forrest Winch, the construction foreman for the engineering company, had been measuring the bridge's movement since nine o'clock. He stayed on the bridge and continued to check the movement with a pocket rule. All day rivets were being sheared off as the buckling continued on the downstream side. Between eleven and one o'clock, the bridge moved an additional seven-eighths of an inch.

After measuring the movement of the rivets on the upstream side, Winch decided to descend into the pit formed by the ice at the base of the bridge and check further. He and a fellow worker, Anthony Morocco, climbed down by way of the roof of Jack Kavanagh's souvenir store and walked a few feet downstream.

As the structure continued to creak and rivets snapped, Winch felt an overpowering sense of impending disaster. He'd been in the construction business since 1919 and suffered a series of mishaps that taught him to be cautious. Now his caution paid off. Winch heard a sharp *snap* close by – another rivet. A sixth sense made him stop and turn around. He glanced down the length of the bridge, looking for a break, and at that moment, the entire structure started to quiver.

"Look out! She's going!" he cried to Morocco. They dashed as fast as they could across the slippery ice and were thirty feet from the bridge when it collapsed.

At the same moment (it was just 4:15 p.m.), William Kirkpatrick, a senior student from the University of Buffalo, was adjusting his camera to photograph the bridge. He was walking a little way back from the American entrance to get a better view when he heard a loud crackle, as if from a campfire, and then a low rumble. He turned about and – too stunned to press the button – saw the whole bridge falling straight down onto the ice – the centre first, and then both ends, pulled loose from the banks. A cloud of snow and ice particles rose 130 feet into the air and then settled over the gorge. In no more than five seconds the entire bridge had collapsed. There it lay, joined together by a twisted mass of steel and cable, looking like a great iron serpent.

All but one of the professional news photographers who had rushed to Niagara to photograph the bridge when it broke apart missed that brief moment. On this bitterly cold day they had repaired to a nearby restaurant for a cup of coffee. But Frank O. Seed of Buffalo, more patient than the others, stayed behind and was rewarded with the only photograph of the collapsing structure.

Within ten minutes, ten thousand spectators had arrived to line the banks and gaze down at the shattered mass below. Scores of small boys climbed down the snow-covered hummocks and onto the ice, crawling over the twisted girders and sliding down the hump in the centre of the roadway.

Late that evening, a fifteen-year-old Niagara Falls, Ontario, boy, Malcolm Perry, slipping and sliding over the snow-covered wreckage, shinnied up the superstructure and removed the bronze plaque that for forty years had marked the international boundary. He had brought with him two wrenches, a chisel, and a hammer, and he worked for an hour to remove the fifty-pound souvenir. He put it into a bag, hoisted it onto his back, and with the ice crunching under his feet and the bag striking hard against his knees made it home in time for breakfast with a gift for his father.

Over the weekend, spurred on by network radio broadcasts in both countries, an estimated three hundred thousand people poured into the two cities by train, bus, and car to see the collapsed bridge. Thirty thousand automobiles lined the seven miles of road between Queenston and Niagara Falls, Ontario. Some seven thousand cars crossed the Whirlpool Rapids Bridge; eight thousand pedestrians walked across it to get a better view. The result was a gigantic traffic jam.

The International Railway Company hired a salvage expert, J.L. Baugh, of Rumford, Maine, to try to save some of the steel. Baugh sought out the best man to ensure the safety of the workers engaged in this perilous task. The best man was, of course, Red Hill. Through long experience, Hill could detect any subtle change in the contours of the ice on which the wreckage was lying and sound the alarm when the ice jam was about to break.

The wreckage presented a potential hazard. If it dropped through the rotting ice and into the river, it could become an underwater barrier that would cause even worse jams in future years. On February 5, Baugh attempted to divide it into sections. Two massive charges of dynamite were set off, shattering windows for hundreds of yards. The bridge was cut into four pieces, but Baugh could not salvage the steel. Not only was the work dangerous but the material was also in a dreadful tangle, and the problems involved in sorting it and dragging pieces up the slopes proved insuperable. Nonetheless, some homeowners salvaged enough of the railings to make fences for their lawns.

On February 6, Red Hill, who had been on twenty-four-hour duty for twelve days, was sent to hospital suffering from exhaustion and pneumonia. The wreckage lay on the ice for seventy-five days. Once again the prescient Hill, now recovered, accurately forecast what would happen. At six o'clock on the evening of April 11, he called the Canadian Niagara Falls *Review* to predict that what was left of the bridge would go to its doom by sundown the following day. At 7:30 the next morning, a section on the American side dropped through the ice with a monstrous splash. A crowd gathered at 8:20 to watch half of the centre disappear.

For more than twenty-four hours the rest of the wreckage lay on the ice. Then, as thousands of spectators gasped in wonder, what remained of the bridge began to move slowly down the river on a gigantic ice floe. The watchers followed it, running along the River Road to keep up with the moving floe. At 4:05, almost a mile beyond its original position, the wreck finally sank. With the ice breaking beneath them, the misshapen girders twisted about, making loud cracking noises and sending pieces of the wooden deck flying into the air. Then suddenly, except for a few floating fragments, the entire mass of wreckage was gone, entombed forever in the deepest part of the river.

The Niagara Parks Commission had been concerned about the bridge's condition for some time before its collapse and was already planning a new structure. The replacement – the Rainbow Bridge – was completed in record time and officially opened on November 1, 1941. Since gasoline was rationed in wartime, traffic was sparse, and horse-drawn vehicles replaced many of the cars and buses. By 1944 the gasoline shortage forced the closing of the bridge on Sundays. Not until the war ended did the real flood-tide of visitors pour in, and only then did the Rainbow Bridge come into its own.

4

Six months after the Rainbow Bridge opened, Red Hill died of a heart attack at the age of fifty-four. Wartime injuries and the hard life of a riverman had taken their toll. He had recovered 177 bodies from the Niagara River and won four Humane Association medals, the last for his efforts each winter to save the wild swans that were swept over the Horseshoe Falls and onto the ice below. Although the ice bridge was officially off limits, Hill went out in the dark of night in his white flannel nightshirt to rescue the stunned birds from the foot of the cataract. He released those that survived. He and his family ate the rest for dinner.

Red Hill never lost his love for the river; it was his life, his obsession. To him, profit was secondary. He was given a small fee for the bodies he brought out, and he dabbled in various enterprises – his taxi business and souvenir store, not to mention a small bootlegging operation. But the river was his real vocation. His wife, Beatrice, felt otherwise. "I hate the river," she said. "I'm afraid of it. I begged my children to stay away from it."

Her pleas had no effect, especially on Red, Jr., who had caught the fever long ago. Stocky, thick-shouldered, and powerful, he asked the press to call him "riverman," the designation in which his father had gloried. Young Red saw himself carrying on the family tradition. His younger brother Corky, who worked on the *Maid of the Mist*, was often by his side when he scaled ledges to retrieve corpses or rescue a marooned climber. It was his phone that rang now when the police needed help. By 1945, the list of bodies he had recovered from the Niagara numbered twenty-eight.

When his father was dying, young Red had vowed he would raise enough money to build him a proper memorial. True to that pledge, he announced in the summer of 1945 that he would duplicate his father's feat of riding a barrel down the gorge, through the Whirlpool, and on to Queenston. For sentiment's sake it would be the same battered barrel that his father had taken in 1931, when young Red had saved his life. This was the barrel in which George Stathakis had met his death; the Hills had had it on display ever since that time.

With the European war over, the big crowds were returning to the Falls. Hill was convinced that a collection taken up among the spectators who lined the bank would be substantial. It would, he hoped, pay for mobile life-saving equipment as well as a monument to his father.

The authorities were now making a serious attempt to stop stunting on the river. To thwart them, Hill had the barrel lowered down the bank at a secluded spot two hundred yards south of the Whirlpool Rapids early on the morning of July 8. A crowd of friends gathered round to mask his movements until he climbed into the red-painted barrel and set off on his perilous journey.

And perilous it was. The unwieldy cask had no sooner entered the Whirlpool Rapids than a gigantic wave caught it and hurled it thirty feet into the air. A crowd of ten thousand lining the bank gasped and groaned as the barrel struck rock after rock. To Hill, crouched in his harness, it seemed as though "a thousand brass bands were playing inside."

Now the barrel was catapulted into the heart of the Whirlpool. Circling slowly, it was pushed near the shore and then sucked back into the vortex as the crowd groaned again. Round and round it went until a favourable current thrust it again toward the shore. Two of Red's brothers, Corky and Major, leaped into a boat, reached the barrel, towed it to shore, and bailed it dry of water. Then the journey resumed.

Bobbing and weaving down the chute of the gorge – moving faster, indeed, than the cars on the road above, which were caught in a traffic jam – the barrel plunged northward to its destination. Standing on the bridge at Queenston, an immense crowd, far larger than the one that had greeted Hill's father, shouted "Here he comes!" as the crimson cask emerged from the white water. A power boat took the barrel in tow. It was so badly battered now that it could not be used again. When Red Hill and his family went out to the cemetery to place a wreath on the grave of Red, Sr., Beatrice Hill was not with them. The excitement over the rescue had caused her to collapse with a heart attack.

Like his father, young Red was no businessman. Unlike the shrewd Farini, he had made no attempt to sell tickets or organize the spectacle for maximum profit. And because the police had infiltrated the area, trying to forestall him, it was difficult for him to arrange a collection. And so, three years later, in September 1948, he determined to try again, using a cigar-shaped steel craft weighing about a thousand pounds. Once again he managed to elude the law and push off secretly from thick woods bordering the river. Once again the waves in the rapids hurled the barrel high in the air – an estimated forty feet this time. Once again the barrel kept circling and slowly filling with water in the heart of the vortex.

The barrel approached the shore two hours after it entered the Whirlpool, and again Hill's brothers towed it to shore. He was badly battered, for his safety harness had broken and he had been forced to tie himself down, an awkward feat with the barrel rolling and tossing in the waves.

The trip to Queenston took another three hours, and when Red emerged he announced that it had been ten times worse than the previous venture. Recording equipment that he was supposed to use to describe the trip broke loose and smashed into his left knee. He emerged, stunned and bruised, to announce, "I'm all through with stunts like this."

But, of course, he wasn't, and neither was his brother Major (his Christian name) Lloyd Hill, who seemed determined to outdo both his brother and his father. In 1949, Major attempted the same trip in another steel barrel, this one equipped with fins worked by levers. These, he said, would allow him to steer himself away from the Whirlpool. They didn't work. Badly bruised after two hours of circling in the maelstrom, he was finally rescued in the most spectacular fashion – hauled up sixty-five feet to the Spanish Aero Car (built in 1916) hanging on its cable above. As he lay in hospital, Major heard Red announce that he would complete the abortive journey to Queenston. That was too much for Major. He left his bed, walked out of the hospital, and made the journey himself.

It was clear that the two Hill brothers were trying to best each other, partly for the honour of the family but also because each saw himself as the legitimate successor to his father. The following July, the thirty-one-year-old Major, a tall and lanky war veteran, announced he would do something that none of the other members of the family had attempted. He would plunge over Niagara Falls in a barrel. Major attempted to surround the effort with an aura of scientific respectability. He wanted, he said, "to disprove certain theories about the Falls." He wanted to show that "there's no rocks in the centre about seventy-five to one hundred feet from the Falls." A more probable purpose was to underline the family's charmed life. "The Falls," said Major, "can't kill the Hills."

A vast crowd turned up on the hot afternoon of July 16, 1950. The press estimated half a million spectators, undoubtedly an exaggeration. They left disappointed. At 1:15, Hill started out from a point three miles above the cataract, but the current quickly drew his barrel under the weir of wire mesh that screened the flow of water to the intake of the Canadian Niagara Power Company. Hill's friends rushed to retrieve the barrel, intending to push it out into the racing stream, but power company employees convinced them the attempt would be dangerous because of large rocks in the current leading to the intake. They hauled Hill from the barrel and, to the disappointment of the throng, sent it plunging empty over the Falls.

Major Hill made another rapids trip that summer but did not attempt the Falls again.

Young Red was miffed. His brother had not invited him to take part in the adventure, and he felt the snub keenly. He also felt the family's honour had been besmirched by Major's failure to make good on his pledge. For years he himself had been toying with the idea of "taking the big drop." Now, the Hills' reputation at stake, he determined to try the stunt himself.

He announced he would go over the Falls in a rubber ball, as his friend Jean Lussier had done. The trouble was that he was broke. A month after his last rapids trip a bailiff had seized his goods and chattels to satisfy his bank, his landlord, and the welding service that had made the new barrel. Strapped for cash, he took his problem to a friend, a local tinsmith named Norman Candler, who devised an inexpensive contraption that Hill dubbed "the Thing." That was an apt name, for it resembled nothing that had ever entered the Niagara River before.

The Thing consisted of thirteen truck tire inner tubes bound together by webbing and encased in string fish net. "This barrel is not something made on the spur of the moment," Hill declared stoutly, but it certainly looked it. In fact, Hill's first reaction on seeing it was one of disappointment. "I thought it would be different," he said.

He went across the river to see Jean Lussier, who told him, "I wouldn't even go on the Chippawa Creek in a rig like that."

"Well," said Hill with a shrug, "that's as far as my money would go."

Its very flimsiness appealed to him, or so he said in what seems to have been a masterpiece of rationalization. "It will ride high and take the knock" was the way he put it.

He had reached the point where he could not back out no matter what anybody said. He had made a public announcement; he had devised a unique craft; and he had the family reputation to consider. One Hill had already backed out of the plunge. This one had no intention of doing so.

Indeed, the prospect of danger seemed to exhilarate him. "I've been watching the Falls for years and I know I can take care of them," he said. At times he seemed to be convincing himself that the journey over the brink would be easy. "There won't be any mistake. I'll ride high over the water. I'll get wet but nothing will happen to me."

His brother Wes, the youngest of the four Hill boys, tried to talk him out of the stunt. "It's too light," he told him. "You're heavier than it is. You're going to shoot out of it like a ball out of a cannon. Not only am I not going to help you, I'm going fishing."

Wes had planned to fish for four days with a group of friends, but he couldn't bear to abandon his brother. A day after he left, he drove all the night from the fishing camp back to Niagara. "Prepare yourself," he said to Beatrice Hill. "You're not going to see him any more."

A friend suggested that Red fake the trip by sending the Thing over empty. He could then climb into it secretly and make money by exhibiting the device and appearing on radio or on television. Red scorned the idea. "It's the Falls I want to go over," he said. "I want that more than the fame or the money."

His mother pleaded with him to wear a life jacket. He wouldn't hear of it. "That would take the kick out of the show," he told her. Yet he seemed in no hurry to make the hazardous trip. "I'll make her soon enough," he told a group of cronies who were urging him on. "Don't get excited."

The date was set for August 5. Red was sitting in the kitchen drinking a cup of coffee when Wes arrived. "I'll see you later," Red said as he headed for the Rapids Tavern. "No you won't," said Wes, glumly.

Hill left the tavern carrying a paper bag containing two

bottles of beer. "I'll see you about 2:30," he told a friend. "I may drop dead before you get back," the friend replied.

A pickup truck brought him to Usher's Creek above Chippawa, where the Thing was concealed behind a pile of brush. Hill took his ease in the truck, drinking beer, waiting for the odd craft to be towed to the mouth of the creek. Helpers pumped up the inner tubes and an air mattress in which he was to lie during the journey. An opening had been left at one end that Hill planned to close just before going over the crest of the Horseshoe. "Just when I feel that last dip before she goes over, I'll jam one of the tubes over the opening and hold it there," he announced. "Then I'll just curl up like a good little boy and ride 'er down."

Hill supervised the final details himself, planning to enter the craft only at the last moment. As he said, "This is my life. I'll feel safe so long as this is run my way." He climbed into a rowboat and smiled ruefully back to the knot of friends on the bank as he was rowed to the main channel. When he reached it, he entered the Thing.

Red took with him a variety of good-luck charms that well-wishers had pressed on him – four silver dollars, a four-leaf clover, a chip from the Blarney Stone, some holy medals, a wreath of heather, a tiny doll, and his father's good luck piece: a small plastic elephant. "I'm not superstitious or religious," he had said, "but when people give me things like this it shows they think a little something of me."

Two hundred thousand spectators – twice the usual number for an August weekend – blackened the banks on both sides of the river to watch Hill's awkward craft dancing, whirling, and shooting through the rapids. It hurtled directly to the crest of the Falls, dropped over in one piece, and vanished in the turbulence below.

A few moments later, two inner tubes that had apparently become detached floated to the surface. Then the rest of the tubes popped up in disarray, "looking like so many doughnuts on a string," in the words of one witness. Clearly the device had not held together but had been torn to pieces by the terrific force of the water. The crowd stood silent. There was no sign of Red Hill.

"Where is he?" his mother cried out. "Where is he? He's my oldest boy. I want him back! I want him back!" She collapsed sobbing on the dock.

Near where the parts of the Thing surfaced the inflated rubber mattress was found floating. Red's shoes, which he had removed after climbing into the craft, also turned up. But the broken body of the riverman didn't appear until the following day near the *Maid of the Mist* landing.

Thus the Hill legend began its tragic end. Corky would die a year later, killed by a falling rock while working on the new Ontario Hydro plant, Sir Adam Beck No. 2. Major Lloyd Hill would die an alcoholic, by his own hand in a jail cell. It was he, standing over the remains of the Thing, who uttered his brother's epitaph.

"Well," said Major, "he put on a great show."

Chapter Eleven

1

Whenever he gazed across the Niagara River at the manicured vistas on the Canadian side, Robert Moses was consumed with frustration. He had been appointed head of the New York State Power Authority on March 8, 1954, charged with the daunting task of building the largest hydroelectric plant in the western world at Lewiston. Directly opposite he could also see the newest Canadian plant, Sir Adam Beck No. 2, taking shape; indeed, by the time Moses got the job, Beck 2 was almost complete. But the American project had now been delayed four years by congressional wrangling. A venomous conflict between the proponents of public power and its antagonists, who attacked public ownership as "creeping socialism," had not yet been resolved.

Moses saw something else on the Canadian side that made him envious. The Niagara Parks Commission now had under its care the entire clifftop from the Falls to Queenston. The handsome drive along the river took tourists past green lawns, public parks, recreation trails, gardens, a golf course, heritage buildings, and historic groves – everything from an art library to a floral clock. By contrast, the dingy American side, apart from the original state reservation, had been left to haphazard exploitation by private interests. The results – a welter of grime-coated factories, railroad tracks, telephone poles, and coal piles – were, to Moses, simply appalling.

The main entrance to the city of Niagara Falls, New York, led along Buffalo Avenue, a dreary, two-mile wasteland of electro-chemical and electro-metallurgical factories – industries attracted to the community by the prospect of cheap Falls power. But now the atmosphere was acrid with fumes rising from the tall smokestacks. Motorists rolled up their car windows when passing through "the Witch's End of Fairyland," as one writer called it.

352

This was the legacy of the heroic age of invention – the reality behind the Utopia that the earlier entrepreneurs had contemplated. The dream city that was supposed to take shape above the cataract had become nightmarish. Pollution was now a fact of life for the citizens of Niagara Falls, the majority of whom worked for or were provided for by the same companies that polluted the atmosphere – Olin Corporation, Union Carbide, Du Pont, and Hooker Chemical. The city fathers cared less about the tourist industry than they did about the thousands of blue-collar jobs the factories provided.

Robert Moses' plan was to circumvent the gritty Buffalo Avenue entrance by building a parkway along the river. "I am a park man," he had said more than once. He had, indeed, invented the modern parkway – a ribbon of divided highway running between two sylvan strips of grass and trees. Besides his new post as chairman of the power authority, Moses was chairman of the State Council on Parks, chairman of the Triborough Bridge and Tunnel Authority, co-ordinator for federal-state highway construction in New York City, and a member of the Long Island State Power Commission. He had been a public servant for all of his career and was used to wearing several hats. At one period he had held ten appointive jobs simultaneously.

Moses had already built 416 miles of parkway in New York State. Now, in his mind's eye, he could contemplate an impressive stretch of parkland running along the American side of the Niagara gorge. He would construct it from the massive mountain of earth, clay, and stone that would be available when the power tunnels and reservoir were excavated. Matching its Canadian counterpart, the park and road would finally frame the Niagara picture, and there was no doubt that once the power project was under way, Moses would pull it off. He had absolute authority and knew how to use it. But even if he had wished to, he could not eliminate the cloud of smog that hung over the city, causing the eyes to smart and the lungs to choke. It could be seen clearly by any air traveller – a dark mantle of greyish brown, masking the land below.

There was far worse pollution beneath the soil, but few were aware of that in 1954 when Moses, the park man, was named energy czar. In the various chemical waste dumps scattered about the area – all within earshot of the great natural wonder – potential disaster lurked.

One of the biggest producers of chemical waste was the Hooker Chemical and Plastics Corporation, named for Eldon Huntington Hooker, who had started his business in a three-room farmhouse and was by 1906 producing caustic soda from salt brine. The waste from Hooker Chemical and other companies stemmed from the revolution in organic chemistry that had occurred in the late thirties and forties. This had its origin in discoveries made just before the turn of the century, when scientists found that carbon, which is the principal component of coal and oil, has remarkable properties that allow its molecules to form long, complex chains and rings. On the eve of the Second World War, chemical companies began to use carbon to create thousands of new medicines, solvents, plastics, pesticides, weed killers, dyes, fabrics, preservatives, transformer fluids, and other products. These ranged from polyester clothing to 2, 4-D and were greeted enthusiastically as the harbingers of a dazzling new post-war world. But in manufacturing the new chemicals, the industry also created waste products that were unknown in nature, many so durable they would remain in the environment for years without breaking down. Some were soluble in fats but not water. Thus they could accumulate in the fish and animals eaten by humans.

By the late forties, with the chemical revolution in full swing and consumers demanding more and more of the new plastics and fabrics, Hooker needed a suitable place to dump the fast-accumulating waste. To the Hooker company, William Love's old unfinished canal, dating back to the 1890s and used thereafter as a winter skating rink and a summer swimming hole, was the ideal dump site. Hooker first arranged with the owner, the local power company, to store wastes in the ditch. In 1947 Hooker bought the site.

The canal was a mile long, fifteen yards wide, and between ten and forty feet deep, built at right angles to the river. The company drained it, lined it with a casing of clay, and deposited in it twenty thousand tons of chemical waste contained in thousands of fifty-five-gallon metal barrels. A thin cap of clay and grass covered the whole. At the time this was considered an adequate safeguard. No one, apparently, foresaw that the barrels might rust or break, or that if they did their contents could leach through the clay with horrifying results. And few, if any, in those days realized there was a connection between the discarded chemicals and a wide range of health problems that included birth defects, liver damage, some chronic diseases, and cancer.

One man did raise a small warning flag. In 1948, a Boston scientist, Dr. Robert Mobbs, wrote in the *Journal of the American Medical Association* that one of the insecticide chemicals in the waste dump, lindane, was a possible cancer-causing agent. Years later, when a Hooker vice-president told a television audience that in the forties his company had no reason to be aware of hazardous wastes, Mobbs was outraged. "Did Hooker come looking for the evidence?" he asked. "Like hell they did. They ignored, minimized and suppressed the facts...." If *he* had known about lindane, he asked, why hadn't they?

That Hooker was concerned about future problems and wanted to purge itself of all liability became clear in 1953. By that time, the grass-covered canal was being using as a children's playground. In May, the Niagara Falls Board of Education, reeling from the pressures of the post-war baby boom, agreed to buy the land from Hooker as part of an urgent plan of school construction. Parents in the burgeoning LaSalle district, in which Love Canal was located (between 97th and 99th streets), were desperate for a school closer to their homes. When Hooker offered the property for a token dollar, the board jumped at it in the belief that the company was acting as a good corporate citizen.

It was no secret that the new 99th Street School would be built next to a dump of waste chemical products. That did not bother the nine members of the board, even though there was more than a hint that Hooker was trying to distance itself from any future controversy or liability involving the devil's brew of chemicals that lay under the grass. There were, indeed, no fewer than eighty-two different substances hidden beside the future school site, including several carcinogens such as benzene, chloroform, lindane, trichloroethylene, and – the most dangerous of all – two hundred tons of trichlorophenol wastes, containing 130 pounds of dioxin, the deadliest small molecule known to mankind.

None of these details, of course, were known to the school board members, nor in many cases had the deadly effects of the chemicals been targeted. That lay in the future. The warning inherent in the Hooker deal didn't bother anybody except the board's attorney. If the deal went through, Hooker made clear, the Board of Education would assume "all risks and liability" involved in the use of the contaminated land. A second clause went further: "As a part of the consideration for this conveyance ... no claim, suit, action or demand of any nature whatsoever shall ever be made [by the Board of Education] ... for injury to a person or persons, including death resulting therefrom, or loss of or damage to property caused by reason of the presence of said industrial wastes."

When the board's lawyer, Ralph Boniello, read this, an alarm bell rang in his head. It was, he said later, "like waving a red flag in front of a bull." He urged the board to hire a chemical engineer to make a study before accepting the Hooker offer. He pointed to the risk and liability it would incur if it took the

356

property on the company's terms. The nine members paid no heed.

The land was turned over to the city, and the 99th Street School was built. Alone among schools in the community, it had neither basement nor swimming pool because of fears that any excavation might damage the waste barrels. The four hundred grade schoolers trotted off to school each morning, often covering their faces with handkerchiefs to screen out the odours pervading the neighbourhood. Later they began to play with "firerocks" they found in a neighbouring field, which exploded with a shower of sparks when thrown against a wall or pavement. These were actually chunks of phosphorus from the Hooker plant. They burned the hands of some children who put them in their pockets.

In 1958, the Niagara Falls Air Pollution Department warned the Hooker company that several children had been burned by similar waste. The company sent two employees out to investigate. They found that wastes had surfaced on both sides of the canal. One, benzene hexachloride, was not only a carcinogen but could also poison the nervous system and cause convulsions. Hooker officials told the school board, but the board took no action. Nor did it warn any of the residents because it feared legal repercussions.

Nobody, indeed, wanted to rock the boat. The city was trying to attract industry, not repel it. Hooker employed thirty-two hundred blue-collar workers, paid taxes, and contributed to the local economy. As for the residents, their jobs for the most part depended on the presence of the big industrial firms.

As the years passed, the noxious fumes grew worse and seemed to be coming directly from the basements of some of the houses. People's eyes seemed permanently red. The paint on some houses turned black. Potholes began to appear in the baseball diamond near the schoolyard. Children who stumbled into muddy ditches emerged covered with a strange oily substance. The city's fire chief warned as early as 1964 that the fumes coming off the former dump could be a detriment to the health and well-being of residents in the area. But nothing was done. These conditions continued for a quarter of a century before the homeowners finally rebelled and Love Canal became a stench in the nostrils, not only of Niagara Falls but of the western world.

2

Robert Moses' reputation as a man who got things done, even at the expense of others, made him an obvious choice to oversee the construction of the huge new generating plant on the American side of the Niagara River. His prime purpose, however, was to beautify the environs of the smog-shrouded community.

Those who were close to him had no doubt of that. John C. Bruel, who was secretary of the board of the New York State Power Authority, thought of Moses as a park man, not a hydro expert. "He didn't know the first thing about electricity," Bruel has said. "If he licked his finger and stuck it in a socket and it sparked, it was alive. That was all he knew."

Moses had reached his seventieth year and was at the peak of his powers when work finally began on the ambitious project that would bear his name. Born of a middle-class Jewish family, he held a bachelor's degree from Yale, a master's from Oxford, and a doctorate from Columbia. In spite of that impeccable scholastic background, he had no interest in an academic life. He had spent forty-five years in the public service, and in the eyes of the press and much of the public he was a hero because of his ability to get things done. He always managed to bull his favourite projects through, pushing aside those who stood in his way and often wreaking vengeance on those who obstructed or criticized him.

His ability to stifle opposition was legendary. "There is little profit in arguing with Bob Moses," the editor of a Syracuse newspaper wrote in 1959. "He is living proof of what a large vocabulary featuring words and terms of scorn, derision, and colossal contempt, can do for a public official when directed at an opponent with machine-gun rapidity. If and when I become embroiled in a controversy with Moses, I will insist in advance on a verbal handicap. There is no percentage in taking him on from a standing start."

Moses himself never shrank from a fight; indeed, he welcomed controversy. "I recommend to my boys that they grow a tough hide rather than cover a thin skin with protective colouring, suntan oil, perfume and deodorants," he once remarked. His mail, he complained, "often takes its tone from whiners and brick throwers." But, he said, he was determined never to be deterred from his purposes. "The armour-plated rhino and the crocodile should be our symbols and our answer to the pea shooters should always be: 'You never touched me.'"

Governor Thomas E. Dewey made Moses an energy czar because of his reputation as a doer. More than any other man, Moses had shaped New York City and much of New York State. He had built sixteen expressways and seven great bridges, including the famous Triborough. He had installed 685 playgrounds. He had torn down acres of slums to put up public housing. His thruways had displaced a quarter of a million people. Peter Cooper Village and Stuyvesant Towers, those monuments to "urban renewal" (the buzz-word of the fifties), were his doing. So were Shea Stadium, the New York Coliseum, the United Nations headquarters, and Lincoln Center.

He had made himself the most powerful man in the biggest city on the continent – more powerful at times than the mayor himself. He was admired, feared, and hated in roughly equal measure. Now, in addition to the several hats he already wore, he had donned a new one. He would be responsible not only for the Niagara project but also for the United States' commitment to the St. Lawrence Seaway.

In the late forties, with the international agreement dividing Niagara's water between the two nations about to expire, and with power blackouts irritating consumers on both sides of the border, Ontario Hydro pressed for a new document. Signed at the end of February, 1950, it changed the previous water allotment, in which Canada had been allowed to draw 56,500 cubic feet a second from the Falls and the United States 32,500. The new diversion treaty simply declared that *all* the water in the river could be used to develop power – after the scenic protection of the Falls was guaranteed.

That meant that not less than 100,000 cubic feet a second must be allowed to flow over the Falls in the summer months. The flow would be reduced to 50,000 between November 1 and April 1, when few tourists paid the Falls a visit. What was left could be divided equally between the two countries.

Four days after the treaty became law, Ontario Hydro had its project under way. Hydro's dynamic new chairman, Robert Saunders, announced that a second generating plant, also to be named for Sir Adam Beck, would soon be built a few yards upstream from the first. It would be designed to produce 700,000 horsepower at a cost of $157 million. That same summer, John E. Burton, then chairman of the New York State Power Authority, offered to build and pay for a similar massive generating plant directly across the river from the Hydro structures.

Saunders wasted no time. Construction on the Ontario plant began in December 1950. But when Moses replaced Burton four years later, American politicians were still wrangling over whether a private or a public company should do the job at Lewiston. The contrast between the two systems – American and Canadian – was never better demonstrated than by the spectacle of the Lewiston site standing idle while its Canadian counterpart was alive with activity. The American concept of grass-roots democracy demanded that every elected politician should have his say before a single foot of turf was disturbed. The Canadian method of dispensing authority from above – a remnant of the British colonial system – was more efficient, if less democratic.

As chairman of the provincially owned corporation, the forty-four-year-old Saunders needed nothing more than the Ontario government's permission to go ahead. With the province facing more power blackouts, it would have been political suicide not to build Beck 2. Saunders, after all, had been the government's choice to head Hydro, which was also deeply involved in the new St. Lawrence Seaway project.

Niagara Falls power seemed to attract powerful men. Like Adam Beck before him, and like Robert Moses, his opposite number in the United States, Robert Saunders was a strong personality. A fireman's son, he had risen successively from farm worker, to truck driver and factory hand, to one of Toronto's most successful and best-loved mayors. A brilliant administrator and a master publicist, he seemed the right man to allay the growing public irritation over the continuing power shortage. Stumping the province in a marathon series of speeches, delivered in a gravelly voice, he levelled with his audience and managed to break through the massive crust of secrecy that had heretofore concealed Hydro's inner workings.

That was why he was chosen. A glad-hander and a collector of celebrities who always managed to manoeuvre himself into the centre of any news photograph, Saunders also knew how to manipulate the press. He remembered the name of everybody he met and with his photographic memory quickly absorbed the minutiae of Hydro development. Soon he was able to astonish colleagues and newsmen alike by reeling off figures on how much power this or that Hydro plant had generated on any given day, or how many farms were served by rural power lines, and even the number of people living on those farms.

The ex-mayor's hail-fellow personality endeared him to

Hydro workers. On seeing a work crew, he would leap from his chauffeured limousine, greet them with a "Hi! I'm Bob Saunders," and ask about the job. Later he would send along cards or letters of congratulation. Every Sunday on Canada's largest radio station, CFRB in Toronto, he'd report to the public and welcome questions. "Good afternoon, ladies and gentlemen, boys and girls, this is your Hydro chairman reporting," he'd announce. He didn't think it necessary to identify himself by name, secure in the knowledge that every listener knew who he was.

He loved the sound of his own voice and would sometimes argue heatedly with his chauffeur, "Swifty," on events of the day. Once, en route to Niagara, the argument grew so heated that Saunders ordered Swifty to stop the car. He eased the chauffeur out of his seat, took the wheel himself, and drove off, leaving Swifty alone on the highway to find his own way to the Falls.

Like Beck before him, but unlike Beck's successors, Saunders adopted a hands-on policy at Hydro. Earlier chairmen had confined their duties to acting as spokesmen for the commission. Saunders, however, wanted a say in internal decisions, which, though it caused some friction with upper management, helped speed the construction of Beck 2.

The boldness of the job fitted the chairman's own personality. From an intake two miles above the Falls, Hydro was blasting the largest underground waterway in the world – a tunnel, five and a half miles long, three hundred feet underneath the town of Niagara Falls. At the lower end of the tunnel the water would race into a two-and-a-quarter-mile canal, constructed in a vast cut two hundred feet wide and ninety feet deep, blasted out of the rock. The other statistics were, as usual, breathtaking. The commission was planning forty miles of new roads. A new community, known as Hydro City, would house 3,000 of the 6,700 workers needed to finish the job. An artificial lake would be gouged out of a 750-acre farm to serve as a

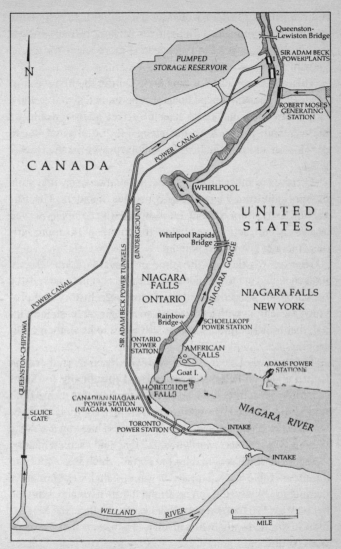

Power canals on the Canadian side

reservoir. This, in effect, would act as a storage battery, holding surplus water drained from the river during off-hours for use during the day when the Falls needed more water for tourist viewing.

This wasn't enough for Saunders. During the first week of June, 1951, he announced that a second tunnel, also five and a half miles long and more than fifty feet across, would be blasted from the rock to run alongside the original cut to develop an additional half-million horsepower for the Beck 2 plant.

There were other headlines that week, however, that stole the spotlight from the publicity-conscious Saunders. The arrival of Marilyn Monroe and a Hollywood film company served as a lively entr'acte played before the curtain of the more serious drama of power and politics.

Monroe was then on the verge of super stardom. Niagara Falls rocketed her to the pinnacle. The great cataract served as a backdrop for a brief scene that made screen history and provided the actress with a trademark so recognizable, so individual, that Marilyn impersonators still use it to hook their audiences.

The movie, of course, was *Niagara*. It co-starred Joseph Cotten and Jean Peters but was tailored specifically for Monroe. Many an actress has walked into stardom, but, as has been said, she succeeded by walking *away* from it. Henry Hathaway, the director, photographed her as no one else had, but it was the famous, voluptuous "Marilyn walk" that made screen history.

A special track was laid for the scene, which was shot from the site of Table Rock. Dressed in a skin-tight black skirt and a flaming red blouse, the actress alighted from a car and wriggled her way for 116 feet through what has been called "the longest, most luxuriated walk in film history." Hathaway shot the scene from behind.

"Mr. Hathaway told me I swerved too much," Marilyn remarked with calculated innocence. "Those damned cobblestones are hell to walk on in high heels." But the damned Niagara cobblestones helped to turn her into a Hollywood icon.

Marilyn Monroe's fortnight at the Falls has become part of her growing legend. Sequestered in the General Brock Hotel, and under orders from Hathaway to give no interviews, she unwittingly contributed to the Honeymoon Capital's mystique by managing to conduct two love affairs while making the film. Her longtime friend Bob Slatzer succeeded in renting an adjoining room in the already overcrowded hotel. There, with the Falls thundering just outside the window, he proposed marriage, and she accepted.

The great cataract's magic did not long endure. Marilyn left Niagara Falls on June 18 and married Slatzer in Tijuana, Mexico – a union that lasted just four days. Later she became the wife of Joe DiMaggio, who had also flown to the Falls to be with her.

When *Niagara* was previewed the following year at the Falls, hundreds of people wrote demanding rooms at the "Rainbow Motel" featured in the movie. There was, of course, no Rainbow Motel. It had been no more than a false front built in a strategic position so that the Falls could be seen in the background. No actual motel, at that time, met the director's requirements.

Ontario, meanwhile was pushing ahead with its newest hydroelectric development almost as fast as Hollywood made films. Hydro was not hampered, as Moses was, by a clause in the international treaty providing that Congress would have the final say in determining which agency would develop the U.S. share of the Niagara power. That simple statement, added to the treaty at American insistence, was to delay the project for the best part of a decade.

The five major private utilities waged what President Harry Truman called "one of the most vicious propaganda campaigns in history" to keep the project in their own hands. Their purpose was to portray the "power socialists," as the chairman of

Consolidated Edison called them, as captives of a foreign philosophy. Ernest R. Acker, president of Central Hudson Gas and Electric, made no bones about it. "We have conducted a vigorous campaign," he said, "to present to the people the dangers of the 'creeping socialism' which is inherent in the proposals of the public power advocates." The campaign had many powerful supporters, including eight major farm organizations. The New York Chamber of Commerce and the powerful General Electric Corporation took full-page newspaper advertisements to publicize their cause.

The advocates of public power were divided, and that added to the delays. Should army engineers build the plant, as a bill before Congress proposed? Or should the New York State Power Authority do the job, as another urged?

In 1953, a year before the Moses appointment, the House of Representatives Committee on Public Works shelved both bills and opted for one urging private development. It passed the House, but before the Senate could vote, Governor Dewey jumped into the fight on the side of public power, which, as he pointed out, the state of New York had been advocating for almost half a century. "If this is creeping socialism," Dewey said, "then it did its creeping forty years ago." The bill was set aside.

The following February, however, Dewey himself bridled at a new bill authorizing New York State to build the powerplant but without federal funding. This bill would have given municipalities and co-operatively owned utilities preference over the private companies in power distribution. Dewey, who faced a rift in his own party when a Buffalo senator denounced his proposals as "pure unadulterated socialism," backtracked. In a remarkable piece of Cold War rhetoric, he declared that there should be no coddling of "those communities which bend the knee to the Moscow concept, abandon private operation of their public utilities, and socialize them."

It was at this point, with the controversy at its height and nothing done on the Niagara River, that Dewey appointed Robert Moses to head the New York State Power Authority. The tough new chairman wasted no time before attacking the private power companies, employing the blunt and colourful language for which he was famous. "The record shows that the worst possible procedure from the viewpoint of public interest would be to turn over the waters of the Niagara to the five utility companies," he wrote to Edward Martin, chairman of the Senate Public Works Committee in 1954. The argument that Niagara power was "divinely preempted for private enterprise" was so much "chatter," Moses said, for "the history of private exploitation of the Niagara frontier in New York State is one of outrageous effrontery that finally was cured by aroused public opinion.... [The] companies ... ignoring the lurid past history of callous exploitation have conducted a campaign of skillful vilification." Moses shrewdly harped on the probability that giving in to the private utilities would cost votes. Any party, he said, that advocated private exploitation of Niagara's power would be thrown out of office in New York.

Bolstering Moses' argument was the obvious contrast with the Canadian venture. While American politicians continued to bicker among themselves, Ontario Hydro was about to open the first phase of Beck 2. "My vocabulary," Moses wrote, "does not extend to the statesmen who find in our sorry record only material for slogans about 'the American way' and 'the matchless spirit of free, private American enterprise.' The Canadians talk less, act faster, and have a better scale of values."

By the end of June, little more than three years after the turning of the first sod, Beck 2 started to produce power. At two o'clock on the afternoon of August 30, the Duchess of Kent officially opened the new power station, which had a capacity of 1,828,000 horsepower. The cost had risen to about $300 million. This was Robert Saunders's big moment – and also his last triumph. The following year the ebullient Hydro chairman was killed in a plane crash.

A month before the official opening, the Niagara River served notice that, in spite of man's attempt to harness its waters, nature was still in control. On July 2, 1954, 185,000 tons of rock comprising most of Prospect Point crashed into the gorge with a mighty roar, largely eliminating the famous vantage point and carving a great wedge-shaped section out of the American Falls, altering its crest line. This catastrophe accelerated plans to stabilize the Falls and restore the crest by narrowing and deepening the Horseshoe on the Canadian side and building a series of control gates a mile upstream to help regulate the flow of both cataracts.

The embarrassing truth was that the United States was being forced to buy much of its hydroelectric energy from Canada. Without a new powerplant, it could not yet make use of its share of Niagara's waters granted by the treaty. With both Beck plants operating, Ontario Hydro was happy to take all the water it could get.

And still the political squabbling continued. Bills that failed to make their way through the committee process one year reappeared in different form the next and were again set aside. Intergovernmental rivalry added to the delays. Washington wanted the job done by the Federal Power Commission (FPC). New York wanted to go it alone.

Moses, who visited Beck 2 in July, 1954, was even more convinced after what he saw that New York should undertake the project. As a park man, he was impressed by the way Ontario had integrated its park system with the hydroelectric development. "The Canadians are away ahead of us," he announced. "They did the job as it should be done; they put the first emphasis on conservation. Power is only one phase of that."

The ponderous legislative process inched along at a maddening pace. In January 1956, the Senate Public Works Committee approved a new bill proposed by Senator Herbert Lehman of New York that would turn the job over to Moses' State

Power Authority. Lehman's bill finally went to the Senate in May and passed by a vote of forty-eight to thirty-nine. But before it could go to the House for approval, nature again took a hand. On June 8, 1956, with a mighty crash and a roar, the cliff supporting the Schoellkopf Power Plant, now part of the Niagara Mohawk Power Corporation, gave way. Most of the structure tumbled into the water, depriving the United States of its main domestic source of hydroelectric power from the river.

3

At five in the afternoon, Bob Frombernad and his wife were strolling through Ontario's Queen Victoria Park, pushing a baby carriage, when it happened. They heard a strange noise coming from across the river – rumbling and grumbling at first, then a thunderous roar. Looking across at the Schoellkopf plant, they stared in disbelief. The top of the gorge began to shake, and for several moments it seemed that hundreds of tons of rock hung in the air as if suspended by wires. Then the entire mass – four hundred feet across and forty feet thick – tumbled down, crushing the roof of the powerplant below. Sherman McKensey, driving through the park along the lip of the gorge, saw it from a different angle. To him it sounded as if a bomber had scored a direct hit. At first there was only a small shower of rocks; but then the entire bank seemed to crumble, and the shower became a cascade.

Inside the plant, Donald Kline, one of the operators on duty, heard a roar that made him think of a jet plane taking off. The workers had been told of dangerous seepage from the cliff above and had been warned to keep a sharp lookout. Now, Paul Batheu, hearing and feeling the rumbling, rushed to a telephone to warn the operator at the switching station on the top of the cliff.

At that moment, the plant's windows began to pop. The floor

heaved alarmingly. A huge crack opened in the end wall of the plant. In less than thirty seconds it widened to a two-foot gap. The building split open. The ceiling began to fall. Kline and Batheu, with thirty-eight other workers, dashed through the building as a blast of water hit one of the generators, blowing it out "like a piece of paper." Thirty-nine men reached the door on the downstream side as the foundations gave way and most of the plant slipped toward the river. One man, Richard Draper, was blown directly out of a window to his death. The rest escaped and, with the elevator out of order, clawed their way 350 feet to the top of the cliff.

Two-thirds of the Schoellkopf station was a twisted mass of steel. It was a devastating blow, not only to its owner, Niagara Mohawk, but also to the entire community. Power from the Falls was already in short supply because of the delay in building the plant at Lewiston. Now, more than ever, the United States would have to depend on a foreign company to fuel the factories along the Niagara River.

It must have seemed to Robert Moses that the long political battle would shortly end in his favour. With the collapse of the Schoellkopf plant, the power shortage in the northeastern United States had grown desperate. The Niagara Mohawk Company called off its attack and urged Congress to pass Senator Lehman's bill; Moses had quietly assured the company that when the American plant was built, the firm would receive a fixed share of the power produced. William E. Miller, the short, fiery congressman in whose district the plant would be built, had also come round as a result of the Schoellkopf collapse. He had fought vigorously on behalf of the private utilities, but now he, too, was prepared to help steer the bill through Congress.

The House Public Works Committee gave its backing to the bill, but a coalition of Republicans and Southern Democrats, which controlled the Rules Committee, refused to clear it for a vote. The original $300-million cost for the project was now

estimated at $405 million, and, as the *New York Times* com-
plained, "we are back where we started six years ago."

All of Moses' problems had been caused by that irritating
clause in the international treaty, giving Congress the right to
approve the project. But was it valid? Moses asked the courts to
decide. That took six months, but in June 1957 the Federal
Court of Appeals ruled that the clause did *not* apply. It turned
out that the FPC had always had the right to license what was
now a $600-million project. More than six years had been
wasted over a rider that had no validity! Political foot-dragging
had doubled the cost.

The new parkland at Niagara was still at the top of the Moses
agenda. He was proposing a $750-million face-lift for the
American side of the gorge to include a new parkway, built on
fill, that would begin at Grand Island and run, eventually, all the
way to Fort Niagara on Lake Ontario. There would be a new
bridge at Lewiston, a new park system, and an expansion of the
original state reservation, including improvements on Goat
Island.

In Congress, Republicans and Democrats hammered out a
compromise bill that would sell half the power developed by
the project to private enterprise and the other half to municipalities, co-operatives, and other power users. Everything seemed
in place for quick Senate approval, but it didn't come. Civil
rights was now a more important issue than public power, and
the Senate plunged into a long debate that delayed the bill's
passage. At last, on August 21, 1957, the exhausting wrangle
was over. The president signed the bill and Robert Moses'
problems seemed at an end.

They weren't. The FPC was bombarded with a series of complaints from the city of Niagara Falls, Niagara County, and the
town of Lewiston. Moses had planned seven thousand feet of
open cut to carry the water from above the Falls to the reservoir
behind the powerplant. The local governments insisted the cut

be covered, and so the FPC was threatening to give no more than a conditional licence to the New York State Power Authority until the matter was resolved.

Moses had planned an elaborate dinner and ground-breaking ceremonies for September 12. He had to scrap them. The FPC hearings dragged on for nine weeks. In November, the city of Niagara Falls gave in. The other two complainants did not. Moses issued a propaganda blast in the form of a glossy forty-eight-page brochure supporting his position. He followed that on December 3 with one of his typically provocative public attacks in which he called the FPC "spineless" and charged that the deputy counsel to the commission was "more interested in his vacation than in putting an end to stultifying delays." The delay, he declared, was costing western New York power consumers at least $100,000 a day.

In the end Moses had to give in. He got his licence from the FPC in January on the condition that the entire seven thousand feet of canal be covered, at an additional cost of $25 million. The following March – eight years after the international agreement was signed – the New York State Power Authority finally began construction of the main powerplant at Lewiston.

4

Robert Moses was all work. He rarely attended the theatre, didn't care for bridge, indulged in no hobbies. His biographer, Robert Caro, called him "America's greatest builder," but Caro was no admirer. He depicted Moses as a man with a hunger for power that was never slaked, and one who was also malicious, spiteful, and arrogant. Moses actually seemed to enjoy expressing his contempt for those he felt were considerably beneath him – a class that included almost everybody.

He didn't just defeat his opponents. He tried to destroy them, and often succeeded. Revenge was always sweet for the power broker. He never forgot a slight, and that was one reason why he was feared. He was not above using the meanest of epithets to bring down his rivals, smearing them as Commies, pinkos, or Bolshies. He kept dossiers on those with whom he had to do business against the day when he would need inside information to bring them to heel.

Moses was a burly two-hundred-pounder with heavy-lidded eyes and a face dominated by a powerful nose. He thumbed that nose at presidents, governors, and fellow park commissioners. "Nothing I have ever done has been tinged with legality," he liked to say, and, "if the end doesn't justify the means, what does?" His was the law of the *fait accompli*, especially when it came to condemning buildings or wooded areas for his beloved highways. While others sought injunctions, Moses put his bulldozers to work before the fact. He did not always wait for legal confirmation of his projects. "Once you sink that first stake," he said, "they'll never make you pull it up."

He was an élitist, who cheerfully shifted the Northern State Parkway three miles south to accommodate the baronial estates of men with such names as Whitney, Morgan, Kahn, and Stimson. But he wouldn't move it an inch when a farmer, James Roth, protested that it would split his property in two. Moses had built overpasses for the powerful so that they could reach their golf courses, but he refused to do so for Roth who, understandably, wanted access to half his land.

The acknowledged overlord of the state's park system and longtime commissioner of New York City parks, he had no interest in building for the lower classes. He cared only for those who drove automobiles – hence his practice of building expressways and thruways. By banning public transportation from the state parks he made them virtually inaccessible to the poor. Similarly, in the city he limited access to parks by rapid transit and made them impossible for buses to reach by building the overhead bridges too low.

Those with dark skins – blacks and Puerto Ricans – were

373

beneath his notice. Because he felt that blacks were inherently "dirty" he made it difficult for buses they chartered to get permits to enter such city parks as Jones Beach. Frances Perkins, Franklin Roosevelt's Secretary of Labor and an old acquaintance of Moses, was shocked to realize that underlying his strict policy of park cleanliness lurked a deep distaste for the masses. "He doesn't love people," she told Robert Caro. "It used to shock me, because he was doing all these things for the welfare of the people…. He'd denounce the common people terribly. To him they were lousy, dirty people, throwing bottles all over Jones Beach. 'I'll get them! I'll teach them!' He loves the public, but not the people. The public is just *the* public. It's a great amorphous mass to him; it needs to be bathed, it needs to be aired, it needs recreation, but not for personal reasons – just to make it a better public."

Moses built few parks in underprivileged areas. In the thirties, he built 255 playgrounds elsewhere in New York City, but only one in Harlem. And when he built the six-and-a-half-mile highway known as the West Side Improvement, which ran the length of Manhattan, he covered all the unsightly railroad tracks except in the section that ran through the black district.

Moses entered the field of slum clearance when urban renewal was the gospel of the day. With the best of intentions, city fathers everywhere were trying to restore the cores of their communities through massive projects that removed the buildings from entire city blocks and replaced them with vast apartment complexes. In New York City, Moses plunged into this war on "urban blight" with his usual enthusiasm and drive, but also with the callousness of an élitist. What was urban blight to the upper classes was home to thousands. But Moses cared not a whit for the old-time neighbourhoods, the corner stores, the small apartments that the people who didn't live there called tenements. Moses got the job done efficiently and with dispatch, but at great human cost. These vibrant blocks, which gave the residents a sense of community, were bulldozed down

374

and replaced by ugly and faceless brick boxes. Thousands of other citizens, displaced by Moses' big expressways, also got short shrift – forced to find new homes, often at double the cost. These people were lied to; Moses' spurious offer of equal accommodation wasn't worth a nickel.

This, then, was the background and the personal style of the man who now proposed to seize 1,383 acres of the 6,249-acre reservation of the Tuscarora Indians. This would form part of the great reservoir, which, like the one across the river, would act as a gigantic storage tank for water that could in peak hours be used to supplement the flow from the conduit and drive the big turbines at the foot of the cliff.

The Tuscarora were an Iroquoian afterthought. The great League of Five Nations was formed in 1451, before the white man arrived to settle in North America. The Tuscarora were latecomers. Driven from their homes in what became North Carolina, they moved north. In the eighteenth century they were accepted into the league, but never as full members. The Oneida gave them land on a temporary basis. Later, the Seneca gave them 640 acres, which they were able to supplement by purchase and grant, on the site of what became Lewiston, New York. As the population of the Falls area grew and new factories sprang up, many Tuscarora men took jobs in industry while the women hired out as domestics. Others farmed.

Moses, with his scorn for ordinary people, especially those of a different skin colour, wanted a good chunk of the Indians' land because he did not wish to disturb the white residents of Lewiston. The taxes that the whites paid would be lost if their land was expropriated; moreover, it would be hideously expensive to purchase the homes and pay the owners for the move. The Indians lived in simple houses and paid no taxes, so very little would be lost. As Moses was certain that their land would go cheaply, the total costs of expropriation, he estimated, would be far less.

In Moses, the Indians were up against a powerful antagonist

who was prepared to go to the Supreme Court, if necessary, and to use every available trick to get what he wanted. Moses hated to lose. But, as it turned out, the Indians were just as intransigent. The three principal Tuscarora leaders, all mild-spirited farmers, were equally ready to fight every inch of the way for their rights. Clinton Rickard was the self-educated founder of the Indian Defense League of America. He had made himself an expert on Indian laws and treaties and considered the Tuscarora a sovereign nation. His eldest son, William, was emerging as a tribal leader. Harry Patterson, chief of the Bear Clan, was a lifelong farmer and former basketball star who, with his six sons, still tilled the rich soil of the reservation, growing crops of fruit, berries, and grain. Elton Greene (Black Cloud) was head chief of the Tuscarora and sachem of the Land Turtle Clan. He had learned English at the age of eleven and in his youth had gone on the road as a vaudeville performer and musician. He had been a Baptist preacher and was a licensed carpenter as well as a farmer. He had a dry wit and a good sense of public relations, cheerfully donning Plains Indian head-dress and beaded jacket and wielding a peace pipe for photographers when the occasion demanded it. ("Do you want me to look mad?" he asked one newspaperman at the height of the battle with the power authority.) Greene was on a first-name basis with most of the civic officials, legislators, and members of the press.

In their two-year struggle with the power authority, the Tuscarora held one high card – the collective guilt of white society about what it had done to the aboriginal peoples since the days of Columbus. The press tended to be on the side of the Indians, running features on Greene and explaining the native attitude toward the land. "We think that our land is very sacred," Greene would declare. "The Indian loves nature. He loves trees. He loves everything that grows…. The way we see it, money evaporates, but the land don't."

The land "is not ours to dispose of," Chief Rickard

emphasized. "We are only its custodians." This aboriginal view of land as something that cannot be sold or bartered, being held in common by all like the air and the water, completely escaped Robert Moses. He didn't understand it, would never understand it, and didn't believe it. The attitude of the Tuscarora baffled him. Why did 634 Indians need 6,249 acres, anyway, especially when much of the land was not being "used"? Moses was convinced that everything had a price. If necessary, he was prepared to pay whatever it took to get a piece of the reservation.

But not at the outset. His plan was to move swiftly and quietly to get the land at rock-bottom prices. In January 1957, even before he got the FPC licence, he made his first move. William Latham, a power authority engineer, knocked on Clinton Rickard's door and asked permission to put a survey crew on the reservation. Latham explained, smoothly, that the authority did not want the land; the survey was solely for the purpose of determining the depth of the soil to bedrock. It would in no way interfere with the Indians' way of life.

Rickard wasn't fooled. "We knew they had an eye on our land," he said later. The Tuscarora council unanimously denied the authority permission to put surveyors on the reservation.

That September, Rickard's suspicions were realized when the Niagara Falls *Gazette* carried a map showing that the authority planned to take 950 acres of the reservation. The chief's council shot off a strong letter of protest to the secretary of the interior, the FPC, and the president himself, without result. "The braves are whooping it up," Robert Moses, in jocular vein, told a meeting of the American Society of Civil Engineers.

In November, a second map was published showing that the state now wanted 1,220 acres of Indian land for the reservoir. The Tuscarora also learned at the last moment that the FPC was about to hold a hearing on the matter. With less than a day to spare, Greene, Patterson, and Rickard rushed to Washington.

The commission and the state power authority tried to stop them from testifying because, having had inadequate notice, they had no lawyer. They were finally allowed to speak on the understanding that this would be their only opportunity. Being placed at a disadvantage, the Tuscarora hired a Washington attorney, Arthur Lazarus, Jr., to represent them.

The hearing was adjourned to Buffalo. There, the town of Lewiston urged the authority to use only Indian land for the reservoir. The authority upped its requirements to 1,383 acres. Moses, in a vague statement, indicated he might be prepared to pay as much as a thousand dollars an acre for Indian land. In February 1958, in an open letter to the Tuscarora couched in blunt, almost insulting terms, he made clear his belief that the authority had the law on its side. "This essential work, already unduly delayed, can and must proceed immediately," Moses wrote. "While we have understood your reluctance to part with land, we cannot delay longer.... We have no more time for stalling and debate...."

"He's bluffing," said Greene. The Indians held fast and posted No Trespassing signs on the reservation. "To us the land was priceless and could never be sold," said Rickard.

But in April, Governor Averill Harriman gave approval to expropriation. A group of legal experts, workmen, and surveyors appeared at the reservation accompanied by thirty-five Niagara County deputy sheriffs, fifty state troopers with riot equipment, tear-gas bombs, and sub-machine guns, and a number of plainclothes detectives. Some two hundred Indians formed a barrier in front of the trucks. Three were arrested for unlawful assembly, a curious charge, since they were on their own land, and one that was later dismissed.

With the entire Iroquois confederacy now pledging support, the Tuscarora stood their ground, preventing the surveyors from working. On April 30, a federal court decision suspended all expropriation proceedings but still allowed the surveyors to have entry to the land. The authority then tried again to deal

378

with the Indians but was rebuffed. "We will not sell at any price," said Greene. Women and children continued passive resistance, blocking the surveyors' transits, but a court order on May 8 finally convinced them it was wiser to yield.

Moses now boosted his tentative offer to a firm $1,100 an acre. When that was turned down, he produced one of the glossy brochures for which he was noted, "smacking more of Madison Avenue than the Niagara frontier," in the words of the *New York Times*. In it, Moses tried to give the impression that most Tuscarora wanted to sell their land and were being blocked by a "small number of recalcitrants." Moses dangled a proposed $250,000 community centre in front of the Indians, displayed in an artist's double-page rendering in his brochure. The Tuscarora weren't interested. One suggested, facetiously, that the power authority might follow the white man's original policy of distributing beads and trinkets.

Meanwhile, Moses' men moved onto the reservation to begin cutting trees and clearing timber and buildings, using the time-tested technique of acting in advance of legal authority. The Indians moved quickly to get a restraining order. A long and complicated court battle was just beginning. Neither side was prepared to give an inch. In June, a federal court judge ruled that the Indians couldn't stop expropriation. But in July they successfully appealed, and all work on the reservation stopped.

Moses now moved to discredit the Indians and their use of the land. In September he sent a wire to a colleague, Thomas F. Moore, Jr., to dig out facts about the band that he could use against them:

"Do we have the basic facts about the Tuscaroras – for public consumption. Apart from the rhubarb about condemnation and pre-Revolutionary and pre-states rights of the noble red men? I mean acreage they have, living conditions, land, cultivation, how much we take, how much we offer, what they could do with cash, what they work at, etc. I don't want a lot of mawkish sentiments manufactured by the sob sisters and other S.O.B.s, it would be a hell of a thing if we had to move the reservoir to cemetery and taxable farmland."

A week later, the Supreme Court gave the Tuscarora a breathing-space by ordering a conditional stay on condemnation proceedings until it could hear an appeal by the Indians challenging the validity of the authority's FPC licence. Moses promptly issued a public statement accusing the Tuscarora of a "fanatical effort to shove the reservoir over onto private property." His timetable for construction would be badly skewed, he said, unless he could build a power line across the reservation. "We have been shunted about and jackassed around from court to court and judge to judge," he said. The courts allowed him to expropriate eighty-six acres of Tuscarora land as right-of-way for his power lines.

The Supreme Court rejected the Indians' appeal, but the Tuscarora got a second reprieve when the U.S. Court of Appeal ruled that the state had no right to take any more land unless the FPC first found that the expropriation would not "interfere" with the reservation. Moses threatened to stop the whole project, a decision that would have thrown 2,726 men out of work. "Disaster threatens the Niagara Falls area," a front-page editorial in the *Gazette* cried. "The greatest economic crisis in the history of our community is imminent."

Moses was now hinting at an unpalatable alternative, designed to arouse public opinion further against the Tuscarora. If he couldn't get their land, he said, he'd have to expropriate land from the town of Lewiston and city of Niagara Falls. That would cost an additional $15 million, wipe hundreds of acres off the tax rolls of the two communities, and force the relocation of 282 homes and two cemeteries.

In November 1958, the FPC opened its hearing to decide whether the flooding of the Indian land would interfere with the purpose for which the reservation was intended. Both towns appeared, taking the side of the power authority. Moses came up with a series of experts who testified that the land was virtually worthless and that, because it didn't amount to much, the Indians had no right to stand in the way of progress.

To Moses the idea of land standing idle – not being *used* – was scandalous. Again, he showed no understanding of aboriginal attitudes. He went so far as to have aerial photographs made showing the location of outhouses on the reservation. As Rickard later put it, "the SPA lawyers decided that the extent of a people's civilization was determined by the number of flush toilets they had. The whole testimony was an enormously expensive attempt ... to belittle our Tuscarora people.... Robert Moses and his henchmen very clearly demonstrated their race prejudice and contempt for Indians. What they were trying to impress upon the FPC was the assumption that since this Indian community did not amount to anything, it had no right to stand in the way of the whites who wanted the Indian land for their own purposes. They respected only power and wealth and might, we had none of these. That such a seemingly insignificant people would stand up to Robert Moses and fight back was the thing that infuriated him most of all, as his hysterical press releases only too plainly revealed."

Meanwhile, Moses had renewed his offer of $1.5 million for the 1,383 acres of Tuscarora land. He had already agreed to pay the neighbouring Niagara University $5 million for two hundred acres. In addition, he had sweetened the offer to the Indians, not only with the community centre but also with promises of new roads and free electricity. He even promised to name one of the big generators Tuscarora. The Indians laughed at this. For the first time, Moses began to talk about building a much smaller reservoir outside the reservation.

Moses continued to press forward in his usual way with construction of the generating plant. As always he was right on schedule. Thirty-five hundred men were now working on the plant and on the huge conduit ditch, one hundred feet deep and four hundred feet wide, being gouged from the

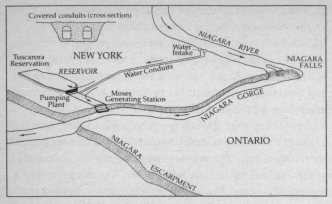

Covered conduits (cross section)

NIAGARA RIVER

Tuscarora
Reservation

NEW YORK

RESERVOIR

Water
Intake

Water Conduits

NIAGARA
FALLS

Pumping
Plant

Moses
Generating Station

NIAGARA GORGE

ONTARIO

NIAGARA

ESCARPMENT

The covered conduits to the Moses powerplant

rock of the Niagara Escarpment. Eight temporary bridges were being constructed, and five million yards of earth and rock had already been removed. Before the job was complete, the bridges would be torn down and the great cut covered over. The estimated cost had now soared to $720 million.

In January 1959, the FPC delayed its findings, hoping for an out-of-court settlement. A desperate Moses was now offering $2.5 million for the Indian land. At a tribal meeting, Lazarus, the Tuscarora's lawyer, urged them to negotiate in good faith. Clinton Rickard's son, William, opposed him, pointing out that the public would think the Tuscarora were simply holding out for more money when they had already said they wouldn't sell for any price. The atmosphere was heated even though the room temperature stood at twelve degrees below zero. In spite of the cold, the debate continued until two in the morning.

Rickard was convinced that Moses was out to create a disunity among his people. Cries of "Sell out! Sell out!" were heard from a minority. The majority agreed to continue negotiations, causing the press to speculate that the Tuscarora *did* have a price. That suspicion was reinforced when Moses upped the ante again to $3 million – more than twice what he had originally suggested he might pay. He set March 1 as a final deadline when the agreement would have to be signed.

The Rickards, father and son, were in despair, for the Indians appeared to be divided as a result of the new offer. "Money is like water in your hands," they had often said. "It falls through your fingers and disappears. But the land lasts forever." Would the Tuscarora heed this message?

The Tuscarora were to vote on Moses' offer on the evening of January 29, 1959. That morning, William Rickard received a letter from a friend describing the struggle for civil rights among the blacks in the South. At the meeting he read the letter aloud. Surely, he said, the Tuscarora could be just as courageous. In forty-five minutes the Indians voted unanimously to reject the money.

Just four days later the FPC handed down its decision, ruling that the use of the Indian land for a reservoir was inconsistent with the purpose for which Indian reservations had been established. The contractors removed their equipment, and Moses announced ruefully that he would build the reservoir on private land expropriated outside the disputed area. By increasing the height of the dikes by ten feet he could cut in half the contemplated loss in capacity.

It was generally accepted that the Indians had won and that Moses was beaten. But Moses was not a man who ever gave in. Apparently, the March 1 deadline was not inviolate, for he now filed a request for a new hearing before the FPC – one that would certainly drag out far beyond that date. Moses had scaled down his demands, announcing that he would now need no more than 470 acres of the reservation for power lines, a road, and part of the reservoir, most of which would occupy land outside the Indian boundaries. Moses had earlier refused to consider this solution.

More delays. The federal government stepped into the dispute, contending that the law, as the FPC interpreted it, applied only to land held by the government in trust for the Indians. The

Tuscarora *owned* their reservation; the government had no power over it. Once again the case moved to the Supreme Court.

The court did not review the case until December and did not publish its decision until March 7, 1960 – and it was a shocker. The court pointed out that the tribe had not acquired their land by treaty but by gift and purchase. By a vote of six to three, the court held that inasmuch as the lands were owned in fee simple by the Tuscarora nation and that no interest in them was owned by the United States, "they are not within a 'reservation' as that term is defined and used in the Federal Power Act...."

The three liberal judges on the bench, Chief Justice Earl Warren, William O. Douglas, and Hugo Black, dissented. "Some things are worth more than money and the costs of a new enterprise," Black wrote. "I regret that this court is to be the governmental agency that breaks faith with this dependent people. Great nations, like great men, should keep their word."

The battle was over. The Indians had lost and Moses was triumphant. "A Niagara of fictional treacle and molasses has been poured on the Indians, a sticky flow finally stopped by the United States Supreme Court," he declared triumphantly in a speech before the New York State Society of Newspaper Editors that June.

But Moses hadn't really won. He did not get his 1,383 acres; he got only 467, which included the land taken earlier for the power line. Most of the reservoir would be outside the reservation after all. Nor was the new plan as devastating to the project as Moses had suggested. The reduction in power would be minor – 1,700,000 kilowatts instead of 1,800,000.

The Tuscarora continued to brood over the court decision. "Many of our white friends have assured us that even though we lost the land, we gained a moral victory," Chief Rickard wrote after the fact. "We unfortunately live in a day when moral victories count for little." The families who occupied the land taken for the reservoir were moved. Those who lost land were

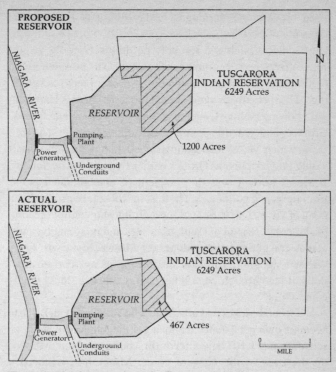

The scaled-back reservoir on the Tuscarora's land

paid for it. The remainder of the Tuscarora received eight hundred dollars apiece.

"The SPA got its reservoir and we were left with scars that will never heal," Rickard said. Some years later he described the permanent damage that had been done by the reservoir. "It has ruined the fishing on our reserve by damming up the inlet. The Northern Pike like to lay their eggs in swampy areas and our reservation provided several such places for them. Now they are gone, along with the other fish that liked to swim in our waters. We have never been compensated by the state for this loss...."

At 11:30 on the morning of Friday, February 10, 1961, the governor of New York, Nelson Rockefeller, pulled a symbolic red-handled switch and formally put into service the largest water-driven power complex in the world. The president, John F. Kennedy, and three of his predecessors sent recorded greetings. The specially commissioned mural by Thomas Hart Benton, showing Father Hennepin at the Falls, was unveiled. Ferde Grofé conducted the premier performance of his *Niagara Suite*, which Moses had commissioned, hoping (vainly) that it would be as popular as Grofé's earlier *Grand Canyon Suite*.

Moses himself was the recipient of unadulterated praise from press and politicians. He was, in Rockefeller's words, "a giant of a man ... a man of unique and almost incredible accomplishments ... a man of fabulous energy and imagination and a genius for getting things done...." Moses' reply was brief. "After long, stultifying and maddening delays and obstructions, it has through persistence and, I suppose, luck, finally come about."

But Robert Moses was not a man who believed in luck. It had been his own persistence that had got the job done exactly on schedule, just 1,107 days after the first bulldozer bit into the sod on the edge of the Niagara gorge. Moses had achieved it through a combination of bulldog tenacity, hard driving, devious politicking, and sheer charm. The powerplant itself was accomplishment enough, but it was the tremendous face-lifting over which Moses had presided that was his true monument. Moses had never seen the powerplant as an end in itself, but simply a means to restore the American side of the gorge by providing the parklike atmosphere needed to enhance the glory of the Falls. This was his larger vision, and he lived to see it completed.

Moses' name was enshrined on both the Robert Moses Parkway and the Robert Moses Niagara Power Plant, but his term at the power authority was about to end. Nelson Rockefeller, with as strong a personality as the power commissioner's, tried to ease him out gently; after all, Moses was long past retirement age. But Moses wouldn't go gracefully. In a burst of anger, he quit all his state posts and issued a furious press release attacking the governor.

That was not quite the end of Robert Moses. In assuming the presidency of the private corporation that was to build and operate the 1964-65 World's Fair in New York, he again put his reputation on the line, only to tarnish it irrevocably. It was not the big fair that interested him. It was his grandiose scheme to use its profits to pay for the greatest city park in the world on its site at Flushing Meadows. The scheme failed, and Moses had to take the blame for his bullheadedness, which antagonized everybody from the European nations that unanimously boycotted the exposition to the press itself. The fair lost $11 million. Moses, by defaulting on the fair's debt to the city, managed to scrape together enough funds to clean up the site. What remained was a far cry from the park of his dreams – a vast 1,346 acres of green space on the rim of the expanding metropolis. But in the view of Moses, the park man, it was still a park of sorts, and for him that was all that counted.

Chapter Twelve

1

The construction of the Moses powerplant turned Niagara Falls, New York, into a city of trailer camps. A total of eleven thousand men worked on the plant, on the reservoir, and on the conduits leading to it. Many, like Frank E. Woodward, a carpenter, had long been accustomed to a gypsy-like existence, moving from city to city, whenever and wherever the work beckoned. Frank's younger child, Roger, was only seven when the family moved to the area in the winter of 1959-60. He'd already been in two schools in two different communities. The 95th Street School would be his third.

The Woodwards and their two children, Roger and Deanne, aged seventeen, lived in the Sunny Acres Mobile Home Park, not far from the job. Frank's foreman, James Honeycutt, lived in Lynch's Trailer Park in the neighbouring community of Wheatfield. Both men worked for Balf, Sarin and Winkelman, building the big conduits.

On Saturday afternoon, July 9, 1960 – a day that the Woodwards would always remember and that would eventually change the direction of Roger Woodward's life – Jim Honeycutt dropped over to Sunny Acres and offered to take the Woodwards for a boat ride. Frank Woodward and his wife declined, but Deanne and Roger eagerly accepted. "Remember to wear your life jacket," Frank called out to Roger, who was just learning to swim.

Honeycutt, an experienced boatman and a strong swimmer with six years' experience as a lifeguard in North Carolina, had done considerable boating on the upper Niagara south of Grand Island. He owned a twelve-foot aluminum craft, powered by a seven-and-a-half-horsepower Evinrude outboard. The trio set off from Grand Island to explore the river. It was a blistering hot day, and Roger wanted to remove his life jacket. But Honeycutt, remembering Frank Woodward's warning, insisted that he keep it on. In later years, Roger Woodward, looking back on the scene, could never understand Jim Honeycutt's purpose in taking the boat under the Grand Island bridge and into the strange and turbulent waters below. Was it accidental, or did he intend to give the children the thrill of their lives?

Roger asked permission to steer the boat as they passed under the bridge; he could see in the distance a pillar of mist rising from the water. The boy had no idea that this marked the crest of Niagara Falls. Indeed, he had no idea that the river down which they were travelling had anything to do with the Falls. For a child of seven, recently arrived, the great cataract had no meaning. To him, Niagara Falls was a city; the Niagara was just another river.

On the American side he could see a small island, no more than a shoal, covered with roosting birds. Suddenly the noise of the motor changed to a high-pitched squeal. The propeller shaft had struck the shoal, the shear pin was gone, and they had no power.

Honeycutt hauled the engine out of the water and called to Deanne to put on the only other life jacket in the boat. Then, seizing the oars, he began to pull furiously for the American shore.

"What's the matter?" Deanne asked fearfully. Honeycutt didn't answer. A moment later the craft was in the rapids on the Canadian side. Goat Island was flashing past. The children began to panic. "We're going to die!" cried Roger. "I don't want to go swimming."

"Don't be scared," said Honeycutt. "I'll hold you."

The boat struck a mammoth wave and righted itself. It struck a second wave, and all three passengers were hurled into the water. Deanne tried vainly to cling to the overturned boat. Honeycutt did his best to hold on to Roger, but the raging water tore them apart.

The boy was terrified. The whole world seemed to have exploded around him. The force of the water threw him against the rocks that protruded from the channel, bruising him badly. Then his terror shifted to anger. He could see people running frantically up and down the Goat Island shoreline and couldn't understand why they wouldn't come out and pull him from the water.

But the anger quickly vanished, and young Roger Woodward found himself at peace. He knew now that he was going to die. His life actually passed before him, all seven years of it. He wondered what his parents would do with his pet dog Fritz, named for his idol, Fritz Von Erich, a local wrestler who lived a few doors from the Woodwards' trailer. He wondered what they would do with his toys and other possessions. How sorry they will be when they learn I'm dead, he thought, for he now gave up all hope of surviving. A moment later, still wearing his life jacket, he was hurled over the Horseshoe Falls.

Meanwhile, Deanne had lost her grip on the overturned boat. Although she was a weak swimmer, she struck out alone for Goat Island.

John R. Hayes, a black bus driver from New Jersey who moonlighted as an auxiliary policeman, was standing near the tip of Terrapin Point with his wife and some others when he saw two black objects bobbing in the white water above the Falls. "It's only pieces of wood," one of his companions said.

"Like hell, they're wood," cried Hayes. A moment later, to his horror, he saw the overturned boat swept over the Falls, followed by two human beings.

A shout went up: "There's a girl in the water. Someone help. For God's sake, someone help!"

Hayes, who had been trained to save lives, spotted Deanne in her red life jacket about to be swept over the brink a few feet from the Goat Island shore. He dropped the camera he was carrying and made a dash for the ledge, climbing over the aluminum guard rail and teetering on the eighteen-inch lip of the bank, a few feet above the water. "Somebody help me! Help my brother!" Deanne was calling.

Hooking one leg over the railing and arching his body as far as he could, Hayes called to the girl to kick her legs. "Kick harder!" he shouted. Deanne was about to give up, but the sound of his voice compelled her to fight. "Swim for your life, girl," called Hayes. "Don't stop." As Hayes reached for her, she just managed to seize his thumb and two fingers. That was her only lifeline. At this point she was no more than fifteen feet from the brink of the cataract.

The force of the water was so strong Hayes could not haul Deanne to safety. He called for help, but the people in the crowd, watching from behind the rail and stunned by the spectacle, seemed incapable of action.

A short distance away, a Pennsylvania sheet-metal worker saw his predicament and moved instinctively. John Quatrocchi, a veteran of five European campaigns in the Second World War, also had a camera in his hand and his five-year-old son in his arms. He handed the boy to his wife, dropped the camera, and raced for the railing, bumping his head as he tried to squeeze underneath. He stood back, leaped over the barrier, and clinging to the bank by the toes of his shoes, helped Hayes haul the girl to safety.

"My brother! What's happened to my brother?" she cried.

"Pray for him," Quatrocchi told her. With tears streaming from her eyes, Deanne dropped to her knees and prayed.

In the vortex below, Clifford Keech, a quiet, pipe-smoking veteran of twenty-three years as captain of the *Maid of the Mist*, had manoeuvred his vessel to within two hundred feet of the Horseshoe, as far as he ever dared go. He was just about to turn it away when he heard a member of a tour group on board cry out, "Man overboard!"

Keech spotted Roger Woodward in his red life jacket about fifty feet away. A crew member threw out a life ring; it fell short. Another followed; it fell short, too. Keech turned the *Maid* in a large circle so that the rope could swing around the boy's body. Roger flung himself across the life ring in a belly flop. "My sister!" he called. "Where's my sister?" On the observation point above, John Quatrocchi saw the rescue and told Deanne that her prayers had been answered.

Roger Woodward, bruised but game, was hauled aboard in his shorts and running shoes. To everyone's astonishment, he asked for a glass of water. The Niagara River, he said, had tasted funny. He was taken to a hospital, where he made a quick recovery, as did his sister in an American hospital. Honeycutt's body was found four days later.

For the next twenty years Roger Woodward kept asking himself why he and his sister had been spared from almost certain death. "You know," people would say to him, "somebody must be watching out over you; somebody has something special planned for you."

The family moved to Florida. Roger studied music and education at the University of Mississippi, spent four years in the navy, became sales manager for a business-machine firm in Orlando, married, and made two trips back to the Falls to show his children where he had almost died.

During all those intervening years, Roger Woodward continued to question his existence. Where had he come from? Why was he here? Where was he going? He had even gone to see the navy chaplain while in the service to ask those questions. The answers, he thought, were unsatisfactory. It was only later that he understood the effect of the plunge on his subconscious – a traumatic experience, whose psychological impact was so powerful that it left an impression on him for life. It wasn't just him, he theorized; anybody who had survived a miraculous brush with death must question the reason for his continued existence. His sister's response was quite different; to this day, Deanne, a mother with two children, doesn't care to talk about her ordeal.

In 1980 a close friend, Ron Cobb, invited Roger to attend a service at an evangelical church. Years before Roger had taken an interest in evangelism through his friendship with Ross

Finch, a member of Billy Graham's Youth for Christ Movement. But it wasn't until he knelt to pray with Ron Cobb and heard the pastor tell his flock, "There is someone here that is lost today," that Roger Woodward felt his questions would finally be answered. Seated in his pew, he "prayed a simple prayer that simply acknowledged Christ as my Saviour."

In 1990, the thirtieth anniversary of his miraculous escape, he returned again to Niagara Falls, Ontario, to preach in the Glendale Alliance Church. "For the first time in my life I knew what God's purpose was in saving me thirty years ago," he said. "Something happened thirty years ago that was very, very special. I lived. Why? So that I could live again ... so that others would come to the saving knowledge of Christ and have the gift of eternal life."

"I did not conquer the Falls," Roger Woodward declared, "and I don't ever want to be portrayed as someone who tried to do that." Nonetheless, his experience was unique. No human being had ever, before or since, plunged over the brink protected by nothing more than a life jacket and lived. And it is doubtful that anyone else ever will.

But even as Roger was recovering from his ordeal in that summer of 1960, a New York maintenance worker was making plans to repeat Jean Lussier's feat and hurtle over the Horseshoe in a rubber ball of his own invention.

To this day, nobody really knows what possessed William Fitzgerald to invest his life savings in a "Plunge-O-Sphere" so that he could conquer the Falls. He wasn't interested in profit. He shunned publicity. He gave a false name – Nathan Boya – and a false occupation to the press. When reporters sought to find out more about his background, he did his best to cover his tracks. He was only the sixth human being to make the plunge and live to tell the tale. But Fitzgerald wasn't telling. He gave no reasons for his decision, and when others who had talked to him advanced theories, he vigorously denied them.

Unlike his predecessor Stathakis, he was perfectly sane.

395

Before he built his sphere, he sought out Jean Lussier, still alive at the age of sixty-seven, and following Lussier's suggestions carefully, he devised a 1,250-pound capsule with a steel frame built around a six-ply rubber core, covered with a skin of laced steel, and sealed with a spray of rubber and vinyl. Snorkel valves made it possible to draw air into the vessel from outside. An easily opened hatch allowed for a fast exit or escape. Hundreds of ping-pong balls stuffed between the inner and outer chambers, together with a number of inflated cushions, contributed to the vessel's buoyancy. One hundred and fifty pounds of gunshot in a chamber below the cockpit would serve as ballast.

Fitzgerald knew from earlier tragedies that the real problem would be the possibility of suffocation. What if the Plunge-O-Sphere, as he called it, got trapped behind the falling waters and remained submerged? He had planned to rely on the reserve air stored in six truck-sized inner tubes cushioning the cockpit, but he remained uneasy about their usefulness. Who knew how badly they would be battered in the fall?

Could the air be filtered through the kind of carbon dioxide converter then being installed in rockets? It could, but the cost was prohibitive. The Sphere was already costing him five thousand dollars; he could raise no more. Instead, he bought a fire-fighting mask and thirteen CO_2 converter canisters. That would extend his air supply to nine hours. He also installed a pair of mouthpieces that would allow him to expel used air from the capsule. He had learned that asphyxiation was caused not so much by the dwindling oxygen supply as by the intake of too much carbon dioxide.

Fitzgerald may have been eccentric, but he was no madman. His plans were rooted in reality, and when he took to the water from a secret site on the American side of the river on July 15, 1961, with only a few to watch him go, he knew exactly what he was doing. The Plunge-O-Sphere shuddered and bumped against the rocks in the channel as Fitzgerald's body strained against the safety belts. He felt a few moments of raw terror and clawed upward for the grip above him just as the big ball tumbled over the brink and deep into the violence of the basin below.

Fitzgerald described the experience in a few sentences: "Before the Sphere's five thousand pounds of lift could reverse the dive, savage forces ripped the hatchgrip from my hands. Soon it flapped back from its welded hinge. Driving spray shot into the capsule, threatening a watery grave." Then, thrust forward by the current, the Sphere burst out of its shroud of vapour and into the brilliant July sunlight. Standing at the rail of the *Maid of the Mist*, Samuel Shifts, a tourist from East Meadow, Long Island, saw it bobbing in the foam and thought it might be a buoy or marker. Suddenly, to his astonishment, a face appeared at the hatch and a hand waved a greeting. The emergency launch, *Little Sister*, knifed out from the shore to drag the Plunge-O-Sphere to safety.

Boya/Fitzgerald did not act like a typical Falls stunter. To all questions and offers, he replied, "Talk to my attorney." He refused to appear on television, even turning down the Sunday night "Ed Sullivan Show," required watching in those days.

It was some time before reporters ferreted out who he was and what he did. When they stated that he worked as a maintenance man for International Business Machines in New York, he flatly denied it, claiming he was a free-lance writer. Jean Lussier filled in with the few scraps of information he had gained from his friend. He was writing a novel, Lussier said. Fitzgerald denied it. Lussier said he had fallen in love with a girl in France ten years before, that they had planned a honeymoon at the Falls, she had jilted him, and "Boya" had made the trip over the cataract to prove his love. Fitzgerald denied that, too. "I did it for my own satisfaction," was all he would say. "Today, in our overcomplicated life, it's hard for anyone to do something for himself."

Yet there are some clues. His words when he was taken from

397

his odd craft in July 1961 give some hint as to his intentions. "I have integrated the Falls," he said. That was the only reference to his colour, but "integration" was very much a buzz-word at the time. The first lunch counter sit-ins, in Greensboro, North Carolina, had taken place the year before, when Fitzgerald was planning his adventure. In May, two months before his plunge, the "freedom riders" began their demonstrations in Birmingham, Alabama.

Equally significant was the alias he had chosen. He had taken the name Boya to commemorate the role of Tom Mboya, leader of the independence movement in Kenya and General Secretary, in 1960, of the Kenya African National Union.

Was Boya/Fitzgerald's plunge, then, a matter of racial pride – an attempt to demonstrate that a black daredevil could compete on an equal level with white daredevils? If so, he made no further attempt to exploit the idea. A later remark, after climbing out of the sphere, was more laconic. "I always wanted to make the trip and now I have," he said, rather like a tourist returning from having "done" Florence.

He paid a fine of $113 for breaking the law and dropped out of the public eye. He returned to Niagara Falls on the tenth anniversary of his plunge to visit with the family and friends of Jean Lussier, who had died the previous year. Again, he was asked to reveal why he'd gone over the Falls, and again he evaded the question. "I'd rather not go into that," he said with a smile.

At that point, he was studying behavioural science and sociology at New York University, having taken a leave of absence from IBM's department of equal opportunity. He graduated with a Ph.D. in 1977 and continued his studies on a post-doctoral fellowship. Then he joined the National Institute on Drug Abuse as researcher and speech writer.

He was in no sense a typical Falls daredevil. Yet in 1988 he announced he would again go over in a barrel, not for money or personal gain, but to throw the spotlight of publicity on the U.S.

government's treatment of minorities and women. "I hurt in every part of my mind, heart and body," Fitzgerald told a press conference. "There is no hurt like a crushing sense of injustice. It is unbearable and debilitating. It becomes the most controlling force in your life." He claimed a white superior would not allow him, a black man, to be given credit for some sociological research he had done on blood pressure. "My losses have been truly staggering. I have lost my dream, my health, and even may have lost my chance to relieve the suffering of humanity.... I intend to make a second plunge over the Falls to protest the U.S. Government's treatment ... of whistle blowers who ethically resist corruption."

He never did it. "I'm trying to talk him out of it," his wife said, "but he's a very determined person." Apparently she succeeded, for Dr. William Fitzgerald, a.k.a. Nathan Boya, the diffident daredevil – like Annie Taylor and Jean Lussier before him – never made good on his promise to tempt the cataract a second time. Nor has he ever explained his reasons for doing it at all.

2

Four years after William Fitzgerald's plunge, eighty thousand square miles of northeastern North America were suddenly blacked out by the worst power failure in the continent's history. The trouble was traced to a small fail-safe device, no larger than a pay telephone, in the Sir Adam Beck Generating Plant No. 2 at Niagara Falls. At eleven seconds after 5:16 p.m. on November 9, 1965, at the worst possible hour, when most people were heading home from work and housewives were cooking dinner on their electric stoves, the device automatically triggered the catastrophe.

Exactly thirty seconds later, in the Robert Moses generating station across the river, operators sensed trouble. The familiar hum of the big generators became a series of eerie, off-key whines as they suddenly changed pitch. Synchronized to produce power at 120 revolutions a minute, they now began to spin at varying speeds. The dials that showed the amount of power the plant was producing went wild. The automatic governors that set the speed of the generators sprang into action, but these were soon fighting each other – one slowing down to compensate for the loss in demand for power, another speeding up as its automatic equipment sensed an increasing demand for its own power production. The needle that indicated the flow of power came right off the paper, producing "more squiggly lines than in an earthquake." The power zoomed suddenly from 1,500 megawatts to 2,250, then dropped back to zero.

Herbert Hubbard, the chief project operator, took three men with him and raced downstairs to begin manual operation of the generators, resynchronizing them by hand individually and bringing them back to proper speed. By 5:45 they were operating normally, but at 6:30 they went out of step once more. Again, it took manual operation to calm them down.

By then the entire northeast power grid was in disarray. In just twelve minutes, thirty million bewildered people in eight states were plunged into blackness; most of Ontario was also affected. Dale Chapman, a United Airlines pilot, was flying at 30,000 feet and looked down at the bright lights of New York City; suddenly he found that the entire city was missing. To him, it looked like the end of the world. Another pilot, Reinhard Noethel, flying a Boeing 707 at 39,000 feet, told his passengers that if they looked out of the windows on the left side they'd see Boston – and then gasped: Boston was gone.

In Niagara Falls, where it all started, power was restored by seven that evening, partly because of the large number of producing stations in the area and partly because of prompt action by the Niagara Mohawk Power Corporation, which quickly cut back power to its industrial customers.

Toronto, with its 670 electric streetcars and 130 electric

trolley buses, blacked out for an hour and twenty minutes at the height of the rush hour. Nineteen minutes later, at 6:54 p.m., it blacked out again. Power was restored at 7:12, but a third outage came at 7:22. Surface lines did not begin running again until 8:32. The subways – with 12,000 passengers aboard – were out until nine o'clock. The result was chaos. Traffic lights stopped working, and in the words of one witness, "the pedestrians went wild, like cattle let out of a pen." At least two men left stalled streetcars to act as emergency traffic policemen. Apartment dwellers couldn't get their cars into garages that operated with electric doors; others couldn't use elevators or even some stairs because these were intended as fire escapes and were reached by doors opened only from the inside.

But Toronto's problems paled beside those of New York City, which was out of power for almost fourteen hours, partly because Consolidated Edison did not move quickly enough to cut itself off from the interconnected systems. The blackout began at 5:27 p.m. Service was not restored until dawn.

Ten thousand of New York's subway passengers were trapped for seven hours; 800,000 were stranded in electric commuter trains. Two trains ground to a stop in the middle of the Williamsburg Bridge, suspended high above the East River. Mary Doyle, an eighteen-year-old commuter, would always remember the sensation, rather like riding on a Ferris wheel: "The wind would blow and the train would sway and some people would scream." With the help of the police, she and the others made their way gingerly across an eleven-inch catwalk leading from the tracks to the bridge's roadway below. This precarious manoeuvre occupied five hours.

Firemen were forced to break through walls in the three tallest skyscrapers – the Empire State, Pan American, and RCA buildings – to release scores of people trapped in elevators. Thirteen strangers squeezed into an elevator on the twenty-first floor of the Empire State Building grew to know each other so well that they organized a Blackout Club that met regularly long after the incident was over. Stranded on the thirty-second floor of another building, a lawyer turned and said to his fellow passengers, "Thank God we've got some whiskey." When the whiskey was gone, they held seances to understand their spiritual selves. Four people found themselves trapped for twenty hours in the RCA Building. One turned out to be a yoga expert. To fight off boredom, he gave the others lessons in various positions, even demonstrating by standing on his head.

Five hundred aircraft had to be diverted from New York City. One thousand overseas passengers found their transatlantic flights cancelled. Some three million cheques could not be cleared at the Federal Reserve Bank. Television went off the air and only transistor and car radios worked. The *New York Times* was the only paper able to publish, thanks to a printing plant across the Hudson in that part of New Jersey unaffected by the power failure.

Yet people groping their way along the dark streets or stranded in the bars and cafés, sleeping on couches and carpets in hotels, remained remarkably cheerful. Fifteen people sang Calypso songs aboard one stranded train and danced in the aisles. Crime, astonishingly, took a holiday. Civil defence was alerted and the National Guard called out, yet there were only a quarter of the arrests made on a normal night. Only two people died as a result of the power failure, one from a heart attack after climbing ten flights of stairs, the other from a fall in the dark. One family's apartment was gutted by a fire caused by emergency candles.

People who had taken the genie of electricity for granted all their lives now came to realize they had become its slaves. The experience of the family of Edwin Robins, a mechanical engineer in Queens, was typical of that of thousands of gadget lovers who suddenly found that *nothing* worked. In the Robins house it wasn't only the lights that went off. The heat went off because the oil furnace was triggered by electricity. The refrigerator stopped running. The stove wouldn't work. The house was a machine that had run out of power. The intercom system didn't work, nor did the multitone door chimes. The Danish dining-room chandelier didn't work. The bedroom clocks didn't work. The hair dryer, the electric blankets, the can opener, the toothbrush, and the razor were all unusable. Even the electric-eye garage door was out of business. The Robins family, who had learned to Live Better Electrically, in the enthusiastic advertising phrase of the day, now found themselves reduced to searing steaks over an outdoor barbecue.

Charcoal fires and guttering candles – the stuff of the Middle Ages – were no longer trendy; they were essential. Harriette Browne, a Manhattan housewife, was forced to use the candles intended for her husband's birthday cake to light the house. People stormed into Ajello's candle shop and snapped up fancy bayberry candles at $7.50 a pair. The New York Hilton Hotel alone used up thirty thousand candles that night.

Nobody yet knew how it had started, and that included the experts. One small boy in New Haven was certain that it was his fault. He whacked a telephone pole with a stick and every light in town went out. He rushed home, weeping, to his mother. A Manhattan housewife who had just finished trimming the ends of some electrical wires, preparing for the painter, experienced a moment of shock when the blackout struck. "What have I done now?" she blurted. Some thought the power system had been sabotaged, probably by the Russians; others thought the Pentagon, experimenting with new weaponry, was to blame.

It took a week to pinpoint the cause of the trouble at Beck 2 and another month for a commission of inquiry to sort out all the details. Ironically, it was the very obsession with safety that helped trigger the blackout – that, and the rapidly increasing hunger for electrical power in North America.

The northeast power grid, known as the CANUSE system (for Canadian and United States Energy), covered much of

Ontario and most of the northeastern United States. It represented a pool of power provided by a loose confederation of forty-two power companies on both sides of the border. Most of this power came from Niagara Falls through the two Beck plants at Queenston and the Robert Moses plant across the river. Combined, they represented the largest generating capacity in one location in North America.

This pooling of resources – the purchase and exchange of power – not only avoided costly duplication but was also efficient, cheap, and reliable. It allowed the transfer of power almost instantaneously to any area that suddenly ran short. The northeast grid was connected to other grids on the continent, so that a housewife in Hamilton, Ontario, plugging in an electric frying pan, might be using power shared by a company in Kansas.

There was, however, a risk. A massive breakdown in one part of the system could create excessive strain and automatically set off a chain reaction throughout the network. Automation had its disadvantages; it required intervention by a human to cut a local system out of the power grid. No fewer than eight buttons at the Consolidated Edison control centre in New York had to be pushed to isolate the city from the rest of the power pool. In the late afternoon of November 9, that had been done too late.

An electrical superhighway of five transmission lines connected Beck 2 with Toronto. On the day of the blackout each of the five was loaded almost to its capacity of 375 megawatts. There was a protective system in operation. If a line became overloaded, a series of circuit breakers, similar to those in an ordinary household, would go into operation and cut off the power. For extra safety, there were backup relays in case a circuit breaker failed to work. Thus there were two sets of failsafe devices standing by to protect the lines going out of Beck 2.

The defect in the system was that Ontario Hydro had not

taken into account the increasing demand for power. The relays were set too low. The backup relay that triggered the blackout had been set in 1963 to operate if the line carried more than 375 megawatts of power. The load the line carried was then much less than the maximum. Now, two years later, although the demand had increased, the relays had not been reset.

Power consumption was building up to its winter peak. The weather was getting colder, and one big steam plant in Ontario was out of operation. The load on the lines to Toronto became heavier. The average flow out of Niagara to Toronto reached 365 megawatts that afternoon, dangerously close to the maximum that had been set in 1963. The flows, however, were not constant; they fluctuated from second to second. On November 9, the flow on one line momentarily exceeded the 375 megawatt maximum, and the fail-safe system automatically disconnected the line.

The remaining lines were already close to being overloaded. When the flow on the disconnected line was transferred to the four still operating out of Beck 2, each became loaded beyond the level at which its protective relay was set to operate. They tripped out successively over a two-and-a-half-second period. With these five major lines disconnected, the Beck 2 generator at Niagara was separated from the rest of the network in Ontario. The Moses plant, too, had been sending power to Toronto, and now this power, together with all the power being generated by Beck 2 – a total of 1.5 million kilowatts – had nowhere to go. It reversed itself, cascaded across the Niagara gorge, and was automatically redirected to other lines in the grid leading south and east. This huge surge of power was more than the lines could carry. It knocked out system after system, as one Hydro account put it, "like box cars piling up after an engine jumps the tracks."

An instantaneous drop in power generation at the big Niagara plants was followed by a rapid buildup that threw the generators out of phase. That caused the breakdown of the New

405

York State transmission system. In effect, the grid had ceased to operate as a pool and was cut into sections. Within minutes, even seconds, the domino effect had forced other hydro plants as well as steam plants to shut down.

In New York City the following morning, weary transit workers walked every foot of the 720-mile subway system to make sure that no one had fallen on the tracks or been incapacitated by injuries. For many New Yorkers, walking was a new experience. Some had trudged thirty blocks or more to get home the night before or descended an equal number of flights of stairs to escape the darkened skyscrapers.

For the first time many people began to realize the extent of the electrical revolution. It was only sixty-nine years since Niagara Falls power had begun to propel the Buffalo streetcars. Since that day, every house had become an electrical machine, and when the power went off, the machine ran down; as the Robins family discovered, everything from TV sets to food mixers stopped functioning.

In spite of the $100-million damage bill for business, the great blackout was no more than a minor glitch in a world attuned to and dazzled by scientific progress. Its chief legacy, and a sobering one, was its demonstration, in the most graphic manner possible, of the utter vulnerability of the modern urban human animal.

3

By the early sixties, the mayor of Niagara Falls, New York, had become seriously concerned about the condition of the American cataract. His city was losing tourists to the Canadian side because not only were the Horseshoe Falls more spectacular but they had also undergone a series of improvements that made them more accessible for viewing.

In 1954, an international control structure had been built out from the Canadian shore one mile above the Horseshoe to replace an earlier underwater weir. Its chief purpose was to hold back the flow of the river so that enough water could be diverted into the upstream tunnels on both sides to feed the Beck and Moses generating stations. But it also controlled the crest of the Horseshoe, allowing the water to spread out to an evener and more picturesque line than in the past.

The following year a great deal of remedial work had been undertaken on both flanks of the Horseshoe by U.S. and Canadian engineers. The riverbed below the old site of Table Rock was cleared of debris and filled in to provide better space for viewing the great Falls. Directly opposite, on the eastern flank of the Horseshoe, an area at Terrapin Point had been drained and back-filled to create another large viewing space.

While the enhanced Horseshoe Falls became an even greater attraction, the smaller cataract on the American side was further diminished by nature itself. Since the big rock slide of 1931, a series of lesser slides had dumped tens of thousands of tons of talus below the American Falls as the cataract continued its slow but relentless movement upriver. The rocks that tumbled from the Horseshoe, producing its notch-shape, dropped into the 200-foot-deep plunge pool below and vanished. But the smaller cataract did not have the force required to remove the talus or the depth of water below to hide it.

The greatest rock fall of all, in 1954, had virtually obliterated Prospect Point and also torn a wedge-shaped section out of the cataract. Prospect Point had lost its glamour, and the view of the Horseshoe from Terrapin Point had been diminished, too. By equalizing the outflow of water over the Horseshoe's crest, the engineers had reduced the amount gushing over the flanks, especially on the American side near the site of the old Terrapin Tower.

The original Cave of the Winds, where tourists in waterproof clothing had ventured behind the sheet of the Luna Falls, was no more. With constant erosion threatening another disaster, the famous site had been blasted away. The name remained, and visitors continued to go down by the elevator that led to the base of the Luna, or Bridal Veil, Falls. There they threaded their way along the catwalks, drenched by a furious blast of spray. It was still an exciting adventure, but not as thrilling as it had once been.

The worst problem was the talus, a mountain of debris growing higher with every rock-fall and blocking off the view of the American cataract. Everything from baseball-sized stones to huge boulders the size of a house lay in heaps outward for fifty feet from the precipice over which the water flowed.

The Falls here were 182 feet high, but in certain spots the mound of talus had accumulated to a height of 100 feet. Every time a prominent feature collapsed, the cataract was further obscured. Photographs taken at the turn of the century show it in all its glory. By the mid-sixties, at least half of it was hidden by the rubble. If the process were allowed to continue, nature would eventually transform the American Falls into a series of tumbling rapids threading their way through a labyrinth of broken rock. Although that calamity belonged to the distant future, the city fathers and the business community could see the Falls already diminishing before their eyes, and they didn't like what they saw.

They were convinced that something must be done. Mankind had already "conquered" the Falls, stolen half the water for power, improved the crest-line of the Horseshoe; now, once again, nature would have to do mankind's bidding. With the help of the Niagara Falls *Gazette*, the mayor launched a campaign to involve both state and federal governments in a gigantic project to clear away the debris. Specifically, the city council asked for "remedial action to prevent further erosion and rock slides, which are endangering tourists and sending them to Canada to view the already stabilized Horseshoe Falls."

With the approval of the International Joint Commission and

with partial funding from Ontario Hydro and the New York State Power Authority, U.S. army engineers carried out, in the summer of 1969, "the most exciting challenge in the history of Niagara Falls." They drained the American Falls dry. Half a mile above the cataract, in the channel between Goat Island and the American shore, the engineers built a massive cofferdam of earth and rock fill. It wasn't an easy job. The channel at this point was 600 feet wide, and the current raced through at more than thirty miles an hour. When the dam was about three-quarters finished and the channel narrowed to a width of 140 feet, the pressure became so powerful that a six-foot section of the dam was torn out overnight. To circumvent the current, the engineers brought in huge quarter-ton boulders and dumped them in the gap. Then they added truckloads of earth taken from the great excavations that had accompanied the building of the Robert Moses powerplant.

By June 10, the curtain of water over the precipice had thinned from a flow of 6,000 cubic feet a second to 500. The roar of the cataract was muffled; bare spots appeared in the channel above the Falls. The next day, all the water was diverted around Goat Island to the Horseshoe. By the following morning, the American channel would be dry.

What lay behind that silver sheet of water, foam, and spray? Thousands waited up all night to find out. Dawn broke to reveal a withered escarpment in all its nakedness – a brown and jagged cliff, riven with cracks and fissures and scarred by two vast wounds made when the rock falls of 1931 and 1954 were ripped from the precipice. Three hundred thousand tons of debris lay heaped at the base.

Halfway up that great rock-fall lay the broken body of a young man; at its base, where a few rivulets still trickled, was the corpse of a young woman – both apparently suicides. Gulls in great clouds, shrieking like banshees, swirled and dived over the dead channel, feasting on the fish that lay flopping in small pools beneath the cliff. Coins flung into the seething waters for good luck glittered among the pebbles in the damp sand of the riverbed. The engineers collected twelve quarts of these.

To the crowds gawking at the unaccustomed spectacle, the sandwich of sedimentary rocks was clearly visible: eighty feet of hard Lockport dolostone surmounting sixty-one feet of softer Rochester shale and below that more layers of other shales and sandstone. The softer shales were already drying out in the hot June sunlight; they would have to be kept wet to prevent their flaking off. A temporary network of pipes drew water from the river above the dam to keep the strata wet until the engineers could install a system of powerful sprays in the rock face itself. On the islands that dotted the dried channel, the poplar trees, too, had to be regularly watered.

The purpose of this expensive and unwieldy operation was to try to find a solution to the problem of the mountain of talus obscuring the view. How much was there? Could it be moved? How deep did it go before it reached the floor of the river? And what, exactly, was causing the harder dolostone caps to break off in dangerous and spectacular rock slides?

The army and its geologists had just five months in which to study the area by drilling into the rock. Once the freeze-up began in late November, the cataract would have to be turned on again. Until that time there would be no American Falls, only the great pock-marked cliff, its rim edged by saw-toothed indentations. Some merchants had worried that the experiment would harm the tourist business. On the contrary, it provided a much-needed boost. That summer, local business almost doubled as people poured in to view one of the great wonders of the world tamed by the hand of man. To accommodate these spectators, the army built flights of wooden steps that led down from Prospect Point to link up with an eighty-foot boardwalk, five feet wide, out on the dry riverbed.

Over the five-month period, the army engineers removed dozens of drill cores taken from borings made in the face of the

410

precipice and in the dry riverbed behind the Falls. Two cages were suspended over the cliff on cables hung from a fifty-foot crane. Workmen in one cage used crowbars to remove any scale or loose rocks that might fall on the drillers. In the second cage, a group of geologists oversaw a meticulous foot-by-foot examination of the rock. Workmen sprayed and sandblasted the ancient riverbed upstream from the cliff, scouring out sand and silt to expose the entire 1,100-foot crest for a distance of 400 feet upriver.

The drilling crews arrived after them and faced the delicate task of boring three-inch test holes in the riverbed and in the cliff face. The cores – totalling a mile in length – had to be in mint condition when they were withdrawn. Special miniature cameras were then dropped down these test holes to gain a better idea of the rock structure.

It soon became apparent from the drilling that this friable cliff was a labyrinth of passageways through which the waters of the river constantly seeped, freezing and thawing over the seasons, expanding the cracks and weakening the shales. The seepage extended under Goat Island and, indeed, was visible to the workers, who could see small jets of water shooting from the cliff face.

In one place, near Prospect Point, the drillers lost both their drill and their rock core in a vast cavity at the forty-foot level. They poured black dye into the hole and waited. Ten minutes and thirty seconds later, the dye emerged in three places thirty feet farther down the cliff. This was added proof that water was percolating through the hard cap of dolostone and into the softer shales.

The entire area was honeycombed with these vertical clefts. Small wonder that so much of Prospect Point had fallen into the river! A wide fissure, one hundred feet deep, had already partially detached a chunk of what was left of the point from the main mass. The crack in the cliff grew appreciably wider as the work progressed, indicating that this would be the site of the next major rock-fall. But when it would be, nobody could tell. It might come at any moment. It might not come for decades. The engineers were taking no chances. An elaborate system of warning sensors had been installed at the outset to give the workmen time to escape, and no workman was allowed to operate below any of the overhangs. Fortunately, nothing untoward occurred.

The geologists made another surprising discovery. The great heap of broken rock that was blocking the view of the Falls was actually acting as a buffer, propping up the crumbling cliff. If it were removed, there was no knowing what would happen.

By fall, nature had begun to blur the edges of the dry riverbed. A tomato plant was discovered growing out of one of the cracks, bearing ten green tomatoes. Carp continued to flop about in the shallow ponds caused by the inexorable seepage. Small poplar seedlings had sprouted in some of the holes.

All this was swept away on November 25, 1969, when the work ended. At 10:43 that morning, a huge crane on top of the cofferdam gnawed a cavity in the wall of earth and rock. Water began to trickle through the gap and pour over the grey, misshapen rocks, to plunge into the gorge below. Within a day the American Falls were back in business.

When the American Falls International Board studying the results of the survey finally delivered its report in February 1972, it was clear that the new conservation movement that had begun in the sixties had affected its decisions. "It is better to allow the process of natural change to continue uninterrupted rather than to give permanence to a particular condition and appearance," the commissioners wrote.

The cycle of erosion and recession should not be interrupted, the report said. The mountain of rubble at the base – 280,000 cubic yards – was "a dynamic part of the natural condition of the Falls." It would be wrong, the commissioners declared, "to make the Falls static and unnatural, like an artificial waterfall in a garden or a park, however grand the scale."

412

The report admitted that the enormous forces of nature might "eventually convert the waterfall into a steeply sloping cascade." But the board added that it had another aspect to consider: "that the visibility of the immense forces at work on the Falls ... is an important part of the dramatic effect, and that any attempt to conceal and interrupt these forces might remove from the scene some element of aesthetic appreciation."

Once again, man had tried to change the course of nature. This time nature was to be allowed to take its own course.

Chapter Thirteen

1

Five years after the American Falls International Board agreed not to tamper with nature, Niagara Falls, New York, was plunged into the worst crisis in its history. The earlier prophecies of trouble at the old Hooker Chemical dump in the Love Canal returned to haunt the city. For well over a century, the Falls had enjoyed an international reputation as a glamorous and spectacular resort. By 1978 that reputation was tarnished.

By shutting off the American Falls almost as easily, it seemed, as turning off a kitchen tap, man had "conquered" Niagara. Decade by decade, more and more water rushing toward the cataract had been taken to produce power. But much of that power had been used to fuel the factories where ordinary carbon was transformed into a satanic mixture that now bubbled up in the basements of families that had bought houses near 97th and 99th streets in the LaSalle residential district of the American city. (There was no 98th Street. That was the site of the Love Canal.)

In 1976, after one of the heaviest snowfalls in history, the situation had become critical. Several years of abundant snow and rain had already turned the old canal into a sponge. Its contents, often disturbed by digging, were overflowing into the surrounding clay and sandy loam, oozing through the old creekbeds and swales that formed swampy channels extending into the neighbourhood. That year, Patricia Bulka discovered a black, oily sludge oozing out of the drains into her basement. Her mind turned back to ten years earlier, when she and her family had moved into the LaSalle district in the southeast corner of the city. Her son Joey had fallen into a muddy ditch, and when his brother, John, pulled him out, both boys came home covered in what she described as an "oily gook." She scrubbed them down and threw their clothes away, but the noxious odour from the muck filled their house for more than two weeks.

At that time, Mrs. Bulka had alerted the Niagara County Health Department. Men arrived, took soil samples, and assured the Bulkas that nothing was wrong. Afterwards, Mrs. Bulka had to endure the indignation of the neighbours, some of whom refused to speak to her for calling the authorities and, by implication, threatening the real-estate values in LaSalle.

Thereafter, Patricia Bulka held her tongue. If she connected young Joey's chronic ear ailment or John's respiratory problems with the incident, she said nothing, even though both problems had begun after the boys went into the ditch. But in the spring and summer of 1976, she found that her neighbours also had basements redolent with the same oily black sludge that was welling up in hers. The Bulkas bought a sump-pump to clear their basement; so did several of their neighbours.

Nobody now attacked Mrs. Bulka for her concerns. Calls began to flow in to the Niagara Falls *Gazette*, which sent its educational reporter, David Pollak, out to the LaSalle district to look into the complaints. On October 3, Pollak reported that "Civilization has crept to the doorstep of a former Hooker Chemicals and Plastics Corp. waste deposit site, and the combination contains the elements of an industrial horror story." The phrasing was melodramatic, but, as it turned out, Pollak had not exaggerated the situation.

Over the past year the Bulka family had worn out three sump-pumps trying to cope with the seepage through cellar walls that were only one hundred feet from the dump site. Pollak had some of this material analysed by an independent firm. Its analysis made it clear that the chemical content came from Hooker wastes. Love Canal, the *Gazette* reported, contained at least fifteen organic chemicals including three chlorinated hydrocarbons, which, the analysts declared, constituted an "environmental concern" and were "certainly ... a health hazard." Anyone who breathed the fumes or touched the substances could be affected. The only immediate action taken by the county health department as a result of these revelations was to state that sump-pumping was illegal and to threaten to take action against anyone pumping out a basement into the sewer system.

Meanwhile, the winter of 1976-77 dragged on, leaving the residents worrying about a problem the authorities refused to acknowledge. The odours abated during the cold weather but returned in the spring. George Amery of the county health department assured everybody that while the fumes might be disagreeable, they posed no immediate health threat to the people living along the old canal. By May 1977 the seepage had been found in at least twenty-one homes. The state ordered corrective action, and in June, the city commissioned a private corporation to study the problem and come up with a solution. Nothing more was heard from officialdom about Love Canal until August, when a dogged reporter, Michael Brown, dug into the human side of the story and sparked the protest movement that, in the end, made Love Canal a byword for pollution in North America.

Brown, a published author, had been born and raised in Niagara Falls. Returning after a five-year absence in 1975, he found a new spirit in the community. Local politicians were proudly announcing handsome new industrial and office buildings. The city seemed to be getting back on its feet after a long decline. In February 1977, Brown went to work for the *Gazette* as a suburban reporter. That summer, he covered a public hearing concerning the existence of a waste disposal firm in the city. A young woman took over the microphone to oppose the company's presence and suddenly, to Brown's mystification, burst into tears as she mentioned another dumpsite ravaging her neighbourhood. That was the first Brown had ever heard of Love Canal. He went to the *Gazette* library and dug out the Pollak articles and some other clippings. Except for Pollak's

418

investigation, the reports were reassuring. The consensus seemed to be that the situation was well in hand, and there was little hard fact to support the young woman's emotional outburst.

He soon changed his mind when he visited the Love Canal area. As he wrote later, "I saw homes where dogs had lost their fur. I saw children with various birth defects. I saw entire families in inexplicably poor health. When I walked on the Love Canal, I gasped for air as my lungs heaved in fits of wheezing. My eyes burned. There was a sour taste in my mouth."

On August 10, Brown wrote his first front-page story, the opening shot in a crusade that would win him a Pulitzer Prize. The state ordered the city to investigate, but when the city found that corrective action would cost $400,000, it rejected it as too expensive. That was a short-sighted decision; within a year the bill for temporary remedies would soar to $2 million. (The total cost of cleanup was later put at $500 million.)

Assured that the story would be pursued, Brown returned to his suburban beat. But the newspaper, under heavy pressure from city officials and industrial leaders, played the story down. "There seemed to be an unwritten law that a reporter did not attack or otherwise fluster the Hooker executives," Brown later wrote. Nothing more appeared in the press until February 1978, after Brown was given the city hall beat. On February 2, in his Cityscape column, he charged, "Government officials are in the throes of a full-fledged environmental crisis." The city was supposed to take action the previous summer, he wrote, but nothing had been done.

By this time the filled-in land over the canal between 97th and 99th streets was a quagmire of greasy mud and potholes. When a city truck tried to cross the field to dump clay into a hole, it sank to its axles. In May, after David Pollak was made city editor, the *Gazette* stepped up its coverage. This wasn't easy because the authorities kept a tight lid on information. The Environmental Protection Agency had at last been persuaded to conduct tests in the basements of the houses on the canal to see if chemicals were present in the air. It took Brown three months to get at the results, which had not been published. A stray memo to a local senator revealed that benzene had been detected on the streets adjoining the canal. This widely used solvent is a carcinogen known to cause headaches, fatigue, weight loss, dizziness, and, eventually, nosebleeds in addition to damage to the bone marrow. The toxic vapours, the EPA survey reported, "suggest a serious threat to health and welfare."

Brown kept up the exposés. He revealed that both federal and state officials were considering declaring Love Canal a disaster area and evacuating some residents. He quoted a state biologist as saying that if he owned a home near the canal and could afford to move, he would. That same month – May 1978 – the state announced at last that it would conduct a health survey based on blood samples taken at the southerly end of the canal area. The results were alarming. The women living in the area had suffered a high rate of miscarriage and given birth to an extraordinary number of children with birth defects. In one age group, 35.3 percent had records of spontaneous abortion – far in excess of the national average. And the people who had lived for the longest period near Love Canal had suffered the highest rates.

It was about this time that a slender, dark-haired housewife named Lois Gibbs found herself involved. She was only twenty-six, painfully shy, politically uncommitted. Love Canal would change her life forever, as it changed the lives of so many others in Niagara Falls, New York.

2

Lois Gibbs had been born and raised on Grand Island, some three miles above the Falls. She married young, as most of her friends did, and after her son, Michael, was born in August

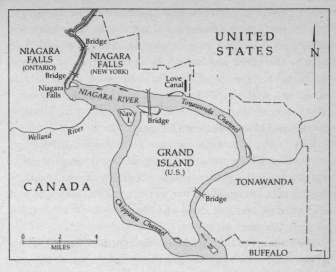

Grand Island

1972, the family moved across to the city so that Lois's husband, Harry, would be closer to his job as a chemical worker at Goodyear Tire.

They bought a three-bedroom house on 101st Street, three blocks south of Love Canal. Mrs. Gibbs had been only vaguely aware of Mike Brown's stories in the *Gazette* and was confused by his references to 97th and 99th streets. These streets came to an end at Pine Avenue (now Niagara Falls Parkway) and commenced again farther to the north. She thought the problem lay some distance away on the far side of Pine. Though she sympathized with the people whose property seemed to be contaminated, she did not connect the problem with her own district until Brown mentioned the 99th Street School. That brought her up short. "Wow!" she thought. "This isn't on the other side of Pine Avenue. This is in my own backyard."

She called her brother-in-law, a professor of biochemistry at the state university in Buffalo, and asked him to translate some of the scientific jargon in the articles. She couldn't quite believe what he told her. It was enough, however, to convince her she should get her son out of the school. She went to the *Gazette* library to read the back files. From these she learned that some of the chemicals could cause a nervous reaction while others might cause blood disease or leukemia.

Lois Gibbs was suddenly very alert. Since Michael had started school the year before, his blood count had gone down and he had begun to have seizures. She had been vainly badgering her pediatrician about her son's condition, which he had diagnosed as epilepsy. Now she began to suspect that there might be another cause.

She reproached herself for her earlier inattention: "God! It's all my fault." Until now she had thought of the grassy expanse that covered the old canal as nothing more than a little park in which her children could gambol. Before Michael started school she had been in the habit of taking him and his younger sister, Melissa, there every day before lunch – *every* day, because, as she was to recall, "being a blue-collar Mom, you have a routine and you never vary it."

Up to this point, Lois Gibbs was, as she herself later remarked, "a typical blue-collar housewife." Her husband was employed on shiftwork at Goodyear. Her own life revolved around the home. As she was to put it, "when you graduate from high school you get married, you have children, the boys go bowling and go for a beer Friday night to cash their checks, and the girls do Bingo with Mom." She didn't belong to any community organizations, had no interest in politics, and voted Democrat only because her mother did. She was a private, inward person, so shy that she mailed in her city taxes rather than paying the bill personally, as others did, because she didn't want to face strangers at the counter.

That is the unlikely background of the woman who achieved

international attention as the determined and effective leader of the activist movement that forced a mass evacuation of the Love Canal district.

Lois Gibbs herself has said that she was the product of an American educational system that puts strong emphasis on grass-roots democracy. If a citizen had a problem, she believed, she had only to call city hall or the local newspaper and the difficulty would be resolved. She soon discovered that it didn't work that way. Over the years she met and had to overcome an inflexible attitude of civic and political resistance. Almost immediately, when she tried to transfer her son to another school, she came up against that resistance. No one would take responsibility for doing something that might establish a precedent. If Michael were allowed to transfer, how many others would follow suit? The superintendent of schools, after a frustrating delay, told her the area was not contaminated and there were no plans to close the 99th Street School.

Lois Gibbs was furious. She had a stubborn streak that was aroused when she grew angry. Now, like a mother bear protecting her cubs, she decided on direct action. She would get up a petition demanding that the school be closed.

She was used to having strangers bang on her door selling something, and so were most of her neighbours. She realized that the women, who were home in the daytime, would be more receptive to her entreaties than the husbands, most of whom worked for the very chemical companies that were under fire. The mother instinct was alive in LaSalle that spring of 1978. It had caused Lois Gibbs, so shy she couldn't face a civic clerk across a counter, to knock on strangers' doors. It would cause others to join her. The campaign that followed was very largely a women's movement.

For young Lois Gibbs it wasn't easy. She felt herself sweating as she knocked timidly on the first door on 99th Street. To her relief, nobody was at home. "What am I doing here?" she asked herself. "I must be crazy." She turned and fled to her own house. Sitting there in the kitchen with her empty petition still in her hands, she screwed up her courage. She realized she'd been afraid of making a fool of herself, but now she reasoned, "What's more important -- what people think or your child's health?"

Next day she ventured out again, not as far as 99th but on her own street, where she knew the neighbours. That made it easier. She started out with people she knew and then, growing bolder, worked backwards to 100th Street, and finally to 99th and 97th, the two streets that bordered the old canal.

She soon developed a set speech that took about twenty minutes. The more she heard from those who would listen, the more frightened she became. It seemed as though every home on 99th had someone with an illness. The problem, she realized, involved much more than the school. The whole community was sick. She quickly found herself at the centre of a small nucleus of activist neighbours determined to force the hands of the authorities. The New York State Department of Health held a public meeting that June to announce its plan to take soil and air samples from the first ring of houses – those whose backyards abutted on the canal – and blood samples from the occupants to see if there really was a problem.

Mrs. Gibbs rose to her feet. She had never spoken in public before, but her anger gave her a voice, especially when Dr. Nicholas Vianna warned the audience not to eat any of the vegetables from their gardens. Obviously, there *was* a problem. Dr. Vianna tried to soothe the audience by announcing that a new filtration system running the length of the canal would be installed to contain the overflow wastes leaching out.

But what, Mrs. Gibbs asked, about the underground streams that fed off the canal? "How will your overflow system shut those springs off?" She didn't get a straight answer.

"How can these kids be safe walking on the playground?" she wanted to know.

"Have the children walk on the sidewalk," she was told. "Make sure they don't cut across the canal."

"How can you say all that when the playground is *on* the canal?" she asked again.

"You are their mother," Dr. Vianna replied. "You can limit the time they play on the canal." Lois Gibbs wondered if the doctor had children of his own.

This meeting, and a second equally frustrating one in July, helped bind the residents of the Love Canal area together. The authorities still wouldn't admit there was a problem, but neither would they say that the area was safe. The neighbourhood was now thoroughly aroused as Mrs. Gibbs and her neighbours stepped up the pressure on the authorities. They shot off letters to state and federal politicians and started to make plans to sue the board of education, Hooker, the city, and the county.

The New York State Department of Health announced an open meeting of Love Canal residents for August 2, 1978. To Lois Gibbs's anger, it would be held at Albany, the state capital, three hundred miles away. She tried to get the venue moved to Niagara Falls without success and so determined to go to Albany herself.

Armed with a thick sheaf of newspaper clippings and a parcel of junk food, she and Debbie Carillo, a 99th Street housewife who had suffered three miscarriages, drove off with Harry Gibbs at the wheel. For the Gibbs family, it was an expensive journey. Harry was bringing home $150 a week. Babysitters had to be hired. The hotel room alone cost forty dollars. But it had to be done.

At the meeting in Albany the next morning, the health department dropped a series of bombshells. First, the residents were again warned not to eat any of the vegetables from their gardens. Second, the department announced that the 99th Street School would be closed. Then came the big shocker. Commissioner Robert Whalen announced that all children under two and pregnant women should leave the district for health reasons.

In spite of these admissions that a problem existed, Lois Gibbs was furious. The state had not said that it would pay for the evacuation, only that people should move. And what was the rest of the family going to do? She leaped to her feet. "If the dump will hurt pregnant women and children under two, what, for God's sake, is it going to do to the rest of us? What do you think you're doing? You can't do that! That would be murder!"

Whalen did not return to the meeting after a ten-minute break. Mrs. Gibbs had arrived with a list of fifty questions for the health officials. None was answered to her satisfaction. "You'll just have to be patient," she was told. "We're doing more studies…. We're going to check on that…."

When the trio got back to Niagara Falls, exhausted, they faced a crowd of angry residents on 99th Street. Hundreds of people were milling about, shouting, screaming, yelling, burning their mortgages and tax bills and calling her name.

Now she found herself, microphone in hand, making the first real public speech of her life, trying to answer the questions that poured from every side, trying to explain what had gone on at the Albany meeting. She spoke haltingly, prefacing and ending each sentence with "Okay?" – only too aware that she was a rank amateur at her self-appointed job. The best she could do was to tell the crowd that the department of health would be holding a meeting the following night in the 99th Street School.

That meeting was as tumultuous as the street scene. Again there were few hard answers. The night after that, in the firehall on 102nd Street, the Love Canal Homeowners Association was formed, and Lois Gibbs was propelled into the presidency. As she took the chair, she asked herself, "How am I going to get through this evening?" But she managed to set four goals for the new association:

1. relocation of all those who wanted to leave the area,
2. an effort to prop up property values,
3. a proper clean-up of the canal, and
4. testing of the soil, air, and water throughout the entire area to see how far the contamination had spread.

On August 7, President Jimmy Carter lent strength to her cause by declaring a federal state of emergency at the Love Canal dump.

3

By the time the governor of New York, Hugh Carey, made a personal visit to the Love Canal, Lois Gibbs had become the personification of an all-out, no-holds-barred campaign. Her small house was jammed with people. Her phone never stopped ringing. Every network as well as the local television stations and every major newspaper were sending people to interview her. The timid young housewife was transmuted, over the months that followed, into a shrewd, tough lobbyist, a forceful public speaker, and a skilled organizer with an ability to manipulate the media. She peddled T-shirts reading *"LOVE CANAL, Another Product from Hooker Chemical."* She turned up on television talk-shows; she learned to talk to politicians in their own language. She made enemies; at one point, her door was kicked in. She rarely had time for her children. It seemed she was never home. Dinner was invariably late. The transformation to shrill activist came slowly. When Governor Carey made his first visit on August 7, she felt intimidated. "My God," she thought, "what am I doing talking to this guy? I can just tell he hates my guts." She had never seen so much television coverage. This is an election year, she reminded herself, and the governor has to take some public action.

As Carey got up to speak, the residents of Love Canal began

427

to scream: "You're a murderer! You're killing our children!"
And then Mrs. Gibbs suddenly heard what she would never
have expected to hear. The governor announced that the state
would purchase 239 homes – the first and second rings of
houses around the canal – and pay for the relocation of the residents. If their basements were contaminated and they had furniture there, the state would pay for that, too, he promised.

Lois Gibbs noticed that one of the governor's key assistants
seemed to be in shock. Clearly, he hadn't expected such generosity. Faced with the outcry from the residents, Carey had
blurted out a solution the state couldn't afford. He had promised to spend more funds than he had federal money to cover.
Carter's federal emergency announcement covered only a narrow band of homes and the Federal Emergency Management
Administration refused to pay any expenses outside that boundary.

The governor had so far promised to move only the people in
the homes immediately adjacent to the canal. Many others
wanted to be moved too, and when this was made clear, Carey
announced that if contamination and health problems were
proven in areas farther away from the canal, the state would
also purchase those houses.

Two days later, Lois Gibbs got her first lesson in political
promises. State officials told her they were not going to buy any
homes in Ring Two. They would relocate only people from
Ring One. They insisted the governor hadn't said what the
entire audience, including the newspaper reporters, had heard
him say. Over the next six months, Lois Gibbs took a new and
practical course in civics, markedly different from the one she
had been given in high school. She discovered that the state's
word meant nothing, that she could no longer believe what she
was told, that promises were made merely to pacify her, and
that rather than retire from battle, as she had hoped, she would
have to keep up the fight every single day.

Love Canal: the emergency declaration area

The governor had promised to move all those who were ill, even if they lived in the outer rings of the canal site. This turned out to be a false promise: no one in that category was to be relocated. Lois Gibbs went to Washington; she wrote to senators, congressmen, and state representatives. She badgered the health department and picketed the new attempts to clean up the canal, which she thought were useless. As a result, she once found herself in jail overnight.

With the help of Dr. Beverly Paigen, a prominent scientist, Mrs. Gibbs conducted a survey of her neighbourhood, proving to her own satisfaction that the disease-producing chemicals had invaded the swales, those low-lying channels that spread

429

out from the canal. In spite of this, the government stuck to its belief that a filtering system and an eight-foot wire-mesh fence around the canal would solve all problems.

Bit by bit, Lois Gibbs's organization was making an impression. The state at last agreed to purchase the second ring of homes, bringing the number of families to be relocated to 239. In October, the remedial drainage and filtration program finally got under way. The state sent in gangs of workmen to uproot trees, tear down fences and garages, and remove swimming pools. It planned to lay drainage tiles around the borders of the canal to divert leakage into wells from which the contaminated water could be drawn and filtered through activated carbon. After that was done, the canal was to be covered with a cap of clay and planted with grass.

The state had announced it would buy no homes outside the official two-ring zone of contamination, a decision that left some five hundred families, including the Gibbses, in jeopardy. Sump-pump samples taken from 100th and 101st streets showed traces of several of the chemicals found in the old canal. In September, the state itself had admitted, after tests of soil samples, that there had been an extensive migration of potentially poisonous materials outside the immediate canal area. Dr. Paigen reported that in 245 homes outside the evacuation area, she had found thirty-four miscarriages, eighteen birth defects, nineteen nervous breakdowns, and ten cases of epilepsy. Lois Gibbs stepped up the campaign to have more families moved.

She was only partly successful. On February 9, 1979, the new commissioner of health, Dr. David Axelrod, held a public meeting to announce that all families with pregnant mothers and children under two living between 93rd and 103rd streets would be temporarily relocated at government expense. Once the remedial work at the canal site was completed, or when their children passed the age of two, they would be returned to their homes.

This caused another uproar. Mrs. Gibbs badgered the new commissioner. Why only these people? she asked. Why not all women who could conceive? The first forty-five days of pregnancy were the most important, she pointed out, yet many women didn't even know they were pregnant in that period. Was the state, then, practising birth control? she asked.

One woman at the back of the hall, tears streaming down her face, cried out, "You can't play games with my life. You have no right to make me stay here." A man took up the cry. "It's too late for my wife," he shouted. "She's already six months pregnant. What do I do if I have a monster because you wouldn't move us out?" Axelrod simply said he was waiting for more data to come in. Just be patient, he advised.

Marie Pozniak, who lived immediately north of the canal, did not fit the state's criteria for temporary evacuation. "Being left behind is the most terrible experience, horrifying," she told Michael Brown. "You know the dangers are still there. You can't get away from them; we all have benzene in our homes. It's a desperate feeling; one of inadequacy. You go out and see someone carrying groceries into their home, in another part of town, and they're smiling and happy and you resent them for it, because they have a safe home. Yours is dangerous. You're afraid of your own home. My family is going to pieces and there are divorces all over this place. My husband is so desperate; there is no way he can get us out, no way for him to protect his family, and that gets to him. That gets to everybody.... Most of the doctors around here don't want to become involved. To be truthful, I don't think they know enough about chemicals.... My children are upset – we can't have a garden this year and they're afraid to go down into the basement. I know a woman who had to take her child for counselling. The kid was afraid of dying.... She had to go too. She's afraid her children will die."

Mrs. Gibbs kept up the pressure. She arrived in Albany with a group of supporters and sent in a baby's coffin to Governor

Carey. She appeared on television with Bruce Davis, then manager of Hooker Chemical (now a subsidiary of Occidental Petroleum Corporation), and lambasted him. After the health department released a statement in April admitting the presence of dioxin in the chemicals at Love Canal, she led a demonstration in the area and burned both Axelrod and Carey in effigy. She went to Washington to testify before the Senate hearings on toxic waste.

The national media were thoroughly alerted. Love Canal became notorious. The ABC network broadcast the documentary "The Killing Ground," greatly distressing the mayor, who said it would destroy Niagara Falls as a tourist area.

Lois Gibbs was no longer intimidated by politicians. The Paigen survey had demonstrated that the chemicals were invading the historical wet areas far beyond the second ring of homes. She now insisted that *all* residents living between 93rd and 103rd streets be evacuated at state expense.

The state moved ponderously. Six months had gone by since Dr. Axelrod had promised that pregnant women and young children would be temporarily relocated, but no action had yet been taken. The Homeowners Association held a candlelight ceremony on the anniversary of its formation. At last, in August, some families who were able to prove illness were evacuated to Niagara University.

The state had already acknowledged that traces of dioxin had been found in seepage from the canal. When Mrs. Gibbs badgered Dr. Axelrod, he was forced to reply that a pregnant woman living in the area bordering Love Canal now stood a 35- to 45-percent chance of miscarriage. Marie Pozniak jumped in. "Are you going to relocate my family?" she asked. After some delay he said, "No."

A school on 93rd Street, four blocks from Love Canal, was now closed for the new term. More families were insisting on the promised temporary relocation. With students returning to Niagara University, the evacuees – now 150 families – had to be moved into hotels and motels at a cost to the state of $7,500 a day. The evacuees announced they would face jail before returning to their homes.

Lois Gibbs and her family left their own home on 101st Street and moved into the local Howard Johnson's. But there was a catch. In order to remain in temporary quarters, all residents had to produce a doctor's certificate saying that their health was at risk if they went back. It took the combined efforts of Mrs. Gibbs's association and fifteen churches to persuade local doctors to issue the documents to the evacuees. "The burden of proof has been thrown onto us, not the state," Mrs. Gibbs declared. "We have to show that we're sick specifically because of the chemicals coming out of Love Canal. But how can we prove that?"

Once again the governor bent to the pressure and announced that between two hundred and five hundred families would be relocated over the next two years. In November, the Gibbs family reluctantly moved back into their own home while a "revitalization committee" was formed to appraise all homes between 93rd and 103rd streets and purchase them. But then the committee found it couldn't spend state money to buy the houses without matching funds from the federal government. These did not come for another year. And so another winter dragged on. And that winter, four-year-old Melissa Gibbs almost died of a rare blood disorder.

Lois Gibbs opposed the revitalization plan. She simply could not believe anybody should be allowed to move back close to Love Canal.

4

On May 17, 1980, the EPA released the results of a study it had made of thirty-six residents of the Love Canal area. The report was devastating. Eleven of the thirty-six were found to have chromosomal damage of a rare type. That meant an increased risk of miscarriage, stillbirths, birth defects, cancer, and genetic damage.

Two days later, a public relations man and a doctor were sent from Washington by the EPA to meet with the community. With the federal government still stalling on matching payments, the residents were in no mood for soothing talk. An infuriated crowd gathered in front of the office of the Love Canal Home-owners Association. "I was afraid," Lois Gibbs wrote later, "that people were going to tear the neighborhood apart." With the tension at dangerous pitch and the crowd cursing the EPA, she tried to clear the air by asking the two representatives to talk to the people. "What a mess this is!" she told herself. "Why did I ever move to this neighborhood? When will it be over?"

Her own mood matched the fighting mood of the crowd on the street outside. When Melissa's life was endangered, Lois Gibbs had resolved never to take her children back to 101st Street. Some members of the crowd were demanding that the two EPA men be held captive. "Let's see how they like being in this neighborhood!" somebody cried. And at that moment, on the morning of Monday, May 19, 1980, Lois Gibbs, the once retiring Niagara Falls blue-collar housewife, found herself the leading figure in a hostage taking.

She told the two Washington visitors they would be confined inside the building and, to soften the blow, said that that was as much for their protection as for political gain. She had no clear idea of what she should do next. "Why didn't I watch TV more carefully?" she asked herself, thinking back to other similar crises.

She took them into an office, locked the door, phoned the White House, and let the cheering crowd know what she'd done. Alone in the room with the men and one woman col-league, Barbara Quimby, she waited for Washington to call back. Suddenly there was a crash as something was hurled through the window, covering the floor with glass. Then the

434

phone rang; an EPA representative from Washington was on the line. Lois Gibbs told him she had locked up his two colleagues for their own protection and had described them as hostages merely to quiet the crowd.

Meetings with the district congressman followed, but no word came from the White House. The FBI arrived and threatened to rush the building. Mrs. Gibbs knew that that would be disastrous. In the end, she gave in peaceably. Her congressman had promised to take up the matter with the president that evening. She said she would hold him to that pledge. "What you have seen us do here today will be a Sesame Street picnic in comparison with what we will do if we do not get evacuated," she told him. "We want an answer from Washington by noon Wednesday." She hustled the hostages out the back door and bundled them into a waiting police car. She expected to be arrested, but her lawyers told her that if she stayed out of further trouble, no charges would be laid against her. The last thing the authorities wanted was a martyr to the cause.

Three things that exacerbated an already tense situation now happened in quick succession. The EPA released a second study showing that some of the residents who had remained in the Love Canal area had suffered nerve damage. Then the Niagara County legislators, by a narrow sixteen-to-fifteen vote, declined to spend any money, even on the revitalization program. (At that meeting, Mrs. Gibbs became so strident that police had to be called to remove her from the room.) Finally, Occidental Petroleum, Hooker's parent, held its annual meeting and turned off the microphones of those who tried to speak in favour of a shareholders' resolution urging the company to take steps to prevent further environmental tragedies. A young nun rose and addressed the chairman, Armand Hammer. "Are you refusing to hear?" she asked. "Yes," he replied, "I am refusing to hear. Go back to Buffalo."

With the situation heating up, Washington acted. President Carter declared a second state of emergency at Love Canal covering a much larger area. Funds were set aside under the Disaster Assistance Administration to allow the evacuation (but not the purchase) of 728 homes in a fifty-square-block area – far more than had originally been contemplated. The residents would be removed "temporarily," but Lois Gibbs was convinced that most would refuse to return.

One Love Canal resident, Ann Willis, wrote of her own feelings in a dramatic lament: "Take another deep breath. Yes, you feel giddy: your heart races; nausea hits you. It is I, myself, that's been vandalized. *Now* you feel the pain. You want to scream out: you open your mouth and nothing comes out. You open the door of your house and you look up the nice street, and you rush to your car and you cry. Yes, your very existence has been vandalized. You look up and down the street once again; your house is noxious; their houses are noxious; the whole outside is noxious! You want to run! But where? You want to scream! But at whom? I don't want a Love Canal house; I don't want to be a Love Canal victim. But, Oh God, I am."

The struggle was not yet over. Once again, the residents were out of their houses and back into motels of their choice, with the government footing the bill. The unsettling effects of this nomadic existence took their toll. Marriages were shattered. Families broke up. The activist wives, obsessed now by the Love Canal struggle, found themselves at an emotional distance from their husbands, many of whom owed their livelihood to the chemical companies. Some small children, after watching television news programs that displayed a backdrop of skull and crossbones, hid under couches or beds and refused to come out. Others were shipped off to relatives hundreds of miles away. With her own marriage threatened, Mrs. Gibbs set out to campaign for permanent relocation.

When she appeared with her followers on the "Phil Donahue Show," she briefed each one carefully on what to say. She had learned the hard way how to get a point across economically and dramatically. In July, she embarked on a speaking tour of

California, which Jane Fonda and her husband, Tom Hayden, helped organize. Lois Gibbs raised enough money to rent a bus for her people to attend the Democratic National Convention in New York. They called themselves the Love Canal Boat People, and, encamped in a strategic spot near the convention hall, cried out their slogan: "President Carter, hear our plea./Set the Love Canal people free."

The president had yet to sign a bill authorizing purchase of the Love Canal homes and matching the state funds with federal dollars. On the ABC program "Good Morning, America," Lois Gibbs accused the EPA and the Carter administration of washing their hands of the entire affair. Ten days after the program was aired, she was told that Carter himself was coming to Niagara Falls and wanted her to be present when he signed an agreement with the state to appropriate $15 million to buy 564 homes in addition to those in the first two rings next to the canal. It was, after all, an election year.

The rest was window dressing. At the crowded meeting in the Convention Centre that followed the signing of the agreement, the president and the governor both spoke. In the midst of Carey's speech, Carter invited Mrs. Gibbs onto the stage while the cameras clicked. She took advantage of that moment to lobby the president for low-interest mortgage money.

By February 1981, more than four hundred families had left the Love Canal area, never to return. Hundreds more were preparing to leave. Some – most of them childless – decided to stay.

Lois Gibbs has won her fight, but not without cost. She had begun as a full-time housewife, with the dinner on the table promptly every night, with her children cared for, with the laundry and household chores done. During the Love Canal battle, all that changed. Harry Gibbs found himself coming home night after night to no dinner; his clothes went unwashed for a week; the house was in disarray; and the two children were consigned to his care while his wife picketed, organized, spoke at demonstrations, and appeared on television – a minor celebrity with a firm set of goals.

He bore it all patiently, even going to Albany with his wife when she needed him. Like many blue-collar husbands, he had seen the women's movement, and Lois's part in it, as a temporary disruption. Once it was over – and now that they were moving away permanently it seemed to be over – he expected their life to return to its even tenor.

But Lois Gibbs was no longer the compliant helpmate he had married. She had, without really understanding it, been thrust into the centre of the expanding women's movement of the seventies and eighties. Like so many of her colleagues, she had thrived on her new independence. For her, activism had become a way of life.

She was convinced that the Love Canal story was not yet over. The federal government had tapped into its new Superfund for disaster areas to compensate the homeowners. The administrator of that fund was charged with preparing an assessment of risk as well as a study of further land use. Neither had yet been done. The Niagara Falls city fathers seemed to think that once the original residents were out of the way, some of the boarded-up houses, especially in the outer rings, could be re-sold to other people, "innocent victims" glad of a bargain. That, she firmly believed, was madness.

She had learned that you *could* fight city hall, if you knew how, and she was anxious to use her own experience to help other communities with similar problems. She and her husband eventually split up, amicably. With her new-found energy Lois Gibbs set about organizing the National Citizens' Clearing House for Hazardous Waste in a small community just outside Washington. She married Stephen Lester, a toxicologist who had helped in the Love Canal campaign and now works with her.

After the family left Love Canal, the children's health problems, which Lois Gibbs had carefully and regularly monitored, began to disappear. She followed her son Michael's epilepsy through medical tests. All traces vanished after six months; he went off his medication and has never suffered another seizure. She also kept track of Melissa's blood count and watched it climb back to normal after she left the area. Melissa, too, required no further medication.

The new activist had plunged into the Love Canal controversy, not from any sense of civic duty, but simply to protect her young. For Lois Gibbs, her children's recovery was payment with interest for that long, exacting battle.

Afterword

The fibres of history are tightly woven into the fabric of the two border cities that face each other across the majesty of Niagara Falls. They are opposites in almost every sense. It is as if each was fashioned by a different force and created by a different environment. Yet both are creatures of the great cataract that is their common parent.

Visitors driving in from the Queen Elizabeth Way on the Canadian side quickly spot the contrasting landmarks that define the character of each community. Even as their hearts leap at the sight of the ghostly spray rising from the Horseshoe, their eyes are diverted by the presence, in the foreground, of a gigantic Ferris wheel looming over an amusement park. As they continue across the Rainbow Bridge, they are entranced by a real rainbow curving above the luminous waters, but the first monument they encounter on the American side is the glittering blue glass office building of Hooker Chemical's parent, Occidental Petroleum.

The carnival ride and the chemical headquarters emphasize each city's priorities. Niagara Falls, Canada, draws the fun seekers; Niagara Falls, USA, is home to the lunch-pail crowd. In an odd reversal of national stereotypes, the Canadians have the guise of Barnum-like showmen, all glitz and sex appeal; the Americans are pure blue-collar – sober, stolid, industrious.

The American community never could compete for visitors with the sinuous sweep of the Horseshoe or the spectacular vantage point of Table Rock, nor did it try. Since the original cluster of shacks and mills adopted the name of Manchester, industrial progress has fuelled its ambitions.

The roots of the Canadian community go back to the town of Clifton and those hard-nosed entrepreneurs, Forsyth and Clark, Barnett and Davis, who exploited the mystery and glamour of the cataract to rope in the customers. Today, the old Front has been reincarnated, albeit with more legitimacy, in the neon midway of Clifton Hill.

In Niagara Falls, New York, there is nothing to compare with this crowded block of fast-food outlets, curio shops, sideshows, wax museums, and motels (complete with heart-shaped Jacuzzis). Since the early 1950s Clifton Hill has been growing and spilling over into side alleys and adjoining lots. A mild-mannered accountant named Dudley Burland controls the east side; the grandsons of Harry Oakes mine the other as assiduously as he mined Kirkland Lake. Here, the Gothic thrills that the Falls once provoked are counterfeited in milder form in Dracula's Castle and the House of Frankenstein.

Visitors flock to the Falls expecting to be entertained – to be photographed against a backdrop of falling water, real or simulated, and to bring home to Toronto or Tokyo an artifact or curio that bears witness to their intimacy with a great natural spectacle. This has been true for more than a century, but life moves more quickly today.

There was a time when such literary travellers as Charles Dickens and Harriet Beecher were content to spend hours, even days, gazing into the unfathomable heart of a cataract not yet marred by surrounding clutter. Although few visitors spend a week at the Falls today, the hypnotic attraction of those boisterous waters is as compelling as it was a century and a half ago. The tinny cacophony in the background cannot compete with the full-throated roar of the green flood frothing above the crest and hurtling into the basin below. For those who lean over the park railing, staring into the depths, or look directly into the deluge from the deck of the *Maid*, the experience remains transcendental.

On the Canadian side the tourists are entertained, on the

American, they are educated. Within the curving contemporary architecture of the Schoellkopf Geological Museum, the saga of the cataract's birth is told in sound and film. In the Robert Moses powerplant, with its spectacular glass-walled walkway, the drama of Niagara's power development graphically unfolds. Each of its characters, from Porter and Evershed to Adams and Moses himself, receives his due. Hennepin is there, too, in Thomas Hart Benton's vast mural.

The most conspicuous human symbol in the New York State Reservation is a larger-than-life statue of Nikola Tesla. In Canada, it is an effigy of Charles Blondin, teetering on a tightrope stretched across Clifton Hill. The two plants named for Sir Adam Beck no longer admit visitors; the emphasis on this side is on doom and daredevils. There are barrels everywhere: imitation barrels for those who want a souvenir photo showing themselves tumbling over a painted cataract, real barrels in which the impetuous and the foolhardy – Maud Willard, George Stathakis – met their fates, and counterfeit barrels such as the replica that Annie Taylor commissioned to stand in for the original that was stolen. (The Annie Taylor mannequin, slender and comely, is as spurious as the barrel itself.)

Others as rash as Annie continue to follow her example, heedless of the authorities on both sides of the river who can – and have – set fines as high as five thousand dollars. The barrel performers, like the tightrope walkers of an earlier day, have become commonplace, yet the parade goes on, with each striving to outdo the others. In 1984, Karel Soucek went over the Horseshoe and billed himself as the Last of the Niagara Daredevils. He wasn't. The following year he lost his life in a plunge at the Houston Astrodome, and he lost his title to Steven Trotter, who, at twenty-one, made the plunge successfully as the youngest daredevil of all (ignoring Roger Woodward, who never claimed to be anything). Dave Munday in 1987 became the first Canadian to go over the Falls and live. Two years later, two of his fellow countrymen, Peter DeBarnardi and Jeffrey

Petkovich, went him one better by stuffing themselves, face to face, into a single barrel, to emerge alive from their tandem journey. When barrel riding became banal, a white-water expert from Tennessee, Jessie Sharp, challenged the Falls in a kayak. He did not survive.

In a specially designed theatre, the Canadian film process known as IMAX concentrates heavily on daredevils. The great exploits of past heroes – of Charles Blondin, Joel Robinson, and Annie Taylor – have been brought eerily to life. The screen is so gigantic that peripheral vision vanishes, the past and present interlock, and the audience feels drawn *inside* the picture. More than most films, this one provokes the kind of nervous thrill – shocking yet exhilarating – that induced a rush of adrenalin in those who witnessed the real thing a century or more ago.

In a curious way, the IMAX production has itself become part of the history of the Falls because its actors had to undertake stunts almost as hazardous as those described in the tourist pamphlets. One cannot fake the Falls or build a replica on a back lot. No film director, no matter how brilliant, no production company, no matter how wealthy, can counterfeit what nature has made unique. The IMAX producers were aware that whoever played the part of Deanne Woodward would have to be flung directly into the furious current on the Canadian side of Goat Island only a few yards from the lip of the Horseshoe – a truly daunting prospect.

No professional stunter could be found to attempt the feat. Apart from Deanne Woodward herself, no human being had ever come within five yards of the cataract's brink without being swept over the precipice. The speed of the water here is close to forty miles an hour. Finally, a twenty-four-year-old Toronto advertising woman named Jan Gordon, eager to break into films, heard about the production and volunteered. Attached to a fifteen-foot leash, she took the plunge and survived as the cameras (one fixed to a gigantic crane) rolled. For her work on the film she received close to five thousand dollars; more important, she got the job she wanted in the motion-picture business.

Once again past and present interlocked, as Deanne Woodward's ordeal was recreated. Standing on the bank with a long, hooked pole in his hands, ready to pluck Jan Gordon from the current, was the last of Red Hill's four sons, Wesley. Employed for fifteen years by the *Maid of the Mist* and now a park policeman, he has had no desire to engage in the ventures for which his father and two of his elder brothers were famous. He still pulls bodies from the river as they did, at $150 a corpse, and has served as an adviser on every recent motion picture about Niagara.

For the IMAX production Wes Hill helped to replicate a deed that many considered impossible: Joel Robinson's 1861 trip through the Whirlpool Rapids aboard a fragile sidewheeler. For this a sturdier craft was built, heavily reinforced with steel and driven by two powerful Chrysler 318 engines. Even so, it required scores of men hauling on a thousand-foot hawser to keep the boat from breaking loose in the Whirlpool and hurtling down to Lake Ontario. The sequence was the most difficult and hazardous the production team had ever experienced and confirmed Robinson's reputation as one of the great figures in Niagara history.

Today such risks are properly confined to the movies. It was once a terrifying experience to clamber down the swinging Indian ladders to the bottom of the gorge. Nowadays, protected by shrouds of yellow plastic, visitors are whisked by elevator to concrete-lined tunnels bored in the cliff face. There, secure from the tempest that all but sucked the breath from Timothy Bigelow in 1805, they experience the thrill without the peril.

If the hazards are gone, so is the spontaneity. The tourists are channelled in clearly defined routes from one vantage point to the next. In 1854, Isabella Lucy Bird scrambled down alone to make her way out to a big rock near the water's edge and to

444

gaze in solitude at the young moon casting its pale light on the shimmering waters. It is hard to imagine anybody doing that today. The margin of the river has been shored up and the crowds – 250 times as large as in her day – conspire against any private contemplation.

Table Rock is long gone. Its name has been preserved in Table Rock House, a park restaurant. The old site serves as a reminder of the remorseless retreat of the cataract, which has moved back at least the length of a football field since Miss Bird "did" the Falls.

The art lover will search in vain for the vantage point from which Frederic Church created his celebrated canvas. It cannot be found because it never existed; Church painted the ideal, not the reality. And now even the reality has been much altered by nature and by man. The waters have long since gnawed their way past the spot from which Church made his preliminary sketches. Framed against the onrushing flood, the silhouette of a derelict scow occupies the foreground – the same scow from which Red Hill rescued two marooned mariners. On the bank above stands the pillared powerplant that Edward Lennox designed for the Electrical Development Company and from whose roof Hill's breeches-buoy was strung. Sealed but not abandoned, the building is to be restored as a museum by Ontario Hydro.

Not far away in Queen Victoria Park, on the site of the old military chain reserve, stands a memorial to Sir Casimir Gzowski, who helped save the gorge for the people. The park is not quite what Lord Dufferin visualized when he talked of preserving the land "in the picturesque condition in which it was originally laid out by nature." The commissioners have long since opted for what Dufferin dismissed as "the penny arts of the landscape gardener." The park, with its edged borders and cropped lawns, derives its ambience from the British colonial style, not the untamed natural beauty of the Canadian wilderness. Supported by fees from souvenir shops and

445

restaurants, the park commission spends $12 million a year just cutting the grass.

The past is well posted on both sides of the river. A guidebook is hardly necessary to find Thomas Barnett's original museum of curiosities – now grown to 700,000 exhibits – or the Oakes Garden Theatre, Prospect Point, and Bloody Run. One landmark, however, frustrates discovery. No sign points the way to Love Canal; no guidebook locates it on a map.

It can be found on the southern edge of town, and it is known today – the part of it that has been declared "habitable" – as Black Creek Village, "A Modern Community," in the sales phrase of the Love Canal Revitalization Agency. The visitor happens upon it suddenly – so suddenly he may not know he has arrived. At first glance, 102nd Street with its row of modest homes looks like any other residential avenue. But something is wrong; the street lacks resonance. Why are there no cars parked in the driveways? Why no children on bicycles, no mothers wheeling baby carriages down the sidewalks? Why are the front yards empty of life – no bent figures weeding gardens, no homeowners pushing lawn mowers?

It is then that a shiver runs down the spine as the visitor realizes that all the windows are boarded up, the eaves troughs are crumbling, the paint is peeling, the front porches are falling apart. Here and there, behind an unprotected and shattered window, the remnants of an old Venetian blind hang limply. And above each doorway a naked light bulb burns day and night, a wan message that the house has been abandoned.

It is an eerie sight, this suburban ghost town. Block after block, the spectacle is the same. Three hundred acres that were once home to twenty-six hundred men, women, and children lie deserted. We are familiar with films and photographs of abandoned mining camps and false-fronted cow towns. But this is not the Old West. This is modern America. Is the shape of things to come to be found here within earshot of the continent's greatest natural wonder? Already another community some three miles away – Forest Glen – has had to be abandoned for similar reasons.

Love Canal is still not free of controversy. People are moving back into the outer ring of homes, two hundred of which were put up for sale by the revitalization agency after a federal survey in 1988 deemed them "habitable." By the spring of 1992, thirty had been sold. But what does "habitable" mean? Only that these houses are no worse off than comparable housing elsewhere in Niagara Falls. For Lois Gibbs, still fighting the environmental battle from her new base outside Washington, that does not mean the houses are free of risk. Even as the new tenants moved in, her organization and several others were planning court action to force a study.

Suits and countersuits drag on. Occidental, which has paid $20 million to 1,328 plaintiffs as the result of a class-action suit, is suing the state, the city, and the school board for funds to help pay the costs of a clean-up. The total cost of litigation has been estimated at $700 million.

This may be only the beginning. The empty homes with their naked light bulbs stand as testimony to the great dilemma of our times: what to do with the unwanted by-products of industry? The problem extends far beyond those ghostly streets. After Love Canal, three more Hooker dumps in the Niagara Falls area were identified, each much larger than the original. Together these alone contain a million tons of waste products. Thanks to the Love Canal controversy, the industries along the river have been cleaned up; they no longer discharge their wastes into the Niagara. But the old dumps remain, some unidentified because no one can remember where the truck-loads of poison were taken decades ago. There are an estimated 250 of these trouble spots within three miles of the river. To find them, excavate them, and remove their contents represents a herculean and hideously expensive task.

The great cataract has become a victim of its own immensity. Its spectacular presence alone was never enough to satisfy those who sought to transform it into a theatrical backdrop for high carnival or to harness its apparently limitless energy to banish industrial grime. The Falls proved a fickle servant. It was that same energy – captured by man, channelled and transformed – that powered the chemical revolution that defiled Niagara's waters. Those early pioneers who talked so enthusiastically of the genie in the bottle did not live to see the havoc caused after the genie escaped.

How bitterly ironic that 89 percent of the pollution that is leached into the Niagara comes from the American side and not from the side show on the opposite shore! Those early pioneers – Porter and Evershed, Schoellkopf and Adams – could not know that the by-products of their vision would some day defile the river. Their purpose was laudable enough – to separate the great cataract from the beneficiaries of its power, to create an industrial community that did not encroach upon the glory of the Falls. The result is Buffalo Avenue, that crowded chemical alley of squat factories and high-tension pylons that leads from the Love Canal area to the business centre of the city. Buffalo Avenue is to Niagara Falls, New York, what Clifton Hill is to Niagara Falls, Ontario. But the much-maligned hill, for all its tinsel glitter, does not befoul the waters.

Yet there is one crowning glory that remains, and it is to be found on the American side. Goat Island continues to provide a haven from the industrial world as it has since the days when Augustus Porter saved it from commercial exploitation. The manicured park land and the encircling roadway of the state reservation are encroaching upon the wild, but thanks to men like Olmsted and Church, some of the original forest remains and visitors can enjoy the kind of ramble in the woods that helped spark the preservation movement of the last century.

Well away from the tourist routes is one little glade where commerce does not intrude. Just opposite little Luna Island on the eastern bank of Goat Island beneath a canopy of birch, black willow, and shagbark hickory, a narrow pathway

448

meanders along the water's edge. Here, beside the slenderest of Niagara's channels, the workaday world is blotted out. The cataract's roar and the hiss of the rapids, racing over the limestone ledges, blur the stridence of the twentieth century. The soft curtain of foliage conceals the jagged silhouette of the skyline beyond.

Here is the peace that Francis Abbott sought. One can easily imagine him in his brown cloak, with his dog by his side, lounging on this very spot and staring into the violent waters at his feet, calmed by the tranquillity of the forest yet haunted by the magnetic pull of the river on its final rush to the brink. Did he shudder a little at the power and treachery of the Niagara River and the Falls beyond? Or did he simply surrender himself to their sorcery? Beauty, danger, terror, and charm are here combined. Over the centuries, poets, essayists, historians, and ordinary visitors have struggled, and often failed, to find words to describe the lure of these waters. Yet in the end, a single word – an old, well-used word – best captures the essence of Niagara. In spite of mankind's follies and nature's ravages, in spite of scientific intrusion and unexpected catastrophe, in spite of human ambition and catchpenny artifice, the great cataract remains what it has always been, and in the true sense of the word, Sublime.

Acknowledgements

A good many people contributed to this book. I especially want to thank George Seibel, historian of Niagara Falls, Ontario, and also for the Niagara Parks Commission. Don Loker of the Local History Department at the Public Library of Niagara Falls, New York, and George Bailey of the Niagara Parks Commission, Ontario, were particularly generous with their time; both responded with enthusiasm and patience to the stream of requests put to them. The Local History Department at the NFPL, New York, is a rich source for anyone studying various aspects of Niagara history, while the Parks Commission has a room in its basement crammed with interesting and useful items.

Dr. Keith Tinkler at the Department of Geography, Brock University, and Dr. Walter Tovell, formerly of the Royal Ontario Museum, were especially helpful in vetting my sections on the geology of the Falls.

Much of the research for *Niagara* was done at the Robarts Library, University of Toronto. Other institutions and individuals helped in various ways: Wes Hill, whose family will always be associated with the river; Kevin McMahon; Dwight Whalen, who assisted us with his extensive research on Annie Taylor; Shane Peacock, for infomation on Farini; Inge Saczkowski and the staff at the Niagara Falls (Ontario) Public Library; Frank Roma and Mary Stessing at the New York State Power Authority; the staff at the Ontario Archives; Paul Odom, Ontario Ministry of the Environment; Bob Smart, Glenys Biggar, Trish Wilcox, Kimberly Bean, Al Breadner, Syd Money, and Chuck Sands, all of Ontario Hydro; Craig Boljkovac and Dave Bruer of the Toronto Environmental Alliance; Burkhard

Mausberg at Pollution Probe; Mary Bell, Buffalo and Erie County Historical Society; Leon Meyer at the Hulton Picture Company; Phillip LeClaire of LeClaire Photography; Melissa Rombout at the National Archives of Canada.

My research assistant, Barbara Sears, who has worked on many of my earlier books, was indefatigable, as always, in tracking down hard-to-find documents as well as the photographs that appear in this book. Without her, the work would not have been possible. My editor, Janice Tyrwhitt, forced me to rewrite several sections and applied a critical eye to the entire manuscript, which, in its finished form, owes a great deal to her suggestions. My copy editor, Janet Craig, caught scores of the inconsistencies, misspellings, and grammatical gaffes to which I am prone. My wife, Janet Berton, subjected the final manuscript to a painstaking line-by-line examination. My badly typed manuscript was recorded on a word processor at top speed and with great accuracy by my secretary, Emily Bradshaw. I also profited from the advice of my business associate, Elsa Franklin, especially on the execution and design of the jacket. If, after this, there are still some inaccuracies and omissions, I can only blame myself.

Select Bibliography

Archival Sources

New York Power Authority, Niagara Falls, N.Y.
Robert Moses files

Local History Department, Public Library, Niagara Falls, N.Y.
Miscellaneous vertical files

Niagara Parks Commission
Scrapbooks

Ontario Archives
W.F. Munro Papers
RG 18 B-O Royal Commission to Inquire into Alleged Abuses Occurring
    in the Vicinity of Niagara Falls, evidence
G.A. Farini Papers
Sidney Barnett Papers
RG 38 Niagara Parks Commission Papers
RG 23 Series B1 File 21.59 Ontario Provincial Police records
Whitney Papers

Ontario Hydro Archives
EDC Minute Book No. 1
OR-101 Administration – History of Hydro – general
1965 Blackout files

Government Documents

Ontario. House of Assembly, Journals and Appendices, 1828.

Ontario. Hydro Electric Inquiry Commission [Gregory Commission],
"General Report"; "General Report – Queenston-Chippawa
Development" [unpublished version at Robarts Library, University of
Toronto, Government Documents section].

Ontario. *Sessional Papers,* 1880, no. 51, "Report Respecting the Recent
Proceedings in Reference to the Niagara Falls and Adjacent Territory."

Ontario. *Sessional Papers,* 1886, no. 77, "Papers Relating to the Niagara
Falls Park."

United States. "Northeast Power Failure, November 9 and 10, 1965:

A Report to the President by the Federal Power Commission, December 6, 1965."

United States. "A Report by the Federal Communications Commission on the Northeast Power Failure of November 9-10, 1965 and Its Effect on Communications," February 1966.

Interviews

Mac Bradden; John C. Bruel; Dudley Burland; Jim Carr; Dennis Dack; William Fitzgerald; Asa George; Lois Gibbs; Jan Gordon; Nicholas Gray; Wes Hill; Fred Hollidge; W.J. Killough; Harry Oakes, Jr.; Jim Simon; Bob Smart; Roger Woodward.

Magazines

Canadian Electrical News, February 1904, June 1906
The Nation, 1 September 1881
Newsweek, 22, 29 November 1965
Time Magazine, 19, 26 November 1965, 11 November 1966

Newspapers

Buffalo *Courier*
Buffalo *Evening News*
Buffalo *Express*
Daily Cataract-Journal
Globe and Mail (Toronto)
Hamilton *Evening Times*, 12 November 1868
Mail and Empire (Toronto)
New York Times
Niagara Falls [N.Y.] *Gazette*
Niagara Falls [Ont.] *Review*
St. Catharines *Standard*, August 1988
Suspension Bridge *Journal*
The Times
Toronto Daily Star, 1921, 1923, January/February 1938, November 1965

Unpublished Sources

Adamson, Jeremy E. "Frederic Edwin Church's 'Niagara': The Sublime as Transcendence," Ph.D. dissertation, University of Michigan, 1981.

Belfield, Robert. "Niagara Frontier: The Evolution of Electric Power Systems in New York and Ontario, 1880-1935," Ph.D. dissertation, University of Pennsylvania, 1981.

Dewar, Kenneth D. "State Ownership in Canada: The Origins of Ontario Hydro," Ph.D. dissertation, University of Toronto, 1975.

McGreevy, Patrick V. "Visions at the Brink: Imagination and the Geography of Niagara Falls," D. Phil. dissertation, University of Minnesota, 1984.

Shields, Rob. "Images of Places and Spaces: A Comparative Study," D. Phil. dissertation, University of Sussex, 1989.

Published Sources

Adams, Alton. "The Destruction of Niagara Falls," *Cassier's Magazine*, March 1905.

Adams, Edward Dean. *Niagara Power – History of the Niagara Falls Power Company, 1886-1918....* Niagara Falls, N.Y.: Niagara Falls Power Co., 1927.

Adamson, Jeremy E. *Niagara: Two Centuries of Changing Attitudes, 1697-1901.* Washington: Corcoran Gallery of Art, 1985.

Album of the Table Rock, Niagara Falls.... Buffalo: Jewett, Thomas & Co., 1848.

Arrington, Joseph Earl. "Godfrey N. Frankenstein's Moving Panorama of Niagara Falls," *New York History,* 49, April 1968.

Banks, G. Linnaeus. *Blondin: His Life and Performances.* London: Routledge, Warne and Routledge, 1862.

Beck, Adam. *Misstatements and Misrepresentations derogatory to the Hydro-electric Power Commission of Ontario by the Smithsonian Institution...examined and refuted by Sir Adam Beck.* Toronto: 1925.

———. *The Public Interest in the Niagara Falls Power Supply.* Toronto: King's Printer, 1905.

———. *Water Power: Statement of Sir Adam Beck....* Washington: 1918.

Bigelow, Timothy. *Journal of a Tour to Niagara Falls in the Year 1805.* Boston: John Wilson and Son, 1876.

Bird, Isabella Lucy. *The Englishwoman in America.* Reprinted, ed. Andrew Hill Clark, Toronto: University of Toronto Press, 1966.

Bird, James. *Francis Abbott: The Recluse of Niagara....* London: Baldwin & Craddock, 1837.

Bocca, Geoffrey. *The Life and Death of Sir Harry Oakes.* New York: Doubleday and Co., 1959.

[Bonnefons, J.C.] *Voyage au Canada dans le Nord de l'Amérique Septentrionale fait depuis l'an 1751 à 1761....* Quebec: Leger Brousseau, 1887.

Braider, Donald. *The Niagara.* New York: Holt, Rinehart and Winston, 1972.

Brown, Michael. *Laying Waste: The Poisoning of America by Toxic Chemicals.* New York: Pantheon Books, 1980.

———. "A Toxic Ghost Town," *Atlantic,* July 1989.

Burbank, George. "The Construction of the Niagara Tunnel, Wheelpit and Canal," *Cassier's Magazine,* July 1895.

Burke, Edmund. *A Philosophical Enquiry Into the Origin of our Ideas of the Sublime and Beautiful* [1757]. Reprinted, London: Routledge and Kegan Paul, 1958.

Cahn, William. *Out of the Cracker Barrel: The Nabisco Story from Animal Crackers to Zuzus.* New York: Simon and Schuster, 1969.

Caro, Robert. *The Power Broker: Robert Moses and the Fall of New York.* New York: Vintage Books, 1974.

Chapman, L.J., and Putnam, D.F. *The Physiography of Southern Ontario.* Toronto: Ontario Ministry of Natural Resources, 1984.

Charlevoix, Pierre François Xavier de. *Journal of a Voyage to North America.* Reprinted, Chicago: Caxton Club, 1923.

Cheney, Margaret. *Tesla, Man Out of Time.* Englewood Cliffs, N.J.: Prentice-Hall Inc., 1981.

Church, Clifford. "River Rescue," *What's Up Niagara,* August 1988.

Clark, Ronald W. *Edison, The Man Who Made the Future.* London: Macdonald and Jane's, 1977.

Cometti, Elizabeth, ed. *The American Journals of Lt. John Enys* [1787]. Blue Mountain Lake, New York: Syracuse University Press, 1976.

Crèvecoeur, Hector St. John de. "Description of the Falls of Niagara, 1785," *Magazine of American History,* October 1878.

Currelly, Charles Trick. *I Brought the Ages Home.* Toronto: Ryerson Press, 1956.

Davison, Gideon Minor. *The Fashionable Tour, A Guide to Travellers....* Saratoga Springs: G.M. Davison, 1830.

Denison, Merrill. *The People's Power.* Toronto: McClelland and Stewart, 1960.

Dickens, Charles. *Works,* Vol. XVII, pp. 384-85, "American Notes for General Circulation, 1842." Boston: 1874.

Dictionary of Canadian Biography, Vols. II, IV, V, VI, VII, VIII, IX, XI, XII. Toronto: University of Toronto Press, 1966-90.

The Distinctive Charms of Niagara Scenery: Frederick Law Olmsted and the Niagara Reservation. Niagara Falls, N.Y.: Buscaglia-Castellani Art Gallery of Niagara University, 1985.

Donaldson, Gordon. *Niagara! The Eternal Circus.* Toronto: Doubleday, 1979.

Dorson, Richard. "Sam Patch, Jumping Hero," *New York Folklore Quarterly* 1, no. 3, August 1945.

Dow, Charles Mason. *Anthology and Bibliography of Niagara Falls.* Albany, 1921.

———. *The State Reservation at Niagara: A History.* Albany: J.B. Lyon, 1914.

Dunlap, Orrin. "The Wonderful Story of the Chaining of Niagara," *World's Work,* August 1901.

Dwight, Timothy. *Travels in New-England and New-York* [1821-22]. Reprinted, Cambridge, Mass.: Harvard University Press, 1969.

Edwards, Junius. *The Immortal Woodshed.* New York: Dodd, Mead and Co., 1955.

Eiseley, Loren C. "Charles Lyell," *Scientific American* 201, no. 2, August 1959.

Elswick, Steven, ed. *Proceedings of the 1988 International Tesla Symposium.* International Tesla Society Inc., 1988.

Fein, Albert. *Frederick Law Olmsted and the American Environmental Tradition.* New York: George Braziller, 1972.

Fleming, R.B. *The Railway King of Canada, Sir William Mackenzie, 1849-1923.* Vancouver: University of British Columbia Press, 1991.

Forbes, George. "Harnessing Niagara," *Blackwoods,* September 1895.

Ford, Alice, ed. *Audubon by Himself.* New York: Natural History Press, 1969.

Frayne, Trent. "William (Red) Hill," *Liberty,* 14 July 1945.

Fredo, Tony. *The Miracle at Niagara.* Chippawa, Ont.: Stetimjob Publications, n.d.

Fryer, Mary Beacock. *Elizabeth Postuma Simcoe, 1762-1859: A Biography.* Toronto: Dundurn Press, 1989.

Gardner, James. *Special Report of New York State Survey on the Preservation of the Scenery of Niagara Falls....* Albany: Charles Van Benthuysen & Sons, 1880.

Gibbs, Lois Marie. *Love Canal: My Story*. Albany: State University of New York Press, 1982.

Gillette, King C. *The Human Drift*. Reprinted, Delmar, N.Y.: Scholars' Facsimiles and Reprints, 1976.

Glassie, Henry. "Thomas Cole and Niagara Falls," *New-York Historical Society Quarterly* 58, April 1974.

Goldman, Harry. "Nikola Tesla's Bold Adventure," *American West* 8, no. 2, March 1971.

Goldman, Mark. *High Hopes: The Rise and Decline of Buffalo, New York*. Albany: State University of New York Press, 1983.

Graham, Lloyd. "Blondin, the Hero of Niagara," *American Heritage*, August 1958.

Green, Ernest. "The Niagara Portage Road," *Ontario Historical Society Papers and Records* 23, 1926.

Greenhill, Ralph, and Mahoney, Thomas D. *Niagara*. Toronto: University of Toronto Press, 1969.

Guillet, Edwin C. *Early Life in Upper Canada*. Reprinted, Toronto: University of Toronto Press, 1963.

Hadfield, Joseph. *An Englishman in America. . . .* Toronto: Hunter Rose Co., 1933.

Harrison, J.B. *The Condition of Niagara Falls and the Measures Needed to Preserve Them*. New York: 1882.

Hartt, Rollin Lynde. "The New Niagara," *McClure's*, May 1901.

Hawthorne, Nathaniel. "My Visit to Niagara," in *The Snow-Image and Uncollected Tales*, in *Works*, Centenary Edition. Columbus: Ohio State University Press, 1974.

Hennepin, Louis. *A Description of Louisiana . . .* Translated by John Gilmary Shea. New York: 1880.

——— . *A New Discovery of a Vast Country in America*. Reprinted, Toronto: Coles Publishing Co., 1974.

Hennessy, Brendan. *The Gothic Novel*. Harlow: Longman Group Ltd. for the British Council, 1976.

Holley, George. *The Falls of Niagara*. New York: A.C. Armstrong & Son, 1883.

——— . *Niagara, Its History and Geology, Incidents and Poetry*. New York: Sheldon, 1872.

Hough, Jack. *Geology of the Great Lakes*. Urbana: University of Illinois Press, 1958.

House, Madeleine, Storey, Graham, and Tillotson, Kathleen, eds. *The Letters of Charles Dickens:* Vol. 3, *1842-43*. Oxford: Clarendon Press, 1974.

Hughes, Ted. "Saunders of the Seaway," *Saturday Night,* 20 December 1952.

Hughes, Tomas P. *Elmer Sperry: Inventor and Engineer.* Baltimore: Johns Hopkins University Press, 1971.

Hunt, Inez, and Draper, Wanetta W. *Lightning in His Hand: The Life Story of Nikola Tesla*. Hawthorne, Calif.: Omni Publications, 1977.

Hunt, Wallace. "Ontario's Hydro Campaign Is Sparked by Saunders," *Saturday Night,* 16 October 1948.

Huntington, David C. "Frederic Church's Niagara – Nature and the Nation's Type," *Texas Studies in Literature and Language* 25, Spring 1985.

―――. *The Landscapes of Frederic Edwin Church: Vision of an American Era*. New York: Brazilier, 1966.

Jameson, Anna. *The Falls of Niagara, Being a Complete Guide to…the Great Cataract*. London: Nelson, 1858.

Jasen, Patricia. "Romantieism, Modernity and the Evolution of Tourism on the Niagara Frontier, 1790-1850," *Canadian Historical Review* 72, September 1991.

Josephson, Matthew. *Edison: A Biography*. London: McGraw-Hill, 1959.

Kadlecek, Mary. "Love Canal – 10 Years Later," *Conservationist,* November/December 1988.

Kalfus, Melvin. *Frederick Law Olmsted: The Passion of a Public Artist*. New York: New York University Press, 1990.

Katz, Sidney. "Why Red Hill Did It," *Maclean's,* 1 November 1951.

Kelly, Franklin. *Frederic Edwin Church*. Washington: National Gallery of Art, Smithsonian Institution Press, 1989.

Killan, Gerald. "Mowat and a Park Policy for Niagara Falls 1873-1887," *Ontario History* 70, no. 2, June 1978.

Kiwanis Club of Stamford, Ontario. *Niagara Falls, Canada: A History of the City and the World Famous Beauty Spot*. Niagara Falls, Ont.: Kiwanis Club, 1967.

————. *Maid of the Mist and Other Famous Niagara News Stories.* Niagara Falls, Ont., 1971.

Leighton, Tony. "Pandemonium Inc.," *Equinox,* January/February 1985.

Leslie, W. Bruce. *Collapse of Falls View Bridge and Ice Jam of 1938.* Niagara Falls, Ont., 1938.

Lewis, Gene D. *Charles Ellet Jr.: The Engineer as Individualist, 1810-1862.* Urbana: University of Illinois Press, 1968.

Lyell, Mrs. *Life, Letters and Journals of Sir Charles Lyell, Bart.* London: John Murray, 1881.

McCullough, David. *The Great Bridge.* New York: Simon and Schuster, 1982.

McGreevy, Patrick. "The end of America: The Beginning of Canada," *Canadian Geographer* 32, no. 4, 1988.

————. "Niagara as Jerusalem," *Landscape* 28, no. 2, 1984.

McKay, Paul. *Electric Empire: The Inside Story of Ontario Hydro.* Toronto: Between the Lines, 1983.

McKinsey, Elizabeth. *Niagara Falls, Icon of the American Sublime.* Cambridge: Cambridge University Press, 1985.

McLeod, Duncan. "Niagara Falls Was a Hell-Raising Town," *Maclean's,* 26 November 1955.

Maury, Sarah Mytton. *An Englishwoman in America.* London: Thomas Richardson & Sons, 1848.

Mavor, James. *Niagara in Politics: A Critical Account of the Ontario Hydro-Electric Commission.* New York: E.P. Dutton, 1925.

————. *Public Ownership and the Hydro-Electric Commission of Ontario.* Toronto: Maclean, 1917.

Moon, Barbara. "The Murdered Midas of Lake Shore," *Maclean's,* 1 September 1950.

Moses, Robert. *Public Works – A Dangerous Trade.* New York: McGraw-Hill, 1970.

Nader, Ralph, Brownstein, Ronald, and Richard, John, eds. *Who's Poisoning America: Corporate Polluters and Their Victims in the Chemical Age.* San Francisco: Sierra Club Books, 1981.

Nelles, H.V. *The Politics of Development.* Toronto: Macmillan, 1974.

"Niagara," *Harper's New Monthly Magazine,* August 1853.

[Niagara River Remedial Action Plan Public Advisory Committee.] *The Niagara River: How Did We Get to This Stage?* N.p., 1991.

[Niagara River Toxics Committee.] *Report of the Niagara River Toxics Committee*. N.p., 1984.

Nicholls, Frederic. "Niagara's Power, Past, Present, Prospective," in J. Castell Hopkins, ed., *Empire Club Speeches...1904/5*. Toronto: William Briggs, 1906.

Nicolson, Marjorie Hope. *Mountain Gloom and Mountain Glory: The Development of the Aesthetics of the Infinite*. Ithaca: Cornell University Press, [1959].

Noble, Louis LeGrand. *The Life and Works of Thomas Cole*. Cambridge, Mass.: Belknap Press of Harvard University Press, 1964.

O'Brien, Andy. *Daredevils of Niagara*. Toronto: Ryerson, 1964.

Olmsted, Frederick Law, Jr., and Kimball, Theodora, eds. *Frederick Law Olmsted, Landscape Architect, 1822-1903*. New York: Benjamin Blom Inc., 1970.

Oreskovitch, Carlie. *Sir Henry Pellatt: The King of Casa Loma*. Toronto: McGraw-Hill Ryerson, 1982.

Parkman, Francis. *The Discovery of the Great West*. Reprinted, Toronto: Ryerson Press, 1962.

Parsons, Gerald. "Second Thoughts on a 'Folk Hero': or Sam Patch Falls Again," *New York Folklore Quarterly,* June 1969

Passer, Harold. *The Electrical Manufacturers 1875-1900*. Cambridge, Mass.: Harvard University Press, 1953.

Peacock, Shane. "Farini the Great," *Bandwagon,* September/October 1990.

Petrie, Francis. *Roll Out the Barrel*. Erin, Ont.: Boston Mills Press, 1985.

Phillips, David. "The Day Niagara Falls Ran Dry," *Canadian Geographic* 109, no. 2, April/May 1989.

Plewman, W.R. *Adam Beck and the Ontario Hydro*. Toronto: Ryerson Press, 1947.

Porter, Albert. "Some Details of the Niagara Tunnel," *Cassier's Magazine,* July 1895.

Prout, Henry G. *A Life of George Westinghouse*. New York: American Society of Mechanical Engineers, 1921.

Ratzlaff, John T. *Tesla Said*. Millbrae, Calif.: Tesla Book Co., 1984.

————, and Jost, Fred A. *Dr. Nikola Tesla*. Millbrae, Calif.: Tesla Book Co., 1979.

[Rickard, Clinton.] *Fighting Tuscarora: The Autobiography of Chief Clinton Rickard.* Syracuse: Syracuse University Press, 1973.

Robertson, John Ross. *The Diary of Mrs. John Graves Simcoe....* Toronto: William Briggs, 1911.

Robinson, Charles Mulford. "The Life of Judge Augustus Porter," *Publications of the Buffalo Historical Society* 7 (1904).

Roebling, John A. "Memoir of the Niagara Falls Suspension and Niagara Falls International Bridge," published in *Papers and Practical Illustrations of Public Works of Recent Construction Both British and American*. London: John Weale, 1856.

Roemer, Kenneth M. *The Obsolete Necessity: America in Utopian Writings 1888-1900*. Kent, Ohio: Kent State University Press, 1976.

Roper, Laura Wood. *FLO: A Biography of Frederick Law Olmsted*. Baltimore: Johns Hopkins University Press, 1973.

Rosenthal, A.M., and Gelb, Arthur, eds. *The Night the Lights Went Out*. New York: Signet Books, 1965.

Ross, Alexander. *William Henry Bartlett: Artist, Author, Traveller*. Toronto: University of Toronto Press, 1973.

Roth, Leland. *McKim, Mead and White, Architects*. New York: Harper & Row, 1983.

Rothman, Ellen K. *Hands and Hearts: A History of Courtship in America*. New York: Basic Books, 1984.

Runte, Alfred. "Beyond the Spectacular: The Niagara Falls Preservation Campaign," *New York Historical Society Quarterly* 57, January 1973.

Schuyler, Hamilton. *The Roeblings: A Century of Engineers, Bridge-builders and Industrialists*. Princeton: Princeton University Press, 1931.

Seibel, George A. *Bridges Over the Niagara Gorge: Rainbow Bridge – 50 Years 1941-1991*. Niagara Falls, Ont.: Niagara Falls Bridge Commission, 1991.

————. *The Niagara Portage Road: A History of the Portage on the West Bank of the Niagara River*. Niagara Falls, Ont.: City of Niagara Falls, 1990.

————. *Ontario's Niagara Parks – 100 Years: A History*. Niagara Falls, Ont.: Niagara Parks Commission, 1985.

461

Severance, Frank H. *An Old Frontier of France*. New York: Dodd, Mead & Company, 1917.

Shaw, Ronald E. *Erie Water West: A History of the Erie Canal 1792-1854*. Lexington: University of Kentucky Press, 1966.

Slatzer, Robert E. *The Curious Death of Marilyn Monroe*. New York: Pinnacle Books, 1974.

Steinman, D.B. *The Builders of the Bridge*. New York: Harcourt, Brace and Co., 1945.

Sturgis, James. *Adam Beck*. Don Mills, Ont.: Fitzhenry and Whiteside, 1978.

Summers, Anthony. *Goddess: The Secret Lives of Marilyn Monroe*. New York: Macmillan Publishing Co., 1985.

Swan, Jon. "Uncovering Love Canal," *Columbia Journalism Review,* January/February 1979.

Szymanowitz, Raymond. *Edward Goodrich Acheson, Inventor, Scientist, Industrialist: A Biography.* New York: Vantage Press, 1971.

Taylor, Anna Edson. *The Autobiography of Anna Edson Taylor.* N.p., n.d.

Tesla, Nikola. *My Inventions.* Zagreb: Skolska Knjiga, 1984.

Tesmer, Irving, ed. *Colossal Cataract – The Geological History of Niagara Falls.* Albany: State University of New York Press, 1981.

Thompson, G.R., ed. *The Gothic Imagination: Essays in Dark Romanticism.* Pullman: Washington State University Press, 1974.

Tinkler, K.J. "Canadian Landform Examples – 2. Niagara Falls," *Canadian Geographer* 30, no. 4, Winter 1986.

Tiplin, A.H. *Our Romantic Niagara*. Niagara Falls, Ont.: Niagara Falls Heritage Foundation, 1988.

Tovell, Walter. *The Niagara Escarpment*. Toronto: Royal Ontario Museum/University of Toronto, 1965.

———. *Niagara Falls: Story of a River.* Toronto: Royal Ontario Museum, 1966.

———. *The Niagara River.* Toronto: Royal Ontario Museum, 1979.

Trescott, Martha Moore. *The Rise of the American Electrochemical Industry 1880-1910....* Westport, Conn.: Greenwood Press, 1981.

Tribute to Nikola Tesla, Presented in Articles, Letters, Documents. Beograd: Nikola Tesla Museum, 1961.

Tumpane, Frank. "Pugnacious Persuader," *Maclean's*, 1 January 1948.

Vanderbilt, Kermit. *Charles Eliot Norton: Apostle of Culture in a Democracy.* Cambridge, Mass.: Harvard University Press, 1959.

Van Rensselaer, Mariana Griswold. *Henry Hobson Richardson and His Works.* Reprinted, New York: Dover Publications Inc., 1969.

Villard, Henry Serrano. *Contact! The Story of the Early Birds.* New York: Thomas Crowell Co., 1968.

Way, Ronald L. *Ontario's Niagara Parks: A History.* Niagara Falls, Ont.: Niagara Parks Commission, 1960.

Welch, Thomas. "How Niagara Was Made Free," *Buffalo Historical Society Publications* 5, 1902.

Weld, Isaac. *Travels through the States of North America....* [1807.] Reprinted, New York: Johnson Reprint Corporation, 1968.

Weller, Phil. *Fresh Water Seas: Saving the Great Lakes* Toronto: Between the Lines, 1990.

Werner, Charles. "The Niagara Falls Tunnel," *Cassier's Magazine* 2, no. 8, June 1892.

Whalen, Dwight. *The Lady Who Conquered Niagara – The Annie Edson Taylor Story.* Brewer, Maine: Edson Genealogical Assoc., 1990.

Wilson, Edmund. "Apologies to the Iroquois – II," *The New Yorker,* 24 October 1959.

Wilson, Leonard Gilchrist. *Charles Lyell, the Years to 1841: The Revolution in Geology.* New Haven: Yale University Press, 1972.

The Wonders of Niagara, Scenic and Industrial. Niagara Falls, N.Y.: Shredded Wheat Co., 1914.

Woolley, Mary E. "The Development of the Love of Romantic Scenery in America," *American Historical Review* 3, no. 1, October 1897.

Index

475